Praise for
New Jewish Feminism:
Probing the Past, Forging the Future

"Extraordinary ... encompasses the broad international spectrum of Jewish feminist advocates and analysts across denominational spectrums, from those who carefully consider halakhic boundaries to those who would remake Judaism from the ground up. Equally impressive, fresh new voices are here added to those of feminist pioneers. This book is a must-read for anyone interested in the renaissance in contemporary Jewish life."

—**Sylvia Barack Fishman, PhD,** professor of contemporary Jewish life, Brandeis University; author, *The Way Into the Varieties of Jewishness*

"For Jews, for feminists, for anyone who believes that we can transform our religions so that they meet the highest ethical standards, this book is required reading."

—**Vanessa L. Ochs, PhD,** associate professor of religious studies, University of Virginia; author, *Inventing Jewish Ritual*

"What a rich chorus of voices! We all know how much thought and creativity has come forth in the Jewish feminist movement over the past several decades. But to see it all together is truly breathtaking. A most impressive achievement!"

—**Dr. Arthur Green,** rector of the Rabbinical School and Irving Brudnick Professor of Philosophy and Religion, Hebrew College; author, *Ehyeh: A Kabbalah for Tomorrow*

"An amazing piece of work! The combination of range and depth, variety and sophistication is nothing short of remarkable. No stone is left unturned, no point on the spectrum unrepresented, no question unasked, no analysis ignored. This book will have 'legs' and will launch the next phase of work everywhere."

—**Blu Greenberg,** co-founder and first president of the Jewish Orthodox Feminist Alliance; author, *On Women and Judaism: A View from Tradition*

New Jewish FEMINISM

Probing the Past, Forging the Future

Edited by Rabbi Elyse Goldstein

Foreword by Anita Diamant

For People of All Faiths, All Backgrounds
JEWISH LIGHTS Publishing

New Jewish Feminism:
Probing the Past, Forging the Future

2009 Hardcover Edition, First Printing
© 2009 by Elyse Goldstein
Foreword © 2009 by Anita Diamant

Library of Congress Cataloging-in-Publication Data

New Jewish feminism : probing the past, forging the future / edited by Elyse Goldstein.
p. cm.
Includes bibliographical references.
ISBN: 978-1-58023-359-0 (hardcover)
ISBN: 978-1-68336-220-3 (paperback)
1. Women in Judaism. 2. Feminism—Religious aspects—Judaism. 3. Jewish women—Religious life. I. Goldstein, Elyse.
BM729.W6N49 2008
296.082—dc22
2008041378

Jacket Design: Melanie Robinson
Jacket Art: Tallit designed by Reeva Shaffer of Reeva's 'riting with ruach; www.reevas.com; (703) 218-3669.

Published by Jewish Lights Publishing
www.jewishlights.com

Dedicated to my husband, Baruch,
and sons, Noam, Carmi, and Micah,
and to all my past, present, and future students at Kolel:
makers of action and speakers of truth.

"It is vain to say human beings ought to be satisfied with tranquillity: they must have action; and they will make it if they cannot find it."

—CHARLOTTE BRONTË

"Truth is always exciting. Speak it, then. Life is dull without it."

—PEARL S. BUCK

CONTENTS

Contents

Anita Diamant's first work of fiction, *The Red Tent*, was published in 1997 and was awarded 2001's Booksense Book of the Year. She is the author of two other novels, *Good Harbor* and *The Last Days of Dogtown*, a collection of essays, and six non-fiction guides to contemporary Jewish life, including *The New Jewish Wedding*, *The New Jewish Baby Book* (Jewish Lights), *How to Raise a Jewish Child*, and *Choosing a Jewish Life*. She is a founder of Mayyim Hayyim, Living Waters Community Mikveh and the Paula J. Brody Family Education Center in Newton, Massachusetts.

FOREWORD

IN THE INTRODUCTION to my first book, *The New Jewish Wedding*, I wrote, "References to the rabbi as him or her do no more than acknowledge the decision to ordain women by the Reform, Reconstructionist, and Conservative movements."

That was in 1985. When I went back to revise the book in 2001, I couldn't quite believe that I'd written those words. I suppose I felt the need to remind readers about what were, back then, relatively new facts on the ground. Even worse, I think I was worried about offending someone by telling a simple truth.

Of course, I left that sentence out in the new edition, as well as a few other apologetic asides that pointed out what has since become ubiquitous and obvious: Jewish women are leaders and teachers, rabbis and cantors, theologians and prophets. Women hold up half of the sky—Jewish women among them.

The arguments about women's participation and inclusive language may linger, but they are vestigial, nothing but rear-guard skirmishes. It's over. We won. Which is to say, the Jewish people have been blessed with a new, vital chapter in our history. *Am Yisrael Chai*, thanks to the work and wisdom of Jewish women, which has led to new paradigms in virtually every aspect of our communal and personal lives, including a flowering of more democratic institutions, more congregational singing, more meaningful rituals, more political action, more books. And women's inclusiveness and inclusion has been the model for the enfranchisement of all Jews, regardless of sexual orientation, race, abilities, or religion of origin.

The publication of this wonderful collection of essays is yet another testimony to the fact that we have lived through an entire generation—thirty years and more—during which the full panel of women's voices have been heard on the public stages of Jewish life.

Everyone knows that we Jewish women have always had our voices and our opinions. We have exercised considerable power from the kitchen table and from the platform of the ladies' auxiliary. We can and should honor the participation of Jewish women behind the scenes and off to the side, just as we can and should be proud of the inherently, and sometimes covertly, democratic tendencies within Judaism itself that have fostered literacy and independence among women and girls.

But twenty-first century Judaism begins in a radically different place. This is the first time in Jewish history that women's voices—not just singular and extraordinary characters but a large and varied chorus—have been added to the public discourse about everything: about God and halakhah, about the governance of our synagogues, about marriage and how we educate our children, about our money, about the substance and fire of our lives.

This unprecedented participation of women results from the passion of what is now nearly two generations of adult Jewish women and men who understand that feminism is nothing less than a profound expression of Judaism's mission and part of the Torah's mandate for justice and the sanctification of life.

The volume you hold in your hands is evidence of this profound change, this life-giving renewal of Jewish life and of Judaism itself. As Rabbi Elyse Goldstein points out in her excellent introduction, this enormous transformation has taken place over an extremely short period of time and yet so much of it is already taken for granted that the revolution is virtually invisible.

Ima on the bimah is just no big deal. How cool is that?

As Jews, we reflexively look back to our sources for prototypes that root change in tradition. We cite texts—the older and more sacred the better—to link us to the past and thus legitimize our innovations. For years now, we have been citing Miriam the prophet as the foremother for many of our leadership roles. We claim Hannah, the spiritual seeker, as the inventor of the personal prayers we have added to communal and private devotion. We explicate Ruth and Esther as exemplars of distinctively feminine forms of courage.

These are legitimate antecedents, well argued and footnoted and expressed by learned and learning Jewish women—and men—who have studied long and deep and, in the process, opened the library doors to the entire Jewish world.

And here is another radical gift of Jewish feminism. Despite our tradition's long-standing reverence for learning, the truth is, serious study was an elite practice limited to rabbis and men rich enough or lucky enough to be supported by their families. Never mind women.

Only in our time, thanks to the advent of a feminist Judaism, which is to say an inclusive Judaism, has it become possible to imagine the entire community—regardless of age or sex or previous Jewish literacy—as a nation of students and teachers. This undercuts the unexamined notion—the fantasy, really—that the Jews of yore were more learned and thus more pious and authentic than we are today. The radical democratization of Jewish learning, with the possibility of universal lifelong learning, is one of the fruits of women's growing participation and leadership in university settings as well as in seminaries and yeshivas.

Hooray for us! But now that we have attained this level of learning and power (with miles to go, I know, I know) it's time to own up to the fact that we are not going to find proof texts for all of our insights and inventions. It's time to be honest that we are creating the Miriam we need—musician, performance artist, prophet—that we give her a timbrel and a place at the Seder and put new songs in her mouth, and that we give her words that speak to our spiritual quests and reflect contemporary models of female leadership. This is perfectly kosher. It's been done by many men before us. It is the juicy, growing part of our tree of life that has kept us from atrophy and death.

We must embrace the fact that we are sanctifying what was not viewed as sacred in the past: the stories of our lives, the power and wisdom of our grandmothers, the sacrifice and triumph of the counter-histories, the counter-narratives, the counter-theologies, of the Jewish past.

Transforming the marginal into the normative is the business of the arts. And so I look forward to a second volume of this book, with chapters devoted to creativity in all of its incarnations. The mandate for *hiddur mitzvah*—the beautification of Jewish life—has never been more pressing; for starters, our dramaturgy—the aesthetic of prayer—is in need of a serious tune-up, from liturgy to music to movement.

Art and culture—homely as cooking, lofty as poetry, challenging as video installation—are going to provide new vocabularies and new avenues of authentic Jewish expression in every sphere, from Torah study to ritual to rebuilding the world. And women will be in the vanguard.

We are at the end of one beginning; we are on the verge of the next.

Mazel tov to all of the contributors to this fine collection. Mazel tov to Rabbi Goldstein for her passion to make it happen. Mazel tov to us and to our daughters and our sons. There has never been a better time to be a Jew.

Can I hear a *shehechiyanu?*

Anita Diamant
Newton, Massachusetts

Acknowledgments

I CAN HARDLY BELIEVE IT was over a decade ago that I sat down to write *ReVisions: Seeing Torah through a Feminist Lens* (Jewish Lights). The title said it all: it was possible to mesh our feminism and our Judaism; it was possible to see the Torah anew, to reread and reteach it with a feminist voice. It was a heady time for us Jewish feminists; the dawn of a new millennium seemed promising. Jewish feminist academics were being appointed to chairs in universities; rabbinic seminaries, once bastions of male power and male culture, were finding new ways to teach about women in Judaism and to make feminist Bible scholarship part of the curriculum. Female rabbis were getting jobs in major congregations, and Orthodox feminist gatherings were large, vocal, and impressive.

After *ReVisions,* I felt that anything was possible, and so I began to compile a feminist commentary on the Torah. During the many lectures and readings of *The Women's Torah Commentary: New Insights from Women Rabbis on the 54 Weekly Torah Portions* and *The Women's Haftarah Commentary: New Insights from Women Rabbis on the 54 Weekly Haftarah Portions, the 5 Megillot and Special Shabbatot* (both Jewish Lights) that came later, however, I felt a quiet discomfort in my soul. It seemed as if so many people in the audiences were completely satisfied with all that had been done, and that these commentaries were the end, not the beginning, of the revolution. They felt that it was now time to "move on." "This is it," they thought. "We are done. Haven't we accomplished what we set out to do? Why keep harping on the feminist stuff?" Then other impressive feminist commentaries followed, and they really seemed to answer many, if not all of our concerns about the text. As I placed the newest commentaries on my shelf next to the plethora of excellent books on Judaism and feminism that had come out over the past ten years, I admit I had the same feeling as those in the audiences. At the rate we are producing feminist works, with the amount of female leaders in synagogues, with the number of women in the rabbinate and cantorate, with the strides we've made in Israel for women, with the changes and advances for women in Orthodoxy, do we still need the "F word"? Haven't we done it all? What's left to be done?

Plenty! I wanted to tell not only my generation, but also the new generation of Jewish women just how vital our insights are and just how important we will be to the future of the Jewish enterprise. I am grateful to Stuart M. Matlins, publisher of Jewish Lights, for his deep commitment to produce serious Jewish feminist books, and for his insight over a Toronto lunch that I could indeed "tell them" through this new book. I discovered after reading only the first few essays of this book just how exciting and true it is that as much as we have done, there is still more to do. I saw just how important it is for Jewish feminists not to rest on the laurels of the past. I also discovered, as you the reader will, that the past accomplishments are worth reevaluating, revisiting, and rediscussing, since they have not only shaped Jewish women but the entire Jewish community as well. Stuart instinctively knew this and inspired me to reach out to many writers and thinkers who all were eager to be a part of the dialogue between past achievements and future tasks.

Once again, as in my other books, Emily Wichland, vice president of Editorial and Production at Jewish Lights, proved to have an invaluable perspective, a keen sense of what's needed, an open ear, and an understanding heart. I was delighted to be offered the chance to work with Rahel Lerner as the manuscript's final editor. I knew her to be a young talented writer (as you will see from her essay in part 5) and a committed Jewish feminist with important things to say. I knew that when she read the manuscript I had edited she would "get it" well beyond the grammar and syntax.

Anita Diamant's Foreword enriches and expands this book. Most of you know Anita's work *The Red Tent*. That novel made the Bible's female characters part of our families and our daily lives. I simply cannot imagine a Torah class anywhere anymore that does not reference *The Red Tent* when reading the story of Dinah. I also know Anita through her other books, most notably *The New Jewish Wedding Book*, *The New Jewish Baby Book: Names, Ceremonies and Customs: A Guide for Today's Families* (Jewish Lights), and *Living a Jewish Life*, all of which have been required reading for years in my basic Judaism classes; and through her mikveh project, Mayyim Hayyim. I consider Anita to be one of the most important thinkers in Jewish life today, and so when she agreed to write the Foreword I was absolutely overjoyed.

A thank-you to all the contributors who wrote from their hearts, minds, and souls, and who share their experiences both old and new in a way that is accessible and inspiring. A thank-you to my extraordinary family: my husband, Baruch, and my sons, Noam, Carmi, and Micah, who are themselves feminists and proud to use that "F word" frequently! I appreciate that my staff at Kolel, Tracey Starr and Esther Scheslinger, took time out of their busy days to e-mail contributors, send back manuscripts, chase down lost essays, and work with the Canadian postal service to ensure this book got done!

A sincere thank-you to all the brave feminists who came before me, and all the brave feminists who will come after me, and all those who work with me now, for breaking glass ceilings, inventing new rituals, naming oppressions, stretching sexual boundaries, teaching new texts, voicing unpopular opinions, breaking popular stereotypes, and challenging received wisdom so that the wisdom that is yet to be received may be born into a welcoming world.

Blessed be the Holy One who has kept me in life, sustained me, and brought me to this day.

Introduction

GROWING UP IN THE 1960S, the notion of a woman rabbi, a woman Israeli Supreme Court judge, or an Orthodox synagogue where women read the Torah from their side of the *mechitzah* (the wall or screen separating the genders) were impossible dreams, even ridiculous scenarios. I never once saw a woman ascend the bimah of my Reform temple, except to light the Friday-night candles; even the mothers of the bat mitzvah girls sat in the pews while the fathers proudly had the aliyah.

In 1968, when I was thirteen years old, I was the only girl in my religious school class who chose to have a bat mitzvah instead of waiting for a "sweet sixteen" party. I will never forget the moment I ascended the bimah, read my portion, and opened my speech. I pushed aside the prepared text—the text that had been written for me by my rabbi—and began to speak extemporaneously. I explained how meaningful and important this day was for me, and then I announced that I wanted to become a rabbi. My family gasped. The cantor broke into tears. And then, the rabbi fell off his chair. When he regained his composure, he announced into the microphone on his side of the bimah, "No, no, of course she means she wants to be a *rebbetzin* [a wife of a rabbi]." "No," I said into the microphone on my side of the bimah, "let my husband be the *rebbetzin*. I'm going to be the *rabbi*." There was lots of laughter.

This is a cute story, but I didn't know at all what it would mean to break a glass ceiling or to do something that had not been done. I was only thirteen and I wanted to change the world, but it was a highly personal, totally individual approach to want to do this through becoming a rabbi. I never thought that women becoming rabbis would shake the very foundation of Judaism, question every assumption of Jewish life, which was based on patriarchal power, or challenge what it meant to be a Jewish woman. I didn't realize that I was in the middle of a quiet revolution, one that would not remain quiet but would eventually echo into the pages of the prayerbook, the board rooms of major Jewish organizations, the seminaries, the yeshivas, and the Israeli government, all within the next twenty years. And indeed it did. In the years following my bat mitzvah, Sally Priesand and the first generation of female rabbis would be ordained, women would become cantors and synagogue presidents. Liturgy would change to not only include the matriarchs but eventually the gender-neutral Hebrew of Marcia Falk and the feminine presence of the Shekhinah. We'd start singing songs of Miriam in summer camp, learn Talmud from Orthodox women, introduce the notion of female spirituality, make feminine tallitot, and redefine sexual politics, all in the span of a few years. We would feel empowered to create midrashim with biblical women named and unnamed, to take on the traditional meaning of the mikveh and reappropriate it to a feminist agenda, to invoke the name of the Goddess. We would reclaim and recast scores of different rituals while questioning the hierarchical nature of those rituals and of the community that "owned" them. We would challenge the Israeli public to rethink the lines between "religious" and "secular," and we would bring the issues of child care, wife abuse, violence against Jewish women, and power imbalances in the Jewish organizational world to the fore.

Today, none of this is new; it is all "normative." The effect of feminism on Judaism cannot be understood without this historical perspective. We have witnessed perhaps the largest-scale change in

Judaism since emancipation in the 1800s allowed Jews to leave the ghetto walls. The public role of Jewish women has evolved so far from the "Yiddishe mama" that it defies all stereotypes. What makes a "Jewish woman" today? How has feminism, both secular and Jewish, affected her identity?

I daresay that no Jewish woman today, even the most isolated or right-wing religious one, is free from the influence of feminism, even if just to have to justify her traditional position. Whereas in the last generation the feminist position was marginal and threatening, today the traditional woman may feel that she is the dying species. She has to explain why the women in her synagogue do not participate ritually or publicly; why there are no women's voices at the Torah study she frequents; why her view assumes heterosexuality or male privilege. That such women are even in dialogue with these questions proves that the questions have entered mainstream Jewish consciousness and thus have become part and parcel of the wider view of the community.

What are the questions Jewish feminism has raised that have so clearly entered our conversation that the tone and content of Jewish life have been forever altered? This book organizes those questions into seven main areas: theology; ritual and Torah study; the synagogue; Israel; gender, sexuality, and age; the denominations; and leadership and social justice. The essays within each of the seven theme areas contain an analysis of what has evolved through the Jewish feminist movement: what has been accomplished and how far we have come, followed by an examination of what is left to be done. The authors of the essays are rabbis, cantors, feminist scholars and thinkers spanning the complete denominational spectrum (and the post- or transdenominational world as well) and reflecting the intergenerational demographic of the Jewish community.

This book looks back and ahead. When you are in the middle of the revolution you can't really plan the next steps. But now we can. This book is meant to spur discussion. It is intended to open up a dialogue between the early Jewish feminist pioneers and the young women shaping Judaism today. It is an ideal reader for bat mitzvah girls, female Jews by choice, university students, women involved in synagogue life in all the movements, and women still on the margins. It can be the basis of Rosh Chodesh and women's study groups, synagogue and *chavurah* (fellowship) discussion groups, and rabbinic seminars. Read it, use it, debate it, ponder it. The reader will find a short biography of each contributor at the beginning of each chapter. In and of themselves, the biographies read as a testament to how far we have come and what we have accomplished.

It has not all been easy, and there has been, and will continue to be backlash, suspicion, fear, and confrontation. A shift in power structure and in consciousness always brings with it the anxiety that we may have been wrong all along and that we may still be wrong; or that our places in the world, once safe and secure, are now tenuous. Perhaps nowhere is this clearer than in the liberal synagogue, with its new emphasis and interest in "the flight of men." Now that women have redefined themselves and their place in Judaism, men are faced with the real and difficult task of redefining themselves as Jews. For some it is just too hard, and they long for the old days when men were the minyan and women served the tea. But those days are forever gone, and there is hardly a synagogue of any denomination where such strict gender roles still prevail, given the realities of women working outside the home and being Jewishly literate and learned, and the cross-denominational relationships we now have that make it impossible to not see another way of doing things.

Our God concepts changed and, with them, our concepts of ourselves as Jews. We used a different language to describe the Divine; it came forth with birth and moon and mothering imagery and thus we began to wonder about what we looked like, made in that divine image. We began to write theology; we corrected the patriarchy of traditional Jewish thought and created our own brand that took into account not only feminist but also ecological and political concerns. We gained a new theological vocabulary, but in doing so we lost God the Father, and some feel adrift and bereft of those comforting childhood notions.

Rosh Chodesh groups lost their "weirdness" and became a normal monthly occurrence in many communities; with that, the "Jew" we had grown accustomed to identifying as the man with long side-curls and a fur hat morphed into the woman with a pink tallit. Women's rituals proliferated and we began to create what was missing from the index of life cycle events: rituals that spoke to the unique biological realities of being women. But we asked, and continue to ask, if our biology is still our spiritual destiny, and if those pink tallitot are really what we want and need.

All this was happening in North America while Jewish feminists were just catching up in Israel. Their battles and concerns are unique; their changes are vast, foundational, and still controversial. Their headway in Israel is changing the whole landscape of what it means to be a Jew in the Jewish homeland. From the kindergarten to the Knesset, the future history of Israel is often provoked by these thinkers in a profound way that no one quite expected. Because "women's issues" were often relegated to the back burner while national security loomed and wider questions of the structure of Israeli society were given priority, women patiently waited their turn at the table, placated by pictures of Golda and memories of bygone women in the Kibbutz movement tilling the soil alongside their male counterparts. Their turn has come.

Then, with the ordination of homosexual rabbis in the liberal movements, all of our assumptions about gender, sexuality, and religion were called into question. We thought it was just about women! It surprised and discomforted many, but we began to see that, like black civil rights activist Fannie Lou Hamer said, "nobody's free until everybody's free."

One of the largest contributions of Jewish feminists may be their ability as women to rise above denominational politics to talk to each other. As women we simply have less to lose when we question those hierarchies and divisions, since we did not create them and have less to win by keeping them intact. We generally haven't flown our denominational banners in each other's faces because our shared concerns often place us in context with each other, not against each other. The interdenominational dialogue now so fruitful in the Jewish world began with women finding commonalities and compromises to make gatherings work, to make women's prayer services accessible, to make discussions of child care a communal agenda item. Can women bridge the denominational politics that riddle Jewish communities everywhere?

In every denomination, and in every sphere, there has been a veritable explosion of Jewish women's learning and scholarship that makes it impossible to assume anything anymore about "women and Judaism." We have learned that we cannot survive as Jews—let alone as Jewish women—without a secure base of Jewish knowledge. It was ignorance that kept us back; we could not argue verse on verse when we were told "you can't" or "you shouldn't," and we accepted the limitations tradition put on us because we simply did not know the text. Bookshelves of Jewish men and women are lined with women's midrash, commentary, ritual, and literature, and this plethora of available knowledge is sometimes staggering. It most certainly means that we know where to look for answers now, and that we can engage in the dialogue as full participants.

With all these vast changes, the Jewish organizational world is also forever changed. While it still may be functionally true in some places that women stuff the envelopes and men make the decisions, and equally true that women of a certain generation are more comfortable with those expectations and roles, the fact that we now *notice* and challenge that scenario is proof of the changes that lie ahead. The fact that the next president of any given organization may likely be a woman will force the issue to the front of the organization's consciousness whether it is ready or not.

Jewish feminists have striven to conserve while changing, to remain faithful to the tradition while questioning and adapting it. We sought to enrich and expand while holding on tight. What a bal-

ancing act! What a tightrope we have walked! That the next generation of Jewish women can navigate it with such grace and ease is a
blessing. But if they think there will be no obstacles in the way, no
boulders on the path, and no detractors on the side, they are wrong,
and in danger of becoming complacent.

Are we witnessing "post-feminist" Judaism, where the gains of
feminism are taken for granted as givens, or has the past twenty
years opened up deeper and even more challenging questions for us
as women? I believe there is still work ahead, and that is why I com-
piled this book. I think by the end of the essays you will feel the same
way. I hope you, dear reader, will find that Jewish feminism has
much to say and many new issues it should tackle, that much is
going to happen that we never thought of before, that many new
voices will join the conversation, and that in probing the past you
will make a commitment to forge the Jewish future.

PART I
Women and Theology

ANY SERIOUS DISCUSSIONS of Jewish feminist issues will begin with the question of God language. And that question will lead to a broader and deeper exploration of what we believe and how we describe it.

God language is not a trivial matter. While language can be poetic, esoteric, or symbolic in nature, it is not arbitrary; language both describes and creates reality. We say what we mean and we mean what we say. So it matters what you say about God, and what you mean about God.

The God of the Torah is taught to us through stories, and we come to know God as a King, a Father, an all-powerful and mighty Being. But as we grow into adulthood, and as we redefine our beliefs in a more sophisticated way, we often find ourselves uncomfortable with those simplistic childhood images. Our spiritual experience, and thus our spiritual vocabulary increases and broadens as we grow, but we often do not understand the depth of what a change in our language means to our belief system.

There is a growing interest among feminists in the image of the Goddess and the notion of Shekhinah. Reawakening what we think might have once been goddess-like aspects of YHVH, and incorporating new goddess symbols for the One God who truly encompasses all things, some women who feel that Judaism did not offer them a spirituality or a voice feel more connected. Women need a personally relevant religious vocabulary, a vocabulary that has been lacking in traditional sources. The search for new images will inevitably bring us to a new way of thinking about God, and a whole new theological enterprise. How do we choose to express our relationship to God? The language of our relationship will have an effect on the relationship itself.

Shekhinah, Goddess, theology redefined or traditionally understood, depictions of God as Mother and/or Father, descriptions of God as indwelling as well as being outside of us, creation theology, hidden metaphors still leave us with this question: Does the Jewish belief system as we have it now, as we have inherited it and continue to practice it, with its attendant language, offer a sense of self-validation and self-esteem to women? Or is it in need of a radical reformation?

Judith Plaskow, PhD, is professor of religious studies at Manhattan College and a Jewish feminist theologian. Cofounder and for ten years coeditor of the *Journal of Feminist Studies in Religion,* she is author or editor of several works in feminist theology, including *Standing Again at Sinai: Judaism from a Feminist Perspective* and *The Coming of Lilith: Essays on Feminism, Judaism, and Sexual Ethics 1972–2003.*

Calling All Theologians

JUDITH PLASKOW, PhD

A REFRAIN I HAVE HEARD throughout my career is that Jews don't do theology: we don't engage in sustained reflection on the presuppositions concerning God, human beings, and the world that underlie Jewish faith and practice. We are a people for whom law is more central than belief, observance more important than speculation. Jews who define themselves as theologians, myself included, have often felt compelled to justify their calling rather than just embrace it—to argue for the role of theology in Jewish life and Jewish self-understanding. I had hoped that Jewish feminists would give the lie to the notion that theology is not a Jewish mode of expression by eagerly embracing it and producing a wide range of theologies that would open up new conversations within the Jewish community. But it turns out that most Jewish feminists haven't done formal theology either, and that if there is going to be a blossoming of Jewish feminist theologies, it belongs to the future.

When I wrote *Standing Again at Sinai* almost twenty years ago, I felt myself part of a burgeoning interest in theological questions. Already in the 1970s, Rita Gross had raised the issue of male God language. She argued that Jewish failure to develop female images for God was the ultimate symbol of women's subordination and that

3

women would be fully included in the covenant community only when God was addressed as "God-She" as well as "God-He."[1] In the 1980s, Marcia Falk criticized what she saw as the idolatrous nature of traditional God language and contended that monotheism should be understood not as the worship of one male God but as the "embracing unity of a multiplicity of images."[2] In the same decade, feminists raised a wide range of theological questions. Drorah Setel suggested that the central challenge confronting Jewish feminists was not so much changing women's roles but overcoming the hierarchical and dualistic modes of thought central to Jewish tradition; Rachel Adler asked whether women had ever been included in the Jewish covenant community; and Ellen Umansky argued for a "responsive Jewish theology" that would combine encounters with the Jewish past with the experiences of the theologian.[3] These works seemed to mark the launch of Jewish feminist theology. It would be not simply a discourse about reimagining God, but a broader exploration of often-unexamined assumptions concerning authority, revelation, God, community, and the nature and origins of gender distinctions. It would make clear the connections between fundamental Jewish beliefs and Jewish attitudes and practices.

As it turned out, however, in the last twenty years, only Rachel Adler, Tamar Ross, Melissa Raphael, and I have published full-length Jewish feminist theologies. My book, Adler's, and Ross's are quite different from one another in their interests and approaches, but they all examine the ways in which women's entry into the Jewish interpretive process challenges and expands the boundaries of Judaism. The core of *Standing Again at Sinai* is structured around the central Jewish categories of Torah, Israel, and God. It asks what these concepts might look like were women full participants in their formulation. I claim that, since Jewish tradition as it has been handed down through the generations is the product of male elites, placing women at the center of Jewish life alongside men would entail reworking many key theological concepts.[4] In *Engendering Judaism,* Rachel Adler maintains that Torah, God, and Israel are not sufficient categories for a feminist Judaism and that feminists must experiment with a wide variety of approaches to Jewish sources and move outside traditional categories in their reconstructions of Judaism. She presents her theology through a close but multidisciplinary reading of particular Jewish texts, offering an especially rich discussion of renewing halakhah that she concretizes through reconceptualizing the Jewish wedding ceremony.[5] In *Expanding the Palace of Torah*, Orthodox feminist Tamar Ross argues that feminism forces the Jewish community to reexamine the relationship between divine revelation and human interpretation in order to determine whether a tradition grounded in the notion of a unique revelation at Sinai can accommodate the changing moral sensibilities of its followers. She develops a notion of cumulative revelation that draws on the thought of Rabbi Abraham Isaac Kook and assumes that revelation unfolds over time through rabbinic interpretation and the prism of history.[6]

Melissa Raphael's book, *The Female Face of God in Auschwitz*, is a feminist theology of the Holocaust and thus quite different in focus from the other three volumes. Raphael roots herself in the feminist critique of the marginalization or absence of women's voices in Jewish texts and argues that writings about the Holocaust have subjected women to a double erasure, adding theoretical invisibility to historical annihilation. She subjects the major post-Holocaust theologians to trenchant criticism, showing how theological discourse on the Holocaust has been patriarchal in central respects. Her own contribution to Holocaust theology begins with women's memoirs of internment and explores the ways in which women managed to be present to each other in acts of washing, holding, and covering bodies. In attempting to preserve their humanity even in the midst of hell, women brought the Shekhinah—the immanent, female face of God in Jewish mysticism—"deep into the broken heart of Auschwitz."[7]

Two other books besides these raise significant theological issues but have as much or more in them of other modes of feminist discourse as of formal theological reflection. Lynn Gottlieb's *She Who*

Dwells Within—a title that refers to the Shekhinah—draws on a range of genres to develop a concept of the feminine divine for today. In seeking to create spiritual paradigms that encourage and reflect an expanded role for Jewish women, Gottlieb uses stories, midrash, prayers, chants, poetry, songs, and ceremonies to address theological topics.[8] Rebecca Alpert's *Like Bread on the Seder Plate* asks probing questions about incorporating the perspectives, dreams, and visions of lesbians and gay men into all aspects of Jewish life and argues that their historical exclusion is rooted not just in contemporary prejudice but in core sacred texts. In expanding the canon on which lesbians might draw in order to transform tradition, however, Alpert is less interested in the theological implications of lesbian inclusion than on gathering a wide range of texts from different disciplines that can be useful in the process of creating change.[9]

One of the reasons it is often said that Jews don't do theology is that Jewish tradition has grappled with theological questions indirectly through storytelling, liturgy and ritual, Torah commentary, midrash, and halakhic reinterpretation. Gottlieb's and Alpert's books illustrate the fact that most feminists have taken a similar approach to theological issues: namely, addressing them through a variety of forms. Thus, at the same time that Rita Gross was insisting that the "Holy One, Blessed be He" is and always has also been the "Holy One, Blessed be She," Maggie Wenig and Naomi Janowitz were writing an English Sabbath prayer book using female pronouns and images.[10] Marcia Falk developed her notion of inclusive monotheism most fully not through theological argument but through *The Book of Blessings,* an extraordinary reworking of Jewish prayers for the Sabbath, New Moon, and daily life that evokes a God immanent in creation.[11] Many other Jewish feminists have responded to the problems with using exclusively male images of God by rewriting Hebrew prayers in the feminine, or in both the masculine and the feminine; creating new liturgies and rituals that address God as Shekhinah; or seeking out and developing other Hebrew names for God with feminine resonances. The question of whether revelation ended at some point in the past or continues into the present has been answered in the affirmative not so much through explicit theological speculation as through a host of new commentaries in which women claim the right to interpret Torah. While the authors or editors of such texts often note the importance of recovering women's missing voices within Jewish tradition, the point of their various projects is not to reflect on theological warrants for women's entry into the interpretive process but to get on with the work of offering fresh perspectives on canonical texts.[12] An explosion of feminist midrash, some of which is published but much of which remains in private hands, also reflects the notion of an open and evolving canon to which women can make vital contributions.[13]

It seems, then, that the question of whether to label a work "theology" is as much about points on a continuum as about clear-cut boundaries. Three of the four texts I have labeled theological are also deeply concerned with feminist praxis and draw on many modes of discourse other than theology. *Standing Again at Sinai* roots itself in the work of a particular Jewish feminist community; explores the theological implications of feminist historiography, prayer, ritual, and midrash; and tries to address the larger social context of Jewish feminism. Adler's *Engendering Judaism* draws together her more theoretical discussions of halakhah, textual interpretation, prayer, sexual ethics, and marriage by rethinking the halakhic basis of marriage and creating a new wedding ceremony that has served as an inspiration for many couples wanting to modify the traditional ritual. *Expanding the Palace of Torah* extensively describes and evaluates halakhic debates within Orthodoxy about the role of women as well as the meta-halakhic theories that underlie them. Raphael's book, while not concerned with contemporary feminist religious practice, draws on memoirs of the Holocaust in order to allow women to speak for themselves.

Given that there are many nontheological elements in Jewish feminist theologies, and that other sorts of feminist discourse are rich with theological implications, what is at stake in calling a particular work theological or not? I do not mean to imply that theology is the "queen of the sciences," or that it is somehow better than other modes of discourse. Indeed, I would argue that one of the great strengths of Jewish feminist theology lies in its connection to concrete issues in Jewish life. If new theologies don't help women to assume leadership in the Jewish community and to become full participants in Jewish study, ritual, halakhic decision making and other arenas, then they become empty speculative exercises rather than genuine contributions to the process of feminist transformation. But I also think that formal and explicit theology can and does play an important role in the feminist enterprise in that it raises valuable meta-questions that emerge out of other forms of Jewish praxis. To call a particular work theological is to suggest that its primary interest is in these meta-questions rather than in other types of feminist expression. Thus, whether or not a certain theologian calls on God as Shekhinah, she might be interested in what the image suggests about the purpose of prayer, the nature of God, and the possibilities for transforming traditional theologies. Whether or not she engages in the exegesis of particular texts, she might consider the fruitfulness of certain textual approaches in relation to their capacity to open up new perspectives on tradition. Whether or not she is committed to certain halakhic changes or to halakhah as an avenue of change, she might be interested in the role of law in religious community or in what specific halakhic arguments reveal about their authors' views of revelation, authority, and the mechanisms of religious change.

In focusing on the underlying assumptions and broader implications of feminist struggles in other arenas, theology contributes to Jewish feminism in several ways: it provides a theoretical framework for other feminist developments, it links the feminist project with larger religious questions about what it means to be a Jew in today's world, and it prods feminist thinking in new directions. First, by reflecting back the assumptions that undergird a range of feminist projects and challenging feminists to clarify our intentions and communicate them effectively, theology provides grounding for feminist work more generally. Do the images of God in a particular

liturgy work in the ways its authors intended? What are the implications for the concepts of chosenness and community of the attention to diversity that has been so central to Jewish feminism?[14] What
notions of authority underlie the struggle for lesbian, gay, bisexual,
and transgender visibility?

One of the areas in which theological meta-questions are especially urgent is in relation to the gender models that inform feminist
theory and organization. For the past forty years, feminist efforts to
transform the Jewish community have generally rested on one of two
concepts of gender, both of which take for granted the existence of
two sexes. An equal-access model has sought entry for women to
forms of religious expression historically reserved for men, and in
doing so, has often expected that women will conform to male
norms. A gender-differentiated model has focused on the neglected
particularities of women's lives, but has sometimes made quite traditional assumptions about what constitutes women's experience. At a
time when feminist theorists and transgender activists are arguing
that the categories of male and female by no means exhaust the social
or physical spectrum of human variation, and Jewish scholars are
calling attention to the rabbinic intersexual categories of *tum tum*
(Talmudic term for one whose gender is not clear at birth) and
"androgynus," Jewish feminists need to reexamine our concepts of
gender as they affect the strategies and goals of the feminist movement.[15] To what extent does feminism require the category of
"woman," and is it possible to hold that category lightly as a social
construct while continuing to organize around it? What would happen to feminist rituals and ceremonies if we assumed that male and
female are just ends of a gender spectrum rather than the only two
possibilities for being human? Might it be useful to imagine God as
transgender rather than as male and female? How would feminist
prayer and liturgy change if we used a wide variety of metaphors for
God that emphasized the fluid and shifting nature of God's gender?

Second, while the category of gender is central to feminism, feminism is not solely about gender and it is certainly not "for women

only." The new forms of leadership that feminists have developed, the initiatives we have taken in producing new rituals and midrashim, the fresh perspectives we have offered on Jewish texts provide models for all Jews who seek to create a meaningful contemporary Judaism in continuity with tradition. One of the tasks theology can perform is to clarify the ways in which feminism represents a specific instance and intensification of the fundamental problems confronting Jews since the rise of modernity. The feminist critique of the patriarchal nature of (most of) the Jewish canon raises the broader issue of whether and how traditional texts can continue to have authority in today's world. At a time when historical scholarship and awareness of religious diversity have made it increasingly difficult to believe in the divine origin of Torah, where does authority finally reside? Feminist efforts to create new modes of Jewish expression that reflect contemporary ethical sensibilities and at the same time are grounded in and faithful to tradition speak to the aspirations of many Jews who find themselves negotiating among multiple communities. Feminist difficulties with male God language and the image of God as dominating Other resonate with the wider challenge of continuing to believe in a transcendent, supernatural deity in a scientific age. Feminist theologians need to be much more explicit in making connections between their efforts to address these questions as they touch on the roles and status of women and the fundamental religious issues with which many Jews wrestle. We need to discuss questions such as the problem of evil and the relation of the God to the Holocaust that feminists have largely avoided. Melissa Raphael's work, with its notion of an immanent deity manifest in the power of human love, is an important contribution to this project. Other feminists have argued for the concept of an ambiguous God, imagining the Divine in the complex and contradictory web of creation and highlighting the mixture of good and evil within all aspects of reality.[16]

Last, theology plays an important role in prodding feminist thinking in new directions. For all its marginal status, feminist theology has inspired a wide range of work that brings feminist perspectives to many aspects of Jewish life and seeks to create a Judaism that belongs to all Jews. But just as Jewish feminism is not solely about gender, it is also not solely about changing Judaism or the internal dynamics of the Jewish community. Jewish feminists have long been involved in the peace movement, in antiracist and environmental activism, in struggles against economic inequality, and in many other efforts to bring about social justice. Yet despite decades of feminist engagement with these issues, there still has not been a full-scale feminist exploration of the connections between the feminist transformation of Judaism and the wider project of *tikkun olam* (repair of the world). Several male theologians have articulated the links between Jewish theological concepts and the imperative toward activism, but Jewish feminists have not yet brought their own unique insights to bear on this conversation.[17] What have we learned from forty years of feminist organizing about both the resources for and obstacles to justice work that flow from Jewish tradition? How do we expose the ways in which the tradition has supported and contributed to sexism, racism, and economic inequality, and at the same time make use of the riches it provides in fighting against these and other forms of injustice? How can we ensure that a commitment to gender justice is part of every struggle for social change, while being clear that sexism is always interstructured with other forms of oppression?

Jewish feminist activists obviously don't need theological analysis in order to get on with their activism. And yet I believe that theology can provide religious warrants for activism that can help to keep it vital, at the same time that serious attention to concrete activist projects would help to expand and deepen the feminist theological agenda. It is this mutually enriching relationship between the meta-questions raised by theology and other modes of feminist discourse and organizing that lead me to hope that formal theology will become more central to the Jewish feminist enterprise. I can only trust that a new generation of feminists will feel the call to engage in sustained theological reflection that is rooted in and nourishes Jewish feminist practice.

Rabbi Donna Berman, PhD, is the executive director of the Charter Oak Cultural Center in Hartford, Connecticut. She holds a PhD in religion and social ethics from Drew University and is rabbi emerita of Port Jewish Center in Port Washington, New York. Rabbi Berman was the editor of a special edition of he *Journal of Reform Judaism,* celebrating twenty-five years of women in the rabbinate and is the author of numerous articles. She recently co-edited *The Coming of Lilith: Essays on Feminism, Judaism, and Sexual Ethics, 1973–2003* with Judith Plaskow.

Major Trends in Jewish Feminist Theology

The Work of Rachel Adler, Judith Plaskow, and Rebecca Alpert

RABBI DONNA BERMAN, PhD

THE JEWISH THEOLOGY we so uncritically accept as "Jewish" was written by men and for men. Yet it is never referred to as "male theology." On the other hand, when women write theology that takes into account their experiences, their needs, the impact of male theology on their lives, their work is labeled "feminist theology." There are two reasons for this. First, in an environment in which maleness has for so long been assumed and male experience universalized, anything that deviates from that "norm" is tacitly required to be made explicit.[1] Second, feminists themselves often insist on this qualifier because, unlike their male counterparts, they wish to acknowledge and make clear the lens they are using to do their work. Sadly, "feminist theology" is too often interpreted as something that excludes men and/or is biased, not as something that is created in response to exclusion and bias. The real goal of Jewish feminist theology is to finally create a theology for everyone.

The exclusion of women from traditional theological discourse within Judaism reflected a denial of women's full humanity. The question for Jewish feminist thinkers and all those who seek gender justice in Judaism is, can we dislodge the manifestations of this denial and still have something that is recognizably Jewish? Or is sexism so intricately woven into the fabric of Jewish law and theology that it is impossible to separate out, rendering any attempt to eradicate it futile?

Rachel Adler, Judith Plaskow, and Rebecca Alpert are among the earliest framers of Jewish feminist theology and ethics to grapple with these questions. They have provided three distinct, rich, and innovative blueprints for change. While others have done work in this field, these three are the only feminist thinkers, thus far, to present fully developed, comprehensive approaches. Their work, therefore, is essential to our assessment of the impact of feminism on Judaism and to the envisioning of Judaism's future.

The Path Forged by Rachel Adler

In her early writing, Rachel Adler brought a scathing critique to Jewish law.[2] In her groundbreaking article, "I've Had Nothing Yet So I Can't Take More," she asks, "Are women Jews?" and concludes that women are, in fact, not considered to be covenanted. She writes:

> The problem is that women will never be validated as complete Jews—moral initiators independent of their fathers, brothers, husbands and brothers-in-law—by proofs from a tradition in which ... women's holiness is purely contextual, depending on whether they are in correct formal status vis-à-vis some man.[3]

In her later, full-length work, *Engendering Judaism: An Inclusive Theology and Ethics,* Rachel Adler envisions the creation of an engendered Judaism that takes into account the impact of gender in the life of the Jewish community, both in the past and in the present. She calls upon us to acknowledge the reality that no traditional Jewish text is gender-neutral and then to wrestle with the implications of that for the lives of real men and women, in the process developing "a way of thinking about and practicing Judaism that men and women recreate and renew together as equals."[4]

Rachel Adler identifies a variety of ways in which Jewish narrative and legal texts can be reconstructed so that the "mending and healing [of] Judaism by encountering, renewing, and reclaiming the holiness in texts" can occur.[5] For example, to explore and decode Talmudic stories, she uses a multidisciplinary, heuristic approach that includes feminist literary analysis as well as object-relations psychology. In conceptualizing what a new halakhah might look like, she draws from the work of legal scholar Robert Cover, who views law as a bridge between two parts of the legal universe: the paidaic (world-creating) mode and the imperial (world-maintaining) mode. It is in the dynamic, chaotic paidaic mode that meaning is created through shared stories and ideas. In the imperial mode, order is created through the imposition of standard social practices that allow the various nomos created in the paidaic mode to coexist harmoniously. The two modes balance each other, maintaining a creative tension between reality and what Rachel Adler calls "alternity," between what is and what could be.

Rachel Adler argues that we live in an impoverished imperial world disconnected from the richness of the paidaic, and thus she calls on feminists to create a new kind of halakhah that would bridge the gap between the two worlds and "regenerate ... a world of legal meaning in which the stories, dreams, and revelations of Jewish women and men are fully and complexly integrated."[6] She claims that to do this we need to read and interpret sacred texts with new eyes, look to the wisdom implicit in "other revelatory stories about Jewish lives," and draw from our own sense of what is morally right.[7] In this way, she sees men and women making concrete their role as covenantal partners with each other and with God.

Rachel Adler explains that a feminist Judaism "keeps faith with texts by refusing to absolve them of moral responsibility. It honors halakhah by affirming its inexhaustible capacity to be created anew."[8] She holds that rejection of these texts for any reason, including the misogyny they too often reflect, is tantamount to rejection of the covenant. Moreover, she maintains that Jewish tradition is multivalent, ambiguous, and contradictory enough to accommodate a diversity of opinion and perspectives, and that patriarchy and the denial of the full humanity of women are not core Jewish values.

The Path Forged by Judith Plaskow

In an early article titled "The Right Question Is Theological," Judith Plaskow argues that the halakhic system presupposes the notion of the Otherness of women. She writes, "Underlying specific halachot, and outlasting their amelioration or rejection, is an assumption of women's Otherness far more basic than the laws in which it finds expression."[9] In her later work *Standing Again at Sinai,* she asks, "What in the tradition is ours? What can we claim that has not also wounded us?"[10]

Judith Plaskow goes on to suggest that it is naive to think that rectifying halakhic injustices will mean that women are no longer viewed as Other.[11] She sees halakhah as the tip of a vast iceberg, an expression of underlying theological assumptions that must be confronted and eradicated. Judith Plaskow suggests that the kind of systemic change in Judaism that is called for necessitates a reconsideration of the basic categories of Jewish theology: God, Torah, and Israel. She calls for an understanding of Torah that acknowledges "the profound injustice of Torah itself."[12]

For Judith Plaskow, the problem posed by Torah is the fact that women are excluded from the pivotal events and moments in Jewish history as it is recorded in the Torah, and that these moments are "not simply history but living, active memory that continues to shape Jewish identity and self-understanding."[13] Therefore, it is essential for Jewish feminists to redefine the past by recovering what she terms "the primordial Torah," or the "hidden half of the Torah," the missing record of Jewish women's history.[14] The tools she suggests for the work of reshaping Jewish memory are feminist historiography, midrash, and liturgy.

In her discussion of Israel, Judith Plaskow focuses on the question, "what would it mean to have a Jewish community that takes women's experience seriously?"[15] She then moves to a larger discussion of the conceptualization of difference in the Jewish community, which she sees as the central issue in a feminist redefinition of Israel. The problem, she asserts, is that difference is, at worst, hierarchized and, at best, tolerated within the Jewish community. We need to create a Jewish community, she argues, where difference is honored. She calls for "equality in our particularity."[16]

Judith Plaskow traces Judaism's relationship and response to difference to the Chosen People concept, which she rejects. She points out that the notion of chosenness arose in the wake of the exile, around 586 BCE, as a source of solace in the midst of disaster and as a way of reframing the disdain the Jewish community experienced. Ultimately, she argues, this resulted in the further erosion of women's status in the community. She writes, "The self-concept that emerged as a compensation for suffering and outward rejection, however, was exaggeratedly elevated.... In this situation, someone had to bear the weight of Otherness reflected in the mirror of the Gentile world...."[17] It was women, Judith Plaskow claims, who were forced to bear that weight.

Despite her rejection of chosenness, she wholeheartedly embraces and celebrates Israel's distinctiveness. She explains, "It is not in the chosenness that cuts off but in the distinctiveness that opens itself to difference that we find the God of Israel and of each and every people."[18]

Judith Plaskow also sees the hierarchical dualism upon which chosenness is based as the foundation for the modern State of Israel's lack of religious pluralism and its attitude toward its Arab citizens.

She writes, "The enduring inequalities of the Jewish community have found new and complex embodiment in the laws and structures of a nation state struggling to secure its existence and survival."[19]

Finally, Judith Plaskow focuses on the remaining element of the Jewish theological triumvirate, God. She reimages God from a feminist perspective and, in the process, provides a powerful critique of the use of exclusively male God language, including its role in the perpetuation of women's Otherness. She writes:

> Feminist God-language does not simply reject this sense of Otherness, but seeks actively to address and undermine it through finding divinity in what has hitherto been despised. In imaging God as female, as darkness, as nature, and as a myriad of other metaphors taken from realms devalued and spurned, we re-examine and value the many forms of Otherness, claiming their multiform particularity as significant and sacred.[20]

Honoring difference is at the heart of Judith Plaskow's call for the reconstruction of the categories of Jewish theology. She urges us to embrace difference rather than hierarchize it, so that no one is seen as Other and there is no longer theological justification for—but rather a clear prohibition against—the domination and exploitation of any part of God's creation.

The Path Forged by Rebecca Alpert

Rebecca Alpert's book *Like Bread on the Seder Plate: Jewish Lesbians and the Transformation of Tradition* is the first and only full-length Jewish theological work using the experience of Jewish lesbians as its lens. In it, Rebecca Alpert asks, "What would make it possible for lesbians to participate fully, as lesbians, in Jewish life?" Her answer is that Jews, Judaism, and Jewish sacred texts "must be transformed from a lesbian perspective," enriching not only Jewish lesbians but the Jewish community as a whole in the process.[21] Rebecca Alpert outlines three steps she sees as necessary to accomplish this goal: new interpretations of traditional texts, the introduction of more contemporary texts that reflect on lesbian existence, and finally, the creation of new sacred texts that are both Jewish and lesbian.

Rebecca Alpert tells us, "For me our textual tradition forms the core of Jewish life."[22] Later she concedes, "[Lesbians] claim a connection to a culture whose sacred texts incorporate ideas that exclude and hurt us."[23] However, she continues to trust in the tradition's ability to respond to her hurt and her need:

> If, however, we assume that Judaism has undergone radical changes over time and that it is in fact the flexibility and dynamism of the tradition that has sustained it, then we may see an opportunity to reinterpret and transform these rules and prohibitions as well as to reject specific ones if necessary and build on a new foundation.[24]

For Rebecca Alpert, there are three ways to read troubling passages of Torah through a lesbian lens: the "Interpretive Method," which refers to what Jews have done for centuries, that is, write midrash and commentaries to make a text relevant to the time in which it is being read, sometimes altering its meaning entirely to enable it to reflect the mores of a new cultural context; the "Historical Approach," by which the text is understood as a human-created product of its era, providing a window onto how a culture lived in a particular time and place; and "Encountering the Text," which means experiencing the text in its immediacy, without the lens of either midrash or biblical scholarship. It is in this third approach that anger and terror are fully felt, as we confront the plain meaning of the words, unmediated by interpretation. But Rebecca Alpert encourages us to move beyond our rage to a place where we can see these texts as "tools with which to educate people about the deep-rooted history of lesbian and gay oppression." She continues, "We begin to use these very words to begin to break down the silence that surrounds us. In this way, we can transform Torah from a stumbling block to an entry path."[25]

In addition to confronting problematic texts with one of the three approaches she outlines, Rebecca Alpert suggests expanding the definition of Torah to include texts such as the book of Ruth, which, she argues, can be seen as reflecting positively on lesbian love. She writes:

> We can find lesbian themes in Jewish texts once we are willing to ask the right questions. In order to read a lesbian perspective into ancient texts, we must search beyond the obvious to explore what the texts could possibly mean to lesbians claiming a place in contemporary Jewish society.... If there are to be lesbian role models, they must be found between the lines through imaginative reconstruction of the text.[26]

Rebecca Alpert explores a play by Sholom Asch and a short story by Isaac Bashevis Singer, contemporary texts that speak to the lesbian experience, encouraging us to expand "our notion of sacred texts to incorporate stories and histories that have been left out of the record."[27]

Finally, Rebecca Alpert speaks to the creation of new sacred texts that are both Jewish and lesbian. She writes:

> As Jewish lesbians we must ourselves take the opportunity to make our own lives part of this story. Our need is not only to transform traditional texts but also to transform our understanding of the sacred. Like Jewish feminists we insist that our lives themselves are text.[28]

Rebecca Alpert turns to lesbian fiction as a way of making lesbian lives a part of the tradition. She does this, she claims, because fiction describes not the reality of lesbian lives, but how we want them to be, in the context of a Judaism that accepts us. She compares these stories to midrash and heralds them for providing role models for Jewish lesbians and for transforming traditional views of holy time and space.[29] She maintains that these texts are crucial to a lesbian transformation of Judaism. She writes:

> They teach the lesson that our lives are the text. It is not enough to study the past and make new interpretations of it. It is not enough to use the text of the past to rethink contemporary practices. We must be engaged in creating new texts that can be passed on to the next generation. In this way, we write ourselves into the Jewish story.[30]

It is at the end of her work that Rebecca Alpert makes clear her position vis-à-vis halakhah: "With other liberal Jews [lesbians] are finding ways to create a Jewish life that is not based on halakhic (legal) precedent but is driven by a Jewish ethics that relies on values gleaned from the stories of our people—both ancient and those we are creating."[31] For Rebecca Alpert, text is the medium through which the transformation she is calling for is possible; telling our stories and having them be heard is the way to create a Judaism that embraces us all and that many who have felt alienated may learn to embrace in return.

The different approaches to theology undertaken by Rachel Adler, Judith Plaskow, and Rebecca Alpert, reflect the fact that the feminist Jewish community, like every community, is not monolithic. Each thinker's work speaks to the needs and concerns of different constituencies. Rachel Adler addresses the issues of those who feel committed to remaining in relationship to halakhah; Judith Plaskow's thought is particularly resonant for non-halakhic Jews who, nonetheless, understand the impact of halakhah and its assumptions on the Jewish community at large; Rebecca Alpert's work speaks first and foremost to the lesbian community, but also to all those who seek justice and inclusion in Judaism.

It has been many years since Rachel Adler, Judith Plaskow, and Rebecca Alpert first presented their work. While we have made some progress—for example, in the use of more inclusive God language in liturgy, the creation of new rituals that mark the milestones in women's lives, and the development of modern midrashim that serve to fill in the gender gaps in the Torah text—there has been very little, if any, experimentation with expanding the canon or introducing new texts that specifically reflect the experiences of women and lesbians. Feminism, to a large extent, remains something that is "tacked on" to Judaism. It is still on the margins, still too often relegated to a specific Shabbat or a special adult education session or Women's History Month. Feminist theology and feminist discourse generally have not made their way into the center.

In 1982, Judith Plaskow wrote, "The Jewish women's movement of the past decade ... has focused on getting women a piece of the Jewish pie; it has not wanted to bake a new one!"[32] Twenty-six years later, this statement feels equally true. How do we get beyond it and create a true paradigm shift? The work of Rachel Adler, Judith Plaskow, and Rebecca Alpert would lead us to create an engendered Judaism in which the Otherness of women, constructed by the tradition, is acknowledged, confronted, and ultimately abandoned as unjust and obsolete; to introduce texts written by women into the canon, so that women's voices are heard and women's experience is honored as sacred; to seriously take into account feminist theology in the creation of our prayer books, not only through the use of more inclusive language, but by rejecting hierarchical images of God and creating a liturgy that better reflects feminist concerns for such issues as the environment and social justice; to organically include feminist thought and perspectives into Hebrew school and adult education curricula.

Rachel Adler, Judith Plaskow, and Rebecca Alpert continue to call us to respond more vocally, more vehemently, and more radically to the patriarchy that remains at the heart of Judaism, even in the twenty-first century. Doing so will create a more dynamic, relevant, compelling, and just Judaism that will challenge, nourish, and at long last, reflect and truly welcome us all.

Rabbi Jill Hammer, PhD, is the director of spiritual education at the Academy for Jewish Religion. She is also the director of Tel Shemesh, a website and community celebrating and creating Jewish earth-based traditions, and the cofounder of Kohenet: The Hebrew Priestess Training Program. She is the author of numerous essays, articles, and poems, and also of two books: *Sisters at Sinai: New Tales of Biblical Women* (Jewish Publication Society, 2001) and *The Jewish Book of Days: A Companion for All Seasons* (Jewish Publication Society, 2006).

To Her We Shall Return[1]

Jews Turning to the Goddess, the Goddess Turning to Jews

RABBI JILL HAMMER, PhD

THERE WAS A TIME when the concept of the Goddess was off-limits to feminist Jews who defined themselves as part of the established Jewish community. God-She, the Divine Feminine, and Shekhinah were all acceptable options, but *Goddess* was a pagan term and therefore unavailable to those who wished to remain within Jewish theology and Jewish community. While pagan women who were Jewish by birth, such as Starhawk, might run off into the woods to celebrate the Goddess, the work of Jewish women was to reclaim Shekhinah, what kabbalists identified as the feminine side of deity. For the kabbalists, Shekhinah represented a kind of tangible female presence emanated from the Divine who could serve as a "bride" or as as a receptacle for the energy of the masculine Divine. Jewish feminists also explored Lady Wisdom, described in the book of Proverbs as a female help-meet or advisor of God. Yet Goddess was across the border, beyond the pale, past the signposts that defined what it meant to be a Jew.

As a young feminist with a traditional Jewish bent, I read many books and essays by Jewish feminists and other scholars in which God-She was considered valuable because her female form offered self-esteem and justice to Jewish women, but the Goddess was carefully excluded. The explanations I encountered commented that while Jewish women wanted equality, feminist theologians did not want to abandon the monotheistic faith of their forebears. While some voices objected to the lines drawn between the Shekhinah of Jewish history and the Goddess writ large, these voices remained few. I remember thrilling to poems about the Goddess with a vague sense of guilt, for if I believed in a Goddess, how could I go on calling myself a *Jewish* feminist? When I went to rabbinical school, my fascination with the wild side of feminine deity (as opposed to the relatively tame feminine of the kabbalists' Shekhinah) stayed underground.

In the past twenty years, something has changed. For Jewish women and men who seek communion with feminine divinity, the word *Goddess* is no longer off-limits. Jewish scholars such as Susan Ackerman and Daniel Dever have reexamined text and archaeology and learned that our Israelite ancestors spent more time with goddesses than the Bible ever let on.[2] Scholars and spiritual seekers such as Raphael Patai, Lynn Gottlieb, and Jenny Kien have shown the connections between the earliest goddesses and the images of the Divine Feminine we find in the Talmud and the Zohar.[3] In recent years, books, discussion lists, websites, and spiritual communities that speak of the Jewish Goddess have proliferated in the United States, Europe, and Israel.[4] Musicians such as Rabbi Rayzel Raphael and Yofiyah sing about the Jewish Goddess. There are even bat mitzvahs and Jewish weddings designed to be Goddess centered. While much Jewish Goddess activity occurs in neo-pagan, Wiccan, and feminist Goddess circles, it is now more common for committed and educated Jews to take an interest in this way of speaking about the Divine. The press has noticed these trends: in an article in the *Forward*, Jay Michaelson interviewed a number of cutting-edge Jews (male and female) about their innovative approaches to Goddess spirituality.[5]

As part of this trend, I have become a cofacilitator of Kohenet, a Jewish women's leadership program that explores Goddess imagery in biblical and rabbinic texts, as well as ancient and modern women's spiritual skills.[6] There is a growing group of ecofeminist or "earth-based" Jews, such as Irene Diamond, Jane Litman, Judith Laura, Rabbi David Seidenberg, and Rabbi Gershon Winkler, who draw on Jewish sources as well as on understandings of God/ Goddess as immanent in Nature to re-vision the Jewish relationship to the earth. While these kinds of spiritual expressions are not, for the most part, heard aloud in most synagogues, it is still true that over time, a shift has taken place. Let us track the unfolding of this Jewish spiritual uprising so that we may understand how and why some Jews, counter to traditional Jewish norms and even to the advice of some Jewish feminists, are choosing to find Jewish language for the Goddess.

Openings: How Jews Experience Goddess

To define what *Goddess* means is not easy. It can describe an experience of God, deity, or divine-within-nature that is non-dual,[7] immanent, holistic, and felt or imagined as feminine. This experience may be consistent with traditional Jewish ideas and images, or it may be different. It may be an experience someone seeks, or one that comes by surprise. Because the term *Goddess* resists easy definition, the best way to define it is to examine some of the spiritual experiences of Jews who use the term.

Rabbi Julia Watts Belser writes the following in her article "Making Room for the Divine She":

> I met God the summer I turned fourteen.... The sky was slowly turning purple, twilight shot through with darkening gold. The wind was crisp and bright against

my face, and the rocks were humming against my hands, pulsing with a kind of kinship I'd never known. She was none of that and all of it: the Presence that flooded through me, the feel of my own body finding center, the press of the balcony rail against my skin, the strange, sudden wideness of the sky. That meeting is the center of my story, the way a stone drops into the center of a lake and sends the water rippling out in slow, certain waves.... This memory is the truest answer I have to give when people ask me how Judaism and Goddess fit together.[8]

Belser's account is beautiful in its specificity, and yet it is typical of Jews who embrace Goddess as a spiritual truth. First, while Belser knows well how to speak theologically, and also knows how to express herself as a feminist, the core of her embrace of Goddess is an experience. Elsewhere in her article, Belser uses traditional Jewish ideas (such as the midrash in Pirkei de Rabbi Eliezer that God is a mirror reflecting each person's vision of divinity) to explain how she can attach to the Goddess and remain a Jew. Yet she speaks out of a personal and spiritual relationship with an entity. She writes: "Goddess is a being, not a belief."

Second, Belser describes Goddess as rocks and sky: as the universe, though she is more than the universe. This panentheism (belief in a deity that comprises all things, yet is more than the sum of its parts) is common among Jewish Goddess believers. The Goddess has a body, and it is all of existence. The femininity of Goddess comes not from an abstract notion of gender but from the way Belser experiences her. This experience is similar to the kabbalists' experience of Shekhinah as the sum total of the souls of Israel and the spiritual presence of the earth itself.

Third, while Belser invests in Jewish ways of believing, she is willing to open herself to experiences that are not bound by traditional Jewish imagery. It is her job to make the Goddess a Jewish experience, but that does not mean the Goddess is Jewish. As Belser herself writes, in the same article, "Religious experiences are not 'born Jewish.' They become Jewish as individuals and communities learn to express them Jewishly, to find a Jewish context for understanding and sharing them.... When communities engage intentionally in this process ... we create Jewish authenticity."

These three factors repeat themselves in the accounts of many Jews who meet the Goddess. In fact, discovering the Goddess is almost always described as "meeting." Kim Chernin, a Jewish woman writer, describes her first Goddess encounter:

> The first time I met Her she did not look Jewish. On the other hand, how should a Jewish Goddess look? Mine was dancing. She had huge breasts that were lifting and flopping. She picked up her knees, stretched out her arms, and bent from the torso in a ponderous dance that was both sacred and ridiculous and seemed to be taking place simultaneously at the center of my head, in my sinews and veins, in the room around me, and nowhere at all.[9]

Like Belser, Chernin describes an experience, not a theology. Again, the Goddess is embodied, in flesh and in the body of the speaker. Yet she is not the sum of the embodied experience; she is also nowhere at all. And, like Belser's Goddess, Chernin's Goddess is not Jewish, or at least she does not look Jewish. She is a universal feminine appearing to a Jewish witness.

Rabbi Lynn Gottlieb had her experience with the Goddess while attending a panel of feminist theologians. As she heard Ann Barstow describe her vision of an immense, many-breasted Goddess giving birth, she was troubled, then moved. Gottlieb writes: "Did She whisper to me then? She said: 'My body is the mountain, My birth waters are the parting seas. Speak these words and you will not be consumed.' What if I permitted other words, other images of God? What if I imagined YHVH as a woman giving birth?"[10]

Once more, the Goddess appears as immanent in the universe. She is evoked through the experience of hearing a woman tell about her. Her presence is confirmed through a whisper inside Gottlieb, a whisper that tells Gottlieb this feminine God-being is authentic and Jewish. Now Gottlieb's process of working the Goddess into Jewish life must begin—but the original experience is what sustains that project.

Rita Gross describes her own experience with feminine prayer language in Jewish contexts by formulating a theology, or theology of Goddess:

> The Goddess gives and She takes away, not out of transcendent power but because that is the way things are. She patronizes both birth and death, and neither is desired or undesirable.... What is born must die, and what dies nourishes life in some form.... The deity does not stand outside and above this round but rather is the round.... Limits, end points, and death are not punishments dealt by an external, transcendent deity but simply part of reality.[11]

This formulation goes far beyond feminizing God, and in fact adopts an attitude toward life that comes from pagan antiquity more than classical Judaism. Gross notes the places where Jewish theology approaches this vision, such as the morning liturgy's blessing over light and darkness, but she also remarks that this theology "develops these insights in significant ways." She concludes that varied and vigorous descriptions of the divine feminine will guard against stereotyping women (and men), and enrich Jewish life.

Gross's sense of the potential of a Jewish thealogy to change how we look at the world is echoed by Marcia Falk, who writes in her groundbreaking liturgy: "Let us bless the fountain eternally giving / The source of life, ever-dying, ever-living."[12] So, too, Alicia Ostriker, a literary critic and midrashist, writes of the Shekhinah: "Womb compassionate pitiless / eyes seeing to the ends of the universe / in which life struggles and delights in life."[13] The Goddess does not stand outside the world, but rather experiences it from within, in all its beauty and harshness.

Other accounts by Jewish women and men who have met the Goddess show similar characteristics. The growing number of Jewish Goddess followers is partly due to the success of the feminist spirituality movement (including popular Goddess-based fiction such as Anita Diamant's *The Red Tent* and Dan Brown's *The Da Vinci Code*); Western exposure to indigenous, Eastern, and shamanic cultures; ecological theologians' recent focus on Mother Earth; and the nature of spirituality itself, which does not always conform to orthodox theologians' wishes.

Most of the thinkers cited here do not seem to suffer the spiritual anxiety of Jewish theologians who have worried about the authenticity and monotheistic credentials of the Divine Feminine. Their experiences are authentic to them from the beginning. Descriptions of the experience may be buttressed by a sense of gender fairness, by midrash, or by kabbalistic doctrine, but the experience stands on its own.

Kabbalah scholar Daniel Matt writes: "The Goddess may have been expunged from the official religion of biblical and rabbinic Judaism, but She re-emerges as Shekhinah in medieval Kabbalah. This new flowering is a testament to the Goddess's enduring hold on the religious consciousness and an example of 'the revenge of myth.' Rendered kosher by the Kabbalah, Shekhinah became immensely popular."[14] Many Jews use the word *Shekhinah*, the term Jewish mystics used for an immanent, feminine aspect of divinity, as a Jewish word for "Goddess." Yet Shekhinah, as it is traditionally understood, represents only one experience of Goddess, by one group of male Jewish mystics, at one point in time. The Goddess may also appear in traditional Jewish forms such as the Sabbath bride or the wise and seductive Torah, but she goes beyond them as well.

Wrestling with the Goddess:
Sounding Out a Jewish Thealogy

As we examine accounts of the last twenty years, we see that Jews who gravitate toward the Goddess act out of trust in an experience shared with much of humanity: the cult of the Virgin Mary, Isis in ancient Rome, Kuan Yin in the Far East, the Shekhinah in kabbalist Spain and Sfat, and Oshun or Yemanja in the modern African diaspora. These Jews also find the *ideas* associated with the Goddess appealing—immanence, the sacredness of nature and the body, the celebration of women—even if many of them wish to balance those ideas with traditional Jewish views of God. How have Jews who accept the language of Goddess resolved the questions of monotheism and of authenticity? How have they answered, and how will they answer, accusations of syncretism, polytheism, and the like?

To begin with, our understanding of how Jewish religious history developed is now quite different than it was thirty years ago. Cynthia Ozick's clear condemnation of Goddess language now reads as an ideological myth rather than history:

> What? Millennia after the cleansing purity of Abraham's vision of the Creator, a return to Astarte, Hera, Juno...? A resurrection of every ancient idolatry the Jewish idea came into the world to drive out?... Without an uncompromising monotheism, there can be no Jewish way.[15]

While the Bible presents the Israelites as monotheists plagued by occasional backsliding toward idolatry, archaeological finds, as well as references in the book of Judges, the book of Kings, Jeremiah, and elsewhere, suggest that many Israelite generations after Abraham lived side by side with goddesses and had little problem with them. The writings of Deuteronomy and the prophets tell us that at some point, some Israelites (and/or some postexilic Jews) sought to expunge goddess references from their religion, but the traces of a lively Israelite interest in figures of the Divine Feminine are still present.

Works like Daniel Dever's *Did God Have a Wife? Archaeology and Folk Religion in Ancient Israel* have shown that the Goddess, in the forms of Asherah, Anat, and Astarte, was present in the lives of ordinary Israelites, probably up until the first Exile,[16] in spite of the prophets' objections. Israeli archaeologists have found beehives from a biblical-era Israelite community, decorated with female figurines.[17] An Asherah tree or pole stood in the First Temple for most of the time that the Temple existed.[18] Ancient inscriptions have been located connecting Yahweh and "His Asherah."[19] The prophet Jeremiah notes the widespread worship of the Queen of Heaven among Israelites of his day.[20] "The tree of life to all who hold fast to her" mentioned in the book of Proverbs is likely a carryover from the days when the Goddess was worshiped as a tree, a comfort for monotheistic Israelites who missed the feminine form of Asherah.[21] Jeremiah's vision of Mother Rachel weeping for her exiled children may be a similar image, allowing the Israelites the consolation of a grieving Goddess: a cognate to Ishtar mourning her young husband who descended into the underworld.[22] Even the Holy of Holies, an empty sacred space cleansed once a year by being sprinkled with blood, can be read as a feminine image: the Goddess cleansing her womb as the seasons move into a new cycle. The transition to monotheism did not bring with it a total rejection of the ancient connection to the Divine Feminine. The connection was transformed, rather than "driven out."

The links between Jews and the Goddess also cannot be limited to antiquity. Raphael Patai, in his foundational work, *The Hebrew Goddess,* traces the link between images of Asherah and Anat and Zoharic depictions of the Shekhinah, and discovers striking similarities.[23] Passover, with its spring birthing of the people through a watery birth canal, evokes the Goddess's birth powers, just as the spring festivals of other peoples did. Many of the objects on the Seder plate (an egg, a leafy green sprig, apples) are Goddess symbols.

Amichai Lau-Lavie notes that the Torah service has Goddess resonance as well: "The ark, the Holy of Holies, is separated by a curtain, like in the Temple, and behind it is the Torah, wearing a silver crown and velvet dress, always referred to in the feminine. Then we bring her out with great decorum, kiss her, undress her, open her up and commence the ritual of knowledge in the biblical sense."[24] The Goddess has never exactly been driven out, but rather absorbed, swallowed, interwoven with the fabric of the tradition that supposedly rejected her.

From this historical perspective, theologians who use feminine God language yet stay away from any terms associated with goddesses will have a hard time separating the two. The Shekhinah is a revision of earlier Goddess images—a revision created by Jews who, having left the Goddess behind, now found they could not do without her. The Zohar knows this, and says: "The truth is that the *Hei* [the letter of God's name that represents the feminine Divine] is called Asherah."[25]

Ellen Umansky posits that "to talk of God the Mother is not the same ... as talking about the Mother Goddess."[26] This is true only if we accept a psychological and spiritual split between God-She and the Goddess, one that does not really exist. Jewish formulations of the Goddess in the Bible (Lady Wisdom) and later kabbalistic literature (Binah and Shekhinah) have been "worked through" Jewish tradition and have been made consistent with monotheism (at least as much as possible). Yet they remain consistent with Goddess literature as well, in that many of the images and concepts (such as the tree of life, the womb of souls, the bride or daughter of the Divine, the divinity of physical matter) remain the same. This dual origin of Jewish language about the Divine Feminine has given Jews a more nuanced view of the "dichotomies" between God and Goddess, and between Shekhinah and Goddess. These nuances pave the way for future feminist understandings of how and why the Goddess was "submerged" in Jewish lore, and what her role might be in the future.

Jews who have experience of Goddess are developing a more subtle relationship to monotheism than their detractors would claim. Their project is similar to one that Rabbi Elyse Goldstein lays out in her book *ReVisions: Seeing Torah through a Feminist Lens* (Jewish Lights): "The Jewish feminist task is one of symbiosis. It involves merging the old goddess imagery, the new ways of thinking about God, and the kabbalistic notions of the Shekhinah ... with a staunch monotheism."[27]

This project of integration is indeed what Jewish Goddess followers have undertaken. However, the "staunch monotheism" Goldstein promotes has taken an interesting turn. We might label many Jewish followers of the Goddess "transmonotheists": Jews who assert the oneness of God without being particularly disturbed by polytheism. Like kabbalists who accepted God as divided into various *sefirot* (realms, energies, or personalities), these Jews understand the various expressions of deity to be "many" and "one" at the same time.

This form of monotheism can dialogue with polytheism by maintaining a belief in oneness while expressing an eager interest in the many ways deity can manifest in the world. Like the early kabbalists, Goddess Jews are reading Jewish texts and traditions in new ways, using a new symbolic system that morphs monotheistic and polytheistic stories and practices into transmonotheist opportunities to explore faces of the Divine. More explicit development of this theology has yet to unfold, and future Jewish feminists must work in this area to develop viable transmonotheist Jewish ways of looking at religion and deity.

This project has taken on some urgency, as Jews who seek the Goddess are well aware of the political and ecological benefits of incorporating this thealogy[28] into Jewish life. These benefits are the third major engine of Jewish Goddess spiritual work. The Goddess can and does support the notion that women's bodies and ways of being are holy (even if goddesses have not supported this notion in all times and places). The Goddess provides women and men with avenues to experience femininity in a sacred way. Further, while the

Goddess as embodiment of Nature may have been regarded as primitive and immoral by many of our ancestors, that earth goddess has a great deal to teach us. If we acknowledge that the circles of nature—life and death, evolution, ecosystem—are as important to our well-being as the unfolding of human progress, perhaps we will treat the earth more humbly. The preservation of the earth is one of the critical issues facing humankind, and theologies that support right relationship with nature are one of our resources for change and healing. Indeed, our struggle to understand our role on the planet will have a powerful impact on our belief system, and the experiences and faith systems described here may be part of that already unfolding impact.

One last benefit of Goddess theology: it punctures monotheistic self-congratulation. Just as Christianity demonized Judaism in order to succeed Judaism spiritually, it is likely that Judaism demonized the paganism being practiced at the time of the writing of the Bible in order to succeed it spiritually. The Bible, in spite of its extraordinary religious insight, is not a reliable witness regarding pagans any more than the New Testament is a reliable witness regarding Jews.[29] When investigating Jewish concepts around idolatry, we can harvest what is good about the relative imagelessness of Jewish tradition while reclaiming the value of spiritual humility.

Conclusion

While many of these observations are radical from the point of view of Jewish tradition, the Jewish project of Goddess reclamation is not so much an introduction of a new concept as an acknowledgment that she has been here all along. It cannot be denied that the circle of life the Goddess represents is a departure from the reward-and-punishment theology of Deuteronomy and from the inexplicably hidden face of the God of history. Yet she has roots in Ecclesiastes, whose author recites, "To everything there is a season," and in Proverbs, which proclaims, "Is not Wisdom raising her voice?" She has roots in rabbinic legend, where the Shekhinah hovers over communities at prayer, and in the kabbalah, where the Shekhinah is described as earth, sea, and moon.[30] While those who have not experienced the Goddess may find her threatening to the fabric of Judaism, the Jews who have met her are finding ways to integrate her into active, faithful, and authentically Jewish lives. The current impact of Jews who revere the Goddess may be small, but like the kabbalists of old, their effect on Jewish experience may indeed be lasting.

Rabbi Karyn D. Kedar is the senior rabbi and spiritual leader of Congregation B'nai Jehoshua Beth Elohim in the Chicago area. She is a distinguished author, and her works include *God Whispers: Stories of the Soul, Lessons of the Heart; Our Dance with God: Finding Prayer, Perspective and Meaning in the Stories of Our Lives;* and *The Bridge to Forgiveness: Stories and Prayers for Finding God and Restoring Wholeness* (all Jewish Lights). She has contributed to several anthologies, is a contributor to *The Torah: A Women's Commentary* and has created liturgical work that appears in the new prayer book for the Reform movement, *Mishkan T'filah.* She and her husband, Ezra, are the proud parents of three children.

Metaphors of God

RABBI KARYN D. KEDAR

THE WORDS WE USE to describe experiences and dreams, fears and aspirations, moments of darkness and moments of transcendence, create our reality and shape for us what we believe to be true. When we wonder, we use words. When we remember, we use words. Words have the power to shape our perceptions; metaphors bring forth images and pictures in our minds. They help us understand what is incomprehensible through mere logical deduction. Stories not only shape our narrative, our understanding of reality; they create it. Words are so important to the human experience and to our perceptions that when we are at a loss for words or, worse, when we are rendered silent and have lost our voice, bad things tend to happen. Ultimately any problem we have with God comes down to the words, metaphors, stories we use to describe that which is beyond description. If we create a God concept that is limited, biased, sexist, or even immoral, instead of rejecting God, we need to reject our concept.

The women's movement entered the world of God language and claimed that the King of the Universe was responsible for narrowing our image of God and, by extension, hindering the status of women. Feminist Jewish clergy neutralized the male-centric language of traditional religion, banishing the King and turning him into the gender-neutral Sovereign. We transformed YHVH into the Eternal. Father was called Parent or simply Aveinu (hoping no one would notice that the Hebrew word translates as "father"). The first generation of female rabbis pushed the envelope, wrote experimental services, played with images of the queen and a periodic goddess while ignoring the king, the warrior, and the punitive father.

Today people wonder if we went too far. I say we didn't go far enough. We banished the King and in doing so became blind to the Mother. If we ask the King to return from exile, we open ourselves to other imagery awaiting our discovery, such as the Birthing Mother. Many of us miss the poetry, the metaphor, the imagery of God language. This is less about God and more about our description of the ineffable. God is not a feminist issue; expression is. Words are power, metaphors transform, poetry inspires, imagery creates belief, and yet, despite our best attempts, God remains elusive. In the meantime, we create an image of God that becomes what we believe to be true, and if our description lacks richness and variety we become blind to other possibilities of expression, limiting the way in which we experience the Divine.

The Invisible Metaphor

For many centuries we have uttered the words, "Blessed are You O Lord our God, King of the Universe." These familiar words have led to the tendency to believe in God as an actual king. The image of the king is seared into our brain, crawling into our quiet places and becoming the dominant image we conjure up, sometimes even despite ourselves. Even today when students, children, teens, or adults are asked to close their eyes and share the first image of God that comes to them, the vast majority will see the king or a man with a white beard or Charlton Heston, all variables of the same image. A small minority sees wisps of color or clouds.

The king has taken over our visual mind and blinded us to other imagery. But one of the most powerful images we have already is God as the Birthing Mother. While she remains invisible to most people, she is at the very beginning of our Bible.

> In the beginning God created the heaven and the earth. The earth was unformed, with darkness over the surface of the deep and the spirit of God sweeping over the water. (Gen. 1:1–2)

The words used to describe pre-creation—*unformed, dark, deep, the spirit of God, water*—are a lovely and powerful description of the womb.

> God said, "Let there be light"; and there was light. God saw that the light was good, and God separated the light from the darkness. God called the light Day, and the darkness She called Night. And there was evening and there was morning, a first day. (Gen. 1:3–5)

God births the world into being. And God sees the light as good. And so to be created in the image of God is to be a creative force for good, to birth into being a bit of the world that is filled with light and goodness. It is a beautiful, empowering metaphor.

Another image for God, similar to the birthing mother, is El Shaddai, the God of Nourishment. Having birthed the world into being, this God must now nourish us with love, protection, and an abiding presence. There seems to be a connection between El Shaddai and the Hebrew word *shad*, meaning breast. We know of Semitic fertility goddesses in the form of small statues with large breasts. El Shaddai, the God of blessing, abundance, nourishment, fertility is known to our ancestors, and is a part of the blessing Jacob gives his son Joseph:

> By the God of your father, who helps you,
> Shaddai, who blesses you,
> with blessings of heaven above,
> blessings of the deep that lies below,
> blessings of the breasts [shadayim] and of the womb
> [rechem]. (Gen. 49:25)

Later rabbinic tradition hid Shaddai in plain sight by placing her on the doorposts of our house, on the mezuzah. Rabbinic midrash teaches that the three letters that make up *Shaddai—shin, dalet, yod*—are an acronym for *shomer delatot Yisrael* (Protector of the Doors of Israel). As we enter and as we exit our home and see the word *Shaddai* on the mezuzah, instead of seeing the God of Nourishment, Abundant and Fertile Blessing, we see God the Protector.

The Hidden Metaphor

One way to hide the metaphor for God without losing its power is to retain the written word while losing the spoken word. Consider, for example, the word *YHVH*. The leaders of the Second Temple period understood that words have great power. They assigned extraordinary power to this particular name for God and allowed it to be pronounced only once a year, on Yom Kippur. The high priest would enter the Holy of Holies to give voice to what was not spoken at any other time. He would utter the "proper" name of God and ask YHVH to forgive the people of Israel for their sins. This moment was considered so precarious and dangerous that the priests who aided in this ritual would tie a rope around the waist of the high priest so that if he were to die from the sheer power of the encounter they could pull him out of the Holy of Holies. But with the destruction of the Temple, the real pronunciation is lost to us; instead we pronounce the four letters, *yod, hey, vav, hey,* as Adonai, which means "Lord."

The root of the word *YHVH* probably comes from *hey, yud, hey* (to be). If God is a verb—such as with the name of God given in

Exodus 3:14, I Will Be What I Will Be—then the word *YHVH* is in the third person future tense masculine—He will Be. But if *YHVH* is a noun, then the ending of the word *(kamatz hey)* renders it feminine, translated as "She is Being-ness." No wonder the word was never pronounced out loud. This female designation for God was too threatening and so she was hidden in plain sight under the utterance of Adonai, or Lord.

The Mixed Metaphor

Literary convention teaches us that mixed metaphors tend not to make sense. However, Jewish literary tradition uses the mixed metaphor to enrich our understanding and experience of God.

For example, on the holiest moment of the year, the start of Yom Kippur services, while we are exhausted, vulnerable, and imploring, we say "Aveinu Malkeinu" ("our Father, our King"), over and over again. This is a classic mixed metaphor. Is God our father or is God our king? The metaphor of God as Father evokes an image of intimacy, love, proximity. Our father is the figure who loves us, hugs us, tells us a bedtime story, and protects us from the monsters of the dark. God the King, on the other hand, is distant, remote, and untouchable. The king lives in a castle on a mountaintop, protected by a moat and guards who do not allow us to approach. The king imposes a debt upon us, wages war, and does not share his wealth. As we say, "Our Father, our King," with hypnotic repetition in the midst of a litany of communal prayer, we are proclaiming two realities barely separated by a comma. We are acknowledging that sometimes we experience God as near, intimate, and loving, and sometimes as far away, inaccessible, foreboding. We are living in a mixed metaphor.

Another example is the phrase, "Av HaRachaman." *Av* literally means "father." The second word, *HaRachaman*, comes from the root *r-ch-m*. This root has two meanings: it can mean "womb" or "compassion." In English we express the power of female emotion as "hysterical," a term referring to both the female emotional experience and the womb (whose root is the Greek *hystera*). However, in Hebrew we take the power of female emotion and identify it with the word *compassion*, meaning "with passion," and then apply it to God. God loves us with the power of a mother who passionately loves and protects the unborn child in her womb. *Av HaRachaman*, best translated as "father of the womb," implies that God is neither father nor mother, but can be experienced as both loving and protective—a powerful mixed metaphor.

Beyond Gender: The Metaphors of Light, Shadow, and Sound

So did we go too far in seeking new ways of thinking about and addressing God, or not far enough?

Our God language has failed us in so many ways. Even rabbinic tradition warns us not to take literally what we hear and what we say. The Rabbis tell us that there are many voices used to describe what is beyond description. Every voice speaks according to a limited vantage point and perspective. Or as the Rabbis understand it, each of us "hears" the reality of God according to our strength, as in the midrash from Exodus Rabbah 29:1:

> I am the Lord your God.... It is written, has a people ever heard the voice of God?... (Deuteronomy 4:33)....
> Rabbi Levi explained: Had it said "the voice of God is in His strength," the world would not be able to survive, but it says instead: the voice of God is in strength (Psalm 29:4)—that is, according to the strength of each individual, the young, the old, and the very small ones. God said to Israel: "Do not believe that there are deities in heaven because you have heard many voices, but know that I alone am the Lord your God, as it says, I am the Lord your God." (Deuteronomy 5:6)

As the metaphors become literal, our perception of God is weakened, and, thus, our experience of God becomes limited. As Jewish feminists, the greatest service we can give is to call upon the poets of our generation to teach us once again that metaphor is symbolic, that God is beyond reach and can only be understood in whispers of meaning through images, and in pictures that are diverse and rich. God is "like" father and "like" mother. God is "like" king and "like" the womb. Above all, God is none of these. And beyond the metaphor of gender, God is my light, *Adonai ori* (Ps. 27:1), and God is wind, *ruach Elohim merachefet* (Gen. 1:2), and God is a silent whisper, *kol damma daka* (1 Kings 19:12), and God is the shadow beneath the wings, *b'tzel kanefecha* (Ps. 63:8).

I believe we can ask the King to return from exile as long as we pledge to become poets. The poets will tell us not to be literal and to look for meaning within meaning. The word for "king" in Hebrew is *melech,* and the three letters that make up that word are the three middle letters of the alphabet, backward—*mem, lamed, chaf*—as if to teach us that God is the center of all we do, all we are, and all that there is. The middle three letters of the Hebrew alphabet are like the marrow of expression, just as God is the central power of the universe. And yet those central letters are rendered as the word *king* only if they are in the reverse order, as if to teach us that when all is said and done, our words will be mere shadows of reality. As if to say: God is the king, the breath of life, the wind, the spirit, the mother of all. But not really.

Ellen Bernstein founded Shomrei Adamah, Keepers of the Earth, the first national Jewish environmental organization in 1988. She is author of numerous articles and books on Judaism, Bible, and ecology including *Let the Earth Teach You Torah, Ecology and the Jewish Spirit,* and *The Splendor of Creation.* She teaches courses on Judaism and ecology at Hebrew College. Learn more about her work at www.ellenbernstein.org.

Creation Theology

Theology for the Rest of Us

ELLEN BERNSTEIN

I HAVE A PROBLEM.

Every time I bring up the term *creation theology*—or even just *creation*—my highly educated friends and colleagues (scholars and rabbis), even my husband, grimace, snicker, or squirm uncomfortably in their seats.

But creation theology isn't creationism. And I believe that creation theology could be profoundly helpful to us as Jews today, particularly in light of the environmental crisis and the Jewish crisis—that is, the crisis of keeping Jews Jewish.

What Is Creation Theology, and How Is It Different from Creationism?

Creationism is the belief that the world was created by God in seven days. Literally.

Creation theology, on the other hand, refers to any kind of reflection on God and the world as a whole, or the elements of the world. It is interested in the nature of nature, and the nature of

42

humanity, and the interplay of the two. It understands God as the continual, creative Presence in the world, as compared to the triumphal, redemptive Presence bound to the nation of Israel. Finally, creation theology derives from the Bible's two creation accounts, but is in no way limited to these accounts. Rather, understanding the ecological language of the two creation accounts can help us to discern the ecological vision alive in the rest of the biblical corpus.

Creation, at least in Judaism, is an ongoing process, not a one-time event. The prayer book reminds us, "Who renews daily the creation ..." Life is an unfolding, evolving process. God does not just originate the world, God sustains the world, is the being of the world, or to use a more ecological metaphor, is the ground of our being. While *creation* does refer to the existence of something new, this does not necessarily entail creating "out of nothing." Much of the creation entails ordering. God works creatively with existing realities to bring about newness. Creation theology answers different questions than creationism. Creationism answers the question, how was the earth created? Creation theology answers the question, what is the nature of creation?

Jews who accept the logic of evolution theory should be relieved to learn that embracing a theology of creation in no way requires a suspension of rational thought or scientific integrity. The ancients paid attention to nature and their environment—they were astute observers in their own right; so much of the sense we can detect in the story results from their own grasp of natural history.

While creation theology is commonly discussed and employed by Christian Bible scholars and ministers, I have not found an adequate definition or framework for its application. Nor have I found more than a handful of Jews who identify their thinking or their work as creation theology.

I believe that naming creation theology as a legitimate category of Jewish thought and interest may help expand the Jewish conversation on the environment, spirituality, outreach, and interfaith matters. And I believe that this discussion could be enlivened and strengthened further through the ideas and values of the feminine in creation.

Creation's Ecology: The Other *Aseret ha-Dibrot*, Ten Principles of Creation Theology

Generally, the high point of biblical religion is thought to be the moment when God reveals the law to Moses. But according to some of the ancient Rabbis, creation was God's first revelation, and inscribed in the creation itself is another dimension of God's law. Unlike Sinai's law, which is explicit, creation's law in Genesis 1 and 2 is implicit. So we begin with a literary reading of these texts to see what we can learn about God and God's relation to the world, and about nature and human nature.

1. God as Creator

The first face of God we encounter in the Bible is God as Creator. Significantly, God appears as the wind, *ruach elohim*, not as the warrior who wrests creation out of chaos. The nature of the Creator God is a gentle pulsing, enlivening energy (Gen 1:2). The Rabbis said that it was as if God were a mother eagle hovering over the fledglings in her nest. Then God's wind/breath crystallized into sound and God spoke the world into being.

In the creation stories, God is artist (Gen. 1), potter (Gen. 2:7), farmer (Gen. 2:9), clothes designer (Gen. 3:21), arborist (Gen. 2:9), provider (Gen. 1:29–30). God is generative and generous, blessing the animals and people with multitudes; feeding every last one (Gen. 1:22, 28–30).

God is constantly in relationship with the creatures: engaged with the habitats in cocreation; engaged with Adam in naming the creatures.

Outside of Eden, the Creator God is the God of the harvest, God of the animals, God of the weather, and God of each person. The Creator God is the One that the biblical ancestors encountered in so many natural settings, whether in an oak tree at Mamre, a burning bush, a stone pillow, a cloud, or a mountain. The biblical characters were no different than many of us today who tend to find God more easily outside of our day-to-day lives, in the stillness and quiet of nature.

2. Goodness

According to the first creation story, everything that was created—light, the sky and water, earth, grasses and fruit trees, sun and stars, days and years, fish, sea monsters and birds, crawly creatures and wild animals, men and women—is good and has value. This value cannot be determined by any human measure—rather nature has essential goodness, simply because it exists; it was created by God. Being itself is related to godliness. This respect for "all that is" is a clear principle of a creation ethic.

3. Beauty

The creatures, in all their diverse forms, colors, and textures, are also beautiful. In his commentary on Genesis 1, Rashbam, the twelfth-century commentator and grandson of Rashi, translated the word *tov*, usually understood to mean "good," as "beautiful." In other words, on (almost) every day, God sees that that all elements of creation—seas, lands, vegetables, swimmers, flyers, and walkers—are beautiful. *Beautiful* has a very different connotation than *good*. The experience of creation's beauty can engage us more deeply in the world; creation's aromatic scents, exotic colors, and rhythmic sounds can stimulate our senses and trigger a full-bodied connection to the world. The experience of beauty can attract; it can inspire and motivate.

We must change our perspective if we are going to see the whole world as beautiful the way that God did. As perceivers, we must be open and vulnerable if we are to experience the fullness of beauty. In surrendering to the beauty of the world, we lose our self-consciousness and gain humility. Beauty is an important part of a creation ethic; it bids us to give up our self-centeredness and can teach us to care.

4. Habitat: A Sense of Place

God's initial actions in the first creation story involve dividing up the *tohu v'vohu* (unformed matter) to form the inhabitable and generative spaces of water, air, and earth. Only when the habitats are secure can fish, birds, and animals emerge, each relative to its specific habitat. In the second story, God starts with soil and water, makes a man, and then breathes air into him to give him life.

In both accounts, habitat (air, water, earth) matters; place matters. *Place* and *habitat* are words from two different domains—culture and biology—that refer to the same thing: the physical environment in which a creature (inhabitant) makes its home. Without habitat, without a home providing food, shelter, and air, no creature can exist.

5. Fruitfulness and Sustainability

Creation, as understood in Genesis 1, provides a vision of a healthy world that is not only able to generate multitudes, but is also able to sustain and diversify itself through the blessing of fertility. The biblical author is preoccupied with establishing a world that will continue on its own into perpetuity (with no help from people). The language also reveals the text's concern with species continuity: the root for the word *seed* is repeated six times in two verses (Gen. 1:11–12), the phrase "after its / their kind" is repeated nine times in five verses (Gen. 1:11, 12, 21, 24, and 25), and the explicit blessing for fertility in Genesis 1:22 and Genesis 1:28 also speaks to the Bible's abiding interest in sustainability. The ending of Genesis 2:3, which in many Bibles is translated as "[God] ceased on the seventh day from all the work that He had made," is literally translated as "God ceased on the seventh day from all the work that He *created to make*"—in other words, *to make more of itself*—providing further indication for God's primary concern with creation's ability to sustain itself into the future.

6. Interdependence, Relationship, Community

In Genesis 1, God depends on the habitats and unnamed others to help in the act of creation. On day three, the text states, "Let the earth sprout sprouts," as opposed to, "Let there be sprouts" (Gen. 1:11). On day six, God, addressing some unknown being or beings, says, "Let Us make Adam in our image, after Our likeness" (Gen. 1:26), furthering the sense of cocreation.

And while all the individual creations are deemed good, only everything all together, the interdependent world completed on day six, is understood as very good. "And God saw everything that He had made and it was very good, and there was evening and there was morning, the sixth day" (Gen. 1:31).

An interdependent universe is inherently a relational one. Creation theology understands the intimate relationship between Earth, human, and animals. God creates *adam* from *adamah,* human from humus. Both human and animals are made of soil, cut from the same cloth. Both fall in the same category of *nefesh chaya,* living souls.

Genesis 2 also describes a relational universe. In the effort to find a suitable partner for Adam, God fashions all the animals from the soil and brings them before him. Adam recognizes the essence of each creature and names it accordingly. We name what we care about. That God would offer the animals as potential partners and that Adam names each one are expressions of the close relationship that exists between the human creature and the rest of the creatures. In naming the creatures, Adam binds himself back to them; he now has a stake in their creation.

7. Language

The language we choose to describe our world matters, because language reflects our perceptions and reactions. Through language, we make sense of the world. The language of the creation stories is vivid and lyrical. Genesis 1 uses highly cadenced, rhythmic language to express a sense of the eternal; the language infuses the creation with dignity, even regalness. By using the same language for the creation of each living thing, the text emphasizes the equal importance of all that is created. On the other hand, the gripping narrative of Genesis 2 is profoundly compelling in its simplicity, physicality, color, and directness.

With all this attention to language, creation theology teaches that throughout the biblical corpus the allusions to land, water, and air, fish, birds, and beasts, barrenness and fertility, rain and drought, famine and harvest are not meaningless or empty. According to the Rabbis, there are no extra words in the Bible; biblical language is not arbitrary. The biblical author would not have wasted words on nature, were it not significant. Indeed, it is impossible to tell the biblical story without the language of creation and the ideas it represents.

Ethical systems do not generally concern themselves with poetry and language. But the medium does contribute to the message. If we pay attention to language we find in the creation accounts a profound sense of place. A sense of place is simultaneously an environmental principle, a literary principle, and a religious principle.

8. Boundaries

In the first creation story, earth, water, and air are created through the establishment of boundaries. Boundaries ensure integrity and protect that which is bounded off.

From earliest times, as evinced by Adam's and Eve's transgressions of the limits God placed on them in the Garden, people have had difficulties respecting boundaries. Like Adam and Eve, we are always craving something more—a quality that has certainly contributed to today's environmental crisis. The boundaries inscribed in the creation (and later reflected in the laws of kashrut) are a regular reminder—to those who choose to pay attention—that the observance and practice of "limits" is essential to a healthy and sustainable world.

In the case of Adam and Eve, the earth is cursed on account of their trespass. Where once the earth was rich, healthy, and bountiful, after they grabbed from the tree that was not theirs, the earth would yield only thorns and thistles. Where once they plucked low-hanging fruits whenever they felt hungry, now they must toil their lives away in the heat of the sun to bring forth grains from the soil to make bread to eat.

There is no such thing as running away or throwing anything away in an interconnected universe. Whether it is a physical pollutant or a spiritual one, what goes around ultimately comes around. This is the meaning of God's oneness. This is the character of the creator God's world.

9. Shabbat: Wholeness and Peace: Time Out

While each individual creature is deemed good, everything together, the interdependent system and its built-in processes of sustainability and dominion, is pronounced very good, and the whole of creation at rest on Shabbat is called holy. A day of utter rest and peace, a day apart, Shabbat offers a profound and necessary respite for humans and all of creation.

A day of rest, built into the fabric of the week, can be a profound environmental practice. The idea of taking one day off a week has been promoted by environmentalists who have suggested that if we "fast" from driving and using electrical appliances once a week, we will naturally learn to cultivate a greater respect for the resources we use (we will come to appreciate what we don't have), and this appreciation will help us to live more environmentally sustainable lives.

10. Humanity's Place: Dominion, Service, and Shabbat

Humanity's place in the creation is not altogether obvious. In the first creation account, humanity is granted dominion over the world. While there is much dispute about the meaning of dominion, I stand firmly with those who argue that it is our job to act as God's deputies on Earth, and it is our honor—indeed, our blessing—and our privilege to ensure the continuity and unfolding of creation on God's behalf: God, after all, not humans, owns the land and all its inhabitants.

In the second story, we are called to serve *(laavod)* and observe *(lishmor)* the land. In addition to these specific roles to both manage and cultivate creation, we are also given Shabbat, a conscious time-out from any interference with nature. On Shabbat we, along with all the other creatures, are called to recognize our creatureliness, our earthliness, and simply rest in nature, content in the deep peace of an interdependent universe. While the work week encourages an active stance in the world, Shabbat is reserved for simply "being" and celebrating the delight of creation.

The creation ethic balances human dominion—which so many environmentalists view in anthropocentric terms and see as the bane of our existence and the root of all environmental problems—with a more creation-centric, bio-centric view of the world: that is, Shabbat.

Creation's Ecology

Creation theology expounds a series of ecological principles, but speaks in a poetic and redolent language to communicate them. And because creation theology is deeply relational, it can be also understood as feminine (women are often described as the gender that is more concerned with relationships: giving birth, raising families, and nurturing all the relationships of the home).

The idea and language of creation most poignantly expresses a sense of human as creature and part of nature, not just master of nature. This idea is in itself an antidote to the malignant anthropocentrism that so many environmentalists see as the cause of the environmental crisis. On the other hand, the word *environment* referring simply to our surroundings, is flat, colorless, and clunky—an abstraction that gives no sense of life to the world that it connotes. The very idea of "environment" perpetuates a subject/object relationship in which nature is seen as separate from us.

As a Jewish community, we need to respond more deeply, and with inspiration, hope, and creativity, to meet the growing demands of an ecologically unstable world. The handful of Jewish laws—*bal tashchit* (do not destroy), *tzaar balei chayim* (kindness to animals), and *shmittah* (sabbatical year)—that are generally referred to as Judaism's environmental canon are not enough.

What we do need are texts, rituals, and language that will be able to inspire and motivate a whole generation. Rabbis and religious and communal leaders have a responsibility to keep the spirit of hope and joy alive in their communities and engage and sustain both Jewish young people and adults as environmental citizens for the long and potentially frightening and dispiriting haul ahead.

As a people rooted in language and story, we must reflect on how our story might provide us the language and perspectives to help us cope with mushrooming environmental ills. In order to do so, we will need interpretive principles or questions to ask of our texts. But at this point in our development, we are like the "simple child" at the Passover Seder, not even knowing what questions to ask.

Keeping Jews Jewish

Creation theology may turn out to be just as important to the Jewish identity, spirituality, and outreach discussions as it is to the environment conversation. Although some would say that theology is all about belief, theology has always had practical implications: how we think determines what we value and how we behave.

One of the primary concerns of the Jewish establishment is how to engage all those Jews who do not feel "at home" in a synagogue or Jewish community, and how to reach those who have abandoned the tradition. Some Jewish seekers leave the fold because they cannot find in synagogue life a spiritually satisfying language, process, or atmosphere. Some don't have the patience needed to give the Bible and Judaism a chance. Others leave because they are uncomfortable with what they think of as the biblical notion of God.

That God's name, YHVH, translates to "Being" or "Existence," and that all of creation is good, may be particularly meaningful to some of these Jews. Many spiritual seekers, especially those thousands of Jews who have abandoned Judaism for other spiritual paths, are often looking for traditions that accept and honor the world as it is, the world of being. These individuals are seeking refuge from today's pervasive idols—the constant grasping, the need to push ahead, the obsession with progress and the future, the belief that more is better, the conflating of success with wealth and status. The language and values of the creation can offer a sanctuary to those who are aching to stop and simply be. Creation values are consistent with a spiritual practice that is interested in a sense of interiority and spaciousness—that seeks to experience life moment to moment.

Grappling with our understanding and portrayal of God is a critical endeavor that does not happen enough in the Jewish community. How we imagine God—whatever God might mean to us— is connected to how we see ourselves and our relationship to the world, how we construct our values, and how we act. Because our understanding of God plays into our own identity, we need to be more cognizant of how certain views and language may create problems for all those unschooled and un-shuled. As more and more Jews turn to nature as their spiritual home, and more and more define their *tikkun olam* (repair of the world) in terms of environmentalism, the Jewish community must "open wide the tent" and establish a Jewish community in which these Jews can feel at home.

Summing Up: Creation's Spirituality

The language of creation has multiple valences; it simultaneously speaks to nature, creativity, and humility. It values the artistry and beauty of the world.

The language of creation is obviously corporeal, embodied. It may be particularly meaningful in an age of ever-increasing environmental problems and in a world that has become increasingly more plastic, where people spend their work lives in front of computers, their leisure time in malls, and their mealtimes eating fast food.

In a world that identifies religion with fundamentalism, it is time to take back the language of creation from the fundamentalists. By dismissing the language of creation, Jews have allowed fundamentalist Christians to set the terms for the meaning and value of creation.

Ultimately, creation theology can be invaluable to Jews. It is inherently generative and hopeful. It speaks the universal language of sand, stars, earth, and heaven. And it provides a common language by which we can express our deepest yearnings, communicate across cultures and beliefs, and work together on the most pressing issues of our day.

PART II

Women, Ritual, and Torah

AUSTRALIAN WRITER Philip Andrew Adams once remarked that "to many people holidays are not voyages of discovery, but a ritual of reassurance." We love and crave rituals because they are reassuring, predictable, familiar, and time tested. They remind us of our past and point the way to the future. They tell us who is in and who is out; who or what is most important to us. They remind us of where our communal boundaries lie. They inform us of our tradition's values and expectations. We come to expect the birthday cake, the anniversary roses, the Thanksgiving turkey as a part of the rhythm of a well ordered life. We color our Simchat Torah flags fondly every year and plan our *simchas* months, or even years, in advance.

Except in rare cases, rituals are more comforting than thought-provoking; they tend not to be experiences of intellect but of heart. They generally do not shock or discomfort us. But when and if they do, we face their change slowly and with some trepidation. We wonder how to reappropriate and reclaim them without having to throw them out and start from scratch. By its very nature, there is no such thing as a "new tradition." So it is in this area of reclaiming and reinventing ritual that Jewish feminism has the most work to do, and where it meets the most resistance.

Ritual has been defined as a customary observance or practice, or the prescribed procedure for conducting religious ceremonies. Using these definitions, we can see wherein lies the challenge of creating rituals that speak to contemporary women. We simply do not have a "customary observance or practice" for menstruation ceremonies. We do not have any "prescribed procedure" for what a women's tallit should be. Should we be creating these "new traditions"? If not, what do we do with the ritual gaps many of us feel when it comes to some of the most significant moments of our lives? And if we do create them, what should be our template? Who will decide if it "works"? Will our children and grandchildren find it normative?

We are poised between two focal points in this generation. On the one hand, we come from a long and hallowed Jewish heritage that has been modernized without losing its central character. Passover Seders may have new Haggadot and new tunes, but they follow the same basic lines that Seders always have. In our increasingly technological world, virtual communities still have not replaced the synagogue or the home, and we still gather to welcome a baby into the covenant whether the medical establishment encourages or discourages it.

But on the other hand, the twenty-first century has a whole new way of doing things. Ashkenazim freely adapt Sephardi customs, and vice versa, with no fears of "divided loyalty" or sanction. Because we can quickly learn from one another across the world, Jewish rituals are often driven by what we can find on the Internet, and put together from a hodgepodge of sources from everywhere both inside and outside of Judaism. Our spirituality is increasingly broad and global. Our denominational communities interact with one another more and more, and Jews connect both formally and informally with other religious communities all the time. Into this mix, throw feminism, with its concern for rituals that will speak to the spiritual needs and experiences of women. Caught between the old and new, we live in a dynamic tension that helps us create and yet prevents us from wandering too far off the Jewish map.

Jewish feminists often feel that they straddle the two stands, trying to be graceful preservers of tradition and forceful agents of change at the same time. Not easy, and certainly never dull.

Rabbi Danya Ruttenberg is the author of *Surprised by God: How I Learned to Stop Worrying and Love Religion*; editor of *Yentl's Revenge: The Next Wave of Jewish Feminism* and a forthcoming anthology on Judaism and sex; and coeditor of a forthcoming series of books on Jewish ethics. She has been widely published in books and periodicals, and was ordained as a rabbi by the Zeigler School in Los Angeles. More information can be found at http://danyaruttenberg.net.

The Hermeneutics of Curiosity

On Reclamation

RABBI DANYA RUTTENBERG

I HAD THE LUXURY of growing up in the eighties, in a Judaism that—thanks to the tireless work of the feminists who came before me—I understood to be gender netural. By the time I had become a twenty-year-old atheist, it seemed patently obvious that the deity in which I didn't believe was neither male nor female. Of course God is a being, not a boy! There was never any question in my mind that women could be rabbis, count in a prayer quorum, or serve in any ritual role that they chose. (It was, rather, quite a shock to discover along the way that a significant section of the Jewish world did not necessarily share my assumptions.)

There are a number of advantages to having your earliest experiences of Judaism as something other than a highly gendered faith that privileged both the divine masculine and the earthly one, and in which both feminine and female were shunted aside as either insignificant or problematic. Earlier feminist work had to correct a

59

long-standing imbalance by jettisioning much of what was down-right hostile to women. This reminds me of the old story (that has no basis in truth) of Elizabeth Cady Stanton sitting on the floor of her church with a Bible and a pair of scissors, snipping away every-thing in the book that was problematic from a gendered perspective, until she was left with a very slim volume indeed.

Now, at this late date, I think that we're able to look around at the scraps on the floor, to think about integrating, on feminist terms, parts of tradition that may have been initially discarded as a necessary part of the feminist process. What treasures are waiting for us to pull them out of the feminist garbage heap?

Some practices might be worth reconsidering with even the most basic deployment of textual analysis. For example, the biblical prohibition against sexual relations with a menstruant carries a long textual history in which women are depicted as evil and polluting—the dark, corrupting force that must be controlled. Stomach-churning examples abound; for example, the Talmud tells us that a woman "is a pot of filth whose mouth is full of blood" (Shabbat 152a), and that "if a menstruous woman passes between two [men]—if it is at the beginning of her menstruation, she will cause one to die; if it is at the end of her menstruation, she will bring strife between them" (Pesachim 111a). These understandings—and many others—of what underlies sexual separation are undoubtedly problematic; the question is, does that indict the practice itself, or only those inter-pretations of it?

In more recent years, some Jewish feminists have argued that this practice of sexual separation during menses *(niddah)* is an opportunity, rather than a problematic symbol of male contempt for women. It can be seen as a way both of honoring the body's nat-ural rhythms, and of designating certain times as worth our atten-tion and our notice, as we do every Shabbat and at innumerable other times in the Jewish year. It can also be regarded as a way of sanctifying intimate relationships, of instilling a sense of a sacred cycle into our partnerships. Some maintain that the traditional observance of *niddah* simply needs to be understood with new eyes, while others believe that a shift in interpretation is accompanied by a shift in praxis. In this case, we might maintain the biblical week of separation but discard the additional rabbinic "white" days that were imposed when healthy menstruation was conflated with bodily emissions associated with illness.[1] Feminist textual and halakhic analysis has allowed us the ability to tease away the neutral notion of sexual separation from later misogynistic overlays—both interpretive and halakhic—that have long determined how we understand what this practice should mean.

But surely, as Jews, we have the power to decide what this, and every other Jewish practice, can, should, and does mean. For, as ritual theorist Catherine Bell puts it: "The obvious ambiguity or overdetermination of much religious symbolism may even be integral to its efficacy."[2] In other words, many rituals, liturgies, and religious practices are open to interpretation, and may even work better when they can mean many different things at once. Therefore, sometimes we can embrace multiple levels simultaneously, and sometimes we can use this multiplicity of meaning to hear the same radio station on a different frequency. At other times, more radical reformulations are necessary. And, of course, there are some things that it may not be possible to salvage. We don't always have to go back, and obviously we don't have to embrace every problematic aspect of our tradition.

I wonder if, rather than operating with the famous "hermeneutics of suspicion"[3]—that is to say, the default assumption that a text or practice is misogynistic until proven otherwise—we might want to try a hermeneutics of curiosity. For example, when we come across something that makes us deeply uncomfortable, we might ask ourselves, what is this ritual (or rule, or piece of liturgy) really about? What are some of the ideas underlying it? How did it get to its current incarnation? How have people understood it in different times and places? And, perhaps most important, what potential does it have? To take a nongendered, but once hotly debated example, the

61

prayer praising God for the resurrection of the dead may have been written as a literal description of the Messianic era, but its underlying message about the cyclical nature of life and death is powerful and porous enough to hold both the ancient notion and more contemporary musings about mortality and existence. The language reveals a truth big enough to carry thousands of years of prayer, and has survived precisely because its wisdom transcends the particulars of time and place.

As feminists, we aren't obligated to accept everything handed to us by our patriarchal tradition. But as Jews, it behooves us to turn our traditions around a few times. Through a hermeneutics of curiosity, we we may not necessarily find everything we need already there from the start, but it's worth the extra spin to see if some notions can help us better learn how to connect to one another and to God.

But what criteria do we assign for an "adequate transformation"? How do we know when something has been sufficiently rearranged to be safe enough for those who care about gender equality in Judaism? A distinction forged by Martin Buber can be instructive here. That is to say, we might think of feminism as one process by which we enable the transformation of I-It relationships into I-Thou ones. In his famous formulation, Buber defined I-It relationships as those in which the other was regarded as little more than an object at one's disposal—a waitress is considered the object that brings food, a cab driver the object that drives to the airport. An I-Thou relationship is one in which one person regards the other person as a whole being, full of hopes and dreams and selfhood, as created in the divine image, in which the relationship is not bounded by a utilitarian framework.

Historically, of course, women have been regarded as "It" by the dominant patriarchal structure. In many traditional Jewish sources, women are portrayed as the "It" who bears children, earns a specific amount of money, mixes drinks, incites sexual desire that distracts from Torah study, puts the opposite sex at risk of ritual impurity.

Women's hopes, dreams, humanity, and needs are rarely recognized—and when they are, it is often with a limiting caveat. For example, the Talmud suggests that a woman who refuses to sleep with her husband on the grounds that he is repulsive to her is not necessarily required to stay married to such a man. Even so, her husband has the power to decide whether a divorce will proceed, and she is sent out without her *ketubah,* the monies designated to her by her husband at the time of marriage. The assertion of selfhood, here, extracts a heavy penalty—one that would be devastating, and quite a deterrent, in the socioeconomic reality of times past. Many women, no doubt, preferred to remain an "It" and sleep with men they found repugnant than to, at best, be cast out, penniless, without any means to feed or sustain themselves.

It could be argued, then, that feminism has been, in part, aimed at the creation of "Thou's." It casts the women who had once been objects as agents. It asserts that women's hopes, dreams, and selfhood must be brought to light, and seeks to change the systems that subvert or repress women's ability to do so. Feminism at its best seeks the creation of I-Thou relationships, and strives to create a communion between equals.

Given the vast number of tools that Jewish feminists have developed from years of interpretation and inquiry, we have untold powers to transform I-It practices into ones that are I-Thou. A hermeneutics of curiosity might show how the wisdom lurking underneath layers of problematic agendas can serve us. For example, with *niddah,* if there are times that sex is taken out of our relationships, perhaps it can help us to see one another as Thou—not only because other means of communication and relating must be employed, but also because sexual connection is not taken for granted.

Or, for another example, the practice of *shmirat negiyah*—that is to say, the custom of not touching members of the opposite sex, other than perhaps immediate family members—is particularly difficult. It's patently heterosexist, assuming first and foremost that men desire women and that women desire men. It presumes binary gender because, according to this formulation, we are all clear on what a "man" is and what a "woman" is, and there are no gray areas in these deliniations. How would people whose biological sex and personal identity don't match our cultural expectations, and people whose biological situation defies these categories, navigate this practice? Perhaps most troubling, *shmirat negiyah* rests on the conflation of sexual and nonsexual touch, transforming even the most benign of encounters into charged confrontations between people who serve as sexual threats to one another. It creates and enforces I-It relationships, rather than teaching us how to meet other people as fully human, fully Thou.

And yet, even with these limitations before us, a hermeneutics of curiosity can challenge us to look for underlying concepts that could be of value. That is to say, touch is a powerful, intimate thing, not to be treated casually. Feminists—those raised as women, particularly—are all too aware of the ways that touch can comfort, connect, confuse, or trouble. Are there ways in which we can think about touch as part of a sacred encounter, and create a series of conversations about how this insight might look in a feminist context? On the one hand, a feminist reclamation would not regulate touch in quite the way that it often is regulated in contemporary communities of *shomrei negiyah.* On the other, respect for individual personal boundaries can certainly be part of how we show respect for the wholly embodied other—the Thou whose own needs may differ from our own.

Another site of classic I-It imposition on women is that of modesty. In Jewish praxis, modest behavior *(tzniut)* is often understood to be one and the same with the regulation of women's dress, speech, and behavior, lest her objectified femalehood stimulate inappropriate desire in the male subject. But this formulation of *tzniut* is hardly the only one possible, or even the original idea behind the theory. Indeed, at the core of modesty, as Maimonides and others have formulated it, is care and consideration for others. Maimonides argues, for example, that modest behavior is reflected in the volume you use to speak to others, in the effort to not show off your money, and, even the way you comport yourself in the restroom.[4] It's about allowing the presence of others to affect your actions.

An ethic of modesty, therefore, can be about intention and the attempt to maintain a connection with ourselves, God, and other people, rather than about the length of a skirt or a hemline. Rather than thinking of the laws of *tzniut* as seeking to transform women into desiccated objects meant for the male gaze, we can relate to *tzniut* as subjects attempting to connect with other subjects. How can we think about modesty in which our embodiment and agency as subjects are paramount, and in which, if we choose to alter our behavior to accommodate others, it is done out of care and respect, and not coercion and shaming? I believe that we can find a way to create a healthy feminist culture in which appropriate measures of interpersonal awareness can be transformative on the individual and cultural levels. It is crucial that we have challenged the normative contemporary execution of *tzniut* as the policing of female behavior. But, at the same time, there are also compelling reasons—Jewish, feminist, and human reasons—to reconsider it now, with all of our tools of feminist analysis and reconstruction at the ready.

While we can't blindly accept practices and traditions inside Judaism that destroy or subjugate women, we have the ability to transform many aspects of our tradition into vehicles that can help us to seek the holy, and to serve God by learning how to better relate to others in caring and connection. It is tempting to leave behind anything that suggests patriarchal domination, but sometimes, mixed in with troubling notions about gender are centuries of questions about how best to live in relationship to the Divine. I think that we do ourselves a disservice when we do not try to find those questions, and when we do not engage them on our own terms. Through a hermeneutics of curiosity, we may be able to help repair a broken Judaism, to turn it into something more whole and complete than it's ever been. And who knows? We may even find ourselves repaired in the process.

Lori Hope Lefkovitz, PhD, is Gottesman Professor of Gender and Judaism and director of Kolot: The Center for Jewish Women's and Gender Studies at the Reconstructionist Rabbinical College. She is executive editor of www.ritualwell.org, and the author of books and articles in the fields of literature, critical theory, and Bible. Lefkovitz has been a fellow at the Psychoanalytic Institute of Philadelphia, has held a Golda Meir fellowship and a Fulbright professorship at Hebrew University, and a Woodrow Wilson dissertation fellowship (for doctoral work at Brown University). She and Rabbi Leonard Gordon are parents of two daughters.

Rabbi Rona Shapiro joined Congregation Bethaynu in Cleveland, Ohio, in August 2007 as its spiritual director. She previously served as senior associate of Ma'yan: the Jewish Women's Project in New York (2000–2007) and executive director of Berkeley Hillel (1990–2000). Rabbi Shapiro was ordained by the Jewish Theological Seminary in 1990. She has written and published numerous articles and is the founding editor of the website ritualwell.org.

The Politics and Aesthetics of Jewish Women's Spirituality

LORI HOPE LEFKOVITZ, PhD, AND RABBI RONA SHAPIRO

These reflections on the relationship between the Jewish women's spirituality movement and the evolution of Jewish women's liturgy and ritual practice emerge from our collaboration as the first editors of the website www.ritualwell.org.[1]

Gender-Neutral Spirits in Gendered Bodies

Women's spirituality movements emerged from the marriage of two distinct challenges to American institutions and social and religious

norms and roles, both enabled by the political and economic conditions of the late 1960s. One offshoot of the sixties youth rebellion
was the spirituality movement, which reclaimed religion from establishment church authority; another was the women's movement,
which invited women to reimagine their collective position in society. While the former championed the individual against the hereto-
fore-unexamined coercive power of large group traditions, the latter
sought to organize women, often disadvantaged by their isolation in
suburban homes,[2] into groups that would become an alternative
base of power. The more particularistic manifestations of these
social trends among young, bourgeois Americans included a bud-
ding Jewish spirituality movement and what may best be characterized as the imaginative possibility of a Jewish women's spirituality
movement.

This fantasy of a Jewish women's spirituality movement was represented notably in E. M. Broner's novel *A Weave of Women* (1978)
and was realized in a smattering of Rosh Chodesh (New Moon)
groups, Jewish variations on secular women's Consciousness Raising
(CR) groups, which were built around the reclamation of an ancient
Jewish festival with a traditional relevance to women.[3] Like CR
groups, Rosh Chodesh groups included personal sharing, but they
also often included Jewish learning and new rituals and foods
related to the Jewish calendar and holiday cycle as well as to the personal, individual life cycle needs of women in the group.[4] At once a
product of a political ideology that imagined building women's
community and of a social ideology that maintained the right of
each individual to unique spiritual self-expression, the Jewish
women's spirituality movement contained the contradictory principles favoring individual creativity, on the one hand, and group solidarity, on the other. Innovative and traditional at the same time,
Rosh Chodesh groups became a laboratory for creative rituals.

In effect, these early women's movements were seeking the normative privileges enjoyed by men, even as what was normative was
being challenged by countercultural critique. In parallel fashion,

the very words *spirituality* and *ritual* carry some competing connotations. Where *spirituality* may be taken as pointing to freedom of expression, individuality, and internal processes of the spirit, *ritual* connotes rote behaviors, shared communal norms, and traditionally prescribed physical actions (often involving props). Spirituality and ritual may even seem to work at cross purposes. From the first, Jewish women's spirituality managed a balance between the freedom of innovation and the tradition of ritual through the creation of what Claire R. Satlof, in her reading of *A Weave of Women,* calls a "counterlife," in which women "seize control of the traditionally male-oriented forms, and more notably create female-oriented ones."[5]

Broner's novel, in which distinctive and very different women gravitate to one another to form a unique community in Jerusalem, is a significant foundation document—even a manifesto—because it inaugurated the Jewish women's spirituality movement with characters who, in Satlof's description, "reply to the traditions of Judaism with new mythic models of spirituality and new opportunities for ritual reenactment."[6] The fiction characterizes these very different women in relation to one another, to their inner lives, and to the sacred: sacred place, sacred seasons, sacred occasions, and sacred events, from birth through death, and much in between. This particular evocation of the sacred is clearly Jewish, but with a clear feminist perspective different from traditional Jewish expressions.

What is important for us here is that these "new mythic models of spirituality" are expressed primarily through new group rituals and begin to establish what Satlof, over twenty years ago, called "a Jewish feminist poetic." According to Satlof, the relationship between spirituality and ritual, in the novel and in Judaism, is rooted in Jewish theology. Theology, she explains, is shaped by sacred stories, and Jews relive aspects of sacred stories through "ritual imitation and reenactment of archetypal events." Participants in ritual performance either imitate the Divine or "assume the holiness and power of the original ancestor, reasserting Jewish belief and history."

For Jewish women, however, "some rituals are forbidden, others carefully circumscribed.... The very world of women—the world of the physical, the bodily, *gashmiut*—is separated from the spiritual, *ruhniut* and only men have traditionally inhabited the latter."[7]

The body/spirit split, in which the female is associated with the body and the male with the spirit, is a well-documented prejudice of Western culture and has been addressed extensively by feminist theory in recent decades.[8] Although traditional Jewish thinking typically presumes a mind/body split, the body nevertheless provides access to the spirit, through the wearing of ritual garb, the physical practices connected with prayer, and other enactments, such as waving a *lulav* (date palm frond); and the body is celebrated as a vehicle for linking one's own spirit to the Divine. Many of these practices excluded women—who, for example, did not don a tallit (prayer shawl) or tefillin (phylacteries)—and there were no rituals to honor what is specific to the female body, such as the onset of menstruation or childbirth. Thus, Jewish ritual reinforced the time-honored prejudices that took for granted women's inferior potential for spirituality and the maleness of the Jewish spirit.

Jewish women's spirituality can be characterized, then, in part, by its investment of spirit into the particularities of the *female* body. The Western tendency to oppose body and spirit is mitigated by rituals in which the body is the vehicle for spiritual transformation, and a first step in accommodating women's spirituality was to grant women access to ritual garb, whether traditional tallitot and tefillin or new and different items designated expressly for women.

Invention or Imitation? Reconstruction and Reclamation

As feminist theory challenges the very premise of a mind/body split, directing us to think about the body as a social construct and about gender itself as a matter of performance rather than essence, the very phrase "women's spirituality" betrays an old-fashioned willingness to countenance deep, socially harmful prejudices: that there is a spirit distinct from the body; that this spirit is somehow gendered; that women's humanity is somehow essentially distinct from that of men. Political feminism, by contrast, requires the category of "woman" for purposes of social organization, even as it seems increasingly counterproductive to assign any essential meaning to the category "woman" itself.[9] One of the first practical feminist questions faced by Jewish women who sought greater participation in Jewish religious life was whether to presume male Judaism as normative and adopt and adapt male practices, or to reinforce female distinctiveness by inventing distinctive women's ritual expressions articulated in a Jewish idiom.

Are male Jewish ritual garments and practices normatively Jewish, and if so, should women adopt them? Should they be adopted as is, or adapted? Alternatively, do we resist adapting male practices altogether and go the route of invention, and if so, how do we undertake that work, authenticate it, and normalize it?

For some women, the demand for women to don tallitot and tefillin indicates that women must in effect become men, by wearing male garb, in order to empower themselves as Jews. Others believe that tallitot and tefillin are the garb of the Jew, and simply because women have not, by and large, had access to this meaningful ritual attire in the past does not mean that they should not wear it now, any more than they would decline to wear judge's robes or surgical scrubs because women came late to the professions of medicine and law. What might be the compromises between these positions, and what are the consequences? More seriously, are we threatening the strength and unity of Jewish women's community by creating further subdivisions among Jewish women, for example, by separating feminist practices along denominational lines? Some, mainly Orthodox, feminists resist adopting the ritual accoutrements of men as a key to equal status; for others, however, the history of separate spheres for women and men at first spurred resistance to traditional women's practices, such as ritual immersion in the mikveh, which seemed tainted by a history of folk prejudices.

From the earliest alternative prayer books of Jewish feminists[10] to websites such as Ritualwell.org, women have sought to revalue menstruation by developing prayers honoring the significance of the onset of menses. How sadly ironic that Judaism, which takes notice of the life force of blood in ritual areas from kashrut (dietary restrictions) to "family purity" (the requirement for physical separation between spouses during and immediately after the wife's menstrual period), offers so little in the way of marking the transition of a body into its potential to create life. Because prayers or ceremonies marking this event would have to be adopted by adolescent girls, it has been particularly challenging to introduce them into Jewish life, since the girls themselves often are reluctant to participate.[11] This is an example of the complex larger question of how Jewish practices that expressly respond to women's biology are to be integrated into the body of established Jewish custom.

There has been comparable neglect of conception and birth, events that have relatively few Jewish prayers or practices associated with them. One particularly lovely suggestion takes advantage of the Jewish folk practice of adding a candle to the Shabbat candelabrum with the birth of each new child in a family. The new ritual marks conception—the exciting but anxious time when new life is anticipated—by adding an unlit candle to the Shabbat candelabrum. It sits unlit until the first Sabbath after the birth, when the candle joins its glowing fellows and becomes a permanent weekly addition. In the unhappy event of a miscarriage, the unlit candle is lit midweek, a mini-*yahrzeit* (memorial) candle for an unrealized promise. The beauty of this ritual comes from the way it addresses the historical neglect of conception, miscarriage, and birth in a distinctively Jewish idiom.[12]

Birth seems self-evidently a moment that requires sanctification, an event that yields easily to the language of spiritual discourse and transcendence. Other transitions seem less clearly religious or feminist by the standards of this rhetoric. However, given what we see as Judaism's fundamental attention to practical matters and urgent life

71

concerns, we included in our broad definition of "feminist rituals" some that either acknowledge the diversity of life or sanctify life's diversity. The acquisition of a driver's license exemplifies a transition that seems to us to cry out for a strong Jewish ritual. In the minds of many contemporary suburban teenagers, the day they receive a driver's license is the most important in their lives after their bat or bar mitzvah celebrations. It signifies real adulthood, power, and independence.[13]

If women were the first to note the absence of ritual for significant life passages—childbirth, miscarriage, menopause, to name a few—that awareness has highlighted the absence of ritual for other significant transitions. A feminist canon, we believe, would enable us to sanctify all such moments. Does this, at some point, become silly? Are there moments not worthy of ritual? Traditional Judaism answers that question in the negative—we have blessings for waking, going to the bathroom, eating, sleeping, and seeing a rainbow. The new body of liturgy and ritual, to which we are midwives, is experimental. Over time, some of it, we believe, will find its way into the canon, while some will fall by the wayside.

Perhaps one of the most interesting aspects of Jewish women's spirituality in the last several decades is that it participates in a larger trend of progressive Judaism to create and institute non-compulsory Jewish practices. Such extra-halakhic innovations may be part of the feminist challenge to hierarchy, though there are many existing *minhagim* (customs) that, while they do not have the status of halakhah (Jewish law), are widely accepted in some parts of the Jewish community; examples include *hag habanot* (a celebration of daughters on one of the nights of Hanukah, once practiced by Jews of *Mizrahi* [Eastern] origin), men's use of the mikveh, *kapparot*, the recitation of *t'chinot* (prayers written for and by women), and so on. We may be working toward the elevation of some new rituals, such as those for naming baby girls, the bat mitzvah, and Miriam's Cup, to the status of "commanded at Sinai";[14] others are in trial stages, and some will remain *minhagim*, practiced by some and not by others. We are mindful, too, of the Jewish principle that repetition (classically, three repetitions of an observance) has the force to transform a custom into a rule.

The sanctification of our individual lives, separately and apart from the national story, is another new emphasis, one that derives partly from the spirituality movement's concern for an individual's personal religious experience. Whether people are seeking to sanctify their life transitions or seeking inspiration for their own creative, more personalized efforts, the increasing popularity of noncompulsory, individualized practices might represent a change in how Judaism will most often manifest itself in the lives of many American Jews. These are bold moves that, in some ways, may affect the face of Judaism far more than our choice of gendered pronouns.

The Politics and Aesthetics of Spirituality

From the fanciful Jewish women's rituals described in *A Weave of Women,* to the recovery of folk traditions and Jewish women's prayers from earlier generations exemplified in the work of Nina Beth Cardin and Chava Weissler,[15] to the new anthologies of women's life cycle rituals and other explicitly feminist liturgies (such as, among others, the Ma'yan Hagaddah, Kolot's feminist Omer counter and egalitarian Shabbat *benscher* [booklet used for blessings at a meal]), and Marcia Falk's *Book of Blessings*), resources for Jewish women's ritual are proliferating. The future of these resources and their impact on the lives of practicing Jews is not yet clear. How to choose among them, moreover, is a problem for every practicing Jew who makes choices, whether it be in planning a wedding ceremony or a Seder, or in deciding whether or not to sanctify Jewishly a daughter's onset of menses. Surely Judaism will evolve, as it always has, in some mysterious natural way. But equally certain is that Judaism will evolve, as it always has, through processes of vigorous debate.

Clearly, there is a process that leads to the inclusion or exclusion of a ritual in the canon(s) of Judaism, and this process points to something that we might identify as the politics and aesthetics of spirituality. The phrase has a paradoxical quality, inasmuch as *spirituality,* with its connotations of intimacy and spontaneity, seems contrary both to the formalism of "aesthetics" and to the all-too-this-worldly concerns of "politics." But what may be called the politics and aesthetics of Jewish women's spirituality seems to us a serious and important area of inquiry as informal Jewish women's expressions are shared in books and on the Internet and make their way into new rabbis' manuals, siddurim (prayer books), *mahzorim* (festival prayer books), Haggadot (liturgies for the Passover Seder), and other publications where living Judaism becomes codified.

The Feminist Criterion

What exactly is a feminist ritual? We envision a world fully inclusive of women, men, and children, their voices, and the range of their experiences—biological, communal, and personal. We strive toward a Judaism that names, embraces, and when appropriate, sanctifies those experiences. Therefore: a bat mitzvah is a feminist ritual because it includes girls where previously they were not included; a ritual for menopause is a feminist ritual because it sanctifies a life passage that our tradition has previously ignored; and a ritual celebrating becoming a father is a feminist ritual because it also sanctifies a passage ignored by tradition and because feminist Judaism sanctifies the experiences of both men and women. We also believe that protecting the earth, working for peace, fighting against racism, striving toward economic justice, and fighting for human rights are feminist causes.

Pronouns: Gendering the Divine

When we begin our conversations about what we mean by feminizing Judaism, we find ourselves on the smallest level of determinations: that of pronouns. In the development of feminist liturgy and ritual, should we compose everything in male and female variations? Jewish feminist theology began with debates about pronouns, famously with the exchange between Cynthia Ozick and Judith Plaskow in Susannah Heschel's early collection, *On Being a Jewish Feminist*.[16] Here the concern was over what pronoun a feminist Judaism could responsibly use to refer to God. Lois Dubin reopened this difficult debate in an article in *CrossCurrents* as recently as 2002.[17]

This pronoun question—how to refer to the deity—is more tangled than the question of including the feminine in our prayers when referring to the worshiper, who traditionally was grammatically male. The questions that feminists have raised are both age-old and modern; in some ways they are very similar to thousand-year-old questions about the nature of divine Being, yet the attention given to issues of gender and hierarchy, which are at the forefront of feminist re-visions of the Divine, are unique to our era. These are hardly simple pronoun questions, but ultimately, they must find a resolution in the words we pray.

Although the masculine formulation, the assumed choice for centuries of prayer, does not necessarily imply a male God, its constant and universal use has had the effect of gendering God as male and reinforcing the equation of maleness and power.[18] To provide blessings in traditional masculine God language on Ritualwell.org would not serve our ends. To provide only feminine blessings would tip the scales the other way, forcing people to use a language that is uncomfortable for many and unacceptable to some. Some would argue that it is no better to address God in the feminine than in the masculine, while others feel that by using both genders we move toward a God who encompasses masculine and feminine attributes. Cautioned by poet Marge Piercy's words, "I serve the word / I cannot name,"[19] we come down on the side of compromise: use both masculine blessings, with a bow to tradition and many Jews' expressed preference, *and* feminine blessings, in the hope that Jews might gain familiarity with them and begin the difficult work of integrating masculine and feminine in the Godhead (as the kabbalists sought to do). The debate about how to refer to God remains unresolved, and many Jewish communities are struggling with the competing, urgently felt needs of their members.

Authenticity and Judaism

It is surely the job of those who publish rituals—on the Internet or in books—to do our best to ensure that the rituals are of high quality and are authentically Jewish. If people use a new ritual, it has authority. If people don't use it, it doesn't gain authority. But, again, questions of determination quickly assert themselves: What is effective spiritual expression? What is authentically Jewish? Can you have one without the other?

Again, there are no easy answers to these questions. Mordecai Kaplan might have said that a ritual is Jewish if Jews do it (though such a broad definition of "Jewish" risks including Christmas trees). Others see the authentic stamp of Judaism in the incorporation of Hebrew, but it seems to us that the mere use of a *she-hechiyanu* does not, in and of itself, mark a successful Jewish ritual. Many people declare that Judaism offers us a plethora of rituals, and we don't need more; or, to the extent that we do, they are defined by halakhah.

In the end, the most compelling criteria, albeit subjective, are: Does the ritual resonate with Jewish tradition as practiced? Does it utilize Jewish symbols in ways appropriate to them? Does it make use of traditional prayers or texts in innovative ways that remain true to their essence? Does it feel Jewish? So, for instance, the ceremony using candles for a baby in utero accords nicely with the custom of adding candles to the Shabbat candelabrum as children are born to a family. Using a havdalah ceremony to mark weaning or a child's leaving home for college also works. According to one member of the Rosh Chodesh group that created Miriam's Cup, "It was as if *Kos Miriam* ["Miriam's Cup"] already existed and was just waiting to be discovered."

Authority and Quality

Who will decide about those small important pronouns, the words our communities speak when they pray? The rabbi? The books we publish? Communities swayed by the winds of the time?

The politics and aesthetics of spirituality continuously raise the question of authority: Who among the creators or users of new Jewish practices has the right to bring them into the Jewish community? Some Jewish feminists have suggested that there is an unofficial, unelected group of women who have been given implicit authority to introduce feminist interpretations and practices into Judaism—Jewish feminist leaders. Others have argued that feminist ritual requires no authorization; indeed, the concept of "an authority" points to the very hierarchy that we are resisting. Like all ritual through all time, ultimate authority rests in the hands of the users. New prayers and practices assimilate into the tradition or fade away in the most democratic of all evolutions.

Some new practices quickly seem time honored; others take hold more slowly; while still others are never adopted by Jews in community. Jews are often surprised by the relatively recent dates of some of the prayers in the classical siddur (prayer book). Some new prayers, such as those that mourn the losses of the Shoah or celebrate the State of Israel, found relatively easy acceptance into Jewish liturgy, while traditional fast days such as the seventeenth of Tammuz have fallen into relative neglect among non-Orthodox Jews. Famously, Jewish authorities in different historical moments sought to omit the Kol Nidre prayer from the Yom Kippur liturgy because of the possibly dangerous confusion that might ensue from this public renunciation of vows. But Kol Nidre and, more vitally, the music to which it is chanted, somehow represent the height of Jewish spiritual expression for enough of us Jews that we have never been willing to let it go.

If our standards for "Jewish" are subjective, our standards for quality are even more so. How could they be otherwise? A few criteria other than the Jewish ones have emerged. A successful ritual must balance the personal and the communal. If it is too personal, it may be opaque to the participants. The personal, however, adds to a ritual's meaningfulness. It is what motivated the person to create the ritual in the first place. So, balance is critical.

Less is more. Sometimes ceremonies incorporate a little bit of everything and fail to be any one thing. Similarly, with explanations: if every symbol and gesture has to be explained, they are probably not working. Many of us have had the experience of participating in a ceremony in which so much is explained that you cannot enter into the flow of the ceremony and participate meaningfully. In a good ritual, explanations are kept to a minimum; if necessary, they can be included in the introduction or provided to participants in a written program.

Finally, since most rituals (here we mean full ceremonies, not isolated prayers or ritual gestures) mark a transition from an assumed "before" (two single individuals, a baby who is not yet a part of the Jewish community, a pre-kindergartner) to an "after" (a married couple, a child who has been brought into the covenant, a child going to school), the ceremony should reflect that movement. The before and after stages should be clear, and "something" must happen in the middle. It is that "something" that gives participants the feeling that they have witnessed an event, that the times before and after the ritual are distinct from each other. A series of readings, poems, statements, and songs, however beautiful, may fail as rituals if they provide no clear sense of movement or demarcation.

Keva or Kavvanah?

Judaism is, after all, a religion that legislates behavior, often by legislating ritual and prayer, with prescribed words and actions for everyday moments and special occasions, for the Sabbath and festivals, and for life transitions. For this reason, the rituals and liturgy of the Jewish women's spirituality movement are now reaching toward codification, demanding their place in the canon of Judaism and in the lived experience of practicing Jews. If the spirituality exemplified in *A Weave of Women* was characterized by spontaneity and passion, the process of codification and legitimation may involve compromising on core ideals that inspired the current spirituality movement in the first place. Ironically, perhaps, Jewish women's spirituality, which developed as part of a countercultural movement to revitalize fixed (and sometimes seemingly empty) religious forms and in response to the neglect of women in classical Jewish rituals, has evolved to a place where remedying the neglect of women in a serious and sustained way requires us to fix their place in Jewish ritual life.

In our work for Ritualwell.org, however, we have become convinced that the movement from Jewish women's spirituality toward a more deliberately egalitarian Judaism has raised the spiritual consciousness of Jews more generally. The creative work of Jewish feminist men and women, who have evaluated traditional Jewish practices and revised and invented traditions to meet current needs for meaningful religion, has made for more spirituality in Judaism at every level of Jewish practice. For example, feminist Seders have wrested families from the routines of their home Passover rituals and redirected people's attention to the religious meanings of the Seder's details. The communal practice of women's model Seders has enriched many family home Seders with new readings and activities, waking participants out of the habits that can flatten what we call "spirituality." The time and attention that parents have devoted to creating meaningful baby-naming ceremonies for daughters where none had existed before has led to the importation of meaningful elements into *brit milah* (circumcision) ceremonies for baby boys, so that what had often become a quick ritual before a bagel brunch has been reinvested with the sanctity that comes from thought and attention.[20]

What may be emerging, as an effect of the Jewish women's spirituality movement, the Chavurah movement, and other outgrowths of the sixties in the Jewish community more generally, is a third path that winds between reified and spontaneous ritual practices—a distinction more classically phrased as that between *keva* ("fixed" liturgy) and *kavvanah* (spiritual "intention" or inspiration). This path is characterized by a democratization of leadership, a reduced role for rabbis and hired professionals in life cycle rituals, and more people feeling free to invent rituals and compose prayers that personalize their occasions. The publication and success of *The Jewish Catalogue* was an early expression of this phenomenon.[21] Today, the Internet is the vehicle for contemporary extensions of this new Jewish spiritual democracy. If the technology of the printing press had something of a freezing effect on the once more flexible liturgical practices of Jews, the Internet may have a defrosting effect, bringing us closer to the creative spiritual practices of our ancestors.

Conclusion

Feminist, idiosyncratic, bold, the Jewish women's spirituality represented in *A Weave of Women* seemed almost fantastic when the novel first appeared. Today, welcoming baby girls ceremonially, performing healing rituals in a mikveh after sexual assault, and other Jewish religious acknowledgments of women's experiences are increasingly finding their way into the mainstream. More important, Jews who are interested in religious practice increasingly appreciate that they are free to express their spirituality outside of the framework of the synagogue and without the leadership of a rabbi. Individuals experiment; the community ratifies. The Jewish women's spirituality movement recognized that Jewish spirituality is rooted in ritual praxis. The democratization of religious spirituality—putting religion into the hands of its practitioners—has been made possible by resources, delivered in books and, increasingly, via the Internet, that make the details of Judaism and the proposed innovations accessible, clear, and compelling. Ritualwell.org is one of the recent instances of this democratization and is a participant in a larger movement to develop a more inclusive Judaism—a goal inspired, in part, by the early expressions of the Jewish women's spirituality movement.

Rabbi Elyse Goldstein, editor of this book, is the director and founding Rosh Yeshiva of Kolel: The Adult Centre for Liberal Jewish Learning, the first liberal adult education center in Canada, and only one of a few in North America. She is one of seven women featured in the Canadian National Film Board documentary *Half the Kingdom*. She is the author of *ReVisions: Seeing Torah through a Feminist Lens* (Jewish Lights) and *Seek Her Out;* and editor of *The Women's Torah Commentary* and *The Women's Haftarah Commentary* (both Jewish Lights). She is the 2005 recipient of the most prestigious award in Jewish education, the internationally recognized Covenant Award for Exceptional Jewish Educators.

The Pink Tallit

Women's Rituals as Imitative or Inventive?

RABBI ELYSE GOLDSTEIN

AT THE SHABBAT morning service during the national biennial conference of the Reform movement, the question of ritual and women became clarified for me once and for all. I stood, preparing to put on my tallit. This tallit is definitely not your average black-and-white-striped variety. It is appliquéd silk, all blues and greens, a full poncho-style garment that reaches to my knees. I put it over my head and adjusted the neck, which has strands of sparkling color and tinkling bells. The top comes over my head as a hood. If there ever was a *cohenet gedolah,* a high priestess, surely this is what she would have worn. I stood silently for a moment, feeling the sensuous raw silk on my back, my front, my arms. I closed my eyes. And from behind me I heard a loud, startled whisper, "What the heck is she wearing?"

Rabbis in the liberal movements in general, but specifically women in the rabbinate, are being approached more and more with the challenge of adapting age-old traditions to a more contemporary reality affected by feminism and the feminist analysis of religion. At the same time, we are also being asked to create new rituals to fill the void where an absence is palpable—around birth, fertility and infertility, menstruation and menopause, growing old. The upsurge in interest in spirituality in our movement has deeply affected us, and women in the rabbinate often are thought of as "experts" in this growing field of the creation and adaptation of ritual for women.

This call for new ways of looking at Jewish ritual is a call many women in the rabbinate have taken personally. After I created a weaning ceremony for my own children, I submitted it to several resource centers and I know it has been copied, modified, and reused by other rabbis for themselves or their congregants. Ritalwell.org is a frequent source for women trying not to "reinvent the wheel" but to find what has already not only been done, but been successful. Mikveh ceremonies for miscarriage, rape, chemotherapy, and midlife milestones are being written and shared through personal contacts or word of mouth. Covenantal rituals for baby girls, more creative than the "baby naming" or the egalitarian ceremony in my rabbi's manual fill my files. Yet, to be honest, many of us experience moments of ambivalence around these creative, invented ceremonies that speak to the soul but seem unconnected to much of Jewish history and shared experience. I imagine us looking at ourselves in the same befuddled way those conference participants looked at my tallit, asking, "What the heck are we doing?"

We have learned through the writings of Lawrence Hoffman, Riv-Ellen Prell, Neil Gillman, and others that rituals provide a marking, a delineation, a framework of meaning around normal events. They sacralize moments that at first glance appear to be mundane because they are in fact so universal, so predictable, and so cyclical. For example, everyone somehow gets born. Those who live to young adolescence reach puberty. In most cultures, people marry or form permanent relationship bonds that create families. Everyone dies.

Participation in a birth ritual, a puberty ritual, a death ritual not only frames this otherwise normal experience, it defines the experience; in essence, the ritual creates the experience.

In Judaism, these central concepts take shape in our rituals. A *brit milah* is a defining ritual. It reframes the perception of the birth of a baby boy from a physical moment in time to a reenactment of the ancient covenant between God and Abraham. Standing under a chuppah (ceremonial canopy) at a wedding is a defining ritual. It identifies the couple as standing under the roof of their newly created Jewish home and is a reenactment of the first "wedding" or coupling—of Adam and Eve. Thus, in Judaism not only do rituals create experience by separating and marking moments, they also serve to create experience in the participant by moving her or him from the realm of "spectator" to the realm of "actor." The baby boy is Abraham. The couple are Adam and Eve. This transformation is achieved not through theories and theologies but through actual drama. Perhaps the best example is the Passover Seder, when we reexperience the bitterness of slavery through the rituals of eating *maror* (bitter herbs), *charoset* (a paste of fruit and nuts), and so on. We reexperience our slavery by acting it out in very specific ways.

So Jewish feminists ask, when do women function as actors in this historical drama? How is a woman's life framed and defined through ritual? How is a woman's experience expressed in Jewish ritual?

We have certainly passed the first stage in answering these questions. Baby namings, bat mitzvah, egalitarian weddings are the norm and no longer the exception. When I was ordained in 1983, doing a covenantal ceremony for a girl in her home on the eighth day or shortly after birth was almost unheard of. Now, at least in my experience, the practice is fairly common. Bat mitzvah is almost standard practice, and some form of it has been accepted in more traditional communities. Women wearing tallitot in synagogues is not the kind of strange sight it was years ago, leading to stares and glares and hostile remarks.

In the progressive movements, we have encouraged what I term imitative ritual. In imitative ritual we redesign the traditional model, but we do not reimagine it. We imitate it, with a "female" twist on the end. Thus a woman's tallit looks no different from a traditional tallit except in color, material, size, or specific design. It may have flowers or rainbows instead of black stripes. It may have lace or be made of silk instead of wool. But it is still a four-cornered shawl with fringes on the end. We take the model of tallit and "feminize" it. A bat mitzvah still includes the traditional rubrics—the girl reads from the Torah, writes a speech, has a party. A baby naming looks like a bris, but without the cutting.

A few years ago I was in Jerusalem, in a Hasidic neighborhood near the Western Wall, surrounded by stores carrying tallitot, kippot, and the like. To my utter shock, prominently displayed in one store's window was a bright pink tallit! I went inside and inquired of the owner, "Who would buy such a color of tallit?" "A bat mitzvah girl of course," this Hasid with sidecurls and knickers said, with no hesitation. Perhaps not the girls in his community, he added, but he was not dismayed at the thought of selling this pink tallit to some Reform or Conservative family for their daughter to don on her bat mitzvah day. The pink tallit is imitative ritual at its best. It adds just a little bit of "femininity" to an established, accepted practice that has been in the male domain for generations. The warning that the pink tallit teaches us, in a crass way, is that women's spirituality is not only about the inner needs of women, it is also about a marketing opportunity and an untapped consumer group. Let's face it, by including women in the "national Jewish agenda," there is money to be made. It's one thing when a feminist artisan creates a Rosh Chodesh necklace. It's another when Hasidim manufacture pink tallitot.

Imitative rituals work best in more formal synagogue settings. They seem to be the modus operandi of Reform and Conservative, and most Reconstructionist, synagogues. Interestingly, because of halakhic considerations, the Orthodox change the "packaging" of women's rituals the most, so as purposely not to imitate. Thus a bat mitzvah for an Orthodox girl is often called by another name—bat Torah or graduation or the like—and looks nothing like a bar mitzvah. The girl does not read from the Torah or haftarah as a boy would; instead she might give a speech or do a community service.

The question is no longer about whether we need rituals that balance the scale, that are "equal" to the traditional rituals celebrated by men. In the liberal movements we have, and we continue to answer that question with egalitarian adaptations of traditional ceremonies. The second-stage questions we need to address have to do with inventive rituals: Do we as women want to merely imitate traditional male rituals or ritual objects—bris, bar mitzvah, tallit, tefillin—or do we want to invent our own? If we choose to be inventive, what will our rituals look like? How will they be uniquely our own? Will they include men? Will they focus on our biological womanhood—menstruation, childbirth, lactation—or a more inner sense of womanhood not defined by physicality? How will they become the normative, established, accepted route of the progressive movements in synagogue contexts?

To be sure, imitative rituals can be extremely meaningful and satisfying. They fulfill the need for balance. They address the exclusive maleness of so much of our traditional life cycle events. They normalize the entrance of women into the public religious life of the community. They make the tradition confront the spiritual needs of women and include women on every level in the dramatic and sacred moments of life.

But on another level, imitative rituals do not satisfy. They say nothing of us as women. They do not mark the unique moments that happen only to women. They do not bond us with other women in a historical way. They wrap us in male imagery, making us "honorary men" for the moment. They express Judaism in ways that still are male ways of envisioning the universe, male ceremonies imagined and invented by men. They are still largely male answers to the question, how shall we mark this moment? We do not know how women would have answered long ago, when many of these rituals were in their infancy. I often joke with my students: If Miriam had been asked instead of Moses, how would she have expressed being bound up with God? I'm just not sure she would have dreamed up black leather straps wound tightly around the arm and a black box on the forehead! Inventive rituals may be the beginning of an answer to the question of how to mark the moments of women's lives.

Inventive rituals reimagine, start from scratch, have no historical bounds or expectations or communal sanctions or communal standards. They ask, is there something uniquely female about this act, about this object? By definition, they are probably not traditional. For example, I once took a woman to the mikveh after a rape. "What ritual will we do? What prayers will we say?" she asked. There was no ritual to imitate, and so we had to invent. The same goes for rituals for first menstruation, for menopause, for lactation and weaning, for pregnancy, infertility, and miscarriage, for divorce, for children leaving home, for hysterectomy, for mastectomy, for rejoining the work force after spending years at home, for rejoicing in the company of women, for forming bonded friendships, for caring for an elderly parent.

A few years ago in Toronto we first staged an event called Succah-by-the-Water. Under silk banners and branches inside a tent, we formed "*lulav* circles," circles of ten women who introduced themselves by their matriarchal lineage, then shook the *lulav* (date palm frond) in honor or memory of women who never could. We made "trees of life," silk leaves with prayers written on them like papers at the Western Wall, then sewed them onto a huge fabric tree that we would bring back to the celebration each year. It is reminiscent of a succah, indeed, but not at all like one. It is an invented ceremony in almost every way. To truly mark not only the significant transitions in our lives as women, the unique moments in women's experience, the drama of womanhood, but also women's perceptions of ritual, women's specific gifts and outlooks and ways of seeing the world, there simply have to be new rituals.

But inventive rituals are risky. They are not linked to thousands of years of practice. They do not look like what your bubbie did. A menstruation ceremony, a menopause mikveh celebration, a silk and appliqué tallit cape with a hood, do not look or feel familiar. It's not the "haimish," folksy Judaism from your childhood. One ceremony does not necessarily link to the next, as Purim links to Pesach, as bar mitzvah links to chuppah. And we miss the knowledge that every other Jew in history and in this time is doing this ritual or marking this event.

We will need to be scrupulous so that our new rituals don't divide us; so that they do not assume heterosexuality or heterosexual marriage and exclude other sexualities and relationships; so that they do not assume childbearing as the norm and exclude women who choose not to have children or who cannot bear them or who do not marry. We will need to be open to the many facets of being female so that we do not fall into the trap of defining ourselves as the patriarchy has defined us—as child bearers, child rearers, caregivers. We are, to be sure, rooted in our physicality, but that is not our sum and total being. There is a danger that we will redefine ourselves right back into the original definition we rejected back in the 1960s: as wombs, breasts, and baby makers.

We will need to be sensitive to language, and we will need to invent new ways of blessing these moments. New rituals that are creative and innovative may feel weird when spoken in traditional prayer language. Can we say *asher kidshanu,* God "commanded" us, to do a menstrual ceremony? Perhaps that very same *asher kidshanu* gives the moment some historical context and a reference point. But on the other hand, new prayer language for old rituals may feel equally out of kilter.

We will need to study and reflect on where these inventive rituals intersect with traditional Judaism and where they do not. We will need to contemplate ways to make these rituals "feel Jewish" so that, while they are not bound to a long history, they speak deeply to us not just as feminists, but as Jews. In this, we find ourselves in a catch-22: These ceremonies don't feel Jewish because Judaism historically has not included women in the discussion of what feels Jewish. These rituals do not feel Jewish because the rituals that do "feel Jewish" have been created exclusively by men. To make them "feel Jewish" we will have to probe into the meaning of authenticity. Why does a tallit look the way it does? What makes any inventive ritual authentic? How do those in a non-halakhic Judaism define ritual and its call upon us?

These questions can be asked, of course, from a viewpoint beyond that of only gender. How do we balance the tightrope between accepted traditional rituals that give us collective context and memory (for example, the Passover Seder), and new rituals that continue our goal of inclusivity and personal meaning (midlife rituals, renewal of marriage vows, blessing our college-bound children, and others)? We add, we subtract, we change, we adapt, and at what point do we say: enough, this ritual is now exactly the way we want it? And what about rituals that mark the lives of men? Should we be satisfied only with what came before? Jewish men in the progressive movements may not feel any more bound to traditional forms than do women. Shouldn't our inventive rituals invent also for men?

And a dark spot remains to cloud these sparks of creativity. Why do these ceremonies seem so hard to find, promulgated mostly in "women's" books, in Rosh Chodesh groups, among women rabbis, or on Internet search engines that women know about but men don't seem to access? Why aren't they more mainstream and widely available, widely practiced? Those of us who do know of these rituals and are in positions of leadership must introduce them into mainstream congregations and organizations so that they can reshape and transform the Judaism we have inherited into a feminist Judaism. We must also be prepared to accept that sometimes inventive rituals do not work. We should not be afraid to try again when a ritual fails, but we also should not discard a ritual if it is awkward after only the first attempt. It may take several times for a ritual to feel natural to the participants (though if a ritual continues to fail on repeated exposure, it may be time to try something else). These practices need to be collected, published, promulgated by the lay and professional arms of our movements. Colleagues who now create and perform these rituals need to be invited into congregations and organizations not only to lecture on the subject, but to lead people in these ceremonies. Women in our congregations and girls in our schools need to be surveyed and asked, "What do you need?"

In the near future, I hope our sons and daughters will see and participate in these rituals as normal, predictable, and cyclical Jewish events, defining moments of a Jewish life. They should not be marginalized experiences of women's groups or periodic, frustrating attempts at gaining meaningful spiritual entree to our congregations, camps, schools, and institutions. In the much nearer future, I hope our male colleagues will take up the call and join with us in this new endeavor, that all in our communities may feel fully served.

Rabbi Geela Rayzel Raphael serves Beth Israel Congregation in Woodbury, New Jersey. She is the rabbinic director of InterFaithways: Interfaith Family Support Network of Greater Philadelphia, and is the visionary behind the Jewish Women's Spirituality Institute. After studying at Indiana University, Brandeis, Pardes, and the Hebrew University of Jerusalem, she was a Wexner Fellow at the Reconstructionist Rabbinical College. Rabbi Raphael is an award-winning songwriter/liturgist and sings with MIRAJ. She is a freelance teacher and ritual maker and is guided by her angels in service to Shekhinah. Her website is www.shekhinah.com.

From Ancient Times to Modern Meaning

Jewish Women Claim Their Ritual Power

RABBI GEELA RAYZEL RAPHAEL

Background

JEWISH WOMEN'S RITUAL life has never been static. The foundation for feminist Jewish rituals begins in the past. We have glimpses of the rituals practiced by biblical women in the oracles of Rebecca in Genesis 25:23, the mourning of the daughter of Yiftach in Judges 11:1–40, the weaning ceremony of Hannah in 1 Samuel 1:24. In the Talmud, Abeye's mother shares her knowledge of incantations and healing (Babylonian Talmud, Shabbat 66b). During the Middle Ages, we have examples of childbirth rituals as well as *t'chinot* (prayers written for and by women) for the mikveh, candle lighting, and challah baking, the three positive commandments for women as well as other occasions in women's lives.[1] And in modern times, on March 18,1922, Judith Kaplan, the daughter of Mordechai Kaplan, was the first bat mitzvah.

The feminist revolution of the 60s, 70s, and 80s built on this rich history, broadening and embellishing older ceremonies such as the bat mitzvah, while filling in the gaps where there were missing rituals. Body-oriented occasions, such as menarche, menopause, childbirth, and nursing, that were once considered private and only women's "territory," were celebrated with new rituals in women's circles. A need for healing rituals from rape, incest, and abuse generated dozens of new ideas. Women began to celebrate aging with a Simchat Hochma,[2] and new calendar rituals such as women's Seders, sukkot soirées, and women's *yahrzeit* commemorations were created.

The themes of the feminist revolution influenced these new events: "celebrate and acknowledge the body," "the personal is the political," "speak your truth," "find your voice." It is now the norm for women to seek empowerment in the public sphere and to claim private, sacred, safe spaces in settings such as Rosh Chodesh (New Moon) groups. It is the continued work of these new rituals to celebrate and educate women, to see women truly *b'tzelem elohim*, in the image of God.

Rituals of the Body

According to Rabbinic Judaism, *tzniut* (modest behavior) was a value for Jewish men and women. Women traditionally wore clothing that covered them well, not revealing shoulders or too much skin. When a woman attended mikveh, a ritual bath at the end of her period, it was done at night so that people wouldn't know who was now sexually available to her husband. A woman's body after menstruation or childbirth was periodically considered *tameh* (impure). In 1969, the first edition to *Our Bodies, Ourselves*[3] was published, giving women access to health and healing information formerly held in the hands of the medical establishment. This book gave women the tools to begin to accept, honor, and heal their own bodies and perceptions of their physicality. It was a source of empowerment. The subsequent evolution of Jewish women's rituals dealing with the body are expressions of women honoring and acknowledging their physical changes in a more public way, often breaking the cultural taboos of the Jewish modesty tradition.

Fertility, conception, and pregnancy were the traditional domain of women. We know that in previous centuries the bed of the mother was surrounded by charms and amulets to keep both the mother and child safe.[4] Red threads were regarded everywhere as anti-demonic and anti–evil eye. To prevent a baby from being removed by demons, the child was sometimes wrapped with red ribbon or thread or wore red coral necklaces. The magical power of the color red derived from its association with the blood sacrifice, for which it was a substitute, and therefore it was believed to appease the power of evil.

Ancient Israel developed other elaborate rituals to ease childbirth and ensure the safety of the mother and child. In some communities it was a popular practice to bring a Sefer Torah to the mother's room and lay it on her, or keep it at her door. Sometimes a red thread was wound from the ark in the synagogue to the laboring woman. To ease labor pains, one prescription was to incise a name of God upon virgin clay and fasten this on the parturient woman, but to remove it as soon as the child was delivered. Another method was to inscribe the name of God, angels, or ancestors on the woman's wedding ring, place it under her tongue, and say ten times, "Go out, you and all the company of your followers, and then I will go out."

Other complex rituals were employed to ensure a smooth delivery. A mother was closely guarded and no gossip was permitted outside her door. Psalms were said, candles lit on her behalf, and she was given the key to the synagogue to "unlock" her womb herself. A circle was drawn around the bed with chalk. And one custom was to lead the woman in labor around a table in order to create a magic circle to keep the demons out.

The mother wore amulets on her neck and arms with biblical verses inscribed on them, such as the priestly blessing (see Num. 6:24), the initial letters of Genesis 49:22, or psalms, especially Psalms 121 and 126. In the Middle Ages, it became custom to put a knife inscribed with the names of angels, the forty-two-letter name of God, or the names of Lilith and her angels on the bed of a woman in labor to "cut" the pains of childbirth. Copies of Psalm 126, with the addition of the names of the anti-Lilith angels—Sanvi, Sansanvi, and Semangelaf—were often placed in four corners of the house to protect children during infancy.

We have certainly come a long way from these rituals and customs as our rational, modern ways of thinking have replaced superstition. Lilith, once thought of as a demon, is now recognized as a symbol of empowerment. Her name is the title of a Jewish magazine that publishes articles with a feminist perspective and new rituals that empower and honor women. And the circumstances of childbirth are vastly different. Men are now present in delivery rooms, for one. But we can still buy red thread that was wound around Rachel's tomb and then blessed, as a symbol of good luck in childbirth and throughout life. There is still a place for ritual that acknowledges the mystery of life and power of the Divine for transformation.

During the Middle Ages, an infertile person chanted aloud passages from the Torah wherein barren women were "remembered" with children. To enhance fertility, women were given pieces of afikoman and the blossom end of an *etrog* (citron) to chew. The direct touch of things used in rituals connected with the Divine was also seen as a cure for barrenness. These rituals have been updated for our times as women have gone through infertility treatments. At my own fertility ritual, women brought pomegranates, with their many seeds, for planting into the womb, and waved a *lulav* (date palm frond), both ancient fertility symbols, as well as chocolate-covered bananas standing straight up, definitely a modern symbol and definitely phallic. My friends brought blessings and even a live rabbit, known for its fertility. Rabbi Goldie Milgram teaches about a ritual she led based on Hagar sitting on Sarah's knees, a pose reminiscent of a woman on a birthing stool.[5] After I gave birth, the father and I buried the placenta in a small ceremony. Rituals for men have also been created as medical practices have been able to identify the male role in infertility.

In addition to childbirth and pregnancy, rituals have been created to commemorate other rites of physical passage that had traditionally been women's domain. For example, in 1998, Nancy Schniederman published a midlife-covenant healing ritual after hysterectomy. In the ceremony she buries her womb and says, "I offer my womb as a covenant, returning it to the earth, honoring the Source of all life. As I plant it in the ground, my mourning is complete and I am released from this part of my life." This ritual signifies that biological fertility is one way for a woman to fulfill her creative potential, but that she can also undertake satisfying challenges in the next phase of life. Schniederman's ritual removes the shame, stigma, embarrassment, and silence from the procedure of a hysterectomy while appropriating the language of covenant for women. She transforms what is culturally seen as a sign of aging and the loss of fertility into a midlife affirmation.

Miscarriage is a painful subject. Usually, it is a private mourning between a woman and her partner, if she has one. However, as women gave voice to their feelings of loss and needed communal support for their mourning, miscarriage rituals were created to foster the healing process. In 1996, after infertility treatments, I became pregnant with triplets. Three months into the pregnancy, I found out they had no heartbeat. A surgical procedure was scheduled for five days later, but I had to carry the dead fetuses in my body for those five days. It was a therapeutic process for me to create a ritual during that time. I drew upon the works of others, my own journal writings, and the traditional mourning liturgy.[6] My husband and I felt it was important to gather a small group of friends around us for support and as witnesses to our excruciating emotional pain. The process of putting together the ritual moved our pain out of our own hearts and into a public sphere to be held with compassion.

In her groundbreaking work, *Tears of Sorrow, Seeds of Hope,*[7] Rabbi Nina Beth Cardin gathers ritual and prayers for healing after stillbirth and the death of an infant. Stillbirth, the death of a baby on the cusp of being born, had traditionally been kept quiet in the Jewish community, and the infant buried with no name. Rabbi Cardin breaks the silence, providing words of comfort, prayers, and poetry for those who have suffered this loss. She also guides those that are mourning the losses of biological fertility, and offers rituals, using mikveh, candlelighting, havdalah, and other modalities, for women who choose to end a pregnancy. The feminist movement gave women permission to choose their destiny, but this decision is emotional and complex. Rabbi Cardin's rituals give voice to the difficulty of this process.

With the increase in breast cancer and breast reduction among Jewish women, rituals have emerged to mark the transition of losing one's breasts. Rabbi Devorah Bartinoff, *z"l,* gathered women to a ritual the night before her mastectomy in 1995. She spoke of why she had loved her breasts, how they had served her as she had nursed her children and made love. She gently said good-bye to them, hoping that the surgery might save her life. She used a blessing-shield bowl made by Lia Rosen, a Jewish potter from New Mexico. The blessing shield is a new ceremonial object, created by Rosen in 1992, used to channel prayers for healing and hope. Three blessing shields were made around the issues of breast cancer, AIDS, and gay-related murder that had touched her life. Lia says, "Since then, the blessing shield has evolved to a custom-made (in consultation with the recipient) healing bowl, used in various ways. It is made from clay inscribed with prayers, names of G-d and thoughts for specific healings; tzitzit are also attached, to help channel kavanot towards the one in need of healing; it is used as a meditation form or aid to prayer."[8]

Women who have elected to have breast reduction surgery for health and cosmetic reasons also need rituals. In my life cycle group, one woman asked us to be witness to the reasons she was deciding to have reduction surgery. Although it flew in the face of the feminist idea of accepting the body, she had realized that her breasts were actually preventing her from exercising appropriately as she aged. She couldn't jog or jump, and even yoga was uncomfortable. Her breasts were weighing her down. Her breasts, symbols of nurturing, were what she needed to shed as she entered menopause and strove to nurture herself and live healthily the second half of her life. Rituals for the loss of gender markers such as breasts and genitals may soon appear as transgender men and women become part of the Jewish landscape.

Rituals for the Life Cycle

Shedding your breasts as an aging ritual is powerful, but it is not the only way to honor the passage of time. In 1986, Savina Teuval created a ceremony called Simchat Hochmah, the Joy of Wisdom. The ceremony reflected events in the life of the matriarch Sarah. In the ceremony, Savina lead a Shabbat morning service, embraced the Torah scroll, read from the Torah, and wore a tallit. She changed into a *kittel* (white robe used as a burial shroud, and for other purposes) during the ceremony because she wanted to acknowledge that she was on the journey to the end of her life. The music created for this ceremony, "Misheberach" and "Lechi lach" by Debbie Friedman and Drora Setel, is now sung in many synagogues. The movie *Timbrels and Torah,* directed by Judy Montell and Miriam Chaya, tells the story of Savina's ritual and other women's aging ceremonies.

Menarche ceremonies are being created for young girls entering puberty. Some are linked to a bat mitzvah; some are separate ceremonies to welcome the adolescent into the circle of women. Penina Adelman writes about a pre–bat mitzvah ritual based on the Eshet Chayil midrash as the foundation of her new book *Praise Her Works.*[9]

Weddings have been transformed with many new interpretations of the ancient rites. In her book *Engendering Judasim,* Rachel Adler argues that a *brit ahuvim*, a lover's covenant, needs to replace the traditional Jewish wedding, which is formulated in terms of acquisition—the groom acquiring the the bride from the bride's father.[10] Many lesbians have created their version of commitment ceremonies using verses from Song of Songs rather than the traditional Hebrew formula of consecration. *Brit am Israel* is a ceremony not based on gender that was created by Drorah Setel. The frequency of divorce has generated new approaches for women to let go of marriages. A friend of mine designed a ritual for the day her husband moved out—the day the marriage was over, but before the *get* (Jewish divorce document), or the legal divorce. She needed to mark that transition. Others have used havdalah as the marker of separation.

Baby-welcoming ceremonies are another marker of feminist innovation. In previous generations a *brit milah* (ritual circumcision) was held for a boy, and girls were welcomed ceremoniously in some Sephardi circles. However, only the father was traditionally called to the Torah to name his daughter. Now Simchat Bat, rituals to welcome baby girls, are flourishing. *Brit milah* has also been affected. More and more couples are choosing to separate the large public naming of the baby from the actual cutting, or creating a covenant ceremony without the cutting at all, suggesting there is room for a covenant ceremony that could be the same for boys and girls.

Rituals of the Calendar

The Jewish holiday cycle is a natural place for women to feel creative about their ritual life. So often women's stories were relegated to the background as holidays were celebrated. The high holy days and their masculine imagery of the King of Kings have now inspired poets to write of the Queen. They transform the traditional prayer Avinu Malkenu ("Our Father, Our King") into Emeinu Malkatenu ("Our Mother, Our Queen")—a change now implemented in many synagogues. Hanukkah has seen the story of Judith and Hannah and her seven sons take new centrality. Women's Passover Seders, begun at Maayan in New York, have spread across the country. Originally conceived as educational events that would expose women to new materials to take back into their own communities, the women's Seder speaks to the freedom experienced through the feminist movement. What began among a small group of feminists has become a widespread women's ritual. It is a celebration and commemoration of Jewish women's journey out of the Egypt of patriarchy. New materials are created just for that night that have no bearing on integration into the family home Seder.[11] These women's Seders also serve as a reminder of instances where women are still not free: when they are trafficked in the slave trade, denied access to abortion, harmed by cliterectomy, and forced to wear burkas.

Rosh Chodesh groups are now an ongoing spirituality process. Since Arlene Agus first wrote her "This Month for You: Observing Rosh Chodesh as a Woman's Holiday" in *The Jewish Woman: New Perspectives*,[12] Rosh Chodesh groups have proliferated around the world. Some are held in private homes; others are sponsored by communal institutions. Rosh Chodesh groups are small, intimate gatherings that lead to deep sharing, bonding, and creativity. They are labs for creativity; in fact, the innovation of a Miriam's Cup, Rosh Chodesh music, and moon rituals all came out of Rosh Chodesh groups.

A woman once said to me, "If I never had bat mitzvah and I never got married, the only ritual I'd have would be my funeral." The Jewish feminist movement has filled the gaps in the life cycle, marking a wide variety of occasions. And, indeed, the opportunities for new rituals are endless. For example, one of my friends developed a ritual when she achieved the age at which her mother had committed suicide. She sent out letters to friends and asked for condolence notes. She invited ten people over as witnesses to her emotions. They sat in the circle, and she held up copies of photos and told some stories, in particular about her anger at her mother for abandoning her. She ripped the photos, then lay down on a large piece of paper while her friends traced her body. When she got up, she glued some photos of her mom onto the picture. Her friends wrote blessings both for her and for her mother, then they cut Elizabeth's shape out of the paper, creating "her own space" for her. Her witnesses held up the paper and she walked through it, separating herself from before and after that time. The torn photos were put into a black cast-iron pot that burned with the havdalah candle, a symbol of separation. The next day she took the ashes out to the seashore with two of her old friends, read poetry, and cast the ashes into the sea.

In her article "Creating Rituals for Relational Healing," Marty Cohen Spiegel writes about a ritual for rage one woman created after finding out her deceased husband had deceived her.[13] "She brought out her wedding photographs, and smashed the frames, broke the glass, and ripped the photographs to shreds while she screamed curses. I had prepared a hole for the wood and glass and paper. When she finished ripping and tearing, we lit a fire in the hole so the pictures and frames would burn into a fine ash. She then planted a lemon tree transforming the pain of the past into the hope for the future."

Rituals of Empowerment

In 1982, Hanna Tiferet Siegel had been acting as spiritual leader in her *chavurah* (fellowship) in British Columbia. Shonna Husbands-Hankin and others, including myself, who were attending a Shavuot retreat, created a ceremony for Hanna, to honor her contribution to the community. It was titled *Eshet Hazon*, Women of Vision, and was a ritual of empowerment and recognition for her spiritual leadership. Since then, close to forty women have received this title as well, and fifteen younger women have been named *Bat Kol*, a Divine Voice, in various communities in the United States, Canada, and Israel. The ritual was created in a time before there were so many women on the rabbinic path, and it serves to highlight women who don't choose rabbinics as their form of leadership. It is the path of Shekhinah, a following of the Divine Feminine. Women are honored for their arts, music, prayer, and creative life, not the amount of traditional text study they have completed.[14]

Music and Art Rituals

Music and art supports the new rituals described above. Various female composers, such as myself, Rabbi Margot Stein, Juliet Spitzer, Hanna Tiferet Siegel, Linda Hirschhorn, Shefa Gold, and of course, Debbie Friedman, have written songs that are woven into new ceremonies. Miriam's Cups for use at the Passover Seder, which mark Miriam's leadership in the Exodus story, are now standard bat mitzvah gifts, while tallitot, kippot, wimples, quilts, chuppahs, and jewelry are used as gifts for new rituals. A cottage industry has sprung up around these new occasions.

Conclusions

Jewish ritual life has developed significantly since women began creating new ceremonies. Other healing rituals, such as celebrating the end of cancer treatments or healing after rape and incest, are now widespread in their recognition and use. Although public ritual mourning for a death has been sanctioned by the community, emotional pain for "women's issues" has not been recognized until recently. The emotional pain that women have held on to in solitude for centuries now has a voice and an outlet. The fact that it has expression in small Rosh Chodesh groups or a minyan of friends, if not in the larger community, is significant. In addition, celebrations of aging are now a source of pride and power.

The era of Jewish women's creative rituals is just beginning. We must translate these groundbreaking ceremonies into Hebrew for accessibility to a global audience. Rabbis, cantors, educators, and other Jewish professionals must be educated about the possibility of using new rituals in their work. Some of the ceremonies that begin in small groups, such as Simchat Hochmah, can be adapted for larger communities, as a way to honor the elders in a larger context. Women must be encouraged to develop and facilitate these ceremonies as ritual leaders, perhaps a role that will someday be respected and honored enough to create a new paid professional position in the synagogue. We need publishers willing to promote and sponsor more books about rituals. Finally, we acknowledge that creating rituals for life's sacred moments is an infinite undertaking, one that we have only begun to address. Someday we may have a ritual for every moment—moments that are both sacred and ordinary, but that we as Jews elevate and sanctify.

Wendy Zierler, PhD, is associate professor of feminist studies and modern Jewish literature at Hebrew Union College–Jewish Institute of Religion in New York. She received her PhD and her MA from Princeton University, and her BA from Yeshiva University, Stern College. Her book, *And Rachel Stole the Idols: The Emergence of Hebrew Women's Writing*, was published in 2004 by Wayne State University Press. Together with Carole Balin, she is editor of the *Collected Writings of Hava Shapiro*. Other publications include a feminist Haggadah commentary in *My People's Passover Haggadah: Traditional Texts, Modern Commentaries* (Jewish Lights), and the introduction, several translations, and an original poem in *To Speak Her Heart*, an illustrated anthology of Jewish women's prayers and poems, edited by Leslie Golomb and Barbara Broff Goldman.

Torah Study "For Women"

WENDY ZIERLER, PhD

IN 1987–88, writer Vanessa Ochs journeyed to Jerusalem to immerse herself in the experience of studying Torah and to write about the burgeoning phenomenon of women's Torah and Talmud study. That spring, we met in Jerusalem. It was my last semester of college. Most undergraduates spend their final months of senior year holding tight to memories of their friends, their favorite professors, their collegiate identity. I, in contrast, traded in the last vestiges of my midtown Manhattan life at Stern College for Women for a semester of study at the Hebrew University of Jerusalem. It was from my tiny room in the Resnick dorms that I would await news of my acceptance into PhD programs in Comparative Literature. It was in the labyrinthine halls of Mount Scopus that I would prepare myself for the years of graduate study and teaching ahead. Among the many courses I took that semester was a creative writing class with Vanessa Ochs. Somewhere mid-semester, having discovered my background, Vanessa pulled me aside, told me about the book she was writing, and asked me if she could interview me about my experiences three years prior, as a student at Michlelet Bruria in Jerusalem, one of the first yeshivot for women that offered the opportunity for serious Talmud study.

The resultant book, *Words on Fire: One Woman's Journey into the Sacred,* which first appeared in 1990, was something of a landmark publication, offering portraits of many of the pioneering, Jerusalem-based institutions of Torah study for women and female teachers of Torah such as Nechama Leibowitz and Aviva Zornberg. In many respects, it was the story of a liberal outsider crashing an Orthodox women's Torah-study party. The idea of studying in Israel had emerged for Ochs as a result of a series of chronic illnesses; despite liberal skepticism and rationalism, a countervailing spiritual yearning had led her to question whether a regimen of religious practice and study might bring a kind of healing that had eluded her in the form of conventional medicine. The occult nature of this quest was mirrored in her foray into the world of Orthodox practice and study. Despite having studied as a teenager at the high school program at the Conservative movement's Jewish Theological Seminary, she seemed ready, at least in part, to assume that authentic Torah study was an Orthodox business. Alienated, however, by the halakhic demands for female modesty and by the religious certainties of many of the women she was meeting, Ochs herself questioned her assumptions: "What was I searching for in Jerusalem? I no longer knew. If learning Torah and decoding Talmud was what I wanted, I should have marched right back into the Jewish Theological Seminary on Broadway and 122nd in Manhattan, wearing whatever I pleased, and gotten down to work among Conservative Jews who accepted me with my naked knees. If it was a woman's perspective I wanted, I could have studied at the seminary with Judith Hauptman or one of several women now on the faculty. Just because all my relatives, with the exception of my parents, disdained non-Orthodoxy didn't mean that I had to be self-loathing. I could have had Jewish scholarship up to my ears. Who needed Esther's learned women, who needed to learn Torah within the context of such blind faithfulness and with such disdain for secularism?"[1]

Back in 1988, I too, though less ambivalently than Ochs, tended to view the whole question of women's Torah study, and indeed, of Jewish feminism writ large, through the singular lens of my Orthodox background. At that point in my life, my feminist agenda involved seeking access through creative reinterpretation of halakhah to what had formerly been off-limits for women: advanced Torah knowledge and ritual and communal empowerment. When Ochs asked me to describe what it was like to study at Michlelet Bruria in 1984–85, I responded euphorically with descriptions of what it had been like to be one of three women that year in the yeshiva who were able to study in the highest level Gemara class. "I felt I was part of a new era," I said, "a pioneer doing something important." No matter that the Reform movement had been ordaining women as rabbis since 1972, and the Conservative movement, since 1983, and that I was studying as part of a movement that still, to this day, does not allow ordination for women. In 1988, I looked solely to the Orthodox world for signs of the unfolding feminist story of Jewish women's Torah study. Little did I know that twenty years later, though still committed to Orthodox observance, I would be writing about Jewish feminism and feminist Torah study from the vantage point of a professorship at the Reform movement's Hebrew Union College–Jewish Institute of Religion (HUC-JIR). All that was far off on the horizon.

Ironically, it was that semester in Jerusalem, while studying at Hebrew University—not just with Vanessa Ochs, but also with Professor Nechama Leibowitz, a teacher whose renown was significant for Jewish feminists, but whose teaching and reading method lacked any self-consciously feminist elements—that I wrote my first work of feminist *parshanut* (interpretations of the Torah written by scholars and rabbis). While still in Jerusalem, I was informed that I had been chosen as valedictorian of my Stern College class and that I needed to write a valedictory address. I knew I wanted to speak about feminism and my desire for the women's division of Yeshiva University to embrace a feminist pedagogical and spiritual agenda. In order to do so, I decided that I would employ what I had learned from Nechama Leibowitz about the various interpretive styles of the classical biblical exegetes; I would use the master's tools, so to speak, to renovate the master's house.

The interpretive "question" I set out to tackle was why it was that the women's division of Yeshiva University was called Stern College for Women while the men's division was simply called Yeshiva College and not Yeshiva College for Men. Professor Leibowitz had taught me that Rashi, following the midrashic authors, tended to cull additional meanings from the appearance of seemingly superfluous biblical words. If one were to ask Rashi about the extra words "for women" in the Stern College name, he might answer that this extra language connoted the special intuition or extra knowledge *(binah yeteirah)* of women. In contrast, Ibn Ezra, a more literal-minded, plain-meaning sort of reader, might answer that the words "for women," came to emphasize that absolutely no men attended Stern College. But were any of these interpretations satisfactory? Might a woman interpreter of this textual problem approach the matter differently?

Simply put, I argued that if the words "for women" were there, they should mean more than that this school was an exception to the male universal, that instead the school ought to espouse a special contemporary mission to empower women. I called for change and I grounded this idea in the act of interpretation. I argued, on the basis of the learning strategies and attainments of a female Torah scholar, that the college needed to live up to its name and define itself around women's issues and feminism. Because it was close to the holiday of Shavuot, I quoted Cynthia Ozick's feminist reading of the book of Ruth as a story of Jewish female personhood and friendship[2] and talked about the need of students like me to be exposed to this kind of reading. That was my world in 1988.

I have rehearsed all of this personal history for you for two reasons: first, because one of the central insights of postmodern thought, in general, and feminist thought, in particular, is that we are always subjective, and that it is important to be honest about where we are coming from when we approach the act of interpretation; second, because I wanted to illustrate how far we, as Jewish feminist students of Torah, have come. Women's Torah study is not a pioneering endeavor anymore; rather, it is a mainstream activity in every sector of the Jewish world. Schools such as the Drisha Institute in New York have produced scores of learned women who have entered day-school classrooms as teachers of Talmud and assumed other communal and pedagogic roles. Vanessa Ochs herself has become an important anthropologist of religion and creative interpreter of the Bible, joining the ranks of hundreds of women who have entered the academy in the various disciplines of Jewish studies. The second edition of her book *Words on Fire* records the "zillion options" that have opened up for women in the area of Torah study, and this second edition is from 1999! To quote Ochs, "It is rare to hear debates about whether Jewish women should be barred from the intellectual life of Torah, just as one no longer hears debates about whether a woman can be a rabbi in the liberal movement: Learned women and rabbinical women are accepted as realities. Even in Orthodoxy, the denomination that does not yet ordain women as rabbis, women have new positions of communal authority and are designated by the temporary-sounding title rabbinic 'intern.'"[3]

In terms of published works of Torah commentary and scholarship written by women, liberal women rabbis have made a major contribution, especially in such volumes as *The Women's Torah Commentary: New Insights from Women Rabbis on the 54 Weekly Torah Portions*, edited by Elyse Goldstein and published by Jewish Lights, as well as *Beginning the Journey*, edited by Rabbi Emily H. Feigenson and published by the Women of Reform Judaism, a collection of insights on three Torah portions that represented a first effort on the part of the Women of Reform Judaism to fashion a women's Torah commentary. Other significant contributions have come from liberal scholars and writers such as Tikva Frymer-Kensky in *Reading the Women in the Bible*; Ellen Frankel in *The Five Books of Miriam*; Alicia Ostriker in *Feminist Revision and the Bible, The Nakedness of the Fathers,* and *For the Love of God*; and Anita Diamant in *The Red Tent.* Similarly important publications have come from the Orthodox community. With her original teaching and writing style that weaves together midrashic, biblical, and modern philosophical and literary sources, Aviva Gottlieb Zornberg, author of *Genesis: The Beginning of Desire* and *The Particulars of Rapture: Reflections on Exodus,* has brought an entirely new approach to Torah commentary. *Torah of the Mothers: Contemporary Jewish Women Read Classical Jewish Texts,* edited by Ora Wiskin Helper and Susan Handelman and published by Urim, brings to light the learning and exegetical insights of several female teachers of Torah. Similarly, although edited by a man, Joel Wolowelsky, *Women at the Seder: A Haggadah,* published by KTAV, features Haggadah commentary by a plethora of learned Jewish women.

Popular anthologies such as *Reading Ruth,* edited by Gail Reimer and Judith Kates, and published by Ballantine Books, have brought together female scholars, writers, poets, and leaders to respond creatively to the biblical text from a variously defined Jewish "woman's perspective." This spirit of diversity, collaboration, and revelation is expressed most eloquently and momentously in the newly published *The Torah: A Women's Commentary.* Edited by Tamara Eskenazi and Andrea Weiss and published by the URJ Press, this anthology brings together more than two hundred women scholars, rabbis, poets, and creative thinkers to respond to each of the Torah portions.

There are several features to this commentary that make it an especially significant marker of the development of women's Torah study up to this point and of areas still yet to be developed. Perhaps the most significant is the scope and "weight" of this volume. It is a large, hardbound, gold-lettered book. It is meant for synagogue use, that is, to be inserted in those wooden slots behind a synagogue pew. One cannot underestimate the significance of this heft and gravity, as they suggest belongingness in the sacred canon. For thousands of years, Jews defined their canon physically in the form of books published in leather or hard, dark-colored binding and gold print. This is the traditional publication form of the *mikra'ot gedolot* (the Rabbinic Bible), of editions of the Mishnah, the Gemara, the Rambam, of responsa literature and Hebrew ethical and philosophical treatises. For the first time, then, we have a work of Torah scholarship that looks and functions like all of that male-authored material but that was authored, edited, and produced by women.

If the primary goals of first-wave feminism—from Mary Wollstonecraft to Elizabeth Cady Stanton—were equal access, enfranchisement, and property ownership, in this realm of Torah study, *The Torah: A Women's Commentary* marks the accomplishment of these goals. It is clear, at this point, that Jewish women now own Torah.

But feminism has also discovered and declared other goals beyond this first wave. It is not enough, we have discovered, for women to gain access to a set of privileges and prerogatives previously accorded only to men if they continue to represent a system of exclusion, hierarchy, domination, and binary oppositions. It is not enough for women to don these Jewish intellectual "pants." Feminism is also about restructuring the system, doing away with the hierarchies, questioning and undoing the binaries. And in that sense, feminism is not only about women. In terms of the whole issue of canonicity, feminism has indeed argued for the place of women within the tradition and has called for a writing of the missing "herstory" of Jewish women's life. At the same time, however, it has called for a redefinition and expansion of the very idea of a canon. Its ultimate goal is to foster pluralism, eclecticism, and collaboration.

In Search of a *Gedolat Hador?*

In this regard, we cannot help but be delighted by the collaborative nature of *The Torah: A Women's Commentary,* which gives voice to so many women across denominational and disciplinary lines. The result is the presentation of a veritable community of Jewish women

108

dedicated to rereading and reclaiming the Bible. Unlike the *"gadol ha-dor"* (great scholar of the generation) paradigm that so much characterizes the publications of classical male scholars, in this Torah commentary no one woman scholar predominates, holds forth, or rises above the others.

It is important to linger for a moment on this point. For centuries, Jews have been trained to study Torah through the eyes of our great male exegetical luminaries: Rashi, Ibn Ezra, Ramban, Sforno, Abravanel, and so forth. We have been schooled in the notion of *gedolei ha-dor* and have been taught that insofar as we have new insights, we need first to pay homage to our predecessors and frame our *hiddushim*—our new insights—in light of these major geniuses of yesteryear. Even if we find the commentaries together in one page, in compendia such as the *mikra'ot gedolot,* we are taught to separate these exegetes from one another, to compare and contrast their analytical approaches. To be sure, modernity and postmodernity have dealt major blows to the ideas of masters and master narratives and have taught us to adopt a hermeneutics of suspicion with respect to the insights of our forebears. And yet, even at HUC-JIR, a Reform rabbinical seminary, we continue to teach our students *parshanut,* which is to say, we teach them how to read, understand, and contextualize the classical exegetical writings of the aforementioned *gedolei ha-dor.*

The feminist enterprise of women's Torah commentary, however, has departed from this model insofar as it has largely resulted in the creation of collaborative anthologies of commentary, rather than masterworks by one author. You can debate whether this is a good or bad thing. In fact, you might argue that among the goals yet to be attained in the realm of women's Torah study—aside from the obvious ongoing lack of ordination for Orthodox women—is the lack of a female *gedolat ha-dor,* a female Torah luminary whose writing is so universally accepted and lauded, even within the Orthodox world, that she has become a widely acknowledged halakhic decisor or interpretive authority. Nehama Leibowitz certainly came closer than anyone else to attaining this stature. I would note, however, that her major contribution was not in offering innovative interpretations of her own, but in teaching us how to read the male *gedolei hador*. Moreover, her books have never been published with gold lettering on the cover, and within certain Orthodox circles, the idea of her teaching men was never truly accepted. And also, certain sectors of the Orthodox world still define the leadership, stature, and public presence of a Torah scholar in stubbornly masculine terms. It is difficult to say what, if anything, can unhinge that way of thinking. Perhaps the rise of a female/feminist *illuyah* (brilliant scholar) is the very thing needed to alter the paradigm. The emergence of such a luminary would depend, however, on the community's willingness to educate such a woman to status and to recognize her as such. In our postmodern, fragmented world, few males have risen to such positions of recognition, let alone women.

The Canonization of Feminist Midrash

For now, then, I'd rather place my bets on the model of widespread proliferation of female Torah knowledge and, as represented by *The Torah: A Woman's Commentary*, collaborative efforts, because they exemplify a model of feminism and of group life that privileges diversity over uniformity and gives voice to those who might otherwise remain outside the conversation. Along these lines, I'd like to call attention to the collection of feminist midrashim and poetry that is included in the "Voices" section of *The Torah: A Woman's Commentary*. For years, a primary goal of my teaching at HUC-JIR and other settings has been to show the ways in which modern Jewish, and particularly modern Hebrew, literary works can be read as an additional layer of interpretation of the Bible and our classical sources. In all my courses, I insist that modern Jewish literature sources be considered part of our sacred, spiritual canon. More specifically, as a scholar of the beginnings of modern Hebrew women's writing, I ask my students to consider what happens when, after centuries of literary silence, women begin to write works of literature in Hebrew and address and enter into this canon. What new questions do women ask about the text? What new details missing from the clipped biblical account do they imaginatively supply? What countertraditional interpretations do they offer?

The range of feminist midrashic interpretations offered in the "Voices" section of *The Torah: A Women's Commentary* is truly breathtaking, including Yiddish, Israeli, German, British, American, Canadian women poets and writers from the eighteenth, nineteenth, twentieth, and twenty-first centuries, poems by women rabbis, by eminent Hebrew women poets, among them the first women to write poetry in Hebrew, poems written explicitly in response to biblical materials as well as others that the editors, through creative juxtaposition, brought into a meaningful conversation with the biblical text by thinking to print them alongside a particular parashah. And because this material is included in a book intended for synagogue use, these alternative voices too have now become part of the canon, in effect redefining what we call Torah.

Men's Commentary

What remains the most vexatious issue with regard to the enterprise of women's Torah study, in general, and *The Torah: A Women's Commentary*, in particular, is the meaning of the word *women's*. Returning to the act of *parshanut* that I described earlier in this chapter, I find myself asking what it means to call this collaborative work of Torah scholarship a women's commentary. Does the word *women's* connote a for-women-only enterprise? If so, the label contradicts the broader feminist project of enabling rather than impeding expression. Given the growing concerns about the place of men in liberal Judaism, do we need to be concerned that the canonization of such a book threatens the place of men? Do we now need an additional canonical men's commentary to give voice to the muted tones of Jewish male involvement?

I would answer yes to all of these questions. In being labeled a women's commentary, the book does indeed claim something for women over and against the entire tradition of Torah commentary, which until relatively recently had been a male-only endeavor.

However, if we take seriously the idea, as asserted by Judith Plaskow, that "feminism is not about attaining equal rights for women in religious or social structures that remain unchanged, but about the thoroughgoing transformation of religion and society,"[4] then we ought to be interested in seeing feminist values applied eagerly to all sectors of the community. That means that the tools we use to analyze the representation of women and the construction of femininity in the Bible, the Talmud, and other such classical sources ought indeed be applied as enthusiastically and critically to issues of masculinity, queer and transgender identity, and the like. Insofar as the Bible legally links women with slaves, deaf and dumb people, children, and the mentally incompetent, the investigation and the critique of the status of all these marginalized groups are, in a sense, part of a larger feminist enterprise.

Already, the Reform movement has begun to generate materials for a men's Seder and a men's Torah commentary. In the words of the Haggadah, I would say, *"Kol hamarbeh, harei zeh meshubah"* ("Whoever expands upon it is praiseworthy"). Feminism has taught us that we cannot allow a male elite to speak and interpret for the entire community. Neither can we allow a female elite, or any singular, narrowly defined sector to speak for all. What we need is many voices, many methods, many metaphors. For women, for men, for all the variegated interests of the Jewish people.

Rabbi Tirzah Firestone is a Jungian psychotherapist and spiritual leader of Congregation Nevei Kodesh in Boulder, Colorado. She is the author of *With Roots in Heaven,* her spiritual memoir; *The Receiving: Reclaiming Women's Wisdom;* and the audio set, *The Woman's Kabbalah: Ecstatic Jewish Practices for Women.*

Transforming Our Stories through Midrash

RABBI TIRZAH FIRESTONE

THIS IS A POWERFUL and even mythic moment, in which we look out over the landscape of the Jewish feminist movement and ask ourselves: *Mah anachnu? Mah chayenu?* What are we? What have our lives been about? And further: In what ways have we successfully expanded the boundaries of Judaism? What is the living legacy that we are leaving for our younger sisters and daughters?

Looking back on a movement to gauge its evolution is something like looking at ourselves in the mirror to see how we are changing with age; it requires both compassion and objectivity. As we gaze, we must not only remember how we once looked, but also keep an eye on the unfolding scene around us. As was true thirty years ago, our lives and work as Jewish feminists are inextricably linked with the era and world in which we find ourselves today.

When we started out thirty years ago, our challenge to expand Jewish liturgy, ritual, and Torah study was necessarily audacious. Many of us had experienced God in our bodies and demanded a way to express this in liturgy, movement, and dance. The feminine face of the Divine was also becoming unmistakable. She, too, pushed her way onto the scene, and with her came an invigorated connection to

113

the female ancestors and holy women who had been buried without mention. All of these pressed upon the crucible of Jewish practice until the tradition groaned, finally expanding and reshaping itself. A generation of new publications, translations, and revisions was born. And all of our feminist innovations bringing forth new God language, God images, and rites of passage, were critical in making a mark on Judaism, in challenging and expanding Judaism in ways that could invite people into fuller ownership.

These elements, now established, are still true and vital, and we celebrate them. But now our gaze must shift to the periphery of the mirror where we find the surrounding scenery of our lives rapidly changing. No longer is it the internal dynamic of the Jewish community alone that grabs our attention. For many of us, our focus has moved beyond the Jewish community to the larger world that we share, to the plight of sisters living under the oppression of emerging fundamentalist regimes, the basic resources that are fast dwindling, and the threat of terrorism that is now a reality in our children's world.

How do our Jewish feminist practices speak to these new existential realities, and what does our Jewish feminist wisdom have to offer us? Can our texts inform and guide us now, at the cusp of such world changes? How can Jewish study inform not just our Jewish practice but also the larger questions stemming from our troubled times?

We might expect to find a plethora of new thinking coming out of the Jewish feminist camp that embraces the issues that surround us: the environmental crisis, globalization, terrorism, random violence, and more. But such is not the case. Even though many of us are thinking about the connection between Jewish feminism and the mandate to engage the present reality, our thinking about the problems at hand has not taken the form of a Jewish feminist creed. Neither have we produced enough articles or publications to give us overarching answers to the newly emerging meta-questions in our lives.

Nevertheless, I would say that Jewish feminism has now taken a surprising turn. Rather than embracing these difficult areas theoretically and academically, Jewish women today are engaging the gravitas of these serious issues through the heart. How? By creating midrash, and thereby working to change the root stories that determine our lives.

I am a teacher of Jewish texts—Tanach, Chasidut, Zohar—that have a unique power to engage and call us into discovery and wisdom. I teach interactively, and I am accustomed to lively discussions. But rarely have I witnessed more eagerness and excitement than when I invite women to enter the text itself, to step out of themselves and into our mythical Jewish narratives, to pour their own life wisdom and personal struggles into the scenes of our history and there to find a deeper knowing. With more aplomb than ever before, today's women are entering the stories and changing them, breaking them open to reveal the places of both wounds and opportunity. They are seizing the chance to transform the stories that guide our lives, and in so doing, they are rewriting the maps that determine the paths we will travel.

What is midrash? Deriving from the Hebrew root *d-r-sh,* to seek out, midrash is the process of interpretation in which we seek out the deeper meaning of a text. "Where the Bible is mysterious and silent, midrash unravels the mystery."[1] Where we find absent or conflicting voices in the text, midrash supplies missing dialogue and harmonizes conflicting voices with a narrative that fills in these gaps. In the formal sense, midrash is the corpus of rabbinic interpretations that was collected over centuries and published between the years 400–1200 CE. But the act and process of interpretation, or making midrash, is one of endless fascination and belongs to all students of the tradition. "Modern midrash" has become especially popular of late, as exemplified by Anita Diamant's bestselling novel, *The Red Tent,* which is based on the biblical story of Dina and the family of Jacob, Leah, and Rachel.

While the study of traditional texts is a big part of midrashic work—we must know the text, the context, and the scope of the rabbinic voices before launching in—we also must take Torah into a first-person experience, as an exploration of our interior land-scape—an experience that can be profoundly transformative and healing.

Creating midrash makes us conscious of the things we don't see and helps us bypass the many religious and cultural filters that screen our wisdom from consciousness. Making midrash takes us from our heads (which may still bark at us that we cannot surpass rabbinic dicta) and delivers us into an open-hearted field of play where we are free to know and be informed by our most human responses.

I have watched with amazement as women of all ages plumb their own depths, creating spontaneous narratives that speak directly to what is unfolding in their world. I have especially seen young women step forward into enormous empowerment by means of their midrash making, tapping depths of wisdom that they did not know were there.

The process of creating midrash might be likened to a laughing brook. While it nourishes, it also stimulates and delights. While it avoids the academic rigor of theology and skirts the intensity required for more in-depth intellectual study, in its own playful way, midrash creates a container for women to use the Jewish narrative as a springboard to engage with the world and their changing reality within it.

The imperative now is to humanize the texts, to breathe life into them and to draw out the wisdom that speaks to us today. Midrash, not theology, is the way Jewish texts will speak to women in human language that is accessible and timely. Midrash is an invitation for Jewish feminists to reenter the mythical soul of our tradition—so long cast through the prism of men's relationships to God and one another. It is a chance to retell our narrative and give expression to our deepest wisdom through the sensibilities of women, sisters, and colleagues. And perhaps more important for our time, creating midrash changes the template of our story as Jews and as women. The very archetypes that have bound and chafed us for centuries and that are still governing our hearts and our politics begin with our primary stories. Midrash actually changes these stories.

The drama of Hagar and Sarah is a good example of a story that can be transformed through midrash. These two women, the archetypal mothers of two nations, sit at the mythic matrix of Jewish-Arab distress. Once intimates, Hagar and Sarah were later divided by issues of competition for prestige and honor, and the Torah offers no story of their reconciliation. The story of Hagar and Sarah and their sons lies deep in our collective unconscious and effects our beliefs about the entrenched relationship with our Arab cousins. To change the rigid story lines requires that we first collectively re-vision and humanize the story of these two women. Many female midrashists have taken up the task of plumbing their relationship. Linda Hirschhorn and Leila Berner[2] are but two who have done this brilliantly in music, articulating the relationship of Hagar and Sarah in the form of midrashic song. To hear the voices of these two matriarchs calling to each other through the ages as they struggle to break free of their ancient roles is chilling. In Hirschhorn's version[3] they understand that to survive they must finally speak each other's name, hear each other's prayers, share each other's dream of a homeland. I have witnessed hundreds of people weeping as they hear this musical midrash, the reaching out in longing and regret of Sarah and Hagar becoming their own, the pain of the centuries and the possibility for healing alive, palpable, urgent. This is but one example of the deep healing that midrash making can provide.

Another example is the myth of Lilith and Eve. In this ancient story, the first wife of Adam demands equality with her mate, and having been scorned, flies off to find autonomy. Because she refuses God's call to return to her husband, Lilith is exiled and relegated to the fearsome realm of night demons, there to play out the negative feminine shadow of Jewish women for centuries to come. Eve comes on the scene as Adam's second wife, implicitly more docile than his first. But in rabbinic tradition, Eve too becomes the object of men's loathing, marking the passage to a fallen existence by succumbing to the snake's temptation.

This story has been reclaimed midrashically using many forms of both written and theatrical exegesis, recasting Lilith and Eve as three-dimensional women.[4] In doing so, the midrashic retellings transform and heal not only these archetypal characters, but also the multilayered stigma that they have been carrying for all these centuries. Good midrash empowers contemporary women and men to penetrate the roles in which we find ourselves stuck, to liberate the archetypal characters of our stories, and in doing so, to liberate our own selves.

The Lilith and Eve myth, like that of Hagar and Sarah, has enormous psychological power over us and begs us to reenter and reimagine it. The rabbinic tradition's tendency to discount and split women by allegiance to their men, subjugating them under a masculine model of hierarchy, is transformed and healed when we filter the story through the experience of our sisterhood and our ability to push toward reconciliation with one another.

As our world has changed in these past decades, so too, our worldview as Jews has toughened. In the past decade I have found students to be less engaged in theological speculation, less God-focused, and more skeptical. The center of gravity seems to be shifting now toward the prescient words *v'Toratcha b'toch may'ai,* the Torah that lives within our bellies (Ps. 40:11).

Women and men who are in touch with the quickening pulse and the rising temperature of our ailing world, who feel the emergence of new and urgent questions, are bringing the feminist enterprise out of the realm of ideas and into the realm of the heart and belly.

It could be that Jewish feminist theological discourse is waning now because our meta-questions have changed. In a world where Jewish faith is rapidly declining, the question is not so much about how to talk about God, but about whether an external deity exists at all.[5] In a world where life has been so gravely devalued, the question we ask is less often, "Where was God then?" and more often, "Where are we now, and what are we going to do to help, heal, and repair?"

At a time when the emphasis is more on self than on nation, on planet than on tribe, when many of our national and religious leaders have lost credibility or don't go far enough in their leadership, the practice of creating midrash calls us into our own power, into a knowing that is rooted in our own hearts and psyches, and has the power to be truly transformative, rather than just intellectually interesting.

Many of us who gaze in the mirror these days can see far beyond ourselves, can see that the next decades are already upon us, bringing with them enormous turbulence and change. How will the Jewish feminist movement respond to these challenges?

I believe we are wealthy in accrued wisdom and tools with which to help penetrate to the roots of our larger cultural problems. We have learned the skill of midrashic vision, to find the malady in the ancient template and shift it—without throwing it away—to reenter the narrative, the collective dream that is guiding us, and heal it. We will heal it by calling forth the humanity, the compassion, and the great ideals that have been lost. May our younger sisters, friends, and daughters look back thirty years hence, and find that the powers we marshaled in the first thirty years of our movement's life were used wisely to transform the stories that guide our lives.

PART III

Women and the Synagogue

BEFORE THE DESTRUCTION of the Temple in Jerusalem in 70 CE, Jewish ritual life was concentrated at one central address: animal sacrifices and priestly roles defined Jewish practice, and all Jews (at least males) were required to attend the Temple three times a a year. Although there were smaller local altars and the beginnings of synagogue-like structures, it wasn't until after the destruction of the Temple in the early second century that Jewish life became decentralized, and the focus of ritual shifted from the altar to the home. The home was called *mikdash me'at*, a small sanctuary, a name that symbolized that shift, placing the home as a mini-substitute for the Temple.

However, from the earliest days of the Diaspora and through today, Jews needed a clear locus of public and communal leadership. We needed a more public place that could become the new center of Jewish life to complement the home, a more private space. Thus it was in the home that Seders happened, *brit milah* was celebrated, and children were educated in Judaism, but it was in the synagogue that communal decisions were made, Talmud was studied, and Jewish law explained and carried out. While both the home and synagogue carried weight, public synagogue rituals—reading the Torah, for example—were critical to communal identity.

The synagogue took on three vital roles, which it retains today:

1. *Beit knesset* (house of meeting): In the synagogue, the important business of the community was carried out, not just its religious rituals. Announcements of communal issues were made, leaders addressed the community, and decisions affecting the entire community were debated.

2. *Beit midrash* (house of study): The synagogue gradually took on the role of educating children, but it also was central in the ongoing learning of the adults, traditionally adult men. Daily *shiurim,* or classes, were attended by those able, and Shabbat learning was common.

3. *Beit tefillah* (house of prayer): The notion of communal prayer—a systematic service presided over by learned lay people and rabbis—developed as a substitute for the systematic animal sacrifice once presided over by the priests.

Women played limited leadership roles in that ancient Temple and in the sacrificial system. Although there is archaeological evidence to suggest that women held some positions of responsibility and leadership there,[1] and both women and men were commanded to bring sacrifices, women did not function as priests. The Rabbis of the Talmud, fashioning the prayer book and the prayer service in the academies of the exile, did not envision a new role for women in the emerging synagogue structures.

The synagogue as a house of prayer, the third area of focus, became the central motif throughout the ages. And so it remains. Thus, as women question their role in public Jewish life, it is often the synagogue that they concentrate on. Can Jewish feminism reimagine and even reinvent the synagogue in the way that the destruction of the Temple invented it? Have female clergy so transformed the life of the synagogue that it is an entirely different institution than the early Rabbis imagined it would be? Is there room for transformation of traditional synagogues? And what would these changes mean for men who have been the primary leaders, supporters, functionaries, and beneficiaries of the synagogue?

Rabbi Jacqueline Koch Ellenson is the director of the Women's Rabbinic Network. She also serves as chair of the Hadassah Foundation. Rabbi Ellenson graduated from Barnard College and was ordained at the Hebrew Union College–Jewish Institute of Religion in 1983. She has worked in a variety of Jewish educational settings, and served as a chaplain at the Harvard-Westlake School in Los Angeles from 1991 to 2002. Now living in New York, she has led a "Rosh Chodesh: It's a Girl Thing" group for four years, participated in a rabbinic cohort of the Institute for Jewish Spirituality, and is a spiritual director. She is married to Rabbi David Ellenson, and they have five children.

From the Personal to the Communal

How Women Have Changed the Rabbinate

RABBI JACQUELINE KOCH ELLENSON

THE PRESENCE OF WOMEN in the Reform rabbinate has caused a revolution within the Jewish community. It is at once an outgrowth of the larger forces of social change that were becoming stronger in the 1960s and 1970s, as well as the cause of continued social change in the Jewish community during the past thirty years. The ordination of Rabbi Sally Priesand at the Hebrew Union College–Jewish Institute of Religion in 1972 was a watershed event. All of us who have been ordained since then owe Rabbi Priesand an enormous debt for putting into action what some had only dreamed of before then.

What have we gained since the ordination of women in 1972? From a small, courageous, and intrepid group of women who braved the barriers to women's ordination in the 1970s and 1980s, women rabbis have become a growing influence in Jewish life. Over the past

125

thirty-six years, we have attained leadership positions in synagogues, instituted prayer book reform, led the way for feminist scholarship, included women's voices in biblical interpretation, and created new prayers and liturgies for life cycle and other formerly ignored and neglected sacred moments. In our day, the presence of women in public leadership roles in the Jewish community is commonplace. In many communities, a girl becoming bat mitzvah is taken for granted, as is a female rabbi officiating at a funeral.

The first stage of women's activism in the Jewish world was in the discovery and recovery of Jewish women's voices from our tradition. The creation of modern, feminist, and inclusive midrashim and other interpretations of text reflected a desire to read ourselves into a textual tradition and history that omitted our experiences. The entry of women into feminist interpretation and deconstruction of text created a path by which our voices would be heard and our experiences would be named. There was a veritable explosion of women's writings in the fields of poetry, midrash, life cycle liturgy and prayer, and historical reconstruction. Ceremonies to welcome baby girls into the covenant, and for weaning, became commonplace. The concomitant entrance of women into graduate schools, and their emergence into the world of Jewish scholarship, contributed to an outpouring of material designed to guarantee that their presence would be acknowledged and incorporated into the corpus of Jewish tradition. They also paved the way for the possibility of women teaching at our seminaries, and providing future rabbinical students with academically strong and Jewishly committed female role models.

Reform women rabbinical students and rabbis joined forces to create an organization that would speak out in support of women in the rabbinate and advocate for women rabbis. We knew that there was a lot of work to be done in the larger organized Jewish community. From their inception, the Women's Rabbinic Network (WRN) and its precursor organizations, the Women's Rabbinic Association in Philadelphia and New York, and the Rabbinic Organization of

Women in Cincinnati were dedicated to the empowerment of women rabbis, to the support of women in the rabbinate, and to advocacy for women in the Reform and larger Jewish institutional world.

The WRN became our central address for support and advocacy. At conventions and meetings, we asked each other the important questions: What should a woman's tallit look like? What should we wear at a funeral? Could we teach about something other than the role of women in Judaism? How would we work with a senior rabbi or a community that was less than supportive? What should we say publicly about family and our commitment to childbearing? Was there a way to be present for our community, and also present for our families? We wanted to create a new model of the rabbinate that was less hierarchical and more cooperative, and to teach a Judaism that was more accessible, more democratic. We knew that, simply by our presence on the bimah as women and as rabbis, we represented new paths of access to the tradition and to leadership within that tradition. At the same time, whenever we arrived at a life cycle or community event, we were, by definition, doing something completely different. We wanted to make this difference more explicit, more meaningful. We couldn't ever imagine that we would be part of the "old boy's network" of the rabbinate, much less that one of us would or could become president of the Central Conference of American Rabbis (CCAR), our national Reform rabbinic organization. Our choice to become active in our own network, and to support one another as we struggled to answer these questions, empowered us to continue searching for answers to our questions. We believed that we could do it all.

Over time, as more women entered the congregational rabbinate, we became increasingly aware that our advancement did not proceed at the same pace as that of our male colleagues, and that our salaries and benefits were also not comparable. Being pregnant or asking for maternity leave was considered the "kiss of death" in salary negotiations. We felt that we had to prove that our primary commitment was to our congregation or our constituency, and we didn't dare provide them with any doubt as to the level of that commitment. At the same time, we wanted to create a new model. We knew that being a rabbi could also, must also, mean having a personal, private life. We could no longer be the type of rabbi known to earlier generations. But it was challenging to confront other people's expectations and our own. Over time, more and more congregations and female rabbis recognized that it was imperative to include a clause for maternity leave in a rabbinic contract. This significant advance continues to require intensive and consistent lobbying, on the part of individual rabbis and the WRN, monitoring of congregational contracts, and confrontation with resistance from synagogues and other institutions. Women rabbis brought their personal issues into the workplace, and in doing so they made pregnancy and childbearing an issue of societal significance requiring a communal response. This concern for parenting, now brought into the public sphere, normalized the conversation about this private concern.

Other women realized that serving in congregational life was not their goal. The possibilities of different types of rabbinic service became realities as women chose to work as educators, Hillel rabbis, and chaplains in senior facilities or hospitals. All of these were rabbinic roles that had been fulfilled by men prior to women entering the rabbinate. Previously, these positions had often been seen as non-normative choices, as lesser, not appropriate, not worthy, not significant ways to be a rabbi. We began to understand that there was more than one way for someone to be a rabbi. As women looked around the Jewish community and examined their professional options, they came to understand that these settings afforded a wider breadth of choices. Soon, women who were wrestling with the tension of raising a family but wanting to work as rabbis were able to search for and find other varieties of rabbinic work. The Jewish healing and spirituality movements became fertile fields for women rabbis and flourished under their leadership. These arenas of hospital chaplaincy, education across the generational spectrum, and Hillel became important venues for the expression of the rabbi as nurturer, a feminine characteristic. As women normalized these positions as a worthwhile manifestation of the rabbinate, men benefited from the growing professionalization of what had previously been a substandard rabbinic choice.

Whereas earlier generations had looked at career advancement and success by counting congregational size, women began looking at success using other variables. Some colleagues developed different, nonhierarchical models of congregational work, such as a co-rabbinate (two rabbis equal in responsibility, power, and authority, instead of the usual hierarchy of a senior rabbi and a more junior assistant or associate rabbi). As women's careers and families grew, some found that raising a family and working full-time did not work for them. The idea of a viable part-time rabbinate, with appropriate compensation and benefits, emerged. The ability to achieve greater balance between the demands of work and the demands of family became a more important criterion for the measurement of success in the rabbinate. Congregations with larger clergy staffs experimented with a rotation of clergy that afforded a Friday night or Saturday morning "off" on a regular basis.

It is clear that the presence of women in the rabbinate made it possible to create possibilities for more than one way of being a rabbi. While congregational work might always be the most obvious choice, different models of the rabbinate, part-time work, and non-congregational alternatives flourished with increased numbers of women in the rabbinate. This growth of the range of possibilities encouraged the growing plurality of women's voices in the rabbinate, and validated our hopes that earlier, more "male" models of the rabbinate could be changed to fit our circumstances and our needs. We created the new models we needed, and then fought to make these choices a reality in the Jewish communal workplace.

Tucked into our successes were the small stories of sexism and discrimination. Only in hushed voices could we allow ourselves to talk about losses of jobs because of pregnancy or sexual orientation. Some delayed pregnancy, or the announcement of a pregnancy, to ensure "getting the job." Some were the targets of sexual harassment from senior staff or congregants. Many women did move up the "ladder" of congregational success, but some did not. Anecdotally, some could not shake the impression that they had not succeeded because of gender concerns. As the numbers of women rabbis grew, women sought one another out more and more to get support with these issues.

At this stage, more than thirty-six years after Rabbi Priesand's ordination, over five hundred women have been ordained by Hebrew Union College–Jewish Institute of Religion (HUC-JIR), the Reform rabbinical seminary, and are among the sixteen hundred active members of the CCAR. Over fifteen congregations of more than six hundred families have a woman as senior rabbi. Over twenty-five women now teach full-time at HUC-JIR. Women are serving in the widest range of rabbinic work that the community has ever seen, and the community itself has grown to understand the myriad possibilities of rabbinic work. As women have been success-ful in redefining their relationship to work and to their workplace, men have benefited as well. Male rabbis, bolstered by their women colleagues' ability to conceptualize and combine work and family/personal life in a humane way that does not jeopardize either their work or their families, have happily adopted some of the alter-native rabbinic models that women created.

These transformations have made possible larger, more complex conversations about leadership. Women may have led the charge for different ways to be a rabbi, but the conversation has been welcomed across the rabbinic spectrum, and across gender lines. We intro-duced the possibility that we didn't have to be "married to our work," and women as rabbinic leaders have moved the conversation toward quality of work-life balance. If we as leaders do not model a healthy balance for our constituents, what are we teaching? This beginning attempt to embody and model equilibrium is one more recent contribution of women rabbis to the field. Leadership need not include denial of self and family. Rather, leadership can embed and integrate the experiences of gender, the experience of family, in daily life. The definition of what makes a good rabbi is changing before our eyes.

Likewise, the entry of women into the rabbinate has brought about changes for other disenfranchised people in the Jewish community. The acceptance of gay, lesbian, bisexual, transgender, and queer individuals into the rabbinate reflects and acknowledges their presence in our communities. The enfranchisement of these individuals could not have happened without the enfranchisement of women.

Women in the rabbinate have achieved so much. The Women's Rabbinic Network has reached many of its goals. There are now many women who have attained leadership positions in our movement. Women rabbis can look with pride at the most recent publishing achievements of the Reform movement, *The Torah: A Women's Commentary*, edited by two of HUC-JIR's professors, Dr. Tamara Eskenazi and Rabbi Andrea Weiss, and published by Women of Reform Judaism and Union for Reform Judaism Press, and the new siddur *Mishkan Tefila* (CCAR Press), edited by Rabbi Elyse Frishman. Both are projects that could only have come into existence with the support, presence, and contributions of women rabbis and academics.

Women continue to choose the rabbinate as a career in ever-increasing numbers. The contributions of women rabbis have breadth and depth. Yet, questions and concerns remain. There are still inequities of salary, benefits, and advancement that must be documented. The Jewish community must continue the conversation about the variety of models of success and leadership. Our community needs more information about the progression and advancement of women rabbis in all areas of the rabbinate in order to assure their continued commitment and contribution to rabbinic service. Women's careers may take a different trajectory; how can our congregations and communal institutions maximize our contributions along our life span? If women step off the congregational career path, can they step back on? As the first group of women rabbis moves into or closer to retirement age, what will their options be? As younger women become rabbis, how can the first generation of women rabbis share their hard-won successes and challenging failures in a meaningful way? As older women and men enter the community as "second-career" rabbis, how can the issue of ageism be confronted in a way that engages the community and enables their inclusion? Concerns about the "feminization of the synagogue" abound and point to a traditional discomfort with women in power. While these concerns must be addressed in a serious and thoughtful way, it is important to note that men are still choosing the rabbinate in large numbers, seeing it as a more holistic career choice than it was a generation ago. While the number of women in rabbinical schools continues to climb, men are still applying in large numbers, and rabbinical schools are recalibrating their curriculum based on that truth. The majority of Reform rabbis are still male, and the rabbinate remains a male-identified field.

The conversation about a successful career continues to change. The question that remains is, shall clergy be chosen because of, or despite, their gender? If women's entrance into the rabbinate has encouraged a vocabulary of access, egalitarianism, and inclusion, that implementation of equality of access and inclusion for men and women must continue to be a priority of the community.

There is still work to be done, because these questions and challenges abound and must be addressed. Our communities still need to learn how to enfranchise both men and women in Jewish life. Women, and women rabbis, will continue to contribute to the evolution of our tradition and to the enrichment of our community. We have worked very hard to bring about this evolution and revolution. However, our community cannot rest on its laurels. Much has been achieved, and much remains to be accomplished. The entrance of women into the rabbinate has been a blessing for our congregations, our communities, and our Jewish world. All of us must commit to extending the influence of that blessing. The future health and continuity of our community depend on it.

Cantor Barbara Ostfeld is history's first woman cantor, having been invested by the Hebrew Union College–Jewish Institute of Religion School of Sacred Music in June of 1975. She served Temple Beth-El of Great Neck as cantor from 1976 through 1988, and went on to serve Temple Brith Kodesh in Rochester, New York, and Temple Beth Am of Buffalo, New York, through 2002. Since 2002, Cantor Ostfeld has held the position of placement director of the American Conference of Cantors. She is married to Todd M. Joseph and has two adult children, Jordana and Aleza Horowitz.

The Ascent of the Woman Cantor

Shira Hamaalot

CANTOR BARBARA OSTFELD

THE CANTOR OF MY childhood synagogue, Martin Rosen, was one of my heroes. Cantor Rosen's voice rumbled like thunder and he had a great, high-pitched laugh. I believed in him, in that rumbling sound, in the fancy prayer words, in the lemon polish smell of the pews, and in the compact feel of the *Union Prayer Book* in my hands. Oh yes, I too would be a cantor one day.

When I was eleven years old, Cantor Rosen let me sing alto in the high holy day choir and made an example of me. He helped me to find a voice teacher and told me tales of student life at Hebrew Union College. I was secure in my resolve until the late winter of 1970, when I called Cantor Rosen to ask him about applying to cantorial school. At that tender moment, he laughed, saying, "They'll never take you."

In spite of Cantor Rosen's laughter, I applied to the Hebrew Union College–Jewish Institute of Religion's School of Sacred

Music. I was admitted and became the first female cantorial student; in June 1975, I became the first invested female cantor. Today, of the 413 regular members of the American Conference of Cantors, 226 are women, and of the 34 students at the School of Sacred Music, 27 are women.

What accounts for the explosion of women cantors in just over thirty years? It is too early to say for sure, but the answer seems to contain five themes: dormancy, germination, the emergence of a seedling, photosynthesis, and flowering. The final chapter, only now unfolding, indicates the promise of renewed fertility.

Dormancy

Jewish law kept women off the bimah for most of our history. Traditionally, halakhah was understood to exempt women from performing many mitzvot. To our sages, this meant that the one who is exempt is not permitted to lead others who are obligated in such observances; thus, women were not permitted to serve as cantors or *sh'lichei tzibbur* (representatives/enablers of the congregation), since women were not obligated to be part of the minyan.

In the Talmud Berachot 24a, we read, "The voice of a woman is *ervah.*" *Ervah* can be translated as either "licentious" or "erotic." This statement is made in reference to the stanza in Song of Songs 2:14, which reads: "Come let me look at you, come let me hear you, / your voice is clear as water, your body beautiful."[1]

The Rabbis teach that here the verse indicates that a woman's voice is erotic, and is thus proscribed. After some discussion, the Talmud concludes that a woman's singing voice should not be applied to any song with biblical verses or heard during Torah study, at the Shabbat dinner table, or indeed at any public gathering.

This conclusion was actually far from inescapable. Indeed, applying this reasoning backward in time would have been disastrous to the women singers of biblical fame. Over half of the Song of Songs would never have been sung, since these lines were intended to be sung by women.[2] Mighty General Barak might have stifled Deborah, whose verse is among the earliest Hebrew poetry in existence (Judg. 4–5). Priest Eli's ridicule would have kept Hannah's song from coming down to us in perpetuity (1 Sam. 2:1–10). And Moses would have silenced Miriam at the shore of the Sea of Reeds (Exod. 15:21).

But until modernity, the rules from Talmudic times were the accepted norm, and for women—specifically for women who sing in public—this ruling lasted until the autumn of 1845, when the leaders of the Berlin Reform Congregation formed a committee that would forever change Jewish history. These early German reformers, appointed to prepare a service for the high holy days, did battle with the notion that Jewish law alone should determine the course of action. The committee suggested, and the congregation adopted, a number of radical measures: they abbreviated the liturgy and added a sermon in the vernacular, a mixed choir accompanied by an organ, and German prayers along with the Hebrew prayers.[3]

What else did they endorse? The religious equality of women with men.

For the first time, at least theoretically, women's singing voices would be permitted, perhaps even advanced. While these were indeed impressive measures, the next 130 years yielded no women cantors.

Germination

So what was different in 1970, when I was too naive to know my question about applying to the cantorial school of the Hebrew Union College–Jewish Institute of Religion would evoke laughter? Everything. Women had "manned" the factories during World War II. The civil rights movement had been born, and the women's liberation movement had already made great strides. The status quo everywhere was under attack. Many young Americans were fed up with racism and war, and with sexism and dishonesty in government. Jews were in the forefront of all of the societal battles being waged.

The collective institutions of Reform Judaism (the Union of American Hebrew Congregations and Hebrew Union College–Jewish Institute of Religion) had long stood at the head of religious innovation. Reform Judaism had also been aligned with liberal social policy. Reform Jews were mostly identified as progressive and, maybe more important, thought of themselves as egalitarian. As individual Jews and as a movement, Reform Jews began to take pride in being part of the backlash against inequalities perpetuated by politics-as-usual. However, the ordination of women as rabbis was hardly a foregone conclusion. After having applied to the HUC-JIR rabbinic program, but before being admitted (as she later was, in 1968), Sally Priesand received some interesting letters from the college-institute. In one, she was directed to education studies; in another, she was subtly discouraged by a statement that the placement opportunities for women rabbis were unknown.[4]

Her battles had been waged and won by the time my application reached the School of Sacred Music two years later. In June of 2008, as I was researching this essay, I asked Dr. Alfred Gottschalk, who was the president of HUC-JIR in 1970, if there had been any controversy with regard to the decision to admit me. He replied that although there was "lots of discussion," my qualities were "outstanding" and there had been no debate. He had been in favor of the decision from the outset. Once I was attending classes, however, several faculty members insinuated that I was less in search of a cantorial career than of a husband from among the members of the student body.

In those early years, many congregations wanted the notoriety of hiring the "first women." They wanted to be on the cutting edge. Consequently, the successful, talented early women cantors secured pulpits without difficulty. Once these women were enrobed and positioned behind their lecterns, dappled with light filtered through stained glass, the question was no longer whether or not there could be women cantors, but whether or not they would take root and would others follow in their footsteps.

The Seedling Emerges

For the most part, the first women were competent and diligent; otherwise, they never would have reached the bimah. Like many women in previously male-only territory, most strove mightily. These factors alone, though, only carried these women up the steps of the bimah. The question remained, what would happen next? Would we be accepted by our rabbinic partners? By our new congregations?

There was no problem with our rabbis. In the late 1970s and throughout the 1980s most senior rabbis in the Reform movement were men. Some of those men anticipated that the fledgling women cantors would be cooperative and nonthreatening bimah partners, and not as competitive as their male counterparts. So it seems that the old saw about women being more collaborative and less insistent in positions of leadership encouraged male rabbis to welcome female cantors, to show their approval of these new colleagues, and to promote their acceptance by their congregations.

The congregational tension revolved around an unfamiliar vocal timbre, alien clothing outlining a womanly figure, a hitherto unknown urge to check out footwear, odd feminine cadences imposed on familiar words, the new concern over the heft of the Torah scroll, and then, of course, the absence of the masculine in all things. Most of my female colleagues will report that these worries, too, are a thing of the past. By the mid-1980s, the answer had became crystal clear: women cantors, by and large, were going to be a hit. In most cases, it would be pure chemistry.

A particular chemistry is found in the synagogue when the call of a female voice is heard from the bimah. The Talmud's use of the word *erotic* in describing a woman's voice may not be precisely on target, but it may not miss the point altogether. The reactions to her voice are not entirely different from what we think of as spiritual responses. Instead of the traditional but problematic translation of *ervah* as "erotic" we might more accurately translate *ervah* as "charged." To say, "A woman's voice is 'charged,'" is true both Talmudically and today. If we couple *spiritual* and *charged,* we would have the full story.

On a basic level, we have the scientific fact that a woman's voice sounds one octave higher than a man's. Surely this alone could not have been upsetting to the Sages. So what qualities in a woman's voice disturbed the Rabbis in Berachot 24a? Perhaps the very attributes that perturbed the Sages awaken contemporary worshipers. The way in which the higher woman's voice conveys the liturgy is indeed different. It may give to prayer-text certain overtones that reading alone cannot convey. People often feel that the female voice humanizes, softens, enhances prayer. The timbre of the female voice may have some salutary effect on prayer.

Is the profound attraction of vocal purity a factor in this chemistry? Men's voices are seldom described as "pure," but "purity" and "clarity" are words frequently used in admiring descriptions of women cantors' voices, something I have noted countless times in my work as director of placement for the American Conference of Cantors.

An additional question: Why do so many of today's worshipers seem to want female voices to be clear and sweet in tone, stripped of earthiness when raised in prayer? Is this a subtle validation of the Rabbis' observation? Or is it a reflection of the pop culture that has made untrained, lighter voices the norm? Only time will answer these questions.

The acceptance and appreciation that early women cantors found from rabbis and congregations allowed them to focus on a far higher hurdle that they had not yet confronted: although women cantors spend much of their professional lives immersed in the details of the Torah, much of the text does not address them. Women cantors sing words in which their ancestral mothers are transmuted into an afterthought, which are not meant for them to intone or even necessarily to heed.

In order to be secure as cantors, women have had to reinterpret the Torah and tradition in order to forge new liturgy and gender-sensitive rituals. They write and read women's commentaries and women's midrashim, and have had to recast such rites as *t'vilah* (immersion) and tefillin. They have had to create ceremonies, such as the covenental naming ceremony for girls, *brit banot,* out of whole cloth. Thus, a woman cantor holds on to the very tradition that once excluded her, and in doing so, she transforms it.

This transformation extends to all ares of Jewish life and ritual. The traditional halakhic divorce, *gittin,* is harrowing for many women. The wife is told by the three presiding (male) rabbis to cup her hands in order to receive the divorce document as it descends from above, released by her husband's fingers. She is then instructed to position the *get* (divorce document) in her armpit and thereafter to turn on her heel and pretend to leave her husband's presence, returning to present the *get* for a rabbinic tearing and final decree that she is "permitted to any man."

To provide a more sympathetic modern practice, Cantor Susan Caro created a woman-focused ritual of separation. In her ritual, the wife herself recites passages from Psalm 27, and others, such as these:

> *K'riah* [tearing] is a Jewish custom which is an expres-
> sion of grief, as it is written: "Rend your garments and
> not your heart ... for God offers compassion and com-
> fort" (Joel 2:13). We are also taught that there is a time
> for everything in this world—a time to tear and a time
> to mend. May the final tearing today leave room only
> for the continued process of mending and healing.
>
> [Tear the *Ketubah*]
> On this day, I depart fully as a free woman from my
> marriage. I stand here as a free agent in the Jewish com-
> munity and in the world, before God, and before myself.
> I stand here, having completed our people's traditional
> ways of unbinding a marital relationship. I stand as a
> Jewish woman with dignity and with strength. I stand
> restored as a whole and complete person.

> Blessed is the Eternal, our God, Creator of the universe, for giving us life, for sustaining us, and for bringing us to this season.

Cantor Caro chose to prevent women from being subjected to what many experience as the humiliation of the traditional Jewish divorce; she wanted instead to give them an opportunity to participate in a rite of passage that acknowledges them as women who have struggled and who have prevailed. In doing so, Susan Caro did more than tweak the ritual of *gittin*. She laid claim to it and bested it in a battle. In doing so, she added to its holiness, infusing it with God's name, absent in the original. In her version, we can sense the sacredness of the rite.

Photosynthesis

The woman cantor, having leaped over the hurdles of investiture, rabbinic and congregational acceptance, and the recasting of ritual, next approached traditional text. As she had done with certain ceremonies, the female cantor resolved her cognitive dissonance with the text of the Torah by ascending the bimah and staking a claim to it. Once she felt comfortable as a leader of prayer and as a reader of Torah, she had given the text her imprint and the space her aspect.

A Jew sitting in the congregation is in the position of listening to a woman chanting a biblical text that indicts her for her sex. For instance in Leviticus 8:1–36, we read a detailed account of the execution of the instructions for the ordination of priests, including the robing of Aaron and his sons. The Torah specifies that only males from the seed of Aaron may officiate in the Sanctuary. The women of these Levitical families are allowed certain privileges (Lev. 21–22), but are excluded from the performance of official functions. When a woman cantor chants these verses, it is discordant in the extreme.

One aspect of this dissonance can be resolved through the acceptance of her leadership: liturgical, educational, pastoral, and spiritual. The more frequently she is seen in these roles, the more natural it seems and the more the sexist mandate of Levitical passages begins to sound as relevant as the one about killing children who insult their parents (Lev. 20:9).

But what about prayer texts? How can they be reinterpreted, and then set to music?

As early as the seventh century, the cantor's role sometimes included creating *piyyutim,* liturgical poetry.[5] This catapulted the job description into a whole new realm. The workaday *sh'liach tzibbur* (person who leads the congregation in prayer) adhered to all forms of ritual and observed the rules of *nusach,* the specific mode in which a prayer is to be chanted that depends both on the day (weekday, Shabbat, holiday) and on the time of day (morning, evening). Perhaps the average cantor improvised a bit within the nusach. But those *hazzanim* (cantors) whose compositional and poetic skills excelled their vocal talents became the superstars of their time. Their words have been immortalized in our siddurim. Witness the *piyyutim* that have come down to us. By design, alphabetical acrostics such as L'cha Dodi[6] or Ashamnu[7] are tunes and words that we can't get out of our heads.

There had been few women writing music for synagogues before the 1970s, though certainly no women cantors doing so before the 1980s. In the 1970s, singer, guitarist, and composer Debbie Friedman began to juxtapose Hebrew and English verses in her compositions to great effect. The sound was new and exciting. Her pieces were accessible. The English embedded within the Hebrew drove the text home. In addition, the melodies sounded instantly familiar. These tunes are simple enough to be singable, yet not so predictable as to be banal. Friedman's compositions began to transform the liturgical landscape. Perhaps inspired by her, it wasn't long after the initial entry of women into the cantorate that women cantors put pens to manuscript paper and began to publish.

The immersion in congregational life of all cantors who also compose moves them to set certain texts to music. The woman cantor, identifying with the bride and the new mother and the matriarch, wants the music for those milestones to be "inclusive and embracing" in addition to reflecting their "great pain and great joy," according to Cantor Lisa Levine, whose many compositions are popular across the country. "The woman cantor/composer creates new forms of worship through compositions that address the life-cycle, the changing months and seasons," says Rachelle Nelson, a Florida-based cantor-composer. Levine asserts that women in this role are also eager to send their compositions out with the subtext of a "woman's increased role and higher visibility in community leadership."

The technique pioneered by Debbie Friedman of inserting non-literal translations of liturgical and biblical texts into musical compositions has opened many minds to prayer. Some of the musical settings that women write for Shabbat worship "aim to convey the emotion that individuals might experience as part of their Shabbat experience: the excitement of passing through the Reed Sea, a sense of Shabbat peace, the meditative feeling associated with personal prayer," according to Cantor Lisa Doob, a new composer on the liturgical scene. Women who are both cantors and composers tend to personalize their worship moments. They welcome the highs and lows that accompany them. They then set out to find ways to connect other worshipers to their own worship moments.

A Flowering

Women cantors are successfully serving in the largest congregations in the world. For example, Cantor Lori Corrsin serves Congregation Emanu-El of the City of New York, which has 2,346 member units. Cantor Roslyn J. Barak serves Congregation Emanu-El of San Francisco, which has 2,623 member units. In 2007 the third woman cantor, Kay Greenwald, was elected to the presidency of the American Conference of Cantors (ACC), having followed Vicki L. Axe (1991–1995) and Judith K. Rowland (1995–1998, 2000–2001). Women cantors serve in many capacities on the faculty of the

Hebrew Union College–Jewish Institute of Religion School of Sacred Music. Only women cantors have served and currently serve as director of music programming at the Union for Reform Judaism (a position that was created first as a directorship of the department of synagogue music in 1996). A woman cantor presides over the alumni association of the HUC-JIR School of Sacred Music, as well. A woman cantor chairs the ACC's endowment fund, and the only two cantors to serve as full-time faculty on the Cincinnati campus of Hebrew Union College have been women. As of this writing, a woman cantor has just begun her term as the chair of the HUC-JIR alumni council, representing rabbis, cantors, educators, communal service professionals, and scholars. Additionally the first nonrabbinic alumni member ever to serve on the board of governors of HUC-JIR is a woman cantor. These groundbreaking achievements are now taken for granted among Reform Jews, further proof of the acceptance of women in the cantorial leadership.

From suppression to connection, and suspicion to esteem, the sound of women cantors has changed Jewish worship forever. The whole scope of the human voice, which spans far more than the notes of the bass or baritone registers, is now heard in our synagogues.

> "Woman of the gardens, of the voice friends listen for,
> will you let me hear you?"[8]
>
> *Adoshem, s'fatai tiftach, ufi yageed t'hilatecha.*
>
> *YHVH, open my lips and my mouth shall speak your praise.*[9]

Sara Hurwitz is part of the rabbinic staff at the Hebrew Institute of Riverdale, where she serves as *madricha ruchanit* (religious mentor). She graduated from Drisha's three-year Scholars Circle Program and for the past four years has studied Jewish law under the supervision of Rabbi Avi Weiss, who is expected to give her the title of *morateinu* (our teacher) this fall. She received a BA from Barnard College, Columbia University. Sara has lectured at Jewish Orthodox Feminist Alliance, Drisha, the Florence Melton Adult Mini-School, the JCC in Manhattan, Lights in Action, Conference on Alternatives in Jewish Education, the National Jewish Center for Learning and Leadership (CLAL), and at various synagogues across the United States.

Orthodox Women in Rabbinic Roles

SARA HURWITZ, *MADRICHA RUCHANIT* (RELIGIOUS MENTOR)

I AM A FEMALE Orthodox rabbi. Well, I'm not technically a rabbi, as I'm not yet officially ordained. But I speak from the pulpit of my Orthodox congregation at the Hebrew Institute of Riverdale and I preside over minyanim at shiva homes. I teach classes to all members of my community, and field late-night questions about keeping kosher and the laws of family purity. I even have a title: *madricha ruchanit*, "religious mentor." In 2008, I will receive a document synonymous with a certificate of ordination after completing three years of study at Drisha Institute, and more than four years of study under the auspices of Rabbi Avi Weiss, senior rabbi of Hebrew Institute of Riverdale. At that time, my title will likely become *morateinu*, "our teacher." So, if I'm not technically a rabbi, what is a rabbi, and what are the barriers for Orthodox women considering this calling?

If you asked a child in the Orthodox community to draw a picture of a rabbi, he or she would likely depict a bearded man in a black hat. While most Modern Orthodox rabbis do not have beards, the picture would not be too far off the mark. The child would be reflecting the community's conception of what a rabbi is. The average Orthodox Jew has a formalistic view of rabbinics. A rabbi must graduate from a yeshiva and receive an official certificate of ordination, called *semicha*. The Orthodox rabbi is a member of a large rabbinical association, and officiates at life cycle events in his capacity as community leader. Within the context of this formal and institutional description of a rabbi, there is little room for women to assume a role of rabbinic authority in Orthodox institutions. Orthodoxy currently forbids the ordination of women, and is not yet comfortable with women in clergy-type roles that were not traditionally theirs.

There is another way, however, of viewing the position of rabbi. I like to call this the functional model. Rather than thinking of a rabbi as an anointed and formal communal leader, I prefer to focus on the day-to-day practical aspects of the rabbinic job. When viewed in this light, we find that women cannot halakhically perform only about 5 percent of rabbinic functions. As of now, Orthodox women do not lead services and women are barred from acting as witnesses for marriage, divorce, and conversion.[1] But beyond these few halakhic constraints, women, with the appropriate training, can fulfill the tasks of the rabbi.

Thus, I believe that it is useful to focus on the actual roles rabbis play in our day-to-day lives. The question then becomes, what do communal Orthodox rabbis do, and what are the perceived barriers to women within each function?

Rabbis Are Well Versed in Texts

Up until recently, many women did not have access to Jewish texts.[2] Women nevertheless made halakhic decisions on a daily basis about how to kasher a utensil, or clean and kasher a chicken. Women's vast knowledge of Jewish law was transmitted from mother to daughter in a rich mimetic tradition.[3] In recent years, however, there has been a shift. Day schools, seminaries, and post-college institutions began offering women access to Jewish textual learning, and women have flocked to these institutions. Many have indulged in Torah study for its own sake *(torah lishma)*, grappling with the Talmud, Torah exegesis, or even works of Jewish mysticism. They often have no intention of applying their studies to any practical use, other than enhancing their own religious lives. However, many of these programs, such as Drisha Institute's Scholars Circle Program, follow a curriculum similar to that of most formal rabbinic institutions. Both require a mastery of the laws of keeping kosher, the laws of Shabbat, and the laws of *niddah* (the laws surrounding menstruation and sexual intimacy). It would be almost impossible for women to refrain from applying this newfound halakhic knowledge to their daily practices. Therefore, empowered by their textual knowledge, women have begun asserting their authority both inside and outside the home. Now women make halakhic decisions based on their own erudition, in addition to relying on what their grandmothers may have done.

Rabbis Are Authorities on Halakhah

Once women have the ability to study text and they become intimately familiar with the pages of the Talmud, the question becomes, why can't women serve as halakhic authorities for the larger community? Since women now have textual literacy, it makes sense for them to be able to make halakhic decisions for others. And in some communities, Orthodox women like myself already do make authoritative decisions about issues of *niddah* and sexuality.[4]

While women as deciders of halakhah is still somewhat uncommon in the Orthodox community, there is precedent for having women in positions of halakhic authority. The Talmud quotes the principle that all who are unfit to serve as witnesses cannot serve as judges.[5] Since women cannot serve as witnesses, women cannot serve as judges.[6]

However, the Pitchei Teshuva Choshen Mishpat 7:5 says, "Even though a woman is disqualified from being a judge, a woman who is wise and learned is fit to render a ruling." [7] The implication is that if women are well versed in law, they can become authorities on any subject matter.

Therefore, the role of women in positions of halakhic authority expands beyond issues relating solely to women. For example, when a woman is about to tear *kriyah* (cutting of a garmet or black ribbon by mourners) for her loss and feels uncomfortable with a male rabbi's assistance, I can help her. When a woman struggles to say the kaddish, I can stand next to her and not only help her with the words, but explain their meaning. I can advise all congregants about which celebrations are appropriate during their mourning period, and which they should not attend.

It is important to distinguish here between answering simple halakhic questions and being a *posek* (halakhic authority). A *posek* must be able to integrate the vast halakhic literature and apply it to our modern era, creatively and independently from an established precedent. There are in fact very few community rabbis who would consider themselves *poskim*. Just as the average pulpit rabbi must often turn to a recognized master when answering a complicated and complex question, women in halakhic authority would do the same.

It remains to be seen how comfortable men and women will feel reaching out to women in all areas of halakhah. It is my hope that the level of expertise that women possess, combined with the appropriate amount of empathy, will ensure that people do seek out women—not because of gender, but because of their proficiency and comfort with halakhic literature. The more opportunities women are given to flex their skills, the more common it will become for the community to turn to female halakhic advisors.

Rabbis Are Pastoral Counselors

Although the role of rabbi is often associated with that of a teacher, the term has come to include family mediator, psychologist, and counselor. People seek rabbis for advice on some of their most private decisions and challenges. Whether the average rabbi is qualified to counsel people is a separate discussion, but there is no reason why women, with expertise and experience, cannot fulfill this role.

In truth, being in a position of halakhic authority requires more than just answering a question. Answering a question is often the beginning of a dialogue; a question may lead to a discussion of more intimate aspects of one's life. Therefore, when weighing how to respond to a question, it is important to respond to the person, not only the technical and analytical side of the question. Sometimes, a question that a woman may ask about using the mikveh, for example, may lead to a discussion about her fears of marriage.

Therefore, women in positions of spiritual leadership and halakhic authority are in a unique position to counsel people on issues relating to sexuality, infertility, and halakhic and emotional ramifications of a miscarriage. But more than that, men or women with a sense of empathy can naturally reach out to people in their time of greatest distress and greatest joy.

Rabbis Are Public Leaders

Beyond being a disseminator of Jewish knowledge and a counselor, a rabbi is also a public figure. From Miriam, who taught the women in the desert,[8] to Deborah, who led the Jewish people (Judg. 4:4), women have been exceptional leaders. However, the image of women standing before the entire community to teach publicly remained fairly uncommon in Jewish life.[9]

We live in a world today where women have reached and assumed significant positions of public leadership. It is no longer noteworthy to see a woman heading a corporation or holding political office. Yet, when it comes to synagogue leadership, women often still choose to stay at home. Perhaps this stems from earlier times when it was not common for women to roam freely in the streets.

Maimonides, living in the twelfth century, paints a vivid picture of the social norms for women:

> It is shameful for a woman to leave her home continu-
> ally.... A husband should prevent his wife from doing
> this. He should not allow her to leave the house more
> than once in a month or twice, according to the need. For
> the beauty of a woman consists in her staying withdrawn
> in a corner of her home, for this is how it is written "All
> the honor of the king's daughter is within [her home]."[10]

In previous times, women prayed at home, not in the communal setting of a synagogue. Jewish law reflects this: women are not obligated in time-bound commandments, and therefore are exempt from communal prayer and do not count in an Orthodox minyan. Their spiritual needs should be fulfilled privately. However, as it became more common for women to enter the marketplace and to gain some autonomy outside of the home, women also entered the synagogue and began asserting their authority in the community at large.[11]

Consider the blessing traditionally recited each morning, *shelo asani ishah*, in which God is blessed "for not making me a women." Despite its negative connotation, this blessing was not considered controversial until women began entering the public space to pray. To accommodate this new phenomenon of women in shul, it became customary for woman to substitute *she-assani kirtzano* ("who has made me according to His will") in place of the traditional "male" blessing.[12]

This precedent can be used as a model for today's changing reality. Orthodox women do go to synagogue services. Many even feel compelled to pray with a minyan, a quorum of ten men, and many do arrive at services on time. And, slowly, women are stepping into public spiritual leadership positions. And, slowly, congregants are becoming more comfortable with this model.

At the Hebrew Institute of Riverdale, I speak from the pulpit during services. This public role is unusual for women, even in

Modern Orthodox services. There are two main reasons for this barrier. First, there are those who think that it is immodest for women to stand and speak before a mixed audience. Second, one of the foundations of an Orthodox service is that men and women pray on separate sides of a physical barrier, called a *mechitzah*. Allowing a woman to address the entire congregation during *tefillah* (prayer) would require women to enter the men's side of the sanctuary, which would likely be disruptive and possibly impermissible. It is therefore generally held to be both immodest and disruptive for a woman to publicly address the community during prayer services.

With respect to immodesty, it has become commonplace to see women in public positions of leadership, both inside and outside of the synagogue. Bat mitzvah girls prepare comprehensive discourses, which they deliver publicly during services. Female mourners deliver eulogies, and many women opt to give *divrei Torah* (short sermons or explanations of the weekly Torah portion) at communal functions. In a Modern Orthodox synagogue, it is no longer shocking to see women address the congregation publicly.[13] Hebrew Institute of Riverdale has circumvented the second problem of keeping both sides of the *mechitzah* separate by elevating the bimah in the middle of the sanctuary. This allows equal access to men and women from either side of the *mechitzah*. When I get up to speak in the middle of services, I do not enter the men's side of the room. As an additional support for allowing women to cross into the men's side when necessary, Rabbi Moshe Feinstein ruled that it is permissible, occasionally, for one or two women to be present in a *beit midrash* or house of mourning during a service without a *mechitzah*.[14] Therefore, on this basis it can be considered acceptable, on occasion, for a woman to stand in the men's section during a regular prayer service to address the congregation.[15]

Rabbis Have a Formal Title

Even if women do step into the role of rabbi, the matter of title will continue to be controversial. On one hand, I am inclined to say that title does not matter. After all, if you are performing the duties in a desired profession, does it really matter what people call you? But then I remember all the times in my professional career where having a formal title would have helped me do my job just a little bit better. For example, when a rabbi walks into a room at a house of mourning, the dynamics are such that he does not have to follow the rules of a house of mourning. A rabbi does not have to sit quietly and wait until spoken to. He walks in with a purpose. He is there to provide halakhic advice, support, and comfort, and the mourner is often more receptive to a rabbi's efforts than words from a fellow congregant. My level of productivity would increase tremendously if I had a formal title. And there is no question that the title "rabbi" is best suited for this profession. While there are different kinds of rabbis, the word conveys the type of services I offer. However, there are several reasons why, for now, the title must remain distinct. For one, the Modern Orthodox world is concerned with remaining separate and distinct from the other Jewish denominations. Thus, giving women the title "rabbi" would make Orthodoxy appear synonymous with the Reform and Conservative movements, a phenomenon that Orthodox leaders living in modernity have always tried to avoid. In addition, the Modern Orthodox community is afraid of being ostracized by the communities to the right. Adopting the title of "rabbi" would become the defining issue for the community, potentially causing the community to split.[16] Finally, the community itself has a visceral discomfort with calling a woman "rabbi," and may be more willing to learn from and respect a woman in a rabbinic role, if she had a distinct title.

Currently, Orthodox women in public positions have an array of titles. Devorah Zlochower is *rosh beit midrash* (head of a Jewish learning school) at Drisha Institute (synonymous with the *rosh yeshiva*, the head of school). Dina Najman is *rosh kehillah* (head of congregation) at Kehillat Orach Eliezer in Manhattan. Rachel Kohl Finegold is programming and ritual director at Anshe Sholom B'nai Israel Congregation in Chicago, but some people call her "Rabbanit" (the female grammatical equivalent of both "Rabbi" and "Rabbi's wife"). Lynn Kaye is director of Jewish life and learning at Shearith Israel, the Spanish Portuguese Synagogue. Elana Stein is resident scholar at the Jewish Center in Manhattan. My title will soon be *morateinu* (our teacher), a title that was affectionately given to Nechama Leibowitz, a noted Israeli biblical scholar. The title *"morateinu"* and some of these other titles can, through use, be reclaimed to have the connotation that the title "rabbi" now conveys, while still retaining the Orthodox philosophy that men and women's roles, at least for the time being, remain distinct. Despite the different titles and without much fanfare, women are slowly taking on ritual leadership roles in Orthodox synagogues. And perhaps, one day, the Orthodox community will simply begin addressing women in positions of ritual leadership as "Rabbi."

Where Do We Go from Here? Successes and Challenges

For now, whatever each of our titles may be, it is my hope that this group of women in leadership roles in the Orthodox community will galvanize and organize our efforts into a professional body of women in positions of spiritual leadership and halakhic authority in Orthodox institutions. This would give us the opportunity to network with one another for resources, as well as provide much needed support as we break into this new field. It may also have the effect of helping young Orthodox girls realize that pursuing a career in rabbinics is a legitimate option. The community has succeeded in opening institutions of higher learning to women both in North America and Israel. Learning for the sake of learning is no longer enough. Now, the learning must be goal oriented. With some guidance, men and women can be equally qualified to take up positions of spiritual leadership in communal settings. Synagogue internships must continue to be created; Orthodox women can be a rabbinic presence at Hillels on college campuses. Federations can hire Orthodox women as their in-house rabbinic presence.

But there are still many obstacles and challenges that women who endeavor to choose this path must face. One challenge often cited as a barrier to women taking positions of spiritual leadership in Orthodoxy is that the community is not ready. But while it is true that people do have a natural resistance to change, change does occur. The first woman to lobby her community to ordain her as a rabbi lived in the late 1800s but it wasn't until 1972 that the Reform movement ordained Sally Priesand as the first female rabbi. The Conservative movement followed about ten years later. The Orthodox movement does embrace change, but the process of change is more methodical and slow. Therefore, it is up to individual lay leaders to take responsibility and lobby for communities to hire women as part of the rabbinic staff. Institutions of higher learning such as Drisha can actively train women to take on positions of spiritual leadership, and then help place their graduates in synagogues. A few mainstream Orthodox shuls have already hired women. It is only a matter of time before other shuls follow.

There is no doubt that the advent of women in rabbinic positions has already and is likely to continue to cause a stir within the Orthodox community. Some even suggest that it will cause a major split in the Orthodox movement. If this were to happen, I believe that the Modern Orthodox movement would be making great strides to sustain itself as a distinct and vibrant movement.[17] The Modern Orthodox movement is slowly but surely looking to establish thoughtful leaders that embrace women in positions of spiritual leadership. As more open-minded rabbis accept jobs in pulpits around the United States, there will be more positions created for women to work in these shuls. And soon, as communities see all that these women have to offer, women will be sought after to become heads of communities, and fulfil rabbinic pulpit positions.

I asserted at the beginning that I am not a rabbi. But I am a de facto rabbinic figure. My community embraces my role, and the rabbinic staff of my synagogue supports my professional development. In truth, I have never thought of myself as a "trailblazer." My desire for synagogue work always felt natural. A vocational test that I took before college suggested that my skill set was best suited for a career in the clergy. At the time I laughed, as this was not an option for Orthodox women. And yet today, not only is entering the clergy within our reach, for many women it has become a reality. And, at least for the community I serve and for the many visitors to our synagogue, I have undoubtedly acclimated people to seeing women stand up on the pulpit and assume roles of leadership.

As for becoming a rabbi de jure, I am certainly willing to accept the risks and responsibilities of ordination if it becomes available. Even if the majority of the Orthodox Jewish community is not entirely ready for a woman to assume a public role in the synagogue, despite halakhic sources permitting these roles, I am prepared and I am ready. And once our community begins to think about the functions of a rabbi, rather than focusing solely on the issues of titles and institutional roles, I believe the barriers to women being accepted as rabbis will be removed. Then the community at large will benefit from a large untapped supply of talent, and will be able to turn to qualified professionals for comfort, advice, and halakhic guidance, regardless of gender.

Rabbi Sue Levi Elwell, PhD, director of the Pennsylvania Council of the Union for Reform Judaism, has served congregations in California, New Jersey, and Virginia. The founding director of the Los Angeles Jewish Feminist Center, a project of the American Jewish Congress, Elwell served as the first rabbinic director of Ma'yan: The Jewish Women's Project of the JCC in Manhattan. A senior rabbinic fellow of the Shalom Hartman Institute in Jerusalem, Elwell edited *The Open Door: The CCAR Passover Haggadah*, served as the Voices editor of *The Torah: A Women's Commentary* and as one of the editors of *Lesbian Rabbis: The First Generation*. The mother of two adult daughters, Elwell lives in Philadelphia with her partner, Nurit Levi Shein.

Feminism and the Transformation of the Synagogue

RABBI SUE LEVI ELWELL, PhD

OVER THE COURSE of the final quarter of the twentieth century, American synagogue life took several new forms. These changes ranged from new approaches to synagogue architecture, to new thinking about leadership, both volunteer and professional; from thinking about liturgy and ritual in new ways, to considering the implications of increasingly diverse membership. What was the impact of women and feminism in these changes? What are the issues waiting to be explored by those who care about creating, re-creating, and sustaining vibrant and healthy inclusive Jewish communities?

Leadership through a Gendered Lens

Like their parents and grandparents in the first half of the twentieth century, those who joined and cared for synagogues in the second half of the century were hoping that the synagogue would serve as a center for community: a place to meet, to worship together, to learn, and to find a mechanism for involvement, as Jews, in the larger community. As the century progressed, however, the individualism that has always characterized American culture intensified, weakening, for some, the sense of need for or responsibility to the maintenance of communal structures and organizations. By the end of the century, the challenge articulated by President John Kennedy at his 1962 inauguration, "Ask not what your country can do for you, but what you can do for your country," had been reversed. For many, the question seemed to be: what can my country, my community, my synagogue do for me?

Concurrently, feminists were beginning to frame questions about and challenges to long-held assumptions and accepted norms in every aspect of organized Jewish life. We were trying to puzzle out the role of gender in shaping the forms of Jewish communal institutions, including the synagogue. By the late 1980s, over one hundred women rabbis were serving synagogues across America and Canada. Whether intentional or conscious feminists or not, every one of those rabbis, myself included, challenged the status quo in the communities they served. Those communities had to adjust their ideas of leadership, power, and authority. We realized that we had not been prepared for a career that was changing, and that, consciously or not, we were part of that change. Some of us went to work with male colleagues who thought that they were ready to work with us, thought that they could welcome and work alongside a female colleague, hoped that their understandings of partnership could include us. Too often, we found that even as we crafted our own rabbinates, we were expected to simultaneously be the educators of these male colleagues as well as exemplars of a new Judaism that embraced the idea of women leaders. This was before we had even begun to grapple with the many challenges that real women bring to any world that has been, for centuries, patriarchal. The fact that most of us were young and without prior work experience was an additional burden, as was the fact that many of us were just beginning life partnerships, were of child-bearing age, and were trying to figure out how to balance work and family life.

At the same time, many of us were stunned by the absence of women from positions of synagogue leadership. While women were very involved in the daily functioning of the synagogue, serving on committees, sometimes overseeing and usually staffing the religious school, raising funds for synagogue programs, and more, few of us worked with women temple presidents or members of executive boards. And if we did, the women were always "exceptional" in some way, often by being the only women to serve among a cadre of men.

But the simple presence of women, professional or volunteer, in any given organization or institution does not mean that anyone thinks about leadership in new ways. Only at the turn of the twenty-first century did some begin to rethink the fixed structural modes and norms that had distinguished synagogue leadership for so many years. Some looked for better ways to strengthen an already effective system. Many others realized that their institutions were flailing and that if they continued to operate as they always had, they would reap the results they always had. The top-down, "top-man" approach that served synagogues in the fifties needed to be reconsidered in the nineties, since that approach was being questioned in all areas of corporate and communal life. In addition, the suburban synagogue of the fifties was undergoing so many changes that its leadership needed to adjust accordingly. The wealthy businessman, entrepreneur, or professional man, long the primary candidate for congregational leadership was complemented by new models of leadership that included women. Some of those women had honed their leadership skills in women's organizations, most notably women's synagogue groups such as Women of Reform Judaism and Women's League for Conservative Judaism, and others had risen through the ranks of synagogue leadership without the benefit of such training.

Welcoming Women Is Only a First Step

Among emerging leadership models, the ones that build on the insights of feminist thinkers are those that recognize and harness the strength and insight of individuals who had formerly been on the periphery. Acknowledging diversity and then bringing talented individuals closer to the center strengthens every organization. Synagogues that have learned this lesson from inviting women in, as both professional and lay leaders, have grown and prospered. And an increasing number of synagogues have extended their reach to other formerly marginal people or members, be they individuals who are physically or mentally challenged, who come from non-normative Jewish communities, whose paths to Judaism and the Jewish community have been through other traditions, who are sexual minorities, who are racially or ethnically different than the majority of the synagogue's members, and more. The celebration of difference is an expectation and an essential value for not just those who are represented in traditional Jewish texts, but for all who study them. In those texts, we hear a wide range of voices that often respectfully disagree with one another. The Talmud includes a broad range of opinions and experiences from those who contribute to an ongoing discussion of life and issues that transcends time and geography. Congregations that manifest respect for diversity thus both reflect tradition and open wide the doors to a vibrant, inclusive Jewish future.

Feminism and the Creation and Transformation of Physical Space

For some members of the Jewish community in the late twentieth century, buildings that had functioned as the physical fulfillment of communal dreams were no longer functional—worship spaces were created for worship and preaching styles that were no longer practiced or valued, classrooms used for years suddenly seemed institutional and lacking warmth, and public spaces did not reflect a changing sense of communal identity. For some, the "edifice complex" was replaced by a desire to return to a romanticized version of the shtetl, creating intimate spaces where Jews could come together to sing, chant, pray, and learn.

Karla Goldman's excellent study, *Beyond the Synagogue Gallery: Finding a Place for Women in American Judaism,*[1] examines the emergence of women and women's concerns in the development of distinctly American synagogue cultures by the conclusion of the nineteenth century. Building on Goldman's insights, we can see the impact of feminism on our own synagogues. For example, Goldman writes about how women moved from the gallery, the physical symbol of the periphery, to the center of synagogue life. By the middle of the twentieth century, the physical plants of synagogues had been transformed by women's presence. Women's increased involvement as both participants and leaders in synagogue life necessitated the construction of better spaces for schoolchildren, as well as play spaces, both inside and outdoors. By the end of the twentieth century, the need for places where mothers could nurse and change their infants was also reflected in an increasing number of public spaces, including synagogues. We began to see changing tables and changing areas constructed in both men's and women's bathrooms in synagogues. Another addition to some synagogues was soundproof rooms adjacent to the sanctuary, which enabled those with small children to be "silent participants" in services.

The design and outfitting of synagogue kitchens also helps us understand the changing dynamics of synagogue life. Who do we expect to be working in and maintaining the kitchen? If we use dishes and serving utensils that must be washed, who does the washing? Is the food for communal events purchased by committee or by the synagogue staff, or is it the assumption that the Oneg Shabbat, the collation after the service, should provide a primary opportunity for sharing both food and fellowship through the potluck system? When "Sisterhood ladies" no longer served tea from a silver tea service, it became clear that the food service at the synagogue needed to be reconsidered. The kitchen rules that are posted in various synagogue kitchens provide a fascinating source of information about the expectations of synagogue leaders and of those who are the most frequent users of the kitchen space.

Synagogue libraries also bear the fingerprints of individual women who established and maintained this physical manifestation of the intellectual center of synagogue life, both in the selection of books and magazines and in an analysis of what books were actually borrowed, read, and returned, or what books were never returned and, finances permitting, were replaced and thus returned to circulation. Many synagogue gardens were established and maintained by female congregants, and the histories of those gardens are a source of additional information about the individuals and groups who made and continue to make an explicit connection between their involvement in the synagogue and their commitment to tilling the soil. The establishment of "brides' rooms," designated spaces for bridal parties to prepare for and store their belongings in preparation for and during weddings, also reflects the involvement of women in thinking about the uses of the synagogue building.

The most recent addition to synagogue spaces is an intentional gathering place that makes available comfortable seating, coffee, and snacks. Building on the popular success of coffee shops as magnets for individuals of all ages to come and sit, at least for the time that it takes to drink a cup of coffee, a growing number of synagogues have sought to create in their buildings a space—and an atmosphere—that entices members to "hang out." These places are particularly popular on Sunday mornings, when parents choose to remain at the synagogue during the hours their children are in religious school.

Finally, those who plan for the construction and reconstruction of the physical spaces in our synagogues are increasingly acknowledging and accommodating members and guests who are physically challenged. Although some congregations are just beginning the work to comply with federal guidelines, other congregations not only already comply but surpass minimal guidelines and make every part of their building and grounds accessible to those who make use of a range of assistive devices to fully participate in synagogue programs. Auditory devices, large-print prayer books, ramps, and accessible bathrooms are a first and necessary step to making synagogues and sanctuaries fully accessible to all. These welcoming changes were brought about gradually. As synagogues began to address the needs of women, the needs of other formerly disenfranchised groups became more visible.

Give Me That Old Time Religion: The Male Backlash

For many Jews, the synagogue is their primary Jewish address. The many jokes that identify "the synagogue I don't attend" point to the importance of the synagogue I do attend, or think I should attend, or feel guilty about not attending. The synagogue is, for many, the place that will almost always take us in. The synagogue is where we create and sustain community and support systems. Synagogue professionals, particularly clergy, are often invited into the most intimate places of our lives when we confront illness, misfortune, and death. So when the synagogue becomes an increasingly female-centered place, panic enters the hearts of some who tragically internalized the deep gynophobia of our culture.

In her disturbing book *Backlash: The Undeclared War against American Women*,[2] Susan Faludi exposed how sexism, both external and internal, was blocking women's full equality at the end of the century that had promised new understandings of gender and unlimited opportunities for all. Nearly twenty years after the book's publication, we are seeing several manifestations of backlash against women's increasing visibility in the Jewish world—particularly against women's leadership in synagogues. There is concern about "male flight" from synagogues and from positions of leadership as women ascend to leadership roles. Attempts to recast and redefine all-male service arms of the synagogue have missed opportunities to rethink gender roles altogether, building on feminist insights and research, and have rather reverted to outdated stereotypes of men's roles in society, culture, and Jewish life. Newly designed publications pitched to a male audience miss the ironies of reclaiming a male Judaism. When asked to contribute to a new volume that would provide a "corrective" to women's Torah analyses, one senior male colleague wrote in a personal correspondence to me, "I have been thinking over your kind invitation to participate in the projected 'Men's Torah' and have come to the conclusion that I disagree with the idea. The new women's Torah is a very valuable addition to any good library of Judaica.... I am really impressed with it. Their work is a very necessary corrective or complement to the traditional misogynistic Torah. I cannot see where a men's slant would add anything. It is not only that the original authors were all men; they very clearly wrote from a male perspective, and their writings produced centuries of men's commentaries. In short, I don't see the need for such a book, and I certainly don't feel that there is a market for it."

In spite of our best efforts, there are those who refuse to pursue peace and choose, rather, to continue to wage a war between the sexes. What are the sources of their fears? For many in the traditional Jewish world, the synagogue was and may continue to be the primary place that men "count" just for being men. Without ten men, a traditional prayer service could not be held. Thus, men were needed simply for their male presence. As women began to be counted in egalitarian synagogues, men lost an important—and for some, essential—reason for their involvement in Jewish communal life. Many have neither acknowledged nor recovered from this loss. Additionally, for many men, the synagogue was a safe, woman-free space where men were unquestionably in control. The presence of women in all of the pews, as well as on the bimah, challenged and changed this formerly male enclave.

Women are also challenging many long-held assumptions about how organizations should be structured and governed. Women's presence on boards and in positions of leadership does, over time, bring change to institutions by bringing closer to the center many who had been on the margins, by making visible the formerly invisible. Women who value relationships redefine professional hierarchies and create new working networks. Women's own experiences as professionals and as members of families and communities have helped reimagine Jewish communal space. Jewish education through a feminist lens challenges every student and every teacher to rethink formerly accepted ideas about the relationship of the individual to the collective, about who does the counting and who is counted, and about how to recognize—and read—text.

Welcoming women is only the first step. There is also a backlash as other formerly marginalized folk begin coming through synagogue doors: the intermarried, individuals with learning differences, the physically challenged, sexual minorities, Jews who come from non-Ashkenazi backgrounds, Jews raised in non-Western cultures, and Israelis. Where some see diversity as an empowering challenge and opportunity, others recoil from our changing community in fear.

Kadima: We Shall Go Forth

Feminism has changed the way we think about the synagogue. For some, the difference begins when we walk in the door and see bins to collect clothes and food to share our bounty with others, or confront ramps and automatic doors that provide greater physical access to our house of worship. For others, the sanctuary itself is transformed because leadership has been diversified. Those leading prayers better reflect those who are sitting in the pews—rabbis and cantors and lay leaders are a mix of genders and ages and backgrounds. The books we use welcome us, with language and print size and transliteration that lowers or eliminates the barriers that kept too many of us from fully participating in communal prayer. And the learning in our schools, for children and for adults, reaches for the highest intellectual challenge while simultaneously acknowledging that learners come from diverse and rich backgrounds, and when difference is shared, all are strengthened. At the conclusion of *Beyond the Synagogue Gallery,* Karla Goldman writes:

> It is clear that the challenges and energy of those who push for change will shape the future course of the American synagogue and the Jewish community. Feminist critiques of worship and theology are generating some of the most creative and serious expressions of liturgical and communal struggle in contemporary Judaism.[3]

As we go forth into this new century, the Jewish community will continue to benefit and grow, thanks to the critiques, insights, and challenges of those who bring together a feminist vision with an absolute commitment to an authentic, living, inclusive, and vibrant Judaism.

Rabbi Joseph B. Meszler is the spiritual leader of Temple Sinai of Sharon, Massachusetts. He is the author of *A Man's Responsibility: A Jewish Guide to Being a Son, a Partner in Marriage, a Father, and a Community Leader* (Jewish Lights) and *Witnesses to the One: The Spiritual History of the Sh'ma* (Jewish Lights). Interested in engaging his male peers in synagogue life, Rabbi Meszler has been a part of founding three different Jewish men's study groups in Reform Jewish settings. He is married to Rabbi Julie Zupan and is the father of two children.

Where Are the Jewish Men?

The Absence of Men from Liberal Synagogue Life

RABBI JOSEPH B. MESZLER

"Mars Has Shrunk"

FEMINISM HAS transformed not only the role of women in society but also the role of men. This is certainly true of Jewish feminism and its impact on the role of men in the synagogue. In the large number of synagogues affiliated with more liberal movements in North America (generally including Reform, Reconstructionist, most Conservative, and those nondenominational synagogues that explicitly promote egalitarianism), what men expect when they come into the sanctuary today is completely different from men's expectations a generation ago.

When men step into a liberal synagogue today, they expect to hear women's voices, not only side by side in family pews and in choirs but also from the bimah. They expect to see both men and women serving as rabbis and cantors. They are not surprised to see women wearing tallitot and kippot and chanting from the Torah.

165

Men assume that they will see such leadership not only in the sanctuary but in the board room as well. Men expect women not only to chair committees and teach Hebrew School but also to serve as congregational presidents and in other such positions. The fact that these are assumptions, now taken for granted as facts of life, is remarkable given that many of these men or their fathers grew up attending synagogues with exclusively male leaders and Brotherhood social events where, as one congregant reminisced to me, "We left the wives at home."

The key phrase in these observations is "when men step into the synagogue." Whereas the synagogue used to be a space of male dominance, liberal synagogues have experienced a growing phenomenon of men simply not showing up. A recent survey of Reform congregations conducted by Doug Barden, executive director of Men of Reform Judaism (formerly the North American Federation of Temple Brotherhoods) reveals some startling facts: There is mounting statistical evidence that any given national North American Federation of Temple Youth event will have a ratio of 65 percent girls to 35 percent boys. A review of enrollment figures for Hebrew Union College–Jewish Institute of Religion, the Reform rabbinical seminary, indicates the ratio of female-to-male first-year rabbinic students is now approaching 70 percent women to 30 percent men. The figure of 80 percent female and 20 percent male is often quoted when it comes to the expected attendee demographics at a local temple adult education program.[1]

The phenomenon of women dramatically outnumbering men in liberal synagogue life has caused Barden, Rabbi Jeffrey Salkin, Rabbi Sheldon Zimmerman, and other authorities to claim that liberal Judaism is experiencing "male flight."[2] Although the synagogue used to be dominated by men and reinforced patriarchal authority, in liberal circles it is now often characterized by men's absence.

The synagogue is not alone in this regard. Churches are experiencing a similar case of male flight. David Murrow, in his book *Why Men Hate Going to Church*, reports, "A typical American churchgoer is a woman.... There are more women (61%) than men (39%) in the pews.... Today 20 to 25 percent of America's married, churchgoing women regularly attend without their husbands."[3]

Other places of a secular nature that were once centers of men's gatherings have also become diminished if not obsolete, such as the fraternal lodge and the barbershop. In the words of writer James B. Twitchell: "Mars has shrunk."[4]

Bringing Home the Brisket

Why have men absented themselves from the liberal synagogue, and what are the consequences of their absence?

One possibility is that because society in general undervalues the work of women, some men no longer value something if women value it, even if this is sometimes a subconscious attitude. If these men now see the synagogue as a place for women, it automatically has less worth in their eyes. Our society is filled with examples of men avoiding tasks, from quilting to teaching kindergarten, that they feel are feminine. But there is a difference between men leaving an area that they traditionally dominated and men avoiding activities that they have not participated in for generations.

Some might argue that the reason men are fleeing is because the synagogue rite has become too "feminized." Others say changes in liturgy referring to God beyond gender and women's involvement in ritual make men too uncomfortable to participate. But this argument is not valid. Changing references to God from "the Lord" to "the Eternal" is already standard practice in many synagogues, along with other liturgical changes. And liberal synagogues have not become places of Goddess worship and unrecognizable feminine experience. These theories explaining men's absence assume an antagonistic feeling between men and women, setting up the synagogue as an arena for competition. While this antagonism does exist to some degree, there are also other possibilities.

Prejudice alone is not a full explanation. While traditional synagogues where men hold full power have not experienced a "male

167

flight," the men attending these synagogues likely hold traditional views toward women's roles. Many of the men who belong to liberal synagogues have more liberal attitudes toward gender roles. Most younger Jewish men have not only accepted egalitarianism as women's ideal but have embraced equality as their ideal as well. Used to seeing equality at home, they have already come to expect it at synagogue.

Despite increased numbers of women in the workforce, men still generally work longer hours than women and therefore have less time away from their careers. In the United States, for instance, the federal Department of Labor reports that out of the total population in 2005, about 60 percent of women were part of the labor force as opposed to approximately 75 percent of men.[5] Of these workers, women were far more likely to work part-time than men, with 86 percent of men working at least forty hours a week.[6] In addition, the number of hours in the workweek, the number of commuters on the road, and the length of an average commute have all gone up dramatically in recent decades.[7] Men are, therefore, working longer hours and spending more time in the car. In addition, there is evidence of a new psychological phenomenon unique to men. In families where both a man and a woman are employed, you might think that the addition of a wife's income would make men less stressed and give them more freedom, but that does not seem to be the case. One sociologist points out that men increasingly feel what has been dubbed "breadwinner anxiety," where they become more anxious over their dependency on a wife's salary than relieved by the support.[8]

Coupled with the still thriving self-definition of "man as breadwinner" is one of feminism's successes, that men now feel a larger stake in being equal partners in marriage and child rearing. In order to meet these demands, however, men want greater flexibility with the time that they work, not fewer hours.[9]

In other words, instead of "leaving the wives at home" to attend Brotherhood meetings at the synagogue, Jewish men are using their limited time away from work and the car to change diapers and cook dinner with their spouses (things their fathers most likely did not do). But they still feel tremendous pressure to "bring home the brisket." And so, when time and work constraints squeeze the modern family, the synagogue may become the easiest cut.

Anecdotal evidence suggests that the programs for which men do show up are those to which they can come with their entire family. In a liberal synagogue, it is not unusual to see husband and wife each wearing a tallit (prayer shawl) and saying the Torah blessings together. When the Hebrew school of my synagogue holds family education programs, men attend in large numbers. In other words, men do come to synagogue when it is designated family time.

This is not the whole picture. After all, even though men generally seem to have less free time and are more obsessed with their work than women, plenty of working women are still making time for the synagogue. Some additional reasons for men's absence come from embarrassment at their ignorance of Judaism, and a lack of feeling needed.

Society compels men to appear competent, even if they don't feel it. Many men feel a special amount of pride in appearing competent. This can manifest itself as reluctance to appearing as a novice. In fact, research has shown that high testosterone levels usually manifest themselves in attempts to demonstrate dominance, not in acts of aggression.[10]

Jewish men therefore resist registering for classes at the synagogue that are labeled "introductory" or "basic" and can feel humiliated at their inability to read Hebrew aloud during public worship. Sophisticated professionals outside of the synagogue, they can often feel infantilized within the synagogue's doors. As many have not stepped foot into a synagogue since they became a bar mitzvah, they are walking around with at most a thirteen-year-old's Jewish education. Ignorance laid open is painful.

If men came from a traditional background, they remember that only men were counted in a minyan in their synagogue. If a man did not show up for services, there might not be the minimum of ten needed to pray the whole service in its completion, including the prayer for the dead, the mourner's kaddish. If a man failed in his obligation to be present, another might not be able to say a prayer for mourning. Now that both women and men are counted in a minyan in an egalitarian synagogue (if the custom of requiring a minyan is maintained at all), there is much less feeling of obligation. In a more traditional synagogue, men have a tremendous sense of obligation and "commandedness," and conventional gender roles hold power. The liberal synagogue today instead subtly suggests that men's presence is optional.

A lack of men in the synagogue also reinforces itself. In any given synagogue bulletin, the programs advertised are inevitably followed with a woman's name as the contact person. Women active in the synagogue are embracing their Judaism and reaching out to their friends, who are also women. Who is reaching out to the men? On this and other levels, the synagogue today too often fails to meet men where they are.

The new generation of Jewish men does not involve themselves in liberal synagogue life for these reasons and more. Add to this mix a high assimilation rate and a decreased ethnic Jewish feeling, and it becomes understandable why Jewish men might question the synagogue's value in their lives. They can either feel relaxed and competent on the golf course, or embarrassed and unnecessary at shul. Simply put, many liberal Jewish men today would rather spend their prized Saturday morning hours recreating or coaching their daughter at soccer than sitting off to the side of a sanctuary, trying to follow along with a prayer service.

How Am I Supposed to Be a Mensch?

With every challenge comes an opportunity, and the synagogue is poised to transform itself to meet the changed needs of a new generation of Jewish men. Most important, the reengagement of men requires the help of Jewish women—women who now feel spiritually engaged, who would stand with men as equal partners and help them grow spiritually. Men have spiritual needs, though often they do not acknowledge this, and both boys and girls need to see men as Jewish role models in the home, the synagogue, and the community. If Jewish men continue to absent themselves from synagogue life, everyone will suffer.

The opportunity comes from the fact that the new generation of Jewish men, whose assumptions have been transformed by feminism, are intensely interested in learning about their responsibilities in the context of their relationships. Jewish men are asking themselves: How do I care for my aging parents? How do I relate to my partner? How do I raise my son or daughter? How do I balance work and home? The synagogue is the ideal place, perhaps the only place, for these discussions to take place among men, and for Judaism to offer some answers.

I have been privileged to be a part of a new effort to found Jewish men's study groups in synagogue life as a way to reengage men in Jewish spirituality. Meeting early in the morning for breakfast before work, we have gathered to see what Judaism has to say about our family roles as well as balancing work and personal needs. The learning that I have done and witnessed has been nothing less than transformative. As much as this new generation of men has shied away from all-male groups (outside of competitive sports), there are things men are only willing to talk about with other men. Just as much as women need one another to reach their fulfilment as women, men need one another as well.

Consider a discussion I once had in a male-only gathering that revolved around a text from the Torah. This passage is featured in the Torah reading on Rosh Hashanah. In the story, Abraham is asked by God to sacrifice his son Isaac. Isaac obediently accompanies his father, unaware of what is in store for him. The two of them travel toward their unknown destination when this short dialogue takes place:

171

> Abraham took the wood for the offering and put it on Isaac his son. He took in his own hand the fire and the knife. And both of them walked together. Isaac said to Abraham his father, "Father!" He responded, "I am here, my son." He said, "Here is the fire and the wood, but where is the lamb for the offering?!?" Abraham answered, "God will personally see to the lamb for the offering, my son." And both of them walked together. (Gen. 22:6–8, translation mine)

The irony of the passage is that the Torah repeats that Abraham and Isaac are walking together, and yet the two of them are not together at all. As much as they emotionally call to each other as father and son, in their minds they could never be farther apart. Abraham seems stunned and overwhelmed. We do not know whether his response that God will see to the lamb is an act of faithful piety or simply an artful dodge. One commentator claims that the story may "be read as a paradigm of a father-and-son relationship."[11]

In the gathering studying this passage, I asked men who they identified most closely with in this story. One man told me he felt like Isaac. "I never knew what my father thought or felt. He always looked upset, like he was carrying a terrible burden. He was always silent."

Another told me he identified more with Abraham. "The best conversations I have with my son are in the car," he confessed. "I don't know why that is. Perhaps it is because we do not have to make eye contact with each other. We can both look out the windshield. We travel like Abraham and Isaac walking together, not looking each other in the face."

Still another said, "My father was my best friend. He would have told God to go to hell."

And so on. The men in the room showed an intense interest in their responsibilities as men, and they were craving learning from each other. Some may have unconsciously felt a certain kind of satisfaction that the learning they were supposed to get from their father, who culturally was not permitted to show emotion, they now received in the context of studying Judaism. Sometimes I wonder if Moses, through the Torah, has become a surrogate father for these men.

It is Jewish men's thirst to be responsible and connected that is a gateway for them into the Jewish world. Men feel the isolation of the office cubicle, and they know that the Internet connects them only superficially. Being truly connected means being present in the lives of others, and men are looking to alleviate their loneliness. The synagogue is precisely the place to meet this spiritual need through creating opportunities for discussion.

Before they started attending, several men in my study group had planned to quit the synagogue after their youngest child's bar/bat mitzvah. They now have no plans to do so. They realize that there is something at the synagogue for them.

This opportunity to reinvent Jewish men's involvement in synagogue life can only take place if men not only share sacred space with women, but also have a claim to it on their own. Just as multigenerational and mixed-gender programming is vital to the health of families, so is the creation of female-only and male-only space. But this new brand of male-only space will not be the kind that was created a generation ago, which excluded women from power and authority; instead it must be a forum for engaging Jewish men for who they are today.

If the synagogue does so, and if men see Jewish spirituality as relevant and enriching to their lives, they will return. In the words of the Reverend Owen Towle, as he grappled with a similar challenge in his Unitarian Universalist Church, "Men ... talk more freely on spiritual and emotional issues when they are just with men."[12]

Time Together and Apart

The rejection of patriarchy in liberal synagogue life has freed men almost as much as it has freed women. In the words of the great activist for freedom Nelson Mandela, "The oppressor must be liberated just as surely as the oppressed."[13]

Feminism has expanded the possibilities of what it means to be a man, and Jewish men have seized upon these opportunities. As partners in marriage, Jewish men no longer need to define themselves solely as providers and breadwinners. Instead, they identify themselves as equal covenantal partners, with each person in the relationship understood to be made in the image of God. As fathers, men are no longer restricted to the role of the disciplinarian and judge who hands down verdicts from the head of the table. Instead, men are now empowered to be demonstrative with their love. And in the realm of the synagogue, men can find themselves lighting Shabbat candles and seeking out new understandings of God beyond the image of King.

The synagogue will only create such opportunities for men if Jewish families stand up and demand it. What does this mean? Just as women celebrate together at a women's Seder during Passover, or monthly at Rosh Chodesh (New Moon) groups, so men need to be able to come together to learn about themselves.

Synagogue leadership needs to create opportunities for men to come together to have these kinds of discussions. It needs to create programs where Jewish men of a new generation can talk about what it means to be a son, a partner in marriage, and a father. This is what the new Jewish man wants to talk about today, and it is a gateway back into organized Jewish life.

It is important that both women and men have time together and time apart. Both genders need to share sacred space, and find their own paths. If Jewish men make the time to do so, they will be able to bring us closer to defining a new "Jewish men's spirituality." They will be able to discover the intangible connections that give life meaning through the lens of Jewish tradition that addresses them in their roles as men. They will hopefully discover that, as much as the world has changed, Jewish men are still obligated to keep the covenant of their ancestors and pass it down to the next generation, renewed this time with their own unique imprint.

Anne Lapidus Lerner, PhD, is the author of *Eternally Eve: Images of Eve in the Hebrew Bible, Midrash and Modern Jewish Poetry,* founding director of the Jewish Women's Studies Program at The Jewish Theological Seminary of America, a member of JTS's Department of Jewish Literature, and a popular scholar-in-residence. The first woman to serve as vice-chancellor at JTS, Lerner is the wife of Rabbi Stephen C. Lerner, founding director of the Center for Conversion to Judaism in Manhattan and rabbi of Congregation Kanfei Shahar in Teaneck, New Jersey. She is also the mother of Rabbi David Lerner, rabbi of Temple Emunah, Lexington, Massachusetts, and Rahel Adina Lerner, an editor.

Pacing Change

The Impact of Feminism on Conservative Synagogues

ANNE LAPIDUS LERNER, PhD

ON A WEEKDAY MORNING men and women draped in tallitot and wearing tefillin are seated throughout the prayer space of Women's League Seminary Synagogue at The Jewish Theological Seminary of America (JTS), the educational institution that trains the bulk of rabbis and cantors for the Conservative movement and has done so for more than one hundred and twenty years. Although all men have their heads covered, generally with kippot, women present a wider range of practice. Some are wearing kippot on their heads; others, scarves; still others, no head covering at all. It is often shocking to visitors to discover that many JTS women, including rabbinical and cantorial students, *daven* bare-headed while in tallit and tefillin. Some newcomers are surprised to see women fulfilling mitzvot traditionally reserved for men; others are shocked that they do not all have their heads covered. Twenty-five years after the decision to admit women to the JTS Rabbinical School there is still no uniform practice even at JTS, while in the majority of Conservative synagogues one finds fewer women who have accepted the responsibility to *daven* either in tallitot or in tefillin.

When I joined the JTS faculty in 1969 its religious services were also an anomaly within the movement. Despite having grown up in an observant Conservative family and synagogue, I was surprised at what I found: the seating in the Shabbat morning prayer space—then Unterberg Auditorium—was gender-separate. While no *mechitzah* served as a visual barrier, the men, in ranked order with the senior faculty first, sat on the left of the center aisle; the women—those who were married wearing hats—on the right. That service still exists at JTS as an option on weekdays, not on Shabbat, although the rank-order seating and the women's hats are now relegated to history. It is not the best attended, and certainly not the exclusive option anymore.

The women's movement has had a strong impact on the roles of women in the Conservative synagogue, but its strongest impact has not been in the pews. It has been, rather, on the clergy. Thus, although JTS prepares clergy and educators for the Conservative movement, its own synagogue has eschewed the practice of most Conservative synagogues for much of its existence. For much of the twentieth century the Seminary's policy for women was to the right of the movement; now it is not clearly defined as left or right. Is it clearly left-wing to have more Jews, albeit women, take on the sometimes onerous responsibility of praying in tallit and tefillin or is it perhaps not more appropriate to call it right of center? In any case, it is different from what one finds at most synagogues around the country. In most places, it is at most a handful of women who *daven* daily in tallit and tefillin. An examination of the roles of women in the contemporary Conservative synagogue necessarily raises a number of fundamental questions. Does egalitarianism mandate that women and men follow the same patterns of observance in the synagogue or does egalitarianism mean those patterns should be different? Does feminism allow for the development of new rituals and liturgies that supplement or replace those of men? What is the nature of religious obligation? Can a movement's tent be so wide as to include comfortably both egalitarian and non-egalitarian members?

A Look at History

It is a truism that Conservative Judaism walks a narrow space between Jewish tradition and modernity, pulled to the side by each of them. Whenever it encounters a challenge to the tradition posed by modernity it must readjust its balance and find a new equilibrium. Because the movement is far from monolithic, its central agencies can set only what they see as acceptable parameters, often leaving rabbis and congregants to negotiate a policy for their own synagogues, as outlined by Gail Labovitz in "Feminism and Jewish Law in Conservative Judaism" (see pp. 323–333).

Women's participation in synagogue life is a good example of the slow—for some too slow, for others, not slow enough—process by which change takes place. The position of women in the synagogue and the roles they take is strongly influenced by the mores of the surrounding culture, as well as by Jewish tradition.

From its prehistory in the nineteenth century, the Conservative movement has struggled with the role of women. "Family pew" or mixed seating, which allowed women and men to sit within the sanctuary without regard to gender, was the norm in synagogues that preceded the establishment of a formal Conservative movement in the United States. As the movement developed in the first half of the twentieth century, women took on roles in synagogues that were consonant with the roles of women in Jewish tradition and in the surrounding culture. The establishment of the National Women's League of the United Synagogue (now the Women's League for Conservative Judaism) in 1918 extended to the synagogue a model in which women most often tended to the domestic sphere. They were concerned with the education of children and provided informal education for mothers who were responsible for conveying a sense of Jewish tradition to their families. They conducted fundraisers, prepared and served food for congregational functions, and they decorated the congregational *sukkah*. In some Conservative synagogues only men were members. If women held office in the congregation, it was usually no higher than secretary. They were not attired in ritual garb. While they might sing in the choir, their voices were not raised to chant significant portions of the liturgy. They led neither in the sanctuary nor in the boardroom, but only in the all-female sphere of the congregational sisterhood.

But by mid-century change was afoot. In 1955, the Rabbinical Assembly's Committee on Jewish Law and Standards (CJLS) dealt with the issue of women's eligibility for an *aliyah* to the Torah. Both of the accepted decisions allowed *aliyot* for women. The majority position limited them to special occasions, while the minority position allowed them across the board. But the permission granted by the CJLS did not become common practice for more than two decades. What did change in the wake of that decision was the spread of the Friday night *bat mitzvah* celebration for girls, generally involving a young woman's chanting a *haftarah* at a late Friday night service, a time when it is not integral to the service, as it is on Shabbat morning. Why were *aliyot* for women not adopted in most congregations shortly after the decision? The reasons are complex, but it was not a hesitation that was rooted in the deep-seated adherence of the Conservative laity to halakhic practice. After all, the decision taken in 1950 by the Law Committee to allow driving to the nearest synagogue on Shabbat—a deeply controversial decision—had followed, not preceded, the widespread lay acceptance of driving on Shabbat. Besides, the halakhic authorities had, with only one vote in opposition, ruled that *aliyot* for women were permitted and had not accepted the one position submitted that denied women *aliyot*. Was a change in gender roles less acceptable than a change in Shabbat observance? Was it a psychological hesitancy rather than a religious one? Or was it that empowering women in the public space of the synagogue ran counter to the post-war idealization of the woman's place in the domestic sphere?

Second-Wave Feminism

By the early 1970s the pace of change had picked up. The confrontation between second-wave feminism and Judaism reverberated in the synagogue. When Ezrat Nashim, a group of Jewish feminists (many of whom had ties to the Conservative movement) accosted the Rabbinical Assembly in March 1971 demanding equal rights and responsibilities for women within Conservative Judaism, they set off a debate that still continues. Pressure began to mount both for the ordination of women as rabbis and for the expansion of synagogue participation to include women. The October 1973 decision by the CJLS allowing women to be counted for a *minyan* precipitated widespread implementation of the previous decision to grant women *aliyot*, as well as the introduction of counting women in the *minyan*. It took another decade for a positive decision on the ordination of women to be reached by the faculty of JTS, then the only school in North America ordaining Conservative rabbis, and four more years for the positive decision on women cantors.

Today about 90 percent of North American Conservative congregations are nominally egalitarian, although there are wide differences in practice and expectations, as we shall see. Further, it is a common perception that egalitarianism is a principle in the Conservative movement, but that is not the case. If it were, there would be no room for non-egalitarian congregations, just as there is no place for congregations that maintain a non-kosher kitchen.

Post-feminism?

For many women today, feminism seems passé. It would appear that the battles have been won and that women and men now can make the same choices in their personal, professional, and social lives. This assumption, not entirely valid in the general culture, is even less accurate in describing the roles of women in Conservative synagogues. Nonetheless, I often hear women rabbinical students echo the general sentiment: "I'm not a feminist, but...."

Women have come a long way toward parity in the political structure of many Conservative synagogues. No longer confined to exercising their administrative and programmatic acumen in the sisterhood, they often serve as synagogue presidents. There does, however, seem to be a glass ceiling on the national scene where only one woman has served as president of the congregational arm of the movement, the United Synagogue for Conservative Judaism (USCJ), in its ninety-five-year history and only three young women have served as presidents of United Synagogue Youth.

The Women's League for Conservative Judaism (WLCJ), the sisterhood arm of the movement, is, like so many other women's organizations, suffering from diminishing and aging membership. Despite first-class educational, social, and religious programming, it struggles to attract the next generation in large numbers. At the same time, its *Kolot biK'dushah* ("Voices in Holiness") program has helped empower more than six hundred laywomen to chant Torah and/or to lead prayer services, helping to move the sisterhood image from baking brownies to ascending the *bimah*. Women who develop these skills are, of course, likely to want to use them and to make their voices heard during the prayer services in their synagogues. The importance of women clergy as accessible role models for women and girls in congregations cannot be overestimated, although in 2008 there are only 242 women members of the Rabbinical Assembly, out of a total international membership of 1,613. Women rabbis and cantors demonstrate that women can carry out the responsibilities of observant Jews with professional skill and intelligence. Conservative synagogues are no longer the spheres of men who allow women to enter, but restrict their participation; they are, with few exceptions, a shared space where women and men have responsibilities and rights.

Future Challenges

However, despite its egalitarian rhetoric, the Conservative movement has yet to work out the implications of that stance for its female laypersons and clergy. For example, the two North American institutions that now ordain women as rabbis, JTS and the Ziegler School of the American Jewish University (AJU) in Los Angeles, have different standards for their women students. JTS requires that women accept the obligation to pray daily in tallit and tefillin; Ziegler does not. In her moving personal essay, "Women in the Conservative Synagogue" (see pp. 186–194), Irit Printz refers to her recollection of a question I asked her at her admissions interview. While I do not doubt that I asked the question, I suspect that it might have been triggered more by what I remember from the other side of the table at that interview—that Irit had never put on tefillin—than by feminist concerns. Neither Ziegler nor JTS requires head covering of its women. As one looks at practices in synagogues around the country, one finds little uniformity in this area. Every Jewish male entering a Conservative synagogue is expected to cover his head and don a tallit; there is no similar standard for women. One may find in a given synagogue that women are expected to cover their heads upon entrance and to wear a tallit if receiving an honor. At a neighboring synagogue one might find that women, regardless of what is on their heads or on their shoulders, can have an *aliyah*, read from the Torah, or even lead a section of the prayers. Are tefillin generically Jewish and therefore appropriate for men and women or are they gendered and male? Does feminism require that women assume the obligations that had previously been exclusively the domain of men or that women devise different ways to accomplish the same goal?

Although it is often the head-covering requirement that is most hotly contested, a tallit is also not always a welcome ritual garment. Whether or not girls receive a tallit upon becoming bat mitzvah, they are less likely than their male counterparts to use it. In those synagogues where a boy is expected to acquire tefillin as he becomes bar mitzvah, a girl is rarely expected to do the same as she becomes bat mitzvah. There is pressure toward conformity that slows down taking on new customs. In my synagogue, where most of the women wear a tallit on Shabbat morning, a woman entering for the first time sometimes hesitates and then, looking at the congregation, takes a tallit from the rack. A Jewish male always does so, in consonance with the behavior of every Jewish adult male. Although the leadership that women rabbis and cantors (and often clergy wives as well) assume on this issue generally has some impact, it does not always influence the behavior of the laity. The Conservative movement is famously the segment of the American Jewish community with the largest disparity between the observance patterns of clergy and laity. Like not riding in cars on Shabbat, the religious practice of women rabbis and cantors and of clergy families may be assigned to the category of those things that clergy do but laypersons do not.

Another area where the impact of the women's movement on the Conservative synagogue remains to be fully negotiated is the area of liturgy. In addressing the nature of the traditional Jewish liturgy, it is important to bear in mind that Hebrew is a highly gendered language. Because Hebrew has no neuter, every noun, adjective, and verb is necessarily feminine or masculine. Since the publication of its first prayer book in 1946, the Conservative movement has consistently attempted to reduce the gendered nature of the language that refers to humans, culminating in the most recent (1998, 2002) prayer books' inclusion of two options for the opening blessing of the statutory *Amidah* prayer, one of which includes the matriarchs by name along with the patriarchs. These changes serve to remind us that women are an integral part of the Jewish community at prayer.

On the other hand, the God language of the liturgy remains in its Hebrew original overwhelmingly masculine. The most recent edition of the Conservative movement's prayer book has revised the 1986 English translations with a view to making them gender sensitive, though not gender neutral. For example, "God's" often replaces "His" when translating the Hebrew. The gendered nature of our metaphoric portrayals of God is to some degree addressed by substituting "Ruler" for "King" in the English, a move that cannot be made in the Hebrew, but it will take time to transform the underlying metaphors. The balance point between liturgical traditions and gender inclusivity remains elusive.

Two issues that have an impact specifically on women rabbis have broader implications for Jewish women as a whole. The first is the question of women serving as witnesses on documents of a religious nature: conversion, marriage, divorce. The initial position of Rabbi Joel Roth, whose rabbinic responsum allowing the ordination of women laid the groundwork for admitting women to the Conservative rabbinate, barred women from serving as witnesses in those areas from which women's testimony had been traditionally excluded. Indeed, many of the women admitted to the JTS Rabbinical School in the mid-1980s agreed that they would refrain from serving as witnesses in these areas that are the professional domain of the active rabbinate. With the passage of responsa allowing women to serve as witnesses, women rabbis and other women are today serving as witnesses to these documents. Some Conservative rabbis consider documents attested by women valid, yet others do not. That members of the same Rabbinical Assembly do not recognize each other's documents both perpetuates a situation in which women rabbis may be perceived as less than full rabbis, and diminishes all women.

Finally, the issue of equality on the job is a significant one for women in the rabbinate and for those who consider joining them. The 2004 "Gender Variation in the Careers of Conservative Rabbis: A Survey of Rabbis Ordained since 1985," commissioned by the Rabbinical Assembly, documented the disparity in income, working conditions, career path, and congregational size between women and men in the same ordination-year cohorts. As a group, the women in the Rabbinical Assembly had lower incomes than men in

183

similar positions and led smaller congregations. While some of the gap may be attributed to choices that men and women make, those choices themselves are often influenced by prospects. The fact that a higher percentage of women than of men have chosen to devote their rabbinate to non-congregational paths such as education and hospital chaplaincy means that fewer of them are in the synagogue as rabbis; it also may reflect the feeling among women rabbis that the congregational rabbinate is less welcoming to them.

Becoming a movement in which egalitarianism is a core principle requires more than pronouncements. It takes the focused attention of leaders, both lay and professional. Change requires both a clear vision of what we are trying to achieve and a focus on getting there. Modeling and persuasion can occur on the national level and on the local level, but what it really entails is changing the perceptions of individuals. In those congregations where a safe space has been provided for women to test these "new" mitzvot, where the clergy has been encouraging, where the school has been involved as an agent for change, the balance is slowly shifting and sometimes women in tallit and tefillin become the majority. Where, for example, a synagogue school develops a policy that encourages or mandates head covering for all its students, boys and girls alike, and educates staff, students, and parents, change is supported. Eternal vigilance is the price of egalitarianism.

Cultivating Future Feminists

Like many others who were deeply involved in the struggle for equal rights for women in Conservative Judaism, I am both encouraged by the changes that have occurred and impatient with the tasks still undone. When the JTS faculty approved women's admission to the JTS Rabbinical School in 1983, my daughter Rahel Adina Lerner, had just entered first grade. I naively expected that by the time she became a bat mitzvah she, along with all the other girls in her class, would accept the obligation to pray each morning in tallit and tefillin. While I was correct in assessing my daughter's wisdom and determination, as you can see in her contribution, "Portrait of the Writer as a Young Feminist" (see pp. 273–276), in this volume, I was wrong about a mass movement. Here and there a girl or teacher would *daven* in tallit and tefillin, but there was no groundswell.

As I write this essay in 2008 my eldest grandchild, my son's daughter, Talya Liat Lerner, is entering second grade. As my daughter before her had been, she is a regular worshiper at a synagogue where her father is rabbi and her parents are strong feminists. As I think about these three generations, and that of my mother, Lillian Green Lapidus, of blessed memory, I marvel at the difference in the worlds we have grown up in—and the similarities. All of us, including my mother, have had the blessing of a strong Jewish education and a home where Jewish observance was seamlessly integrated into daily life. My mother, who was a lifelong member of Conservative synagogues, had her first *aliyah* to the Torah at our synagogue when she was in her sixties because women were not yet accorded that right at hers. I was in my thirties when I had my first *aliyah* and my daughter has no memory of a time when women did not have a place in the public ritual of her synagogue. Will my granddaughter, like her aunt and grandmother, be one of a handful of women who choose to be obligated to the mitzvot of tallit and tefillin? Will she become part of a cohort in which these and other mitzvot formerly reserved for men are no longer deemed male but generically Jewish?

In the grand long view of Jewish history, change has taken place at breakneck speed; measured by the pace of change in today's fast-evolving world, it is rather slow.

Rabbi Irit Printz was born in Bucharest, Romania. Her family made *aliyah* in 1973. Rabbi Printz worked for many years as a high school math and science teacher, and later earned a masters of science curriculum development degree from the Hebrew University in Jerusalem. She entered the Rabbinical School at The Jewish Theological Seminary of America in 2000 as the recipient of the prestigious Crown Fellowship. She was ordained in May 2005 with a master's degree in Bible. Rabbi Printz served as the assistant rabbi at Ahavath Achim Synagogue in Atlanta, Georga, and is currently teaching at the Essex and Union Solomon Schechter Day School in West Orange, New Jersey

Women in the Conservative Synagogue

Some Personal Thoughts and Observations

RABBI IRIT PRINTZ

Gender Issues? What Gender Issues?

Dr. Anne Lapidus Lerner, the former vice-chancellor of The Jewish Theological Seminary of America, director and founder of the Jewish Women's Studies Program, and director of the Jewish Feminist Research Group, was on my rabbinical school admissions interview committee. At the time, I had no idea who she was. The interview itself is no more than a blur now, but I clearly remember one question Dr. Lerner asked. Why was it, she wanted to know, that I did not feel it was necessary to address any sort of women's issues in my application essays?

I remember being completely astonished. I do not remember what I said, but I do remember being vaguely insulted by the question.

Were the male candidates asked why they did not address men's issues in their application essays? It simply never crossed my mind that there were issues I should have raised. Asked about the great challenges facing the Jewish community in the decades to come, I wrote about identity, identification, and the growing sense among my peers that Judaism mattered very little in the larger scheme of things. I believed, with the certainty of the naïve and inexperienced, that there were no such things as "women issues" as opposed to "men issues." There were just "Jewish issues." To some extent, I still believe that today.

I am not an obvious choice for inclusion in this book. I spent my formative years in Israel, where—like everyone I knew—I had almost no connection to Judaism. My only exposure to synagogue culture was the yearly midnight school trip to a *slichot* service. No one in my circle of friends and family had any religious friends. We studied Jewish texts and traditions in school, of course, but they were largely divorced from their inherent Jewishness. I must have been aware of a gender divide within Orthodox Judaism (the only Judaism visible to me at the time), but I didn't care at all. What difference could it have possibly made if I wasn't allowed to do a bunch of things I had no interest in doing in the first place?

By the time I became seriously interested and involved in Judaism I was living on the Canadian West Coast. I was a member of Beth Tikvah, a synagogue just outside of Vancouver, and studying with Rabbi Martin Cohen, who eventually became my mentor and friend, and whom I still hold responsible for my decision to become a rabbi. It was there that I learned to chant Torah, lead services, and become invested in Jewish tradition. I was one of many women who engaged in these activities on a fairly regular basis. When Rabbi Cohen and I talked about rabbinical school, my gender never came up. When it came to being a rabbi, I did not see gender. It was irrelevant. And it was infinitely less interesting to me than other issues, such as how to foster a sense of excitement and wonder about Judaism and all it has to offer in disconnected, disinterested young adults—both women and men.

I was a few years into rabbinical school before I realized that my belief in the irrelevance of gender and my passionate focus on outreach work were both borne of luxury. I have the luxury to address issues I am deeply passionate about and that happen to transcend gender precisely *because* of the intense focus on gender issues that gave birth to egalitarianism, the ordination of women, and a myriad of new rituals that speak to women and their unique moments. Dr. Lerner, like many of the writers in this book, spent most of her life addressing feminist issues in Judaism. That I could apply to rabbinical school without giving a second thought to my gender or the issues I might face because of it—a little more than a decade after the very first woman was admitted into the Seminary I could now attend—is astounding. My reaction to Dr. Lerner's interview question is, in some ways, symbolic of the great success of Jewish feminism.

Evidence of the Work to Do

I have spent the three years since my ordination in Atlanta, Georgia, serving as the assistant rabbi at a large, established, very old synagogue. My personal experiences as a female member of the clergy, as well as observing my congregation's life, opened my eyes to the long road Jewish feminism still has to travel before it can declare itself "done." My congregants—male and female —often interacted with me in vastly different ways than they did with the male senior rabbi. They physically touched me more often. I faced many more inappropriate comments. ("Is it ok to kiss the rabbi?" "How can a rabbi be so sexy?") Beyond the issues I faced personally, it seemed to me that the genuine concerns of my female congregants were often dismissed as frivolous or petty. A congregant who had been denied a *get* by her ex-husband for many years was told that the reason he continued to receive synagogue honors was because "we (in the synagogue) don't take sides" in family disputes. A woman whose husband had been convicted of assaulting her felt like she was the one being shamed by the congregation for "making a fuss." Those of my female conversion students who happened to be single found their motives constantly questioned since they had no Jewish boyfriends to "convert for."

Last Rosh HaShannah I spoke from the bimah on the topic of domestic violence and sexual abuse in the Jewish community, a sermon inspired by the surreal media frenzy surrounding Michael Vick's dog abuse case at the same time that a profound media silence was the only reaction to several domestic violence incidents perpetrated by other football players. This particular sermon drew extreme reactions, both positive and negative, from both men and women. Many congregants thought it was an inappropriate topic for a High Holy Day sermon since it was essentially a "women's issue" sermon. I found myself reassuring congregants that relationship violence is a community issue, as if it would have been a less legitimate choice to address a topic that primarily affects women.

At the same time, the synagogue has one of the largest sisterhoods in the United States. These women are engaged and active. They are significant contributors to the Conservative movement's Women's League—both monetarily and in terms of personal dedication. They attend and organize conferences. They offer adult education classes through the Sisterhood, and attend classes all over town, including the two-year Melton program. No one could ever accuse these women of being uninvolved or uninterested in Judaism and what it has to offer.

The synagogue I worked for is almost fully egalitarian. Women play significant roles in leadership, and have done so for many years. They have the opportunity to lead services, read from the Torah, offer comments and *divrei Torah*, and do anything men can do—including wear pants on the bimah (this last barrier was crossed in 2006). The only thing women cannot do is recite the priestly blessing. Women at the synagogue were offered the opportunity to have a bat mitzvah ceremony as far back as the early 1950s—a Friday night ceremony where they chanted the haftarah and offered a small *dvar*

Torah. These days there is no distinction between bar and bat mitzvah ceremonies, except that girls may choose to decline wearing a tallit and tefillin but boys may not.

However, the demographics of the shul skew toward the older members, and many of these women are extremely uncomfortable with egalitarian practice in reality, even though they fully support it in theory. Most will not accept *aliyot* (going up to bless the Torah) without their husbands by their sides. Almost none will take on chanting the Torah, even though they are encouraged to do so and individual training is offered. Many own tallitot, but few wear them. Only one woman I know wears tefillin. Most families give beautiful tallitot to their daughters and grand-daughters. We created a beautiful ritual for this, the parents wrapping their child in a brand new tallit as part of the bar or bat mitzvah ceremony. But while the boys always wear their tallitot when they attend shul after their bar mitzvah, the girls almost never do. I understand that this is a common phenomenon in Conservative synagogues. One of my colleagues, Rabbi Rachel Brown, shares a telling story. A couple of years ago she purchased a beautiful and feminine tallit to wear only on Shabbat. A year or so later, the tallit began to shred and unravel. When Rabbi Brown took it back to the store she was told, "Of course it ripped, it wasn't designed to be worn every week!" As another of my colleagues, Rabbi Diane Cohen, points out, the girls and their families seem to consider the tallit a garment of passage, not a garment of commitment—a sentiment retailers are clearly aware of.

Post bar and bat mitzvah children who attend one of the three non-Orthodox Jewish day schools in Atlanta are expected to wear tallitot during morning prayers. The boys are also expected to wear tefillin. But when I tried to push the tefillin issue with the girls, I met tremendous resistance. They felt too exposed; each felt too much the odd woman out. A year ago I worked with a group of particularly bright and engaged students. Among them were four girls who were to celebrate their bat mitzvah ceremonies within weeks of each other. They all thought the tefillin ritual was "really cool." I suggested they start a trend at their particular school. They were tempted but eventually declined, convinced that they would be ridiculed. Only one of their teachers wears tefillin, they said, and everyone knows she is a "feminist." (This was stated in a hushed tone, like the teacher was suffering from some fatal disease.)

The synagogue's ritual committee is open to any member, but currently only one woman serves on it. She brought up, and pushed, the issue of the inclusion of the matriarchs, the *imahot*, in the Amidah, which already mentions the patriarchs. It is now standard synagogue policy to include the *imahot* in the public prayer. Some simply refuse—some men *and* women choose to remain silent during the portions in the Amidah that mention the *imahot*. But most people don't seem to care one way or another. The reason for this apathy is not entirely clear. Partly, I think, it comes about because of a general disinterest in prayer. Partly, it might be due to the fact that most congregants do not understand Hebrew, so that the blatant maleness of the language is not immediately evident to them. But mostly, I think, they feel the issue is one of political correctness and not one that affects reality one way or another.

The Jews (Women) in the Pews

But how has Jewish feminism affected the average Conservative Jewish woman? When I asked a group of female congregants to share their thoughts on Jewish feminism, most of them readily acknowledged its influence on their involvement and connection to synagogue life. This is a group of women who mostly grew up when it was scandalous to imagine a woman could ever set foot on the bimah. For them, Jewish feminism changed the very contours of the religion they grew up in. They largely feel that feminism has opened the door to a deeper engagement, to a more meaningful way to be Jewish. Yet, when I asked them about the biggest challenges facing the Jewish community today, not one of them raised an issue that could be classified as a feminist concern. Few of them believe that

Jewish feminism has run its course or that there is nothing left to address. In fact, when specifically asked about appropriate feminist focus in the future, they raised a variety of issues—from meaningful rituals to fairer *get* practices. It is telling, however, that none raised issues relating to synagogue life, or that none of them thought these feminist issues could be classified as among the most significant challenges faced by the Jewish community as a whole.

My job as assistant rabbi largely focused on outreach. Specifically, I was to create activities that might draw under-identified, disaffected, and unaffiliated young Jews in their twenties to forties to our synagogue. With this demographic, the story—both Jewish and feminist - changes significantly.

This demographic, my demographic, is unlikely to attend any synagogue events, even ones directly catering to its needs and interests. So one of the earliest programs I instituted was a monthly Jewish View Café held at my home. It was a social gathering with a purpose. The idea was to discuss issues already of interest to young Jewish adults, and to bring into the discussion whatever Judaism had to offer on the month's topic. We discussed end-of-life issues; ethics of war and torture; sex before marriage; interdating and intermarriage; privacy in the modern world; the existence (and relevance) of God; and many other topics. Most of the topics discussed over these years were suggested by members of the group. Despite the large number of women in the group, the only feminist topic we addressed was when the Georgia legislature attempted to pass a law that would redefine the beginning and end points of life; the group asked to discuss the Jewish approach to abortion. This was the exception that proved the rule. Feminism, Jewish or otherwise, holds little interest for anyone in this group. My generation is by and large a post- generation: post-denominational, post-feminist, post-isms of any kind.

In contrast to my older female congregants, the women in this group do not feel that Jewish feminism shaped them. There is no question that it did, of course. All of them—without exception—

begin with the assumption of choice. Whether they go to synagogue or not, whether they attend fully egalitarian *minyanim* or Orthodox ones with a *mechitzah*, whether they actively participate in Jewish rituals or shun them entirely, whether they date in or out—they all begin with the assumption that they could do anything, Jewishly speaking, if they wanted to. Jewish feminism is a baseline for the women of my generation—yet another sign of its widespread success. Still, there is little awareness of its success or desire to identify with it as a continuing cause.

This generation of women, just like this generation of men, tend to stay away from organized forms of Judaism. But this isn't a sign of indifference. They find many of the trappings of institutional Judaism dull, irrelevant, or stifling. They feel they do not have a voice, that their concerns are not heard. They are not sure whether Judaism has anything important to say about the things that matter to them. This generation, like ones before it, is looking for a meaningful Judaism. It's simply the shape of that meaning that has changed.

For my older congregants, meaningful practice meant participation in the organization. When I asked them what made synagogue attendance meaningful for them, they talked about contributing to synagogue life, their ability to influence the direction their synagogue took, and having a voice. For the young women in my outreach group, meaningful practice means an intimate setting, music, uplifting spiritual experiences, being in a participatory environment (almost all of them mention sermons and old-style cantorial solo singing as things that make them feel disconnected). Unsurprisingly, these are the same things the men in this cohort cite when describing meaningful practice.

The young women in my outreach group are not looking for a Jewish feminist identity. They are not, in fact, looking for a Jewish identity at all. Both the women and the men in this group already have an identity—they have a sum total of interests, concerns, ideology, and philosophy—with which they are perfectly satisfied. What they are searching for is a way to foster Jewish connections, to integrate Jewish ideals and traditions into their life—but only if these connections, ideals, and traditions prove compatible with the ideals and values they already hold.

Is Passion for Jewish Feminism Truly Gone?

It is difficult to draw general conclusions from my observations. My sample is small, and it is not exhaustive; my personal experiences thus far are limited. While Jewish feminism and its future are not a central concern for most of the women I have encountered in my very brief time in the rabbinate, it may be a geographical issue (the southern United States) or a generational issue. It is possible that the lack of passion for Jewish feminism I have witnessed represents something much deeper. Is it that the questions asked by involved synagogue-attending Jewish women are not even on the radar for those on the margins? Perhaps this lack of involvement in the issues of Jewish feminism symbolizes a discontent with synagogue life itself? It is also entirely possible that there is plenty of feminist passion in the Conservative movement that I have simply not yet had an occasion to witness. In fact, there is only one thing I can state with certainty: If I were to write my rabbinical school application essays today, Dr. Lerner would not have to ask me why I didn't see fit to mention anything about the challenges Jewish women are currently facing.

PART IV

Women in Israel

IT USED TO BE that you could easily distinguish between "kinds" of Jews in Israel. A person was either totally religious (*dati* in Hebrew) or totally secular (*chiloni* in Hebrew). You could point to the signs: fur hat and sidecurls for the religious, going to the beach on Yom Kippur for everyone else. Today this stereotype is miles from the truth. Many Israelis, especially young people, are well read and well traveled; they have experienced egalitarian, liberal, and modern forms of Diaspora Judaism on their visits abroad. Many now understand the nuances of being "traditional" without necessarily being Orthodox. But what is much more significant is that, over the past twenty years, there has been a steady birth of a "homegrown" Israeli brand of the liberal movements. No longer can someone say with surety, "it is only Orthodox or nothing" in Israel. No longer can anyone claim that Israeli Reform, Conservative, and Reconstructionist synagogues are only products of foreigners or the misplaced longings for home of newly immigrated North Americans. While it may be true that those synagogues are the "spiritual homes" of those immigrants, a whole new generation of *sabras* have wholeheartedly embraced the egalitarian message of the liberal movements.

Not only that. A new kind of egalitarian traditional synagogue has been born—one that is remarkable in its insistence on adherence to traditional forms (Orthodox prayer book, full traditional service, a *mechitzah* separating men and women), while offering, within all possible parameters of halakhah, full privileges for its women members. In Jerusalem and across Israel you will see vibrant, young synagogues filled with Israelis *davening* (praying) in separate seating arrangements, with a woman leading the prayers up front; when the Torah service begins, the *mechitzah* is pulled back a bit and women get aliyot or read from the Torah from their side and men from theirs. It is a sight to behold: an Orthodox mother, complete with hair covered and modest dress, standing beside her daughter who is having a bat mitzvah and reading from the Torah, all from the women's side of the service. The rest of the congregation—men and women— listen and watch with full reverence and respect. No one snickers and no one complains; no one even seems to notice that they are in the middle of a revolution. This kind of service is also being imitated and initiated across North America. Who would have thought it possible?

And it also used to be that we could rest easily on the laurels of women's successes in Israel: after all, we have women drafted into the army, and we had Golda, Israel's female prime minister! (About whom it was said, "She's the only man in the Knesset.") Women in Israel now know that those days of heady pioneer equality are over; the swamps are drained and the time has come for the hard work of ensuring true equality in all levels of government, politics, religion, economics, education. Those of us in the Diaspora who love and support Israel need to let go of some of our old-time caricatures of the woman soldier and woman pioneer and start working for the woman denied her Jewish divorce, the woman who desires advancement in the army, and the woman reaching for the top of today's government.

It used to be that "national security" pushed aside any mention of women's rights, women's struggles, or women's issues. That will all have to wait, we were told, until peace. Until economic security. Until forever. But it's a new day in Israel, and there is no more waiting.

196

Rabbi Naamah Kelman is a descendent of ten generations of rabbis, becoming the first woman to be ordained by the Hebrew Union College in Jerusalem in 1992, where she is currently the associate dean. Born and raised in New York City, she has lived in Israel since 1976, where she has worked in community organizing, Jewish education, and rabbinic training, all to help establish and support a thriving Progressive (Reform) movement in Israel. She is a board member of Rabbis for Human Rights, MELITZ, and the Tali Education Fund. She also is deeply committed to interfaith dialogue. Naamah lives in Jerusalem and is married and the mother of three children.

A Thirty-Year Perspective on Women and Israeli Feminism

RABBI NAAMAH KELMAN

THIS CHAPTER IS dedicated to the memory of Penina Peli z"l. Penina was the first Israeli religious feminist to speak out loudly and passionately on all these issues. She encouraged and supported my journey from my first days in Jerusalem.

A year or so after I arrived in Israel in 1976, I was invited to speak at the Women's Center in Tel Aviv. This was one of the first such feminist-oriented centers in Israel. Much to my shock, I was there to debate a formerly Orthodox woman who had become secular. In the eyes of these Israeli feminists, it simply was not possible to be a "religious feminist." They had to put a stop to the "propaganda" I was propagating. I was stunned by the whole arrangement. First of all, where was the concept of sisterhood? Had I come all the way (it was a much longer drive then) from Jerusalem to be attacked? Second, it

197

dawned on me as the evening wore on that they had simply no idea what it meant to be a non-Orthodox religious woman. As someone who embraced the self-definition of "religious," I must be part of the patriarchal, political, official rabbinate in Israel that was systematically oppressing women. The evening ended better than it had begun. I managed to convince them that I was on their side. But the encounter was another reminder of the vast gulf between Israeli Jews and North American Jews.

I had arrived in Israel riding the tidal wave of Jewish feminism in the United States. In 1973, I had attended the "big bang" birth of the American Jewish feminist movement—the very first convention held at the McAlpin Hotel in New York. Some five hundred Jewish women gathered for the first time to discuss, argue, envision, create, and galvanize to change the face of Jewish religious and organizational life. The place was exploding with energy, as if we had been holding our collective breath through five thousand years of Jewish history … written by men, run by men, told by men. Now it was our turn to talk, laugh, scream, cry, pray, rejoice!

That gathering certainly changed my life. I was nineteen years old and was struggling with conflicting desires. My family biography destined all the men to become rabbis; women simply married them. My rabbi father and the Conservative movement that I grew up in had been taking its first steps toward women's increased involvement in prayer and synagogue life. And yet, despite the heroic steps of Sally Preisand at Hebrew Union College–Jewish Institute of Religion in 1972, when she became the first woman ordained in the United States, I could not find in myself any desire to become a rabbi. That would take another twelve years or so. I had become deeply involved in the Chavurah (fellowship) movement and had eagerly relearned all the synagogue skills. I was a full and equal participant in *tefillah* and was poised to consider reaching for leadership in the organized Jewish world. I say "relearn" because, like many girls raised in the Conservative movement, I had been encouraged to lead parts of the service. In 1968, my bat mitzvah ceremony consisted of reciting the haftarah on Friday night from the bimah. I was not called to the Torah, I did not offer a *d'var Torah,* but I did learn to read the haftarah and lead other *tefillot.* Ironically, a family friend approached me after the service to congratulate me and offer these words of "consolation." He said, "Too bad this is the first and last time you will be allowed to do this!" Indeed, when I moved over to the post–bar mitzvah side of camp, I was relegated to calling out the pages for our *tefillah.* That was my feminist "click" moment! It wasn't until the early seventies that I could reclaim my place with a vengeance.

Israel seemed completely insulated from these developments. I arrived in Israel in 1976 ready, like many Americans, to create an Israel in my image. What, there are NO egalitarian minyanim? Then I must create one! What, *feminism* is a dirty word in Israel? Well, we have to change the image of who considers themselves feminists! While political feminism had found a clear but marginal voice in Israel, there were few signs of the kind of Jewish feminist revolution that was taking hold in North America. There was only Penina Peli back then, an Orthodox woman who was in dialogue with her American counterparts. With no support and hardly any recognition, she created some of the first dialogues, seminars, and *davening* (prayer) spaces for women.

The progress in recent years, however, has been tremendous. In 2006–2007, two Israeli women rabbis were named as among the top ten most important people by their respective local newspapers. This could not have happened even five years before. So what has happened over thirty-some years that Jewish religious feminism has gone from almost complete invisibility to a visible and vocal movement across the religious and secular spectrum?

The rise of religious feminism goes hand in hand with the rise of the liberal denominations taking root in Israel. In the late 1970s there was a small but active political feminist force at work. Although Israel has some of the most liberal laws regarding women's equality and women's rights, it has been a constant struggle for women in almost every aspect of life to see these promised rights realized. The great social democratic tradition of equality that the early Zionist pioneers hoped to establish fell short in every critical part of society: women in the military, women in the workplace, family responsibilities, and status in rabbinic courts. Israel was and remains a highly militarized and patriarchal society, and in these critical areas women are second-class citizens. The military remains the most important springboard for politics and industry. Since women are, for the most part, not in the elite military units and networked, they are at a major disadvantage for gaining entry into the highest echelons of government and business. But much worse is the fact that the Orthodox and, increasingly, the ultra-Orthodox control the state rabbinate and rabbinic courts. Women are subordinate in marriage ceremonies; women are at the mercy of husbands and all-male rabbinic courts when it comes to granting a divorce; and women cannot be witnesses. When the State of Israel was established, the so-called unifying Orthodox rabbinate was to be Zionist and mainstream. Therefore, all weddings were Orthodox, as were conversions and divorces. Even funerals were handled by the Orthodox rabbinate, and if the deceased had only daughters, the recitation of kaddish was handed over to a male relative or friend. For the first thirty years or so, this seemed to work for most Israelis; they had little use for the actual ceremonies. They tolerated them so long as they could live secular lives undisturbed. With the rise of an Orthodoxy that was becoming both messianic and nationalistic, secular Israelis felt more coercion, less unity, and deeply uncomfortable.

The late 1980s and 1990s ushered in a new era for the non-Orthodox movements. A few incidents and developments converged giving the liberal movements greater press and eliciting much more sympathy. They included the fact that North American liberal *olim* (immigrants to Israel) now had children to raise. The new, expanded Hebrew Union College campus opened to much fanfare the same week when, coincidentally, a significant new Jerusalem Reform synagogue was "raided" by a local state-funded ultra-Orthodox rabbi. Then-mayor Teddy Kolleck responded dramatically by donating land to the congregation. No less significant was the fact that for the first time, the United Jewish Appeal, due to pressure from American Reform and Conservative rabbis, began to fund the fledgling movements in Israel with an annual budget. Israel. This put liberal Judaism on the map. For the first time, secular Israelis were offered an alternative: egalitarian, accessible life cycle ceremonies, including weddings, bat mitzvah and baby namings for girls. Liberal congregations in key urban centers and scattered throughout the country drew thousands of Israelis to life cycle events, Shabbat and holiday worship, adult education and a network of nursery schools. In 1986, when there were no progressive schools for my children, places that my eldest daughter and other girls would be full Jewish citizens, we simply founded a school. At this school, we Progressive Reform parents joined the established Tali system. Tali was founded by Conservative movement rabbis and activists in 1976, creating a state-recognized school system where parents could determine the extent of the Jewish enrichment. Our particular school is very much identified with Reform ideology, but this is not necessarily true of the other schools, which successfully maintain a non-affiliated but Conservative ideology–inspired network.

We established the bat mitzvah ceremony tradition. Since 1992, ours has been the only school where our sixth-grade girls celebrate a group bat mitzvah and are called to the Torah. All girls bless and some read from the Torah, and all read the haftarah. This tradition continues today as whole families attend this lively celebration, the only one of its kind in Israel. Out of the thirty-some girls in the class each year, about eight or so go on to have their own full bat mitzvah service. I served for many years as rabbi in that school. We used to joke that the boys would ask me if men can be rabbis too! While more schools, both secular and Orthodox, seek some kind of meaningful ceremony for their girls, we in the Progressive movement continue to press for equality, rather than alternatives to this coming-of-age ritual. Unfortunately, bat mitzvah has not become the mainstream Jewish practice it is for boys in Israel, where even the most secular family will go to their local Orthodox synagogue for a bar mitzvah ceremony. However, there is progress; our non-Orthodox synagogues in some communities, such as Tel Aviv, have become the "synagogue of choice" for both bat and bar mitzvah for secular families.

Our school programs and systems have grown significantly over the past twenty years as well. When we opened our first preschool in 1986, there were no materials or curricula available in Hebrew that offered a liberal, egalitarian view of Judaism. Every picture of synagogue showed men and boys at prayer, women lighting candles. We embarked on a mission—to gather photographs, posters, and curricular materials, and to attend teacher-training workshops and seminars—that has slowly affected the schools our Progressive movement works with. Over the years, on a few occasions, I have been a feminist "censor." I once visited one of our preschools only to discover the doctor's play area had a poster of a male physician and female nurse. I suggested that they find some additional posters, since I was sure that a number of the parents included women physicians. But that type of change is easy. Getting girls or teachers to wear kippot is the real challenge. The problem remains unresolved; we do better with convincing them in the early years, and they agree to wear them at the bat mitzvah ceremony, but in between, we have not found the right balance. And this is just in our Jerusalem school—in the rest of Israel, the fact that our secular students are praying, and that parents come to holiday celebrations, represents huge strides.

Another countercultural trend, surely inspired by feminism, is the return to Jewish text study, now for men and women together, and rituals in a small but important circle of organized secular Jewish life. There are numerous secular "study houses" or *battei midrash,* and a few *chavurot* that are creating prayer alternatives. They are alternatives to the Reform and Conservative movements, as these institutions define themselves as secular.

All these forces, liberal and secular, working in parallel and sometimes together, have begun to redefine Judaism in Israel. Weddings have sustained the most dramatic change. For the first fifty years of the state, the vast majority of Israelis had no option aside from a state-sanctioned Orthodox wedding, officiated at by a rabbinate-approved Orthodox rabbi. In the last ten years, however, thousands have opted for a non-rabbinate wedding, even when they were eligible to have one. This is a not-so-quiet social protest led by couples who prefer egalitarian and personally meaningful ceremonies that express who they are as Jews and as Israelis. Israelis can now choose from an array of secular and liberal ceremonies whose common denominator is equality.

Israelis who choose a non-Orthodox ceremony are obligated by the Reform movement to have a civil ceremony outside of Israel and sign a prenuptial agreement guaranteeing the woman's basic rights in case of divorce. More important, the egalitarian ceremony that allows for double ring exchanges, modern *ketubot* (Jewish wedding certificates), and other forms of women's participation have had a ripple affect on the Orthodox rabbinate. As thousands opt out of rabbinate marriages, the rabbinate's only recourse is to be more responsive to these feminist demands. A typical rabbinate wedding today will allow for women to give their husbands a wedding ring at the conclusion of the ceremony. This would have been unthinkable without the work of Reform and Conservative Judaism in Israel.

Orthodox feminism has taken root, too, notably the courageous work of Orthodox feminists actively struggling to break the stranglehold of the Orthodox rabbinate on women whose husbands refuse to grant them divorce. I believe that the pioneering work of the non-Orthodox feminists set the agenda for the Orthodox. In 2000, I participated in the Kolech Conference. This gathering of Orthodox women invited me and Professor Alice Shalvi, the matriarch of liberal Jewish Israeli feminism, to speak from our Reform and Conservative perspectives. Alice had "brazenly" and publicly exited Orthodoxy. The founder and former principal of a liberal Orthodox girl's school, Alice's departure was both highly publicized and highly controversial, as she walked straight into the loving and welcoming arms of the Schechter Institute of the Conservative movement.

The giant ballroom was packed as we addressed the crowd. There was a great deal of emotion regarding Alice's typically brilliant, eloquent remarks. There was both a sense of betrayal and a clear vote of approval expressed. Overwhelmingly, the sense was that there must be an Orthodox way for women to participate in Judaism. I stated simply that this gathering would not have been possible without the path-breaking work of the liberal movements in Judaism. "Whether you like it or not, or care to hear it," I said, "we have set the bar; we ask the tough questions. You may not like our answers, but we push the boundaries."

When I was the first woman to be ordained in Israel in 1992, CNN was there to cover the event, but *Ha'aretz*, Israel's most important newspaper, was not. There was some coverage in the local Jerusalem press, and eventually I did appear on a number of interview shows, but overall, the international press was more excited than the Israeli press. Now *Ha'aretz* has an impressive group of journalists covering many aspects of Diaspora and Israeli life. Since my ordination, another twenty women have been ordained in Israel. More women serve congregations than men. Women have chaired our rabbinic council. Perhaps most important is that Israelis see the Reform movement as synonymous with equality between the sexes; for many this is positive; for others, negative. Recently, *Ha'aretz* published an article about the work of Dr. Tzvia Waldan, linguist and activist, who explored the question of how a woman rabbi is addressed; why some women use the Hebrew title *Rav* (the masculine form of "rabbi") and others have chosen a new title, *Rabbah*. *Rabbah* as a feminine rabbi is the creation of Israeli-born women who want the gender-specific title. Others, including myself, prefer the profession-specific title, despite that it confuses people grammatically. Waldan determined that this is a generational issue. The first women rabbis mimic their male counterparts, while the second and third feel liberated from this. Time will tell if this theory holds true, but it is another indication that we haven't quite found the language in Israel for the phenomenon of women rabbis. It is symbolic of our struggle, to find our unique voice yet be grounded in a glorious past.

The struggle is far from over. The Orthodox rabbinate's control of marriage and divorce renders women second-class citizens. Orthodox feminists and Modern Orthodox rabbis are trying to put a more caring and compassionate face on the religious court system. Sadly, the Israeli political system, still beholden to the ultra-Orthodox minority, capitulates to their extremism. Rabbinic court appointments have become an additional battleground. Liberal Orthodox forces attempt to get Modern Orthodox rabbis on these courts, to lessen the ultra-Orthodox majority. So far it has been a losing battle.

But we are winning on the ground. Women are emerging as scholars of Judaism in all the pertinent fields of study. Theater, movies, and the arts are looking at Jewish women with a feminist lens. Women rabbis are not an oddity. We are no longer the "bearded lady" in the circus. We are now invited to panels and seminars where our voices are heard. The educational system has become more and more sensitive to these issues. Even the Israeli Defense Force is looking for ways to give women more challenges, more involvement, better opportunities.

This is not the Israel I encountered in 1976. Now my daughters are second-generation feminists and 100 percent Israeli progressive Jews. They and their sisters are now shaping Israel in their image. Thirty years from now, I pray, the liberal religious options will long have become mainstream. Torah will be taught and studied and celebrated from a women's perspective, seen as just another layer of the myriad layers of Jewish commentary. Women's studies will not be a separate and marginalized discipline but, like Jewish mysticism or Hasidism, another subject of Jewish studies. I no longer agree to appear on panels about Jewish feminism or the role of women in Judaism. Instead, I choose to talk about Judaism. Thirty years from now, the Judaism we see in Israel will be irrevocably altered by the next generation of women and men. Equality and pluralism will not be a privilege, but a basic right.

Rabbi Dalia Marx, PhD, tenth-generation in Jerusalem, is married to Roly Zyl-bersztein and is the mother of Tom, Niv, and Noam. Marx earned her doctorate at the Hebrew University in Jerusalem and her rabbinic ordination at Hebrew Union College–Jewish Institute of Religion (HUC-JIR) in Jerusalem and Cincinnati (2003). She is a professor for liturgy and midrash at the Jerusalem campus of HUC-JIR and teaches in various academic institutions in Israel, the United States, and Europe. She is involved in various research groups and is active in voicing progressive Judaism in Israel. She writes for academic journals and the Israeli press, and is engaged in creating new liturgies and midrashim. Marx is currently in Berlin with her family, where she was invited as a guest professor to Potsdam University and Abraham Geiger College.

Gender in Israeli Liberal Liturgy

RABBI DALIA MARX, PhD

THE WAYS IN WHICH gender is depicted in the liturgical language[1] is one of the most heated issues faced by contemporary liberal Jews.[2] The discussions dominate the religious and academic spheres as well as the public arena.[3]

The fact that most Jewish liturgical texts, and certainly all the public prayers were composed, performed, and preserved throughout the ages by men and in the presence of a quorum of men is not new, of course, but it went almost unnoticed until just a few decades ago. The achievements of the feminist movement that led to ever-increasing numbers of women serving as rabbis, cantors, educators, community leaders, and prayer leaders shed a new light on the imbalanced provenance of these central religious texts. It is also well known that the traditional prayers mention almost exclusively male characters from the Jewish tradition (such as Abraham, Isaac, and Jacob), refer both to the Divine and to worshipers in the synagogue in masculine language, and address God by means of masculine attributes and metaphors that hardly relate to feminine experiences. Traditionally, women had an at best marginal public role in most life cycle events and virtually no active part in synagogue worship.

In recent decades, Reform, Reconstructionist, and to some extent, Conservative Jews have made it a priority to mend this situation and to make the liturgy more egalitarian, balanced, and inclusive. It appears that most, if not all, liberal Jews would agree on the importance and need for such changes, but the movements and the different Jewish centers differ in the means, tone, and extent of changes that they are willing to make.

The intense interest in gender language in the Israeli liberal liturgy has clearly been imported from liberal Judaism in North America. Whereas in the United States gender in liturgy has been a central topic since the late seventies,[4] in Israel the discussion became significant only in the last fifteen years. The first Israeli Reform siddur, *Ha-Avodah Shebalev*, published in 1982, reflects so little interest in gender issues that the American liturgy scholar Erik Friedland wrote: "The Israel religious progressives' apparent unconcern with gender terminology might reek of rank heresy to their American siblings."[5]

The second edition of *Ha-Avodah Shebalev*, published in 1991, pays more attention to gender issues, as does the Conservative siddur *Va-Ani T'filati* from 1998 (although the innovative approach is not always accepted in the congregations and organizations of the Israeli Conservative movement). But only in more recent informal prayer handouts and semi-formal publications does the treatment of the gender issue reach its full extent.

Although the gender discussion has gradually become more central on both sides of the ocean, there are unique considerations that Israeli women and men have to take into account when seeking a more balanced language. We face a host of challenges that are unique to a gendered language such as Hebrew, and to Israel's rather traditional society. Since the outset of Reform liturgy in general, many of the changes and innovations of the liberal liturgy were made only in the English, leaving the traditional Hebrew barely touched. In this way, the prayerbook editors could hold the stick on both ends: presenting a comprehensible and ideologically acceptable text to worshipers while maintaining the feeling and linguistic authenticity of the traditional and familiar Hebrew prayers.

Needless to say, the liberal Israeli liturgists do not have the advantage and privilege of using this compromise. The fact that the liturgical language is akin to that of the vernacular (although in a higher linguistic register) is a double-edged sword. On the one hand, it is more urgent for the them to alter imbalanced liturgical language, since it cannot be mitigated by altering the translation; on the other hand, any change would be more conspicuous. Even secular Israelis are sensitive to traditional liturgical language, since they fully understand it and are used to hearing it.

An example may illustrate this complexity: An experienced teacher in an Israeli progressive-Judaism kindergarten told me about an ongoing discussion she has had with one of the female rabbis in the movement. This rabbi claims that since equality is an important Reform value, it is crucial to use balanced liturgical language in the kindergarten. She suggested that some of the blessings be recited in the traditional way *(Barukh ata Adonai ...)*, while using feminine language *(B'rukha at Yah)* for others. The teacher, on the other hand, felt that the mere fact that children coming from secular families (where many parents are suspicious of any form of religious observance) are experiencing daily prayer, not to mention having girls wearing kippot and taking an active role in the leading of the service, is odd enough for their parents, and that changing the well-known blessing formula would seem altogether unnatural, and in fact alienating, to them.

Indeed, contemporary Hebrew speakers constantly have to choose between the comfort of the well-known text and their ideological, theological, and aesthetic approach. This makes their task quite complicated and at the same time extremely interesting.

The discussions around these issues that are most passionate in Israel (as in the Diaspora) are those dealing with God language—the ways God is depicted and referred to in the prayers. There are no less than four levels[6] of reference to gender in the liturgy of Israeli liberal movements:

1. Use of Inclusive Language to Refer to Worshipers

Liturgical phrases that are perceived as offensive to women, such as the blessing, "Praised … who did not make me a woman," were omitted or revised from all liberal prayer books right from the out-set.[7] In some, but not all, cases when the prayer text appears in the first person, such as the early morning prayer, "I thankfully acknowledge," the feminine form is added: *"Mode/Moda ani."*[8]

Regarding nonverbal aspects of prayer, women in Israeli liberal circles tend to wear tallitot and sometimes kippot. The use of tefillin is widely accepted among women in the Conservative congregations in Israel. It is interesting to note that the editors of the Israeli Conservative siddur chose a picture of a woman wearing tefillin to demonstrate its proper use.

2. Addition of Representative Female Characters

Although using different liturgical means, both the revised edition of the Reform siddur (1991) and the Conservative siddur (1998) add the matriarchs to the first blessing of the main prayer that is recited in every service, the Amidah. This is a clear adoption of the American liberal liturgy.

It is noteworthy to add that the *hatima* (ending formula) of the blessing in *Ha-Avodah Shebalev* differs from the American Reform one. It reads, *"poked Sarah"* ("the One who remembers Sarah"); the American version reads, *"ezrat Sarah"* ("the help of Sarah"). The Israeli version was chosen since it is closely related to the words of Genesis 21:1, "And God remembered [*pakad et*] Sarah," and thus reflects a close awareness both of the biblical text and of the grammatical structure.

A few methods of including the matriarchs were used. Here is the version that appears in the 1991 edition of *Ha-Avodah Shebalev*:

ברוך אתה אדני אלהינו ואלהי אבותינו ואימותינו
אלהי אברהם, יצחק ויעקב,
אלהי שרה, רבקה, רחל ולאה ...
ברוך אתה אדוני מגן אברהם ופוקד שרה.

Praised are you Adonai, our God and God of our fathers
and mothers
God of Abraham, Isaacs and Jacob,
God of Sarah, Rivkah, Rachel and Leah ...
Praised are you Adonai, shield of Abraham **and the One
who remembers Sarah.**

The Israeli Reform youth siddur mentions the matriarchs side by
side with the patriarchs:

ברוך אתה ה'
אלהי אברהם ושרה
אלהי יצחק ורבקה
ואלהי יעקב לאה ורחל ...

Praised are you Adonai,
God of Abraham **and Sarah,**
God of Isaacs **and Rivkah**
and God of Jacob **Leah and Rachel** ...

In the Israeli Conservative, or Masorti, movement the addition
of the matriarchs to the Amidah met a great deal of objection. Rabbi
Professor David Golinkin, president of the Schechter Institute of
Jewish Studies in Jerusalem, wrote a halakhic response on this
topic.[9] He suggested that "the authentic and traditional way" to
include the matriarchs would be to add *piyyutim* (liturgical hymns)
to be recited in the middle of the blessing and not in its ending,
which, he claims, cannot be changed, according to halakhah. As an
example, he quotes a hymn composed by Rabbi Dr. Einat Ramon,
dean of the Schechter seminary:

נבואה אוהלי שרה, רבקה, רחל ולאה.
ותהי גמילות חסדיהן לפנינו
בכל עת ובכל שעה.

Let us enter the tents of Sarah,
  Rebecca, Rachel and Leah.
May their acts of loving-kindness
be an example to us at all times.

For now, some Conservative congregations add the matriarchs at the opening and closing of the blessing (as is the custom in all Israeli Reform congregations), while other congregations simply don't mention the mothers at all.

In the blessing of Ge'ula (redemption), said after the recitation of the Shema, Miriam is mentioned. A uniquely Israeli inclusion of women is found in the *Mi Sheberakh* prayers for the men and women who are about to begin their military service. It reads:

מי שברך לוחמינו
יהושע, דוד ויהודה, דבורה, יעל ויהודית,
הוא יברך את _____ המתגייס/ת
לצבא ההגנה לישראל

May the one who blessed our warriors Joshua, David
  and Judah, **Deborah, Yael and Judith,**
Bless _____ who is about to join the service of the
  Israeli defense forces.

3. New Rituals and New Ritual Opportunities

On both sides of the ocean, old rituals are being adapted so that they are inclusive and incorporate women, and new rituals are been created to celebrate the feminine experience—that is to say, to mark what has been unmarked.[10] While not categorically refraining from women-only activities and rituals, Israeli liberal women are generally less apt to have their own separate rituals. Yet, in recent years we have witnessed a rise in the number of prayers and services created by and for women. Some are reclaiming old rites while adding a feminine aspect, and some are new rituals that have to do with women's unique experiences.

One example of a ritual reclaimed for women is an Israeli women's Haggadah, edited by *Yalta*, an organization for Conservative female rabbis and student rabbis. The editor, Rabbi Idit Lev, writes: "This is a journey of searching for a new meaning in an ancient *seder* and addition of new texts. This is a search after a contemporary Israeli voice."[11] Instead of four sons, this Haggadah expands on four daughters, "one possessing wisdom of the heart, one rebellious, one simple and one who cannot ask questions."[12]

Another example of rituals reclaimed is the variety of *piyyutim* (liturgical hymns) asking for rain that are recited on Sh'mini Atseret. Traditionally, these hymns mention the merit of our patriarchs in relation to water; liberal *piyyutim* add the experience of the matriarchs. One such poem was composed by the Renewal rabbi Ruth Gan Kagan.[13] Here is the first stanza, referring to Sarah:

זכור אם ברוח קודש סוכה כמים

צחוקה מתגלגל כפלגי מים

אורח כנשים השבת לה כמים

בנים הניקה כשפע מים

בעבורה אל תמנע מים

Remember one who laughed, cascading laugh like water
Whose way of women You resumed,
blood flowing out as water
The babes of kingdoms from her breasts
she nursed with milk like water
Her children You made numerous as sea sand by the water
For Sarah's sake send water

A comparison of the Hebrew to the English version (composed by the author) is a good opportunity to demonstrate how the literary qualities and scriptural allusions are are especially vivid and multi-layered in the Hebrew text.[14]

Examples of Israeli rituals for women only are found in the multitude of Rosh Chodesh (New Moon) groups in liberal con-gregations, and a host of new rituals marking life passages, such as first menstruation, joining the military service, the beginning of a spousal relationship, becoming pregnant, miscarriage, abortion, fertility treatments, divorce, and menopause. In many cases, these texts reflect deep acquaintance with biblical and rabbinic sources, as well as contemporary poetry and literature. For example, here is a paragraph from an immersion ceremony for a woman who experienced a miscarriage, composed by Reform rabbi Tamar Duvdevany:

ארפא גופי ואטבול במים

תרפא נפשי במים חיים.

יישטף גופי בתוך המים

תיטהר נפשי במים חיים.

ייעטף גופי בחיבוק של מים

תירחב נפשי במים חיים.

I'll relax my body and immerse myself in water
May my soul be healed in living water.
May my body be washed by water
May my soul be purified by living water.
May my body be embraced by water
May my soul be nurtured in the living water.

This prayer is quoted from *Parashat Ha-Mayim*, a book edited by four Israeli Reform female rabbis that contains a variety of texts and rituals of *t'vilah* (immersion).

It may be a cliché, but it is not untrue that women tend to be closer to their bodies than men are to theirs. I believe that the reincorporation of the body and physical aspects that were previously considerably neglected in liberal worship (especially in the classical version of the Reform movement) has to do with the role women have taken in participating, leading, and creating in Jewish worship. Composition of rituals that have to do with physical experiences contributes to this process.

While most of these themes are not unique to Israeli women, both their content and form reflect Israeli experience and style. Prayers written by North American women inspire Israeli liberal liturgists, but the cultural reference is often different. Sometimes North American liturgical pieces are criticized for being too "touchy-feely" for the *sabras* (native-born Israelis).

Interestingly, Rivkah Ben-Sason, an Orthodox woman, was quoted recently in the Israeli press after publicly expressing the need to compose a ceremony to mark divorce.[15] Her pioneering, public call may stem from her familiarity with such ceremonies in the non-Orthodox realm (and indeed, people from the Orthodox camp denounced her as "Reform," as often happens to innovative Orthodox women), and may also forecast future involvement of the Orthodox in the endeavor to mark women's lives with meaningful ritual.

4. Gender-Inclusive and Gender-Balanced Metaphors of God

While avoiding referring to God in a gendered language is relatively easy in English, since *He* can be easily changed to *God*, it is practically impossible to do this in Hebrew, since all nouns, verbs, and adjectives are gendered. Also, as we have indicated above, many feel that it would be too extreme to change the formula of the traditional blessing too radically, as, for example, Marcia Falk does.[16] Instead of changing the traditional liturgy, other texts may be added. *Kavanat Ha'Lev*, the Israeli Reform Machzor (1991), prints next to the *piyyut* "Avinu Malkenu" ("Our Father, Our King") another poem, "Sh'khina Mekor Khayeinu" ("Shekhinah, Source of Our Lives"), and a third *piyyut* that is gender neutral. This Israeli inclusive innovation later also found its place in North American liberal liturgy.

In a mikveh ceremony for a bride's mother composed by Reform rabbis Maya Leibovich and Alona Lisitsa, the blessing before the immersion is: *"B'rukha at Yah, Mekor Hakhayim, Hamekhadeshet et horuti"* ("Blessed are you Yah, the source of life, who renews my motherhood"). After the immersion, the mother says:

שכינה מקור חיי

האירי הורותי החדשה

לב חכם טעי בי ורוח נכונה חדשי בקרבי

לקבל את בן/בת זוגה של בתי

Shekhinah, source of my life
enlighten my new (form of) motherhood
Create in me a wise heart
and renew a true spirit within me
to accept the spouse of my daughter.

In informal or semi-formal prayer sheets and booklets, Israeli Reform liturgists take more freedom to use feminine language when they refer to the Divine. I'm not aware of such attempts in the Israeli Conservative movement. As for Reform congregations, at least one change, initiated by Rabbi Levi Weiman-Kelman, is adopted in many synagogues. It is the ending for the Shabbat Hashkiveinu blessing:

ברוכה את יה, הפורשת סוכת שלום עלינו

ועל כל עמה ישראל ועל ירושלים.

Praised are you Yah, who spread a shield of peace over us and over all **her** People Israel and over Jerusalem.

It seems that the merciful and compassionate depiction of God in this blessing made it suitable in the eyes of many for its use of the feminine form.

Summary

An intriguing paradox underlines the treatment of gender in Israeli liberal liturgy: on one hand, the fact that Israelis fully comprehend the language of the liturgy makes the exclusion of women more acute and disturbing; on the other hand, the comfort and familiarity with the traditional text make it more difficult to radically change it. As for the general public, the challenge is twofold: many Israelis seem to be reluctant to engage in religious observance, and also reluctant to publicly embrace feminism (although many of them incorporate both in their lives), and therefore may perceive any change in the liturgy as "unauthentic."

The treatment of gender in Israeli liberal liturgy is greatly influenced by the liturgical innovations in North America. However, because Israeli liberal liturgy operates in a more traditional environment, and because Hebrew is a highly gendered language, its creators seek their own unique voice.

It seems Israeli liberal liturgists are more willing to relate to the symbolic aspects of liturgical language, and to realize that total balance is hard to achieve under any conditions, let alone in Hebrew. A personal example to illustrate: I was once criticized by an American editor who claimed that a prayer I wrote was not sufficiently gender sensitive. I replied:

> As a female Reform rabbi in the state of Israel, I am devoted heart and soul to women's issues. Making our prayers accessible to women of all ages is one of my main personal commitments. This is why it is painful for me that sometimes I think we shoot ourselves in the foot when we are not willing to understand some of the

liturgical terms as metaphors, which can be used and understood in more then one way.... Please, don't take from me the precious words my foremothers and my forefathers used when they prayed to the creator of the world.[17]

We have to admit that, for now, liberal Judaism and liberal liturgy, let alone gender-balanced liturgy, are still marginal in Israel, treated with ever-growing overt hostility by the Orthodoxy and with a great deal of suspicion by secular Jews. That said, it is equally important to note that Israeli liberal liturgy has an appeal in nonliberal circles: Modern Orthodox women are beginning to seek liturgical responses in nontraditional liturgical language, and secular women are finding new life cycle rituals meaningful and valuable.

Time will tell what the affects of these modern liturgies will be both inside Israel and out, and how they will influence Jewish practice in general. In the meantime, we in Israel continue to pave the way here, in small, but hopefully significant steps.

Rabbi Einat Ramon, PhD, is the dean of the (Masorti) Schechter Rabbinical Seminary in Jerusalem. Coming from a family of three generations of cultural-secular Zionists in Israel, Rabbi Ramon was the first Israeli-born woman rabbi. In the 1990s she taught at Kibbutzim College of Education and supervised a Masorti *chavurah* in Tel Aviv. She teaches modern Jewish thought and literature and Jewish feminism at the Schechter Institute of Jewish Studies. Among Rabbi Ramon's publications is her book *A New Life: Religion, Motherhood and Supreme Love in the Thought of A. D. Gordon* (Hebrew). She lives in Jerusalem with her husband, Rabbi Arik Ascherman (together they constitute Israel's only rabbinic couple), and their two children.

Masorti (Conservative Israeli) Women

RABBI EINAT RAMON, PhD

WHEN THE MASORTI (Israeli Conservative) movement was founded by Rabbi Moshe Cohen of Ashkelon in the 1970s, the question of women's equality and empowerment was secondary.[1] The thrust for establishing the early Israeli Conservative congregations was to provide an alternative to the religiosity of the dominant Orthodox community, and to reach out to Israeli "secular" Jews who were growing more and more alienated from their own religion and from halakhah.

As the movement approaches a celebration of thirty years since its establishment, it has a membership of approximately forty-one small congregations and *chavurot*. The number of congregations has remained relatively steady for the past twenty years, which suggests the need for the movement to review and seriously analyze its achievements and goals. It must ask why, despite the immense efforts of its Israeli rabbis (among whom we find some of the most talented rabbis in the worldwide Conservative movement), the movement's theological message—the importance of bringing halakhah closer to the Jewish people and the people closer to halakhah—has not yet reached the majority of Israeli society.

One thing, however, is clear: Despite the lack of social recognition and very slow educational influence on Israeli society, the Masorti movement has given rise to extremely dynamic women: lay leaders, *rebbetzins,* and rabbis, all of whom have advanced a Jewish women's voice within the movement and worldwide. However, the often independent nature of their personalities and work, a lack of historical consciousness on behalf of the Masorti movement, their own emigration out of Israel, and serious ideological and personal differences among the women themselves have all led to the fact that Masorti women's work has often gone unrecognized. What is needed is an attempt to map, mention, and evaluate the individual achievements of key Masorti women and their contribution to Jewish and Israeli cultures.

Masorti Women Lay Leaders

The absence of a thorough historical record of the Masorti movement and its congregations conceals, in particular, the untold story of many female lay leaders who were pivotal figures in establishing the early Masorti communities in Israel. It is important to note that women lay leaders have never been united on the issue of egalitarian services. An example where strong, committed women sided with two opposing views on that issue is the movement's oldest congregation in Israel, Kehilat Moriah, in Haifa, founded in 1954. Sharone Meital—a psychologist and mother of four who in the 1980s founded not only a Tali school in the area[2] (Tali schools are Israeli public schools affiliated with Masorti that offer an enriched curriculum in Jewish studies), but also a women's Rosh Chodesh (New Moon) group in the 1990s—was instrumental in moving the congregation toward egalitarian prayers in the 1980s.

At the same time, Julia Slonim, an English teacher and one of the founders of the Moriah congregation in Haifa, objected to egalitarianism all the way through, yet stayed with the congregation until she died at a very old age. However, Brenda Kaplan and Sarah Goldenberg left the congregation for Orthodox shuls, the former because the egalitarian synagogue was not suitable for her father, the latter because she regarded women leading services beyond the pale of halakhah.[3] Likewise, in Eshel Avraham, the Masorti Congregation in Beer Sheva (founded in 1976), one-third of the members, men and women, left the congregation when it became fully egalitarian in 1979.[4]

Masorti women's lay leadership has been reflected in a variety of national volunteer projects and positions, culminating at the beginning of the twenty-first century with the election of Dr. Irit Zemora from Congregation Eshel Avraham in Beer Sheva as the first woman chairperson of the movement. Three other women from the "founding" generation, Rachel Lior, Joan Kedem, and Diane Friedgut, established projects extending the spiritual message of the Masorti movement to soldiers and to women around the country. Rachel Lior, who was the founding principal of the first Tali school and one of the only native Israeli women among the founding generation of Masorti Jews, worked with Israeli officers in the Israeli Defense Forces (IDF) to create a program in which Masorti rabbis were regularly sent to introduce the Masorti religious perspective to Israelis. Joan Kedem, a member of Moreshet Yisrael at the center of Jerusalem, has established a program that reaches out to hundreds of "lone soldiers" (soldiers who do not have family in Israel) in the IDF. Her home phone number is circulated among soldiers, and upon their requests, she matches them with Masorti families for Shabbat hospitality, sends them *Mishloach Manot* for Purim and goods for other Jewish holidays.[5]

Under the auspices of the Israeli branch of Women's League for Conservative Judaism Diane Friedgut has, since 1998, organized four women's study days each year in central locations throughout the country. The study days feature the movement's most talented women rabbis and teachers and draw hundreds of women, mostly immigrants from North and South America and the former Soviet Union, to study texts together, thereby creating a network of Masorti women.

Rebbitzens

Another group of women whose talent has advanced the Jewish world via the Masorti Movement are three outstanding and active wives of Masorti rabbis. In this category is the prolific writer Naomi Graetz, wife of Rabbi Michael Graetz, the founder and rabbi for over twenty years of congregation Magen Avraham, founded in 1973 in Omer, a small city close to Beer Sheva. Naomi Graetz has written pioneering books on the topic of domestic violence in Jewish sources as well as feminist midrashim.[6] Another key person in the history of the Masorti movement was Dr. Barbara Spectre. A talented educator, Spectre had served as the de facto rabbi of Netzach Yisrael congregation in Ashkelon when her husband, Rabbi Phil Spectre, served as the second director of the Masorti movement in the 1980s. She was also the first chairperson of Schechter Rabbinical Seminary's board. Following the end of her husband's tenure as the leader of the Masorti movement in 1998, the couple moved to Stockholm, where she became the director of Padea: The Institute of Jewish Studies in Sweden.[7] A third rabbi's wife whose active participation was widely felt in the movement is Ziva Nativ, the wife of Rabbi Gil Nativ, the current rabbi of Magen Avraham in Omer. Ziva Nativ is a renowned Torah reader and bar/bat mitzvah teacher, and in 2004 took over the Masorti project the Bar/Bat Mitzvah for the Special Child. The program, which was initiated and cultivated for its first twelve years by the educator Judith Edelman-Green,[8] trains children with special needs to read or be called to the Torah, taking into consideration each child's unique learning ability.

Women Rabbis

The female rabbis of the Masorti movement have been trailblazers in a variety of ways. I am the first *sabra* (native-born Israeli) woman ordained as a rabbi.[9] Raised in Jerusalem in a Labor Zionist background, prior to my ordination I worked as the programming director for Noam, the Masorti youth movement in Israel. I was ordained by the Jewish Theological Seminary (JTS) in 1989.[10]

A year later, in 1990, Rabbi Gilah Dror was ordained at JTS. Dror returned to Israel immediately following her ordination, and in 1991 became the first Masorti woman to serve as a pulpit rabbi. A few years later she again made history when she was elected chairperson of the Israeli branch of the Rabbinical Assembly, thus becoming the first woman in the world to head a rabbinic organization. Dror was rabbi of Eshel Avraham for ten years, after which she decided to return to the United States and serve there as a pulpit rabbi.[11]

The decision to ordain women at the Schechter Institute of Jewish Studies was a topic of debate for many years within the movement. Finally, in 1992–93 the Israeli Law Committee, chaired by Rabbi David Golinkin, decided to ordain women.[12] Rabbi Valerie Stessin, a French-born graduate of B'nei Akiva, was the first woman ordained at Schechter, in 1993.

The ongoing budgetary crisis of the Masorti movement has hurt its women rabbis severely. Due to a lack of funds to pay rabbis, various women serving as Masorti rabbis in Israel ordained by Schechter Institute, such as Rabbi Amy Levin (formerly of the Masorti congregation Beit Hakerem, in Jerusalem) and Rabbi Florian Chinsky (of Kehillat Yaar Ramot, in Jerusalem) had to emigrate. Iranian-born Rabbi Shira Yisrael, a talented teacher of Jewish mysticism, had to leave the profession (though not the vocation) in order to make a living. Unfortunately, a number of Masorti women rabbis today are still currently unemployed or underemployed, as there are fewer job opportunities for women. Masorti women rabbis also face the difficulty of balancing work obligations with family obligations. Cur-

rently, three women rabbis serve Masorti congregations: Rabbi Sandra Kochman, Rabbi Chaya Roen-Bekar, and Rabbi Chagit Sabagat
Eshel Avraham in Beer Sheva. Rabbi Debbi Greenberg serves as the
rabbi of the Masorti youth movement, Noam. She had followed the
footsteps of Rabbi Claudia Kreiman, Noam's first rabbi.

Some women rabbis have been employed by the Masorti movement's national office. I was the spokesperson and political organizer
of the movement in 1996–97, the year when the struggles for non-
Orthodox representation at the municipal religious councils and at
the Western Wall were at their peak. This was also the year when the
Ne'eman committee was established to resolve the parliamentary crisis over non-Orthodox conversions in Israel. Rabbi Tamar Elad-
Appelbaum has been recently appointed as the coordinator of
weddings and of a new program for community administrators.

Other women rabbis found good rabbinic jobs in institutions
that are linked to the movement, though not officially affiliated with
it. Rabbi Valerie Stessin is a high administrator in the Tali school system, which in 2007 numbered over one hundred elementary
schools, currently serving as the assistant director of that educational system. For the past four years, Rabbi Idit Lev has been a
human rights worker, focusing on economic justice on behalf of the
multidenominational organization Rabbis for Human Rights.

In order to address some of the challenges facing women rabbis
in Israel, and following a gathering with North American colleagues
in 2000, Idit Lev and Valerie Stessin founded *Yalta*, a forum of Israeli
women rabbis and rabbinical students. The forum, named after the
learned and courageous wife of Rav Nachman (mentioned in
Berakhot 51b),[13] intends to empower Masorti women rabbis and
rabbinical students. It originally focused on two major initiatives: an
Internet discussion group and regular social gatherings for the
group's members, and feminist Seders based on an "in-house Haggadah" edited by Rabbi Idit Lev, which are led by *Yalta*'s members at
Masorti locations throughout the country. In the past, *Yalta* also
supervised fellowships allowing women rabbinic students to intern

at various congregations. In 2005, some of its members had left it and it no longer serves as a support group for all of the Masorti women rabbis and rabbinical students. In recent years the group has focused on promoting the signing of prenuptial agreements.

Some of the greatest breakthroughs for Masorti women have eventually happened subsequent to the appointment of Professor Alice Shalvi as rector in, and eventually acting president of, the Schechter Institute. With Professor Shalvi's appointment, a new feminist era began at the school. Shalvi had previously been principal of Pelech, an Orthodox girls school in Jerusalem, and founder and director of the Israeli Women's Network, work for which she won the Israel Prize in 2007. Among other dynamic educational initiatives in her time at Schechter Institute, Shalvi founded the Center for Women and Jewish Law in 1999, together with Rabbi David Golinkin, and helped launch *Nashim: A Journal of Jewish Women's Studies and Gender Issues* (in 1998), the only academic journal dedicated solely to Jewish women, copublished with Brandeis University, and later with Indiana University Press. The Center for Women and Jewish Law has trained superb women scholars of halakhah, including Rabbis Diana Villa and Monique Sziqind-Goldberg, who have been researching topics related to women and family law, in particular, thus paving the way for the advancement of women in Jewish society.[14]

In 2005 when I was a lecturer at the department of Jewish women's studies at Schechter and an advisor for women at the Schechter Rabbinical Seminary, I was asked to step in as an acting dean of the rabbinical school. The nomination became formal as of 2006, which made me the first female dean of a Conservative seminary. Since then there have been many changes in the roles of women at the rabbinical school. I recruited two women rabbis to the faculty, Rabbi Sarah Ben Moshe in the Talmud department (she is also the first Sephardi on the faculty) and Rabbi Diana Villa in halakhah. As a result, half of the Talmud courses at Schechter Rabbinical Seminary are currently offered by women. In addition, the class "Introduction to Jewish Feminism" is a required course in the curriculum, thus exposing all of Schechter's Israeli students to the various feminist streams and theologies. Schechter Rabbinical Seminary also prides itself on regularly admitting non-Ashkenazi women, which is rare in other religious feminist circles in Israel. One-third of the current student body at Schechter is non-Ashkenazi.

Religious Thought and Theology

With such a wide range of activities that still, nevertheless, engage a very small number of people (ten thousand at the most), we Masorti women must recognize that the task ahead not only involves reaching out to new populations (a complex mission that necessarily requires creative thinking), but also a clearer religious Jewish feminist message. I believe that the vision that we Masorti women must convey is one of a partnership of women and men on all levels of human and Jewish life.

Over a million Jews living in Israel have been exposed to communist and socialist ideas—whether in communist countries or in the avowedly socialist and secular kibbutzim—both of which regarded religion and the traditional Jewish family an obstacle to an egalitarian utopia. Current statistics indicate, however, that Israelis are tired of social experiments and extreme reactions to modernity, both religious and secular. Most Israelis, even those who do not identify themselves with halakhah, are traditional in their outlook.[15] Our struggle is to move forward without rejecting the tradition.

Early Zionist feminist thought provides a helpful direction for Masorti women. When we look at the vision of second aliyah feminist thinkers we realize how both secular feminists (whom we now know to be more sympathetic to Jewish tradition than originally perceived) and Modern Orthodox feminists have emphasized the importance of intertwining traditional models of motherhood and family structures with women's national and intellectual leadership. According to that feminist-Zionist vision, men were perceived as necessary partners both in intimate relationships at the home, and

225

in local and national communities. It was men's rejection of that partnership that angered the early pioneer women, though not to the point of giving up that vision. The vision was first articulated by the pioneers' main thinker, A. D. Gordon:

> When both the man and the woman learn to live their entire selves … they will be able to deepen and enrich themselves through their partners' selves. This is the secret of love between a man and a woman, the secret of mutual attraction between worlds that are so different from one another and yet which so complement and renew one another.[16]

Gordon's students; his daughter, Yael; the literary analyst and thinker, Rachel Katznelson-Shazar; and Ada Maimon, the founder of the feminist Labor organization for women have all further developed his thought on the matter.[17] Ada Mainom, in particular, embodied that vision with a bit of humor as a Knesset member in the early years of the state.

> As we all remember, on one occasion in Jewish history the wise men of the Persian monarchy decreed: "Every man shall reign in his home." Once and only once. I sincerely hope that members of the Knesset have no aspirations to identify with the ideology of King Ahashverosh.[18]

Beyond her humor, Maimon, herself an observant Jew, conveyed a deep faith in Judaism and in its message that could potentially be achieved in our generation: men and women ought to come together in the image of God if they are to overcome the obstacles of modern and ancient patriarchies. This was her perspective on how rebuilding the State of Israel could be a step toward the messianic world. The Masorti movement, acknowledging and celebrating a new feminist vision, could be a true partner in that work.

Professor Margalit Shilo, PhD, is head of the Land of Israel studies and archae-ology department of Bar Ilan University, Israel. Among Shilo's books are *Princess or Prisoner? Jewish Women in Jerusalem, 1840–1914* (Brandeis Univer-sity Press, 2005), finalist for the National Jewish Book Award and Bahat prize from Haifa University; *Voices of Jerusalem Women;* and *The Challenge of Gen-der, Women in the Early Yishuv.*

The First Decade of the Orthodox Women's Revolution in Israel[1]

The Case of Kolech

MARGALIT SHILO, PhD

The Plight of Orthodox Women in Modern Society

THE WELL-KNOWN VERSE, "All is the glory of the princess within," from Psalm 45 notwithstanding, systematic observation will demonstrate that in Jewish society from time immemorial, it was exactly those women who "went public"—such as the prophetesses Miriam and Deborah, and Queen Salome Alexandra—who earned the greatest renown and esteem. Despite these exceptions, however, Jewish women were traditionally excluded from the power bases of society: institutions of Torah study, public service, and active partic-ipation in communal religious services. In traditional Jewish society, women were regarded as a "people unto themselves," credited mainly with enabling their men-folk to achieve greatness.[2]

227

In the twentieth century, with new societal norms being established all over the world, many new opportunities are becoming available to women in Israel, too, including Orthodox women. The possibility of obtaining higher secular education in all disciplines, coupled with the almost unlimited professional prospects of advance in their profession, have only emphasized the limitations and barriers still in place in Orthodox society. In Orthodox institutions such as synagogues and houses of Torah study (yeshivot), doors have been closed to women throughout history, and they remained closed in the modern age. According to the traditional interpretation of Jewish law, women are exempted from the mitzvah of Torah study, and though there are two contradictory views in the Talmud concerning their right to study, a positive one and a negative one, through the ages most Rabbis opposed women's learning.[3] Orthodox women's desire to continue their observance of religious tradition has brought them face to face with a dissonant reality: impressive progress in secular society, submission, and self-effacement in Orthodox society.

Is this paradoxical situation a ticking time bomb? In Orthodox institutions, discrimination against women is twofold: they are absent, and their interests are viewed only from male perspectives. On the one hand, Orthodox women consider themselves obligated to observe religious law and adhere to the framework dictated by patriarchal institutions. On the other hand, they have attempted to penetrate this patriarchal system and challenge its masculine character. Characteristic of the Orthodox women's revolution, or, put differently, the goal of creating a new social order consonant with the feminist revolution as a whole, is, I believe, a desire to avoid a total break with Orthodox society while at the same time reshaping that society. In other words, Orthodox women would like to continue to maintain uncompromising loyalty to the overall framework (family, congregation, community), while at the same time making exhaustive efforts to modify that framework and invest it with new, egalitarian content. (Though the term *egalitarian* is part of the rhetoric of the Orthodox feminists, its exact meaning has so far not been clarified.) You might say that the Orthodox feminist revolution is epitomized by the desire to have the best of both possible worlds.

On July 7, 1998, a group of nearly twenty women gathered in a private home in order to establish a women's organization named Kolech: Religious Women's Forum,[4] which would advance women's participation in Orthodox institutions, help in solving women's plights, and raise the Orthodox public's awareness of women's status and needs.[5] Without a formal declaration, Kolech started to lead the Orthodox feminist revolution—that is to say, the movement to create a new social order in the Orthodox community.

Before going any further, I have to make a personal statement. My profession is history and I specialize in the history of Jewish women in pre-state Israel. I am also a very active member of Kolech. Being an integral part of this organization gives me access to much information; much of Kolech's printed material is in my personal collection. I also interviewed the founder, Dr. Chanah Kehat, and many other active members. The most important sources dealing with Kolech's concepts and ideas are four volumes of articles based on papers that were presented at Kolech's five international conferences.[6]

First Steps toward an Orthodox Women's Revolution

Over the last thirty years, Orthodox society in the State of Israel has witnessed several innovations that potentially challenged the male hierarchy of the system. These innovations have been of major importance in empowering Orthodox women, heightening their sense of empowerment, and stimulating their desire to organize for the achievement of their goals:[7]

- The establishment of Torah study centers for women (*midrashot*), where the oral law (sometimes including the Talmud) is studied on a high level. Although young boys are offered Talmud study beginning in elementary school, *midrashot* for girls (they are not called yeshivot!) are post–high school. (On the high school level, the Pelech Religious Experimental High School for Girls was apparently the first Orthodox school in Israel to introduce Talmud for girls in a *beit midrash* setting.) The argument they aroused as to whether halakhah permits girls to study the Talmud died down quite quickly. It has become clear that, although Jewish women were excluded from higher Torah study throughout the ages, there are no solid halakhic grounds for such exclusion.[8]

- Women are being trained as rabbinical advocates *(yoazot rabbaniot),* whose function is to help other women appearing before rabbinical courts.[9] The need for these advocates springs first and foremost from the awareness that rabbinical courts—which in Israel have exclusive jurisdiction over matters relating to matrimony—frequently treat women in a humiliating manner. The initiators of the concept of female rabbinical advocates had a twofold agenda: first, to reinforce the voice of women, who felt that they were being silenced and discriminated against in the rabbinical courts; second, to support them in halakhic negotiations and heighten their awareness of their rights according to halakhah. So far, approximately one hundred women, some of them active members of Kolech, have been trained as rabbinical advocates.

- The need for halakhic advice with regard to the specifically female and delicate topic of *niddah* (halakhic impurity, the ritual state of a woman during and after menstruation) has received new attention thanks to the training of women with Torah knowledge in the relevant laws *(yoazot niddah).*[10] Prior to the development of this position, women in need of a halakhic ruling on such matters have had to consult male rabbis, a matter of considerable discomfort and embarrassment. There is now a clear understanding that in this intimate area women will more readily seek advice from other women and that women themselves can provide authoritative halakhic answers to such questions.

- Nearly two decades ago, an Orthodox woman was appointed for the first time as a member of the religious council in the small development town of Yeruham. Religious councils are charged with providing religious services to the community, such as ritual baths, kashrut supervision, burial facilities, and the like. Until 1988, all members of religious councils were men, and the Orthodox establishment tried to maintain this position. However, thanks to the struggle of one Orthodox woman, Leah Shakdiel, the Israeli Supreme Court ruled in favor of female membership in religious councils. This was the first venture of a woman into a civic institution in charge of religious affairs.[11]

The Founding of Kolech

The formation of women's organizations, as distinct from the absorption of women into men's organizations, is perceived as an extremely effective strategy for the achievement of women's goals,[12] since it enables women to strengthen their own self-awareness and refrain from adopting masculine norms. As it happens, the initiative taken by Orthodox women toward the end of the twentieth century to organize with a view to ameliorating their second-class legal status in halakhah was not the first of its kind. In 1922, a group of Orthodox women in England, headed by Lizzie Hands, a learned woman, established the Council for the Amelioration of the Legal Status of the Jewess.[13] This organization quickly branched out to the Continent, and even to the United States, Canada, and Australia, and got together to fight for deserted wives *(agunot)*, women denied a *get* (halakhic divorce), and those needing release *(halitzah)* from Levirate marriage. But one of the main differences between this past endeavor and Kolech is the level of education of its women members. Due to the recent advances in women's learning, Kolech's learned women can propose new halakhic solutions and do not have to rely solely on male initiatives.

Orthodox women in Israel were also encouraged by developments in the United States. The example of the Jewish Orthodox Feminist Alliance (JOFA), founded in 1996, inspired a few dozen Orthodox women from Israel who were seeking a platform for a new initiative. One of the most important assets of the Israeli organization from its inception was its leader, Dr. Chana Kehat. Kehat was raised in a distinguished family of *haredi* (ultra-Orthodox) Torah scholars, and later became an Orthodox Zionist. She possesses extraordinary leadership qualities. Over and above her intellectual capabilities and her knowledge of halakhah and Jewish thought, she demonstrated tremendous sensitivity, perseverance, and dedication to the organization and its goals. A gifted speaker and mother of a large family, her personality captivated all those who met her. Representatives of the press frequently interviewed her, seeking and airing her views on a wide variety of topics affecting women and halakhah. The organization was virtually identified with her persona until she retired from it.[14]

The Overall Goals of Kolech

The name of the organization, Kolech: Religious Women's Forum, was chosen with the express intention of bringing the female voice to center stage, inspired by a verse from the Song of Songs: "Let me hear your voice, for your voice *[kolech]* is sweet."

Kolech was not created with a defined agenda. Even the crucial question—does it aim at achieving full egalitarianism for religious Jewish women?— has no simple answer. The organization's public goal is "adherence to halacha and gender equality."[15] It is questionable if Kolech's aim is fully attainable. The founders entertained the somewhat messianic hope that, in keeping with the religious belief in *tikun olam* (improvement of the world), women too can be part of this process through their spiritual contribution. In a lecture delivered at the First International Kolech Conference in 1999, the philosopher Yehuda Gelman cogently expressed the concept that equality of women "brings us toward the future realization of an absolute morality."[16] Gelman convincingly conveyed the sense that Kolech was not an organization with the sole purpose of improving the lot of women in Orthodox society; rather, she argued, its mission was to purify Judaism, to transform it from a situation of "temporary morality" (that is, a deficient world) to a situation of absolute morality (that is, a perfect world).

Kolech—From Theory to Practice

Kolech, the only egalitarian Orthodox women's organization in Israel, first attracted public attention with a series of pamphlets published under their organization name that discussed the weekly portion of the Torah reading. The novelty of these pamphlets was the fact that they were, for the most part, written and edited by women who voiced their thoughts on the weekly Torah portion, halakhic issues, homiletics, and various Torah subjects—topics that had not previously been within the purview of Orthodox women. It is true that the celebrated Bible teacher Nechama Leibowitz had published a weekly page on the Torah portion many decades earlier, but in contrast to Leibowitz's Torah interpretations, which were "gender blind," the articles published in Kolech placed the emphasis on women's interests. The innovative element of these pages was so obvious that it aroused the antagonism of the former Sephardi Chief Rabbi Mordechai Eliahu, who actually ruled that it was forbidden to read them.[17]

Kolech achieved its most impressive public presence in five international conferences, held in Jerusalem in 1999, 2001, 2003, 2005, and 2007, each attended by over a thousand active participants, mostly highly educated, professional women. Over the years, the fear that the feminist initiative would undermine the Orthodox framework has in some measure died down. The plenary sessions of

Kolech conferences have dealt prominently with women's social concerns and difficulties, such as *agunot* and sexual abuse, and the attitude toward abusers in Orthodox society. These questions have been deliberated on both theoretical and practical levels. The presentation of problems from a personal, emotional viewpoint, as well as on a theoretical level, was a most powerful demonstration of Kolech's role not just as an organization for academic deliberations, but also as a supporting arm for Orthodox women who, on the one hand, refuse to be silenced but, on the other, do not want to abandon their religious way of life.

Along with concern for the halakhic issues surrounding the role of women, an educational team was established to draw up curricula for different age groups, to teach girls and boys egalitarian concepts. Realizing that a most important channel toward equalizing relations between the sexes is through education, the members developed a number of educational programs for various age groups. Likewise, many other problems plaguing the Orthodox community, such as the large number of women who remain unmarried or marry late, point to the need for innovative education, to help young men and women maintain relationships in the new egalitarian society.

New initiatives in religious Orthodox circles point to the vibrance of these modern egalitarian concepts. The Gender Studies Program for MA/PhD at Bar Ilan University, founded in 2000, attracts over a hundred students and paves new roads in the study of feminism. The opening of congregation Shira Hadasha in Jerusalem in 2001 was an attempt to answer the growing need within the Orthodox community to reinterpret the place of women in the synagogue. Shira Hadasha tries to harmonize between halakhic obligations and women's religious needs. Its members want both men and women to have a meaningful role in the synagogue within a halakhic framework, including the right of women to read from the Torah and have an aliyah, all from their side of the *mechitzah* (the wall or screen separating the genders). The most controversial initiative of all was the foundation in 2005 of Bat-kol: The Religious Lesbian

Organization, which aims to allow women to embrace both their religious and lesbian identity.

Is an Orthodox Women's Revolution Possible?

Though the Orthodox women's revolution takes place in a unique society, its aim to establish a new social order is in some ways parallel to the suffragists' revolution, which aimed at not only getting the vote for women, but also at establishing a new egalitarian society.[18] Is the aspiration to create a new social order, to alter women's image and their status in religious society, a "mission impossible"? Perhaps the claim made by opponents of Kolech, that the Orthodox framework cannot be changed and at the same time preserved, is correct? Opposition to Kolech in the Orthodox community has not died down, and the expression "Hold back your voice" (an out-of-context quotation from the prophet Jeremiah) is heard more loudly than the verse "Let me hear your voice" (Song of Songs 2:14). Indeed, while the preliminary achievements of Kolech are promising, they are also disappointing. The most serious problems, such as relief for *agunot,* still await solutions. One wonders whether the slowness of the campaign is not an indication of the impossibility to achieve its goals.

Yet, progress has been made. Some rabbis agree to collaborate with Kolech in the fight against sexual harassment in Orthodox circles and in promoting the "Agreement for Mutual Respect,"[19] which is to be signed by a couple prior to their marriage in order to help prevent difficulties in obtaining a *get* in case of a divorce.

An analysis of the process of the radical changes that have taken place in the Israel Defense Forces (IDF) over the past decade may reveal strategies to achieve societal changes. The two major changes are the inclusion of women soldiers in combat fighting units, including as air force pilots, and the abolishment of the *Chen* (Women's Auxiliary Corps). Three factors brought about this change: first, a handful of women who untiringly demanded reform of the military system and were willing to lead the way; second, cooperation with part of the male sector (in this case, the judicial system); and third, social perceptions elsewhere (such as in the U.S. Army) as to the priority of egalitarian considerations in the military framework. A similar analysis of the efforts of Orthodox women reveals that the Orthodox women's revolution is also dependent on three conditions: first, women's accomplishments in Torah study and their subsequent demand for equality; second, close cooperation with at least some part of the male sector; and third, acceptance throughout the Western world of the principle of an egalitarian society.

Is it possible to define the correct strategy in order to achieve Kolech's goals? Will organization, loud protests, and publicity promote the desired goal, or should Kolech opt for nonthreatening but intensive behind-the-scenes activities? At first glance, the success of the Torah study centers for women (midrashot) might indicate that underplaying their importance is effective; inroads are being made slowly but surely. However, the status of women in the rabbinical courts is perhaps a counter-indication. The rabbinical advocates help women but are totally dependent on the rabbis who run the rabbinical courts. Cooperation with the system has brought only slight and slow results. Can conclusions be drawn from other struggles of women? Esther Yeivin, an active member of the Federation of Women for Equal Rights, founded in Eretz Israel in 1919, whose motto was "one law and one constitution for men and women in Israel," wrote in no uncertain terms: "In this battle [for voting rights for women in Eretz Israel] women have learned an important lesson, namely, that the solution of important problems cannot be postponed, and that one cannot depend on others, always remembering 'If I am not for myself who will be for me? and if not now, when?' (Avot 1:14)."[20]

Kolech's Impact on General Israeli Society

The Fourth International Conference of Kolech in June 2005 provides a good opportunity to try to evaluate its impact on Israeli society. The conference, which was held in Jerusalem and attracted well over one thousand participants (among them over 150 lecturers, some of them men), received coverage in the Israeli media. *Kolech* has become a household word in Israeli society. Feminist circles agree that Kolech is the most active group in Israel today advocating feminist aims within Jewish society. This view is usually the perspective of the secular segment of society. From the perspective of Orthodox Zionists, however, the picture is quite different. Although some important innovations had preceded the establishment of Kolech, the Orthodox Zionist public as a whole seems to see the women of Kolech as a threat to the fragile fabric of their society. Kolech's agenda—to make Orthodox patriarchal society egalitarian—is seen as pressing for a change that may undermine their very existence.

Nevertheless, a profound desire to adopt the new egalitarian ways of modern society is discernible, mainly among the younger generation of Orthodox Zionists, including a small group of rabbis. Kolech's existence lends important moral and practical support to Israelis who believe in combining the new, modern concepts with the old tradition. Kolech, and its vision of a halakhic, Orthodox feminism in Israel, empowers Orthodox men and women to believe in their ability to conduct new, democratic ways of life while adhering to their cherished traditions.

PART V

Gender, Sexuality, and Age

I ONCE HEARD Rabbi Yitz Greenberg remark, "It used to be that you would be born an Orthodox man in Brooklyn, and you would die an Orthodox man in Brooklyn. Today you can be born an Orthodox man in Brooklyn but die a Reform woman in Paris." I thought about how astute that comment was, and how much this reality has caused those in my generation pause and reflection. In the old days of feminism, we thought men were men, women were women, and we just needed equality between the two. We thought in binary. We thought in opposition. We thought feminism was about women's rights, women celebrating being women, biology as spiritual destiny, *Our Bodies, Ourselves*. My generation's feminism was introductory. It was about equal pay for equal work. It was about proving that we women could do anything a man did, and we would not be defined by men or "male" values. But we seemed to know what those "male" values were.

It certainly "pushed" my father's envelope of comfort to have to get his own fork when he sat down to dinner. It stretched my university's envelope of comfort to offer women's studies as a respected major. It pushed my rabbi's envelope to see women do more than light Shabbat candles on "his" bimah. But that was then, this is now. My own envelope has been stretched very far by a new generation of thinkers, and new words have entered my vocabulary: *grrls, transgender, intersex, transitioning.* The new generation of thinkers has taught us that feminism widens the conversation about gender altogether. What is a gender? What does being "feminine" or "masculine" mean anyway? Does our biological sex or the genitalia we were born with still define us?

I grew up at the edge of the sixties, when *revolution* was a household word and we were proud to buck any system we could. We would fight "the man" and we would win. And in many ways, we did win. So now who is "the man"? What if "the man" is now us? Young Jewish girls don't feel the need to buck the system anymore. They are comfortable with the battles we won for them and the gains they have as a result. The dragons they slay will be of their own choosing. They don't need—or want—consciousness-raising groups. How passé, how last century!

So, is there still work for us and them to do? Do they have the spunk and the guts needed to go the new distance? And do we of the "first" generation of Jewish feminists have the guts to let them pass us when they do?

Marla Brettschneider, PhD, is professor of political philosophy at the University of New Hampshire with a joint appointment in women's studies and political science. She is cofounder and past coordinator of the UNH queer studies program and currently serves as coordinator for women's studies. Her latest book is *The Family Flamboyant: Race Politics, Queer Families, Jewish Lives*. Other publications include: *The Narrow Bridge: Jewish Perspectives on Multiculturalism; Democratic Theorizing from the Margins;* and *Cornerstones of Peace: Jewish Identity Politics and Democratic Theory.*

Jewish Feminism, Sexuality, and a Sexual Justice Agenda

MARLA BRETTSCHNEIDER, PhD

JEWISH FEMINISM, as feisty and creative as it is, does not exist in a vacuum. It does its thing amid numerous constricting and productive trends, historical legacies, and any moment's current conditions. Jewish feminist developments in the area of sexuality have been shaped by multivalent discourses, including those regarding women, Jews, race, class, and sexuality that have been constraining, and related discourses that have seemed "progressive." In all, Jewish feminist engagement with sexuality in the last century has been quite active and intense, though it has not steered a straight course or been able to leave the "constraints" in the so-called dust bin of history.

A helpful entry point in discussing specifically U.S. Jewish women's and feminist engagements with sexuality is the national response to the mass of immigration from Europe at the turn of the century and the early part of the twentieth century. This focus on a defining moment for Eastern European Ashkenazi Jews is crucial to exposing how Jewish feminist sexual justice agendas are rooted and continue to be located—for all that is fabulous and all that is problematic—within this raced and culturally specific historical frame. Until we are better at naming the raced and classed nature of how we got to where we seem to be on the frontiers of feminist sexuality explorations, we will be limited in our work for sexual justice.

In response to millions of new immigrants on these shores in the early twentieth century, most fields of public and academic discourse were mobilized to respond to the "shock," "manage the problems," and plan for the future. Though the United States always had a lower economic class made up of various groups, and a fear of workers standing up against the tide of capitalist progress, the mass European immigration set the nation on edge in new ways. With more access to new technologies and faith in science, more pockets of "knowledge" could be brought together for an attempt at a systematic response to a human flood that "threatened" to wash out the shining qualities of our national character. The United States needed the people power and cheap labor of these new immigrants, but these people would also have to be housed and fed; they might be seen on the streets before or after work hours; they would need some degree of education for themselves and their children; and they would inevitably "multiply like rabbits," exponentially expanding the enormity of the threat they posed.

Turning to science, women's sexuality and reproductive habits became a focus of interest. When the IQ test was developed, minions of researchers went to a likely place, where they could gather a large data set from a relatively captive population: Ellis Island. Subjecting Jewish and other immigrants to newly developed IQ test experiments in English, researchers quickly proclaimed Jews, Poles, and most of the others in the data set "feebleminded." As this flawed research suggested such a high percentage of the feebleminded in these grouped populations, researchers quickly concluded that this feeblemindedness was genetic. This meant that not only did U.S. policy makers, health facilities, housing boards, and other legal venues have to confront what they perceived as the challenge of the masses of feebleminded Jews before them but—since the feebleminded were "infamous for reproducing"—plans had to be made with haste regarding the real threat of potential future generations of the "unfit."

Jewish women were targeted in plans of hygienic campaigns. Their cultural, domestic, sexual, and reproductive habits were studied, and reformers set out to (re)train them. Jewish women, among others, were likened to animals, and their habits were seen as "naturally primitive." Thus, the hope was that new scientific techniques could be utilized in their human training, and that the training would allow them to be included in the human family. For this, Jewish women needed education, guidebooks, carrot-and-stick incentives (which included many state-sanctioned severe punishments) to "learn" how to keep themselves and their homes, families, food, neighborhoods, and workplaces clean. Germ theory was still somewhat new, and reformers set about their project to save the populous from infection by "germs" all too easily spread by the new immigrants. Again, though many populations of the new immigrants faced similar fates, Jews bore a special burden for fighting their infectious habits, since the Polish, Italian, and Russian immigrants were, at the very least, Christian, and therefore less threatening (even if so many were Catholics).[1]

Eugenic discourse flourished in the effort to slow down the growth of this lascivious and infectious population, and to limit its effect on the national scene.[2] In similar ways, with sometimes differing motifs, Jewish men and women were seen as sexual perverts, prone to unnatural (yet innate) behaviors such as masturbation, lesbianism, excessive voluptuousness and desire, wanton procreativity, and irresponsible displays of affection of all sorts. The response by reformers was to constrain Jewish women's sexuality as much as they could. Jewish women disproportionately found themselves among the imprisoned, institutionalized, and the subjects of social worker reform. Their sexuality was seen as powerful and dangerous; they were more likely to be deemed hysterical and thus were "protectively" placed in the custody of the state, health "care," and criminal "justice" systems.

Yet, these eugenic trends also found a home among many Jews who participated widely in the dissemination of beliefs regarding, and cures for, these ills. For new Jewish immigrants, the idea of science as savior was persuasive. Social reformers did often appear to be able teach Jews much sought-after "modern" ways. No one in the immigrant community wished to be considered feebleminded and dangerous, but, rather, to be proper "Americans." Jews wanted to make a contribution to their new home and leave behind what was cast as the clannish, unclean, primitive ways of their ancestors in Europe. New, clean, shiny, healthy, educated, social reformers and their message seemed the antidote to the confines of patriarchal traditions, overbearing parents, and small-minded shtetl attitudes.

Many writers have discussed the ways that by mid-century the Jewish community, associated then with European immigrant roots, underwent a race- and class-based reassignment in the taxonomies of U.S. hierarchical thinking.[3] Doors stood somewhat more open for Jews to enter middle-class professions, and the perception of the community as a whole went from "other" and non-white to the possibility of "American" and white. Many Jews were cautious, as the costs of leaving behind aspects of what was Jewish in becoming "American" seemed great. At the same time, many wanted their second-class, suspect, and sexually and racially "other" status to end. A common U.S. mode for ending discrimination against "others" is to try to wash out what is "other" about them. Like our earlier twentieth-century feminist forebears, there was much that was appealing for Jewish women in this mid-century bargain.

It is not easy to resist the attraction of a potential rise in socioeconomic status, access to education, better housing opportunities, loss of a despised public image of one's group. Again, desires for freedom and things that suggest freedom brought many rather willingly into new versions of what might be considered a Faustian bargain. Freedom in the United States comes in a package resembling moneyed, white, Protestant people and cultural norms. Jewish, exotic, wild, alluring, Semitic sexuality (rooted in European anti-Semitism, a fiction as much a creation of "America" as it reflected anything about our actual experience) was slowly eclipsed by a fictive image of a whitewashed suburban housewife and the preparation of Jewish girls for such a "free" and "successful" future. Few actually can survive such whitewashing. Few can emerge seamlessly refigured. Not everyone accepted the bargain in the first place. Not everyone thought they even had a shot—if the class ladder seemed too crowded for them to climb, if their coloring was just not white enough, their body shape too Jewish to pass in good Christian company.

It was these tensions that created the conditions for more contemporary Jewish feminist explorations regarding sexuality. For some, assimilation in these ways was deemed neither possible nor desirable, and these women had to find alternate paths to freedom, self-esteem, and fulfillment. It is not a criticism to point out that these very aspirations placed these Jewish feminists firmly within the historical moment, moving onward from such mid-century developments mentioned above. The "mythic promise" offered to some groups in America of assimilation in America isn't just a gift; it is a kind of exchange. You are promised the goods but the bargain is that you have to give up quite a bit in return. Many were still caught in the winds of change and inspired by the hope of promises of freedom. What were some of the issues specifically? One significant arena was birth control. Jewish women had been primary targets in eugenic campaigns earlier in the century, before Nazis made *eugenics* such an explicitly nasty word. Many people deemed "progressive" social reformers were part of the eugenics movement. Margaret Sanger's work to create a movement for birth control was driven largely by eugenic conceptualizations, and she clearly allied herself with eugenic groups. At the same time—to the degree that new technologies might become available to change the inevitability of large families, the dangers and burdens of both pregnancy and childbirth without much agency—birth control was simultaneously appealing for many women. Jewish radical free love activists such as Emma Goldman participated in the new birth control movement precisely because it held promise for women's sexual freedom even as it was making headway in large part by people and ideas who sought to limit Jewish birthrates for eugenic purposes.

In each era, the early twentieth century, mid-twentieth century, and more contemporary times, we find Jewish women and feminist organizations at the forefront of reproductive rights campaigns as expressions of our insistence on sexual freedom. This work has two primary areas of focus: increasing access to limiting births, and increasing births. Usually, reproductive rights issues such as legalization, safety and choice in birth control, and abortion are in the camp to limit births. Sometimes the work to enhance safety, such as protection from sexually transmitted diseases, falls within larger movements to limit births or to enhance them. For example, some options for birth control, such as condoms, are also promoted as safe sex methods.

The mass movements in the United States for birth control and abortion have been criticized by some minority groups as taking over the agenda of the reproductive rights movement. Jewish women seemed to have turned the eugenic origins of birth control and abortion into apparently unproblematic matters of freedom and gender justice. The days of our being primarily targeted for forced sterilization, institutionalization, and sexual surveillance have been significantly slowed due to that mid-century racial and class reassignment. Other groups, such as Mexican American, Native American, and African American women have not lost their target status to the same degree as Jewish women, and thus a reproductive rights movement that focuses on the "right" to limit births remains unseemly. Many women still are targeted for forced-sterilization programs, disproportionately under state surveillance, and subject to punishment for their sexual lives and reproductive activity. Thus, diminished social justice work on these issues in the mainstream reproductive rights movement is seen as evidence of a callous collusion with continuing racist eugenic practices. Jewish feminists remain in the forefront of the mainstream reproductive rights movement. Many of us are proud of this. Simultaneously, many of us are also aware of the fraught history of the "right" to limit births, its base in raced and classed eugenic discourse, and are active in movements to end the continued practices of forced sterilizations. Many of us are proud of this as well. What is a recommendation for a future agenda here? Jewish feminists must work to bring together groundbreaking developments on both sides of reproductive rights work as part of a larger feminist vista of sexual justice.

In the past twenty years, however, our engagement in aspects of a movement not only to limit births but also to enhance fertility has been no less fraught. One branch of eugenics was called "positive" eugenics and focused on enabling populations deemed worthy to have more children and make the birthing process safer. Again, the dual nature of such work is evident: shouldn't all well-meaning people want to work for women's health, to ensure pregnancies are wanted, to enable safer pregnancies and births? There has been a fine line between highly problematic right-wing efforts and those of the "progressive reformists" in these arenas. Many times, the focus of these political groups is not women and the realization of their full humanity, but care for potential fetuses and the angelic "unborn."[4] Living women often lose out when ideas about fetuses and the rights of guiltless unborns are pitted against them. Many of the new reproductive technologies such as ultrasounds, genetic testing of people and fetuses, in vitro fertilization, and surrogacy have passed the "culture police" due to their ability to fit into and promote fundamentalist Christian anti-women agendas.

At the same time, Jewish doctors and scientists, and Jewish women as subjects, have again been in the lead on the research and use of these techniques. Damningly, these movements for the freedom to have children have somehow been divorced from the movements of other minority women to have children (such as the movement to end forced sterilizations and other moves to curb "overpopulation"). Again this development places Jewish feminist leadership in certain facets of the reproductive rights movement seemingly at odds with other women engaged in this social justice area. Plenty of work remains to be done on a reconfigured agenda where Jewish feminist organizations (which now have much organizational strength) can play a part in new frontiers for sexual and reproductive freedom.

One more example of the multilayered role of our historical routes to contemporary Jewish feminism in the area of family planning relates to adoption practices on a social justice/sexual justice agenda. Jewish women are involved at a slightly disproportionate level in adopting children and in adoption rights activism. Efforts to allow single women, older women, working-class women, women with some disabilities, and women outside the heterosexual norm to adopt children have spurred Jewish feminists to their historic activist selves. Included in this agenda has been the initiative to remove the ban on transracial adoptions, seen from that vantage point as a remnant of Jim Crow antimiscegenation racism. All of these aspects of adoption activism are figured as fair access issues, a conceptual framework with which liberal Jews are historically quite comfortable. The frame of fair access makes sense to a population that wanted access to the goods and bounty of a nation that thinks of itself as abounding in riches. Being denied access to the "goods" that the nation has to offer (in this case, children) is a marker of discrimination, and we Jewish feminists proudly put ourselves on the line against discrimination.

Similar to the other reproductive rights issues mentioned above, these aspects of the adoption rights campaign are hauntingly severed from parallel recognition and rights movements by those who, as communities, have not undergone reassignment from "other" to "member." A simultaneous movement exists to call attention to the fact that adoption policies focused on access in the ways named above gain ground at the direct expense of other minority and poor women.[5] The pool of children from which adults seek to gain access comes from somewhere. Easier access to adoption has been made possible by clearing a path toward certain forms of terminating parental rights. It is no coincidence that the groups disproportionately found among the early terminations are poor women, women of color, and women of developing nations, who in this example are generally not Jewish. The domestic growth of a prison-nation, with skyrocketing numbers of women in prison and on parole, has meant more children than ever before in the foster care system. The movement for adoption access has tried to move children from foster care to an adoption-available status with greater ease and swiftness. This also makes it far more difficult for poor women and women of color in the criminal justice and welfare systems to hold on to their parental rights to their children or to fight to keep their children in foster care and out of an adoption track. Again, options for future agendas for Jewish feminists abound, including closing the gap between these two social justice movements in which Jewish women play such central roles—as activists, lawyers, policy makers, researchers, social workers, community organizers, comrades, birth mothers, and potential adoptive mothers.

In all of this it remains fatally misleading to assume that the Jewish feminists involved are now "reassigned" and "are" white and middle class, whereas the "other" feminists are poor and people of color who are not Jewish. We are at a crossroads in Jewish feminism where we must recognize the politics and costs of the racial positioning of Jewish feminists who understand themselves and/or are often perceived as "white." Our image of our communal selves must come to include—and be transformed in the process—the millions of non-white/Ashkenazi/European-heritage Jews among us.[6] There is much Jewish multiracial and multiheritage engagement in feminist movements for sexual freedom, despite the fact that much of Jewish leadership (individually and institutionally) remains largely European-heritage/white. Jewish feminist leadership in certain aspects of work for sexual justice does not fully reflect the range of Jewish feminist experience and activist potential. We can work together to reshape the nature of our work in sexual justice movements in ways that also directly reflect how Jewish women of color face antifeminist and race-sexual profiling in the United States today.

Rabbi Jane Rachel Litman has served as the rabbi of Reform, Reconstructionist, Conservative, and Gay Outreach congregations, and has taught at the University of Judaism, California State University Northridge, and Loyola Marymount University. Rabbi Litman has consulted with the Metropolitan Community Churches, the National Conference of Christians and Jews, and the National Council of Churches on moral education for diverse families. She is the author of numerous articles and essays on feminism, creative liturgy, and contemporary theology. She edited the award-winning *Lifecycles, Volume 2: Jewish Women on Scripture in Contemporary Life* (Jewish Lights) with Rabbi Debra Orenstein.

If the Shoe Doesn't Fit, Examine the Soul

Jewish Feminism and Gender Expression

RABBI JANE RACHEL LITMAN

THIRTY YEARS AGO, feminist theorist Gloria Steinem rhetorically asked, "If the shoe doesn't fit, must we change the foot?" This rather graphic physical metaphor expressed Steinem's understanding of gender and gender roles. The "foot" in question was biological gender or sex, and the "shoe" represented social gender roles. Steinem's point conveyed mainstream feminist theory of the time, that gender roles needed to be expanded. Her remarks also critiqued the emerging option of transsexual "gender reassignment." Steinem believed that the answer to gender discontent was to transform social gender roles, a worthy goal, rather than medically change one's biological gender/sex.

However, Steinem's metaphor bears further analysis. For Steinem, there are two genders just as there are two feet. There's a left foot and a right foot, a male body and a female body, a left shoe and a right shoe, socially defined femininity and masculinity. For Steinem, transsexuality meant changing the foot to fit the shoe—that is, changing a male body to fit a feminine role or changing a female body to fit a masculine role. Since there were only two possible roles (albeit in need of expansion) and two possible genders, Steinem and many other feminists believed that the emerging transsexual movement was a reactionary strategy to medicalize (rather than politicize) gender, pathologize those who could not conform to prescribed gender roles, and undermine feminist efforts to expand possibilities for women. Given the long history of pseudoscientific attacks on women, and particularly on women who didn't conform to the feminine gender role, it's not so hard to see why Steinem opposed the very idea of transgenderism.

Steinem's understanding was based on then-current political theories of gender rather than actual contact with transgender people. In the intervening time, these abstract theories have not proven true on the ground. Rather than reifying traditional concepts of biological and social gender, transgender people have called into question the entire notion of binary human gender. Are there really only two feet and one pair of shoes? Perhaps there are hundreds of feet and thousands of shoes.

The underpinnings of gender category revolt were already existent in the days of Steinem's seventies feminism. The late-twentieth-century feminist movement found itself in a quandary about lesbian sexuality. Some mainstream feminists were loathe to take on the issue of gay rights, while the more radical lesbian wing of the movement declared that "feminism is the theory and lesbianism is the practice." Seventies feminist politics aside, lesbian sexuality, in and of itself, hints that all might not be perfect in the world of left and right feet. Lesbianism conceives that two left feet (or two right feet) might see themselves as a valid pair. Lesbian and gay male sexuality speak to the possibility of a nonconforming nature of sexual attraction. If right feet don't automatically go with left feet, what is the meaning of binary feet? Who really needs two left feet? Might one foot or three feet be equally useful?

Radical lesbian feminists argued that binary male-female power inequities were inherent in heterosexual family structures. In their view, liberation from heterosexual sexual identity was the ultimate expression of liberation from constricting gender roles and female oppression. According to lesbian separatist theory, and to rephrase the then-popular bumper sticker, a left foot (a woman) without a right foot (a man) is "like a fish without a bicycle."

In its critique of male-female power dynamics, political lesbianism expressed considerable unease with the butch (masculine) and fem (feminine) gender roles that had been a cultural facet of earlier lesbian life. Seventies political lesbians claimed that such roles recreated male-female power inequities within feminist circles. However, this critique ironically called into question the very idea that there are only two genders. If a political lesbian was neither masculine nor feminine, perhaps then she was not a foot at all, but some different organ altogether? The very insistence on lack of complementary binary gender roles, even among lesbian women, perforce created new gender possibilities.

In addition, seventies political lesbianism also implied that it is possible, in essence, to convert sexual identities, for a formerly heterosexually identified woman to consciously choose a lesbian sexual identity. Feminist bisexual theory of the eighties explicitly voiced this idea. Bisexual writers explored the unfixed nature of sexual attraction. In their view, a left foot could pair with either a right foot or a left foot as a choice. Most bisexual feminists explained that there was nothing "bi" about their sexuality, that they were attracted to individual people rather than specifically gendered partners, either of the same or opposite sex. This ideology could require an entire wardrobe of new shoes, needing a veritable Emelda Marcos–sized closet of sexual identities. Just as seventies lesbian feminism called the male-female dyad into question, so eighties bisexual feminism called into question fixed sexual categories altogether. If a person could be attracted to both men and women, masculinity and femininity, or something in between, the rigid walls of oppositional pairing would rapidly crumble.

By the nineties, the politics of the feminist movement changed. The movement worked to broaden itself and become more inclusive. That meant taking in a more wide-ranging world of feminists, including feminists of color, women making more traditional life choices, butch/fem lesbians, and feminist men. As the feminist movement broadened its base, it also changed its goals. Seventies feminism was about analyzing the oppression of and achieving more rights for women. Nineties feminism began to link oppressions based on class, sexual identity, age, race, physical appearance, and ability with the oppression of women. This analysis of interlocking power imbalances brought forth a more comprehensive political agenda.

The politics of the gay and lesbian rights movement also changed. Like feminists, lesbian and gay rights groups became more inclusive. Organizational names changed to reflect this new inclusivity, as formerly gay and lesbian groups redefined themselves as LGBT (lesbian, gay, bisexual, and transgender) or just "queer." As the transsexual movement evolved, its politics changed as well. The early movement was heavily anchored in surgery, medical interventions, and psychiatric theory. Some transsexual people fulfilled feminist fears of reinforcing gender stereotypes. However, over time, the movement became more about authenticity, integrity, and personal sovereignty than fulfilling external definitions of gender. As transpeople came together for social and political support, their goals and language developed in a quest for gender freedom, not gender conformity.

In addition, the growing transgender political movement served to heighten awareness for intersex people. Medical ethicists began to question the practice of surgically and hormonally pushing intersex children into male or female biological sex and social gender. Ironically, this position upheld Steinem's original point, that the misfitting foot needn't be altered. However, gender reformers came at the issue from a different perspective—not from the view of content, but of methodology. Both transgender and intersex activists promoted the idea of personal sovereignty and choice. That is, they believed that people who don't want to choose one gender (or are too young to decide) should not be medically confined in a gender, but people who so desire should have the opportunity to shape and reshape their body—and their cultural gender status—as they wish.

Transgender emergence created new thinking about sexuality. Theorists sought to define and explain the confluence of sexuality and gender, which, in the closet of left and right shoes, is taken for granted. Heterosexuality is an unspoken norm that requires two unexamined opposite genders. Gay and lesbian sexuality obviously do not require two genders, and in practice both the gay and lesbian communities tolerate a fairly wide expression of gender, at least compared to the mainstream world. Bisexual people show that sexual identity can be fluid and not based in gender. Transpeople show that gender identity can be fluid and tied to a range of sexual identities. In our day, much of the complexity of gender and sexuality is yet to be explored.

Throughout the nineties, feminists Talmudically debated the status of transpeople, gender, and sexual identity. Over the years, feminist institutions and organizations (with a few notable exceptions) came to the conclusion that inclusion was better than exclusion. Twenty-first-century feminists and queer activists are more likely to believe that gender expression is a matter of personal integrity, and that justice and feminist values are ultimately served through supporting a broad spectrum of gender expression, both biological and social. Not only is it okay to change misfitting shoes, but it's also good to change misfitting feet, to go barefoot, to ride a scooter, and to question the aptness of the analogy of gender and feet.

The discussion taking place in the larger society about gender categories impacts the cultural, religious, and political life of the Jewish community. Like that of the larger society, the Jewish feminist movement of the seventies and eighties had its mainstream and radical wings, often (though not always) divided along the lines of sexuality. In addition, concerns about gender status have religious overtones in Jewish practice, since a number of observances are traditionally divided into male and female gender categories.

It is therefore interesting to note that traditional Jewish religious literature is comfortable with naming varieties of gender identity. The Talmud (throughout, and especially in Yevamot), Mishnah, and Tosefta (Bikkurim) explore varieties of nonbinary sex/gender identity. The study of these Talmudic texts on gender identity has become a trend among Jewish feminist, gay rights, and trans scholars and activists. The scholarly mission of understanding the world of the past is often fraught with projections from the present, and in this case, contemporary expositors simply do not agree on some basic assumptions of these texts.

Rabbinic literature conceives of at least four (and perhaps as many as six or seven) "genders," with specific characteristics and legal rights and disabilities. Two of these "genders" are male and female, but the others have no obvious English equivalents. It is tempting to wonder if—like the Eskimo language's multiple ways of describing snow—the Talmudic linguistic richness in regard to gender indicated something about contemporaneous Jewish culture. The rabbinic texts discuss gender in relation to biological conditions such as menstruation and genital emissions. They also explicate gender in relation to the gender of the marital partner (what we might call sexuality), religious duties, and inheritance rights.

It is not entirely clear if in the other gender categories the Talmud describes only individuals who are biologically/genetically neither male nor female, or if it also discusses those of variant social gender status, people who might currently be called butch or fem. *Tum-tum*, the Rabbinic Hebrew term for "androgyne," may deal with those who our society describes as "intersex," or may describe people who don't fit male and female heterosexual identities. It could also refer to people who do not fit societal gender roles or reference some mix of all of the above. One thing is clear: the Talmud's gender categories differ from those of contemporary society.

There simply isn't a consensus about what the texts mean, even about whether their intent is to diversify the binary gender assumption or to reinforce the binary gender through naming and disciplining unruly variant forms. It is true that the Rabbinic method is usually hostile to ambiguities, however although multiple genders represent ambiguity in our culture, such might not have been the case in the world of the Rabbis. It fact, the Talmudic text itself quotes Rabbi Yose as saying, "An androgyne, he is a case unto herself, and the Sages could not decide whether it is a man or a woman" (Mishnah Bikkurim 5:11).

In the days of the Talmud and ever since, Jewish conceptions of gender have been located in a context of family, community, culture, and history. Jews tend to be tied to their families and communities as a cultural value. Many modern-day non-Jewish gender revolutionaries cut ties with their unsupportive families to pursue their own expressive paths. In past times, Jewish political rebels did the same, but today's Jewish gender rebels are more likely to want to keep some connection with the Jewish community and their families. Transgender writer Kate Bornstein movingly describes her return to her large extended Jewish family and community at her mother's funeral. The baffled responses of those in attendance became secondary to the religious and communal task of mourning.

Historical Jewish expressions of gender do not match those of secular Western civilization. For centuries, the idealized gender expression for a Jewish man was a life of study, and the idealized gender expression for a Jewish woman was a managerial role. To return to the shoe analogy, if the gender expectations of mainstream society are Nikes and open-toe high-heeled sandals, then Jewish gender roles are scuffed loafers and sensible low-heeled walkers. Faced with this contradiction, contemporary Jews express gender in relation to both Jewish tradition and the norms of secular society.

The late-twentieth-century Jewish feminist movement, like its secular counterpart, was primarily concerned with analyzing women's oppression and creating new opportunities for Jewish women, both religiously and communally. This often translated into support for a single androgynous gender category or the elimination of religiously based gender altogether. For Jewish feminists, achieving milestones such as the rabbinic ordination of women, new liturgies about women's life experience, and the affirmation of same-sex/gender unions or marriages by the liberal denominations have created a new climate.

Jewish feminists of the twenty-first century are less reactive and more introspective, searching for a Jewish theology of revisioned gender expression and gender roles that focuses on authenticity rather than simplistic categories. Even in the face of considerable antifemale and antifeminist backlash in both the secular and the organized Jewish world, Jewish feminists are understanding gender in new ways. As in the larger secular society, Jewish feminists are making the links between forms of oppression. Gender expression is interwoven with class, race, age, sexual identity, physical form, and—as Jews are particularly aware—religious culture. It can change over time, and is both internally motivated and culturally significant. It is both biological and social.

Gender expression touches on a wide variety of human and Jewish endeavor. It can be about hormones and hair, about clothing, about sexual identity, about accent and employment, about prayer practice and spiritual aspirations, about inchoate inner sensibilities. What exactly is a woman? What exactly is a man? What is an androgyne or a *tum tum*? Are there other possibilities? What are they? Today we realize that the subject in question isn't about the nature of the shoe or the foot, but rather of the soul.

Beth Cooper Benjamin, EdD, is a senior associate at Ma'yan: The Jewish Women's Project, a program of the JCC in Manhattan. She has worked extensively with single-sex programs for girls, as a researcher, a practitioner, and a consultant. She received her doctorate in human development and psychology from the Harvard Graduate School of Education, where her work examined the topic of girls' leadership and the intersection of femininity and social class privilege.

Jodie Gordon is a senior associate at Ma'yan: The Jewish Women's Project, a program of the JCC in Manhattan. A graduate of Brandeis University, she has over ten years of experience working with Jewish teens and young adults in a range of both pluralistic and Reform organizations. Jodie currently resides in Brooklyn, where she is active in the Jewish community.

Koach Banot (Girl Power)[1]

Talking Feminism with Jewish Teen Girls

BETH COOPER BENJAMIN, EdD, AND JODIE GORDON

JANUARY 15, 2008: In the back corner of a fluorescent-lit basement classroom at the Jewish Community Center (JCC) in Manhattan, two women and three teenage girls are arranged in a loose circle on the floor. Originally set up for small children, the room is filled with child-sized chairs upturned on squat, rectangular tables, and now atop the chairs rest a variety of cast-off backpacks and winter coats. Around the circle of bodies there are plates piled with pizza and salad, cups of soda and water, and assorted shoes and cell phones; at the center is a digital voice recorder, silently logging.

These five have gathered this evening to discuss the *other* F-word: *feminism*. And more specifically, Jewish feminism. The girls—Tamar, Natasha, and Rachel—have just wrapped up an eight-month research training internship with Ma'yan: The Jewish Women's Project, facilitated by the authors of this chapter. In addressing young women's perspectives on Jewish feminism, we decided that even we ourselves, in our late twenties (Jodie) and early thirties (Beth), simply weren't young enough to be reliable witnesses. In their internship, however, these girls had spent much of the past year studying their peer group—American Jewish teen girls—and their identities and interests as Jews and as young women. Theirs, we had already discovered, are voices worth listening to.

The method for this chapter is based on an innovative piece of feminist qualitative research: an article published in 1992 titled, "Over Dinner: Feminism and Adolescent Female Bodies," written by the social psychologist Michelle Fine and her colleague Pat Macpherson.[2] Curious about young women's relationships with and attitudes toward feminism, the authors invited a small group of girls from various backgrounds to join them for a series of informal dinner discussions. These discussions illuminated the gendered issues and assumptions shaping the adolescent girls' lives and identities, but they also challenged the authors' own assumptions about what feminism is and is not. In re-creating this scenario, we sought to gain some similar perspective: learning how feminism is understood and embodied by Jewish girls today, and learning something about our own unexamined beliefs as well. In this regard, the project did not disappoint.

Energetic and highly principled, Tamar is a junior at an all-girls yeshiva day school (which, she is quick to mention, teaches Gemara and Torah), and has lived her whole life on the Upper West Side of Manhattan. The eldest of five girls, Tamar comes from a tight-knit Orthodox family. She is the only one among the group who self-identifies as a feminist. Natasha carries herself with a grace that belies her young age. A sophomore in high school, she has attended the same private school in the Bronx (where she also resides) since kindergarten. Natasha's family belongs to a renowned Reform congregation on the Upper West Side, and they have been instrumental leaders at the JCC in Manhattan. Rachel's enthusiasm and intelligence shine in her eyes, and though she speaks quietly, her insights command attention. Rachel had the longest commute to our meetings, coming from her home in a middle-class suburb on Long Island, where she lives with her parents and her twin brother. An athlete and an avid reader in the eleventh grade, she is active in her Reform synagogue.

Living Feminism

It has been said that there are as many feminisms as there are feminists. While this multiplicity makes for a rich and diverse movement, it also makes clarity and common agreement difficult. As we were interested in considering how the girls' lives and beliefs reflect and embody (or resist and reject) feminism, it seemed important to clarify how we ourselves relate to feminism. Beth can't remember a time when she did not consider herself a feminist. She was raised by a feminist mom who gave her choices (milk or apple juice? pants or a skirt?) so that she would learn she has a right to ask for what she wants. Growing up in Rochester, New York, home of Susan B. Anthony, she was surrounded by American feminist history, and she counts in her own lineage a remarkable Jewish feminist: the garment industry union organizer and author Rose Pesotta. For Jodie, the journey to developing a feminist identity was traveled with a family who let her find the path herself. Jodie's mother had grown up with strong messages about what "girls didn't do," which in her family, included going to college. And so, from a very young age, Jodie was shown the world through a series of wide-open doors. Jodie grew up with the sense that if she couldn't do something, it was because she hadn't tried—not because she wasn't allowed. The granddaughter of a Columbia University alumna and founding editor of *Soap Opera Digest* magazine, Jodie remembers many of her first feminist messages coming from her grandparents.

In their ambition and their expectation of high achievement, Tamar, Natasha, and Rachel are living proof of feminism's impact. They are already accomplished athletes, performing artists, and activists. They are deeply engaged in Jewish communal life, both spiritually and socially. Sounding much like the (largely affluent and white) "alpha girls" characterized by the psychologist Dan Kindlon,[3] they dream big, and they foresee no structural or cultural barriers to their success. Natasha, for one, dreams of a career as a chef; last summer she talked her way into an internship in the kitchen of one of the finest restaurants in the city. Rachel's expectation of personal achievement admits no constraint. As she puts it, "I feel like if there's something standing in my way, then I'm gonna find a way around it." These girls seem to take as an article of faith that they are entitled to equal treatment and equal opportunity.

Other evidence of the girls' lived feminism emerges in the sophistication of their social criticism. Keen interpreters of the world around them, the girls are quick to name bias where they see it … even if they don't always see it affecting them directly. When the conversation turns to subtle gender bias (as opposed to structural inequality), Natasha mentions an article she's just read profiling the former child television star Danica McKellar, now an accomplished mathematician, who has written a book designed to make math less intimidating for young women. Though Natasha finds the idea admirable, she is offended by the implicit sexism she finds pervading the book, which in her words tells young women, "You should know how to do division because you can tip your manicurist." A hot topic of conversation in the group, based on the research they did as Ma'yan research training interns, is the JAP (Jewish American Princess) stereotype. Tamar has taken a special interest in examining the JAP issue. She argues that even though many respondents in the girls' survey didn't associate JAP with Jewish girls in particular, it is still a form of anti-Semitism: at the end of the day, the stereotype plays on and reinforces narrow ideas of Jewish womanhood.

Though all three girls have become bat mitzvah (another obvious way their lives have been touched by Jewish feminism), their experiences are quite distinct. For Tamar, as an Orthodox woman, the opportunity to read from Torah, and to stand alongside her mother and great aunt on the bimah was powerful. Natasha recalls making the choice to become bat mitzvah with the rabbi she felt most connected to, though it meant not having her service in her synagogue's main sanctuary. Rachel's bat mitzvah was billed in her invitation as a "double-header," an exercise in compromise as she and her twin brother reconciled a part formal, part sports-based celebration that reflected their distinct personalities. But questions about the intention of the bat mitzvah experience set our conversation rolling. Tamar, to our surprise, announces that she regrets holding the party that followed her service, and she has concluded that twelve or thirteen is simply too young to become bat mitzvah:

> I just wasn't a real person [then] ... now, I really am much more confident, and aware of who I am as a Jew.... [If we were to become bat mitzvah at age sixteen] I would just be constantly thinking about what it actually means to take on this whole new role, and how I could have this chance to decide which role I want to take.

Knowing Feminism: The F-Word Cometh

As practitioners working with adolescent girls, we expected that the word *feminist* would bring up a complicated set of reactions, ranging from allegiance to ambivalence to negativity. As feminists ourselves, with a deep stake in the perception of the word and the future of the movement, making room for the girls' reactions and opinions around the "F-word" was a real challenge. Fine and Macpherson describe this experience in their own discussions with girls:

The re-vision that is central to feminist process gets very tricky when applied to adolescence, because our own unsatisfactory pasts return as the "before" picture, demanding that the "after" picture of current adolescent females measure all the gains of the women's movement. Our longing is for psychic as well as political completion.[4]

Watching the girls wrestle with the social stigma of the feminist label, observing the absence of collective political consciousness or awareness of how their own fates and choices are constrained—in Judaism and American society alike—by living in female bodies, we struggled to bite our tongues. We were committed to the "re-vision" of feminist process that Fine and Macpherson describe, and in order to learn from these girls, we had to get past our impulse to dismiss their resistance to feminism as naive and uninformed, to resist our urge to make them over in our own image.

Rachel: I wouldn't call myself a feminist, but I definitely see what Tamar says, and why shouldn't women be considered equal to men in those kinds of aspects. But, for me, I guess it's kind of different cuz I'm Reform.... If there is something that's traditionally not for women, I kind of just do it, and ... I haven't really been shut down. But I'm not, like, active, so that's why I wouldn't call myself a feminist. And I'm not going out and rallying for the rights of women, like as a whole but, if there's something that I wanna do, then I'm just going to do it, in some way that I can.... I'm not gonna cause an uproar for something that I don't feel is as important or pertaining to me. I know that kinda sounds selfish.

For Rachel, feminism at its most basic means a belief that men and women should be treated equally. In that regard, she recognizes herself as benefiting from a legacy of feminist action within the

Reform movement. But with such a sense of open opportunity it's hard for her to see how feminism today might be "important or pertaining to me." When Beth draws the girls' attention to how the word itself is viewed, Rachel recalls a teacher who was "a complete feminist," and how her strident identification made Rachel and her classmates uncomfortable:

> **Rachel:** If [you] walked up to her and asked her, "What are you?" she'd say, "I'm a feminist, nice to meet you."… She was just always preaching and that almost gave the word *feminist* a negative connotation to me…. I remember saying something about feminism to one of my guy friends and they were, like, "Oh, are you just one of those feminist, crazy people or something?" And I'd be, like, "No! I'm not a feminist!"

In the absence of structural barriers and visible gender bias, and in the face of social stigma, Rachel has plenty of reasons not to take on this particular mantle.

> **Natasha:** I've never really been faced with being discriminated against because I'm a woman. Um, because I've grown up in really liberal circles. But, like, to hear the experience of feeling like a second-class citizen really angers me, and I'd love to do something about it. I mean, on many things … in the wide scope of feminism and women's rights—right?… Like, I went to Washington and marched for the woman's right to choose…. But I don't know. I don't think that if someone asked me to identify as a feminist, I would. Like, maybe I am feminist, but I don't admit that I am [laughing]. I feel like I have the mentality of a feminist, but I wouldn't coin [*sic*] myself as a feminist.

> **Beth:** So then the obvious question is, why not?

Natasha: I haven't really thought about it that much. I just—it's just not something that would—if I were to describe myself with twenty adjectives, it just wouldn't pop into my head. It's sort of like second nature for me; so many of the ideas that feminists are fighting for, I think, have been handed to me. Which is very selfish. Again, I probably should think about how my world is very, like, insular, and different from the rest of the world—but, um, it hasn't ever been necessary for me to define myself as a feminist.

Natasha's commitment to women's rights is, to her, self-evident ("second nature to me"), the byproduct of growing up in "really liberal circles." Yet she openly admits her reluctance to take on the label of feminist. Though she tries to decouple the two—feminism and women's rights—as she speaks, she herself grows increasingly critical of this stance. Listening to her, it became more and more difficult to classify Natasha's relationship to feminism. Notably, Natasha is keenly aware of how her own insularity and privilege (though compared to what, or whom, she does not say) have contributed to her lack of identification as a feminist, stating that "it hasn't ever been necessary" for her to take such a stand.

It is interesting that both Rachel and Natasha describe their rejection of the feminist label as "selfish," a self-recrimination that reminded us of the feminine expectation for self-sacrifice and serving the needs of others. It is selfish not to be a feminist, they seem to suggest, because it is *a failure of care* for those others whose lives are directly affected by gender inequity. In a frustrating perpetuation of women's caretaking role, the girls imply that claiming feminism on behalf of other women is a more honorable position than claiming it for their own benefit. In this view, in fact, the girls suggest that their privilege, be it liberal, economic, Reform, or American, renders feminism needless in their own lives.

> **Tamar:** I just feel like women are equal to men, and we have just as much the power to do anything that we could do, just as well as they can. And ... I don't know, I feel like women are put down a lot, just like, they aren't given a lot of opportunity. In Judaism also. Like they don't count, in the Orthodox daily life, like a minyan, they can't count as a witness ... just a lot of things that as I learn them, really bother me. Cuz why, how are we any less of a person?

Tamar, who even in her internship application identified as a feminist, speaks with an intensity that conveys the excitement she feels in claiming her place as a Jewish woman. With the support of her family, Tamar has availed herself of opportunities that most young Orthodox women never see. Having led services at her bat mitzvah in an all-women's prayer group, and having her father, a rabbi, observe from a distance, Tamar has an appreciation for her rights and responsibilities as a Jewish woman that is distinct from her peers'. The stake, for her, is personal, as she describes herself simultaneously as the beneficiary of Orthodox feminism and as an active participant in an ongoing movement toward equality for Jewish women.

Tamar alone describes being personally affected by gender bias, and attests to the pride and solidarity she has gained from her work with other Orthodox women:

> **Tamar:** We made a women's [prayer group], that's only with women, so that empowers us, because then we run it ourselves, whereas in the main shul we sit in the balcony and no one *davens* [prays] and everyone just talks.... [When] we're in [this group], it's just much more meaningful, just the women *davening*. It's just, like—you want to have a part.

Recognizing the spiritual costs of inequality, Tamar's feminism is both a legacy and a living enterprise. It is a conviction of equality and a commitment to working in pursuit of justice. At the same time, she seems to struggle when articulating how she reconciles feminist equality with the gendered divisions of Orthodoxy:

> **Tamar:** For Orthodoxy, at least, we accept that we each have our different rules, and that's fine, people just have different things that they need to do ... and they're just as important as each other ... just as long as the other one that's not doing the thing isn't meanly put aside. Like, it doesn't really happen with this kind of thing, but you wouldn't be, like, "You can't be in the room when I light the candles." You know what I mean? Like, we don't discriminate against them when we're doing our thing.

Curious where the girls' ideas about feminism came from, we asked if they thought their parents would identify as feminists. For Tamar, not surprisingly, the answer is a resounding "Yes." Feminism is openly discussed and highly valued in her family, with emphasis on expanding the role of women in Orthodoxy. Rachel and Natasha, meanwhile, seem unsure of the answer—*feminism* doesn't appear to be a term much used in their families. Instead, they reason out the question based on the evidence they see. For Rachel, though she doesn't think her parents would identify with the term *feminist*, does see evidence of feminism in their politics and the pleasure her mother derives from connections to other women: "I think they're liberal enough to support feminism—and I think my mom would identify with it before my dad would, because we go to this women's Seder at my temple and she loves it.... She loved being identified as a woman and having some kind of connection." Like Rachel, Natasha finds it easier to imagine her mother as a feminist than her father (suggesting that these girls see feminism as a movement for and largely relevant to women), but she questions this logic when she remembers her father attending Ma'yan's feminist Seders.

Generational Issues and the Future of Jewish Feminism

Along with femininity and Judaism, woven through the girls' language and their ideas is another often invisible influence: social class privilege. From their ambivalence about elaborate bat mitzvah celebrations to their ambitious professional goals to the impression—for the non-Orthodox girls—that the Reform movement and their own insular privilege has rendered feminism unnecessary, affluence intersects with gender and Judaism in shaping their worldviews. Indeed, Rachel and Natasha are correct when they suggest that their class advantages render gender bias more difficult to see in their daily lives (the structural inequities that persist in Orthodox Judaism help make it easier for Tamar to recognize bias). In a surprising inversion of previous critiques of American feminism as a privileged white women's movement, Rachel and Natasha instead see its utility largely as addressing gross inequalities in less "liberal," and presumably less economically privileged contexts.

Growing up in an era during which "girl power" has become a tool of mass marketing, the girls seemed to wrestle with the issue of choice.

> **Natasha:** I think the real problem in feminism … if someone doesn't want to make the choice to be a home-builder [sic] and stay-at-home with their children, and maybe not have a job while their children are young, I don't think that person should be disdained…. Everyone should have the right to … lead their life in the way they want to, as long as it's lawful or whatever.

All three girls similarly were troubled by their impression that in the pursuit of equality, feminism winds up turning women into men, or suggesting that feminist equality requires the eradication of any acknowledgment of gender difference. Like Judy Chicago's *Dinner Party*, or more recently, the third-wave feminist movement to reclaim women's traditional crafts,[5] or even Jewish feminism's reclaiming of the Rosh Chodesh (New Moon) observance, there is a strong tradition within contemporary feminist movements of reclaiming and honoring women's traditional spaces and skills. Yet the girls seem unsure about how legitimate this option is actually considered; as Tamar states, "When it [feminism] first started, it was like they looked down on anybody who was a homemaker … cuz it was, like, 'How dare you put yourself down?'… But it's more level-headed now. We don't want to be men. We just want equal opportunities. We want to be just as much women as anything."

Here, again, we wonder if class privilege is playing the silent partner in the girls' debate. These girls are growing up in a context of intense pressure to excel academically, where high school is seen largely as the gateway to an elite university.[6] Perhaps, we wonder, their desire to validate women's traditional role as homemaker is a form of resistance against the achievement pressures they feel from their families and communities. When the Ivy League and a law degree are the ultimate goal, we can imagine that a girl might yearn to be supported in choosing to "opt-out."

Listening to these girls speak about feminism, we sense that this generation has created a new vocabulary for describing and understanding their identity—both Jewishly and secularly. While their occasional lack of appreciation for the hard-earned gains of their mothers and grandmothers was frustrating to hear, we also heard a very distinct opportunity. This generation has seen women on the bimah, the women's Seder is an established family tradition, and they seek new ways of understanding their role as Jewish women. Thus, in many ways, this generation is poised to revitalize and reenergize American Jewish life like none before. They are technologically savvy social entrepreneurs who have been raised to reach for their goals and hold on tightly with both hands. Dr. Jonathan Sarna, professor of American Jewish history at Brandeis University, points out that, in fact, some of the most creative ideas for revitalizing Judaism have always come from the bottom up—or from those who exist on the periphery.[7] Jewish youth have marked Jewish history with innovation, and with thoughtful repurposing of Jewish ritual and celebration. Throughout contemporary Jewish history, we have watched traditional notions of belonging, identity, and practice be challenged and redefined by those who existed outside the boundaries of traditional Jewish power structures.

It is important to locate this discussion and these girls in the broader context of contemporary American Judaism. As Sarna points out, we are seeing a strong return to secularism in modern Jewish life. Jewish innovators are finding ways to create significant cultural ties for young Jews that do not rely on traditional notions of ritual and practice. These organizations tie Jewish values with global action, resulting in opportunities for the formerly disenfranchised populations of "unaffiliated" young Jews to find a community in line with their personal values. This is not to say that the institutional pillars of our communities will become disused monoliths to this generation; rather, it is these very institutions that can cradle and nourish the visions that these young women describe for the future.

For Tamar, the future is something she has already begun to carefully consider; she has given much thought to how she intends to raise her children. Her religious conviction plays a strong role in deciding what path she will take, which she describes as her own "evolution." She envisions a future rich with Jewish tradition, balanced with an open mind and open heart toward who her children choose to become. For Rachel, a tentative toe dipped into the well of Jewish spirituality (in the context of a peer-led havdalah service) proved to be a very positive experience. Rachel represents more than the sum of her Jewish communal parts: she has just begun to notice the various options available to her that transcend her notion of what it means to be Jewish (a notion rife with stereotypical visions of strict adherence to meaningless ritual). For each of these girls, the message is clear: the pathways into adult Jewish life must remain wide enough to accommodate their constantly evolving sense of self and Jewish identity.

As Anna Greenberg writes, Jewish students are personalizing their individual form of Jewishness, ordering a "Grande Soy Vanilla Latte with Cinnamon, No Foam"[8] from among an infinite set of ethnic and religious options. This lack of boundaries in ascribing traditional notions of belief and identity extends to the way in which Natasha, Tamar, and Rachel view their relationship to feminism. The surge in young, Jewish "out-of-the-box" organizations, or independent minyanim, reflects a very important trend. Young Jews are connecting with independent and informal organizations rather than seeking out formal religious ties. These communities provide customized experiences that represent the mark of this millennial generation: they are seeking spiritual and interpersonal connections in an environment that validates their varying and ever-changing identities.

Our conversation with these young Jewish women indicates that their Ma'yan internship experience has become a springboard for their own self-reflection. Although taking the girls' voices and viewpoints seriously proved deeply challenging to our own sense of ourselves as feminists, we were also thrilled to recognize a familiar process unfolding during this evening's discussion: good old-fashioned feminist consciousness-raising. As facilitators, our job was to remain probing and objective; as mentors and as women, older enough to feel a sense of protectiveness and a desire to *teach*, we often found ourselves tempted to react, rather than respond. And as we worked to hold this tension—sometimes staying silent, sometimes challenging their thinking or revealing our own beliefs—we witnessed moments of transformation that suggest to us a great opportunity for Jewish feminist intervention with the next generation. By drawing the girls' attention to the word *feminist* instead of what feminism is, for instance, we enabled them to distinguish between feminism as a movement and an ideology and their own distaste for its negative reputation. With this, they were able to question their own reluctance to identify with a movement whose goals and objectives they found largely agreeable, even important. In fact, the mere occasion of our convening this discussion let the girls know that we, whom they have come to trust and admire, feel the topic is important. If this weren't enough to convince us that Jewish teen girls might be open and responsive to such feminist conscious-ness-raising, we will close with Rachel's final thoughts—the message she wanted to be sure we would convey to Jewish feminists:

> Girls our age and coming up, I feel like education is so important. I think we're getting that a lot more, as we move forward.... Just keep educating people about what you believe, because that helps so much. Because this stuff has ... especially the feminism word is so scary to so many people that those generalizations can just grow. As long as people are more familiar with it, that'll definitely stop, and there are so many people that are open to learning ... about things like that, to make things less scary.... And, just, that teenagers are willing to learn, and we're not totally closed off to anything you have to say.

The conversation is needed, but as far as Rachel, Tamar, and Natasha are concerned, the door is wide open.

Rahel Lerner is a freelance editor and writer. She has a BA in comparative literature from Columbia University, and has worked for publishers including Farrar, Straus and Giroux, Pantheon and Schocken Books, Random House, and Stewart, Tabori and Chang. She is also an editorial consultant for *Nextbook* and a frequent contributor to *Lilith* magazine.

Portrait of the Writer as a Young Feminist

RAHEL LERNER

I'VE ALWAYS BEEN proud to call myself a feminist. And it's a good thing, because a picture of me with nine other Jewish women in tallitot and tefillin has taken on a life of its own as a feminist image, in ways that I certainly never imagined it would when it was taken fifteen years ago.

It's hard, perhaps impossible, to recall what I thought when the picture was taken. I can look at the image of my sixteen-year-old self life-size in a museum, but it's very hard to access what I was thinking behind those huge glasses. I remember that the photo shoot took forever, that it was terribly uncomfortable—my head tilted at an odd angle, my arm held stiffly to better display my tefillin. I remember feeling honored to have been chosen, to be in the picture with some of the rabbinical students I knew and admired, among whom I hoped someday to study. I remember feeling somewhat exultant that the makeup person had insisted on applying lipstick to my mother, who never indulged in such frivolities, and who was constantly puzzled by my passion for makeup and glitter. But I don't really know what I thought would come of it, and once that long photo shoot was over, I don't think I thought of it much at all. I finished high

273

school, spent a year studying in Israel, and returned to New York to start college.

And that October, *Jews: America: A Representation* was published, and the picture was suddenly everywhere. In the pages of *Lilith*. In *The Jewish Week*. In *Life* magazine. I was getting phone calls from friends, "I saw you in the doctor's waiting room!" Apparently a minyan of women in tefillin had a shock value second only to the lesbian daughters of Holocaust survivors—every publication that reviewed the book seemed to publish this same picture.

As I looked at the picture over and over again, I felt used. I didn't see myself in it, or my mother, or the other women I knew. Instead I saw the photographer's projection of what women in tefillin must be like: angry. He hadn't let us smile during the shoot—I had remembered that—but I hadn't foreseen the effect of our unsmiling faces. We looked, to me, like a caricature of angry scowling feminists. The photographer, Frederic Brenner, had insisted that we all wear traditional black-and-white striped tallitot, instead of our own more varied and individual ones. He'd said at the time that he wanted a unified look, but when I looked at the picture, I saw angry women in the traditional, very masculine tallitot—women grasping at male ritual symbols; I had never thought of tallitot as gendered before.

For me, *davening* (praying) in tallit and tefillin had never been about women claiming the right to engage in rituals that had been limited to men. To me, the tallit and tefillin were how Jews should pray, and I had never, until I saw myself in that picture, worn them as an act of feminist defiance. Obviously, I knew that most women did not *daven* in tallit and tefillin, that halakhah had long-since considered women exempt from this mitzvah, but it had never made sense to me that men's prayer, or the garb that accompanies it, should be different from women's. I *davened* in tallit and tefillin as a Jew, rather than as a woman, and hoped that other Jewish women would join me in what I saw as a fundamental Jewish observance.

I know I am unusual in not seeing tallitot and tefillin as male. My mother began *davening* in a tallit before I was born, and has been *davening* in tefillin for as long as I can remember. Most women who take on the mitzvot of tallit and tefillin must reach past an assumption of these ritual articles as masculine. But to me they were Jewish, and mine. I certainly knew that most Jews did not share my assumptions about tefillin. I hadn't grown up in some sort of utopian egalitarian bubble. I had gone to an Orthodox high school where I'd fought for—and failed to win—the right to *daven* in my tallit and tefillin. I knew that in my own Conservative movement, *davening* in tallit and tefillin had been a requirement for women seeking ordination as rabbis and was an important part of the Conservative movement's growing trend toward egalitarianism. To me, the right to *daven* in tefillin in my world had long since been won, and I saw it as one of the many feminist advances for which I should thank my mother, and could then take for granted.

But I couldn't get away from the picture, which showed such a defiant feminism. For years, when I was asked about it, I laughed it off. I called it the "Scary Amazon Women in Tefillin Picture." When I was in Israel one summer I had the shock of seeing it full-size for the first time at the Diaspora Museum. As a counselor for a United Synagogue Youth trip, I had the opportunity to talk to my campers about why I had chosen to take on these mitzvot—not out of defiance, but out of the conviction that the habits of daily prayer and of physically binding yourself to God can be tremendously powerful. I talked about my conviction that Jewish observance need not be gendered, that all Jews can participate fully in religious life. Tefillin wasn't about defiance or about making a point, I said, it was about God, and one's relationship to the Divine.

But over time, something unexpected began to happen. I started to get angry. I saw the female professors I admired in college denied tenure. I saw the Jewish community blame working women for a declining birth rate. I saw women who had entered the Conservative rabbinate struggle for equal respect and consideration for prominent pulpits even twenty years after that historic decision. I entered the workforce and saw women heavily represented in the lower ranks, and not in senior positions. I saw my friends have babies and struggle to afford child care. And I realized that the optimistic feminist I was at sixteen had been a bit naive. There was much more left to be done than I had realized when I was entering college. And I am far angrier about the treatment of women than I ever thought I would have cause to be.

I don't think Brenner was somehow prescient in his portrayal of us in his photograph. I certainly don't think that he was predicting my own personal disillusionment. I still think that in characterizing us as defiant he neglected to include the essential love of Judaism, of *tefillah*, of ritual—whatever it was that had brought each of the ten very different women in his picture to take on the mitzvot of tallit and tefillin. But I now recognize myself in that picture, and the fact that I do is a terrible disappointment.

Ruth Andrew Ellenson received the National Jewish Book Award in women's studies for her anthology *The Modern Jewish Girl's Guide to Guilt* (Plume, 2006). The book has also been translated and published in Israel. A journalist who lives in Los Angeles, she is the daughter of Rabbi David Ellenson and the stepdaughter of Rabbi Jacqueline Koch Ellenson, also a contributor to this book.

The Pink Ghetto

RUTH ANDREW ELLENSON

FOR MY GENERATION—those of us born in the 1970s and 1980s, after women were already being ordained as rabbis—the issues of Jewish feminism have less to do with overthrowing the patriarchy, and more to do with the sociological fallout of that revolution.

Despite all the strides Jewish feminism has attained for women in the community, there has been a backlash against that progress. Like teachers and nurses before them, the modern Jewish professional world is coming to be perceived as a women's domain.

The term "pink ghetto" has come to describe what happens when a profession is seemingly overtaken by women. Men are no longer attracted to the field because it has come to be seen as women's work, and the field finds itself falling victim to the classic penalties of institutionalized sexism: lower pay and less prestige. The term can also be used when women's concerns are pushed to the side and marginalized.

It's somewhat ironic that a generation of women shaped by the ideology of Jewish feminism—we were given copies of *Deborah, Golda and Me* and *Our Bodies, Ourselves* for our bat mitzvahs—are now confronted with this anxiety over Jewish feminism.

Over the past few years, I've come into direct contact with the pink ghetto fears—both professional and ideological—in a way I never

277

expected to: by working on a book about Jewish women. Through that process, I not only came to see the fear of the pink ghetto develop, but also witnessed the tension between generations as they struggle over the definition of what it means to be a Jewish feminist.

The struggle took me by surprise. In 2005 I edited an anthology with what I thought was a rather funny title: *The Modern Jewish Girl's Guide to Guilt*. A title such as *The Modern Jewish Woman's Guide to Identity, Post-Feminism* might have been more accurate, but wasn't quite as catchy. The book was a collection of essays by Jewish women writers about their lives at the dawn of the twenty-first century. Jewish American women were due for some self-reflection on the current state of post-feminism. I hoped the essays exploring that would display a deep thoughtfulness, a strong candor, and a sense of humor. The ambition of the project was this: now that Jewish women could speak for themselves, with all the strides they had gained, what did they have to say?

The book was, in my mind, a feminist endeavor. Jewish guilt was a cultural stereotype that had been invented by Jewish men in the 1960s and 1970s—think Woody Allen and Philip Roth among others—to deflect their anxiety over assimilation onto Jewish women. It was easy to make women the butt of the joke. Stereotypes of clingy mothers, nagging wives, and Jewish American Princesses abounded, and they were embraced. In the 1960s a bestselling book called *How to Be a Jewish Mother* by Dan Greenburg was as much an instruction manual as my book was a guide to feeling more guilty—which is to say, not at all.

In the introduction to my book, I wrote about how thirty-plus years after the Jewish feminist revolution of the 1970s, women had choices that our *bubbes* could have never dreamed of (according to family legend, my great-grandmother almost fell out of the women's balcony in her longing to be part of the men's service below, while my stepmother is a rabbi who regularly leads the service). Yet, despite the opportunities I was given, it wasn't clear which option was for me.

I would not be relegated to one side of the *mechitzah* (the wall or screen separating the genders), but I also didn't want to be the *gabbai* (the person assisting the clergy in a servcie). As I pondered my choices, I was overcome by guilt for not wanting to take all of the hard-won opportunities I was given. But I couldn't help it. I didn't want to sit in the women's balcony for the service, but the thought of having to lead the service made me want to fall off a balcony. And so, in the middle of all these muddled thoughts, the book was born.

Right off the bat, I got some flack for the title. Jewish feminists weren't supposed to use the term *girl*, much less feel guilty about anything. The controversy the title sparked seemed to break on generational lines. Many people over fifty seemed to find the title offensive; under fifty, not so much. The irony was that *because* of the title, the book probably reached young Jewish women who would never normally contemplate a Jewish book, much less one on feminism. They liked the title because to them it seemed cheeky. Perhaps what marks one generational difference is younger women's ability to be irreverent about being Jewish and female without fear.

Despite strong sales, disapproval of the title continued. One of my father's colleagues remarked that the book was actually quite good regardless of its "horrible title." A Jewish studies professor I greatly respected told me that when she heard the title of the book she thought, "Oh no! What has Ruthie done?"

These criticisms stung. They were more often than not delivered by women my mother's age, whose example as Jewish feminists had deeply influenced me and profoundly shaped my perception of what was possible as a Jew and a woman. I felt indebted to them, and had created something I thought was a manifestation of the legacy they pioneered—that the narratives of Jewish women's lives were as important as men's—and found myself chastised for it.

In my mind, the book marked the fact that Jewish women had earned enough security and power to discuss their ambivalence publicly. Even my embracing of the term *Jewess,* which several writers in the anthology used with evident delight, seemed to be a sore point. I was not of a generation that would ever consider the term *womyn* necessary, nor the term *Jewess* offensive. We were post-feminists, and the legacies of feminism, both good and bad, were ours to embrace as we saw fit. If anything, the criticisms I received from older feminists made me doubt aligning myself with them.

Simultaneously, the book began to receive the "pink ghetto" label. I received criticism for not including Jewish men in the book. Didn't I know that by focusing on Jewish women, I was making men feel excluded from a Jewish experience? In a time when young Jewish men were increasingly leaving the community, and women were outnumbering men in Reform and Conservative rabbinical schools, didn't I realize I was contributing to the problem? As much as I might have been having trouble relating to older feminists, these criticisms raised my feminist hackles. How could these seemingly well-meaning people think the Jewish community was under threat by having strong female leadership? Why did the supposed feminization of the rabbinate (which the facts strongly disputed) even merit discussion, much less deserve to be seen as a liability? When men were in charge there were no allegations of the "masculinazation" of the rabbinate.

Still, the pink ghetto charge haunted me. I was getting flack from both sides for focusing on Jewish women. On the one hand, did being a feminist mean that I had to sacrifice my sense of humor? On the other hand, was focusing on Jewish women as opposed to men really a cause for criticism? I was left with more questions than answers, and the meaning of Jewish feminism seemed more complicated than ever.

Isn't Jewish feminism supposed to be a countercultural, subversive movement? Older Jewish feminists who had broken the glass ceiling were now, to me, themselves status quo. They seemed rigid in maintaining their definition of a movement they had founded and expected us, the next generation, to carry on. And yet, when the status quo *was* broken, it sparked a deluge of criticisms for focusing on women's lives.

To engage young Jewish women of my generation in the next phase of Jewish feminism, there has to be willingness to allow the definition of Jewish feminism to evolve. Clinging to earlier definitions or preconceived assumptions of what the term means excludes younger women. It doesn't help instill a sense of values or community; in fact it alienates them from it. And that community is needed when the critiques roll in about too much focusing on our Jewish experiences as women qua women.

If academics, activists, and rabbis who are on the leading lines of Jewish feminism want to show the importance of the cause to younger generations, there must be room for a questioning of the standards of what has been received. It's not a rejection of the gains the women before us have gifted to us, but it is a reexploration of how we will use those gains. For my generation, living with feminist privilege is a matter of course, not a cause.

Jewish feminism is not the sole province of women who want to fight the patriarchy of Judaism. It is about embracing the experiences of Jewish women without an agenda and looking at what constitutes reality for Jewish women today with honesty, humor, and saucy affection. When we have an open dialogue concerning those experiences, we can move out of the pink ghetto together.

PART VI

Women and the Denominations

THERE'S AN OLD JOKE about an army captain trying to determine the religion of his men for their dog tags. He calls each man's name, and each steps up and answers affirmatively: "Jones." "Catholic, sir...." "O'Donnell." "Protestant, sir...." "Smith," "Unitarian, sir...." Then Davidson is called. "Davidson!" The private gets up and stammers, "Well, sir, you see, my family wasn't really religious, we did some of our traditions, but mostly we...." And the captain interrupts and says, "Jewish!"

We are a funny people. Ask a Catholic if they are Catholic and you get a straight answer: yes, no, or lapsed. Ask a Protestant and you'll get their denomination. Ask a Jew and you get a dissertation! They'll answer your question with a question, "What do you mean by that?" That the uncomplicated statement, "I am Jewish" can be so complicated is at once fascinating and also telling. Though there will be a variety of opinions in every group, being Jewish seems quintessentially a question in search of an answer.

That brings us to the denominations. The average Jew joins a synagogue not based on its tenets, or the movement it belongs to, but on whether he or she likes the rabbi, enjoys the services, and feels welcome by the community. Most Jews leave it up to their rabbis to debate platforms and come up with definitions as to what Orthodox, Reform, Conservative, Reconstructionist, Jewish Renewal, Traditional Egalitarian, Modern Orthodox, Neo-Hasidic, or any other jumble of names might mean.

I once attended an interdenominational conference about the uses of the mikveh where I was touched more deeply by the cross-denominational dialogue than by all the scholarship. You see, the Orthodox "mikveh lady" and I became fast friends, and I wondered how that happened so naturally. She and I would not feel comfortable in each other's shuls, for sure. She believes liberal Judaism is seriously misguided on some key issues, and I believe exactly the same about Orthodoxy. She is wary of change in Judaism, and I embrace it. And so on. But she was willing to see that, despite her misgivings, I am a committed passionate Jew. And I was willing to see that, despite my misgivings, she is also a passionate committed Jew. We know we are both on the same "team," though we disagree on how to play the game. We know that the other cares deeply and is willing to do anything in her power to help Judaism not only survive but thrive. We respect the other's right to do it her way. And we respect her right to be wrong, even if only in our own opinion.

Rabbi Yitz Greenberg, an Orthodox rabbi, wrote in the foreword to *Revisions: Seeing Torah through a Feminist Lens* (Jewish Lights),[1] "At a time when relations between the denominations have become poisoned, we must reassert the unifying power of Torah.... We must restore dialogue by 'talking in Torah.'" The mikveh lady and I did not have a meeting of the minds—we had a meeting of the hearts, because we were both "talking in Torah."

I have always felt that Jewish women have the power—and the challenge—to bridge the seemingly intractable denominational gaps. Once outsiders to the system, women who are now insiders can affect great change. This "commonality of womanhood" can supersede even the thorniest of philosophical disagreements. We can form our own "teams" and show a new way of playing the game that doesn't end in a lose-lose outcome.

Each of the major denominations has had to struggle with both how much it is willing to expand the walls to make room for women, and also how much it will allow the definitions, rules, and regulations of traditional halakhah to define what *equality* will mean. Each of the denominations looks completely different now from how it looked twenty years ago; women's issues have pushed other issues into the limelight as well. It may appear that Orthodoxy still has the farthest to go, but sometimes what is easiest to reach is the last thing we take, so Reform, on the other hand, also has its distance. No one is really "in the middle" anymore.

Idana Goldberg, PhD, a graduate of Barnard College, worked as a research associate for the Andrew W. Mellon Foundation and received her doctorate in history from the University of Pennsylvania, where she studied modern Jewish history and gender and feminist theory. Idana serves on the executive committee of the board of directors of JOFA (Jewish Orthodox Feminist Alliance). She currently works at the Jewish Funders Network in New York and is a faculty member of Me'ah, a two-year intensive adult Jewish learning program. She is the coauthor of *Crafting a Class: College Admissions and Financial Aid 1955–1994*. Idana lives in White Plains, New York, with her husband, Michael Kellman, and three children.

Orthodoxy and Feminism

IDANA GOLDBERG, PhD

THE BOOK OF GENESIS teaches the commandment of *brit milah*—the covenant of circumcision—through the story of Abraham, who circumcised himself and his two sons, Ishmael and Isaac, upon God's command. But only a few verses after the Torah describes this rite, it also makes clear that the *brit milah* is insufficient by itself to forge the covenantal link for God's chosen people.

God tells Abraham that it is only through Isaac that Abraham's covenantal line will flourish and multiply; only Abraham's children with Sarah will inherit the destiny of what will become the Jewish people. Perhaps in response to God's explicit inclusion of Sarah in the covenantal promise, Rabbi Menachem Meiri, a thirteenth-century French commentator, describes how, on the same day that Abraham had his *brit milah*, Sarah underwent her own transformative *brit* by immersing in a mikveh.

While certainly far from the plain meaning of the text, this reading of Sarah's parallel transformation evocatively reinforces the notion that the covenantal destiny of the Jewish people was formed through the partnership between Abraham and Sarah. Sarah has a complementary *brit*—one she passes down to her daughters, one that insists that their motherhood is a necessary prerequisite for covenantal entry and that they are themselves entered into God's contract upon birth.

It is precisely this legacy of Sarah as equal covenantal partner that Orthodox feminists strive to maintain, transforming Orthodox Jewry into a community that recognizes the essential need for both women's and men's full participation in Jewish communal, ritual, and family life and that takes into account the spiritual and religious needs of both men and women.

When faced with the challenges of modernity in the nineteenth century, Orthodox Judaism adopted a strategy of self-preservation epitomized by the Hatam Sofer, a leading Hungarian rabbi, who famously pronounced "there is nothing new under the sun." This attitude allowed the Orthodox community to evolve in response to modernity, even as it denied doing so.[1] The transformation in the role of women in Jewish life over the last century—and especially in the last thirty years—has been among the most dramatic challenges to Orthodox Judaism. In that time, Orthodox women have become extensively and intensively educated, have assumed leadership positions in religious and communal institutions, and have begun to participate in public ritual ceremonies to a greater extent than at any prior point in Jewish history.

Yet despite the advances achieved by Orthodox women, feminism, as a movement that promotes equality of opportunity for women and men, poses particular challenges to Orthodox Judaism, precisely because of the elements that continue to distinguish Orthodoxy from other movements within Judaism. The belief in an ongoing covenantal promise initiated with Abraham and Sarah combines in Orthodoxy with the belief in the enduring divinity of a binding halakhah. At least in principle, these twin convictions leave little room for human agency and deny the possibility that contemporary belief systems can or should have an impact on Jewish life.

For those women and men who subscribe to dual allegiances of halakhic Judaism and equal opportunity—Orthodox feminists— the challenge is how to find strength within the halakhic system for changes that prima facie seem to go against the system. Solutions created by Orthodox feminists range from distinguishing between legitimate halakhic positions and traditional social behaviors to using a dynamic understanding of halakhah to create space within halakhah itself for innovation.[2]

Positive Developments

As a movement for change, Orthodox feminism is gaining support. In 1997, following the first International Conference on Feminism and Orthodoxy, a group of women led by Blu Greenberg founded JOFA, the Jewish Orthodox Feminist Alliance. With a current membership of five thousand women and men, JOFA seeks to educate the larger community about ways to expand women's meaningful participation within Orthodoxy. Employing an online library of articles, regional conferences, film screenings, halakhic publications, and curriculum development, JOFA educates and advocates for change.[3] The emerging strength of JOFA as an institution represents the attempts by many thousands of Orthodox women and men to enhance their own ritual and communal participation and to strengthen Orthodox life.

Rituals—both public, synagogue-based ones such as prayer and Torah reading, as well as those that mark private family transitions or delineate sacred time and space—make overt statements about an individual's relationship to her or his family, community, and God. Because of the ability of rituals to define identity and set boundaries, they are both theologically and socially important. They can change the way individuals conceive of God and covenantal inclusion, as well as how a community constitutes who is included and who is not. Orthodox women's demands for greater ritual inclusion—both public and private—reflect this importance.

Orthodox women have creatively carved out roles and won acceptance from halakhic authorities in many Jewish rituals—domestic, liturgical, and life cycle.[4] It has now become common in many modern Orthodox communities to find women participating in the rituals around the Shabbat table, including blessing the wine or the challah, or leading a *zimmun* (mini-quorum for the blessing after meals) of three women—offering opportunities for women to more actively sanctify the Shabbat and model a vision of shared religious participation for children and friends. Life cycle rituals for welcoming a new daughter and for bat mitzvah recognize the role of Jewish girls in the divine covenant and their obligations in mitzvot; the widespread acceptance of these rituals also highlights the advances that Orthodox women have made. Contemporary Orthodox wedding ceremonies often include rituals to create a more equitable ceremony that still remains within the bounds of traditional halakhic interpretation. Brides engage in reciprocal gestures with their grooms and invite their female friends and family members to add their voices to the ceremony. Mother's names are routinely included in many *ketubot* (Jewish wedding certificates), which are sometimes even read by a woman.

Orthodox women's participation in the public rituals of prayer has also evolved over time. Many women today regularly *daven* (pray) with a minyan at daily *tefillah*, and many choose to honor their deceased parents by reciting the mourner's kaddish thrice daily during their year of mourning. The vibrant women's *tefillah* network—groups of "women-only" services led by women, for women—has prepared a cadre of talented women to read from the Torah and lead the prayers. Most recently, in a number of cities in North America and Israel, Orthodox minyanim have formed in which women lead portions of the prayer service and partner with the men for aliyot and Torah reading. Anyone who has witnessed the joy of a woman seeing the inside of the Torah scroll for the first time, reciting a blessing for her first aliyah, or dancing with the Torah on Simchat Torah appreciates the profound and visceral connection that Orthodox women feel when they encounter the Torah, perhaps more so even than their feminist counterparts in other denominations of Judaism, who have for many years had this as a "normative" Jewish experience.

Inclusion in Jewish activities becomes even more valued and vital as the education of Orthodox girls becomes more extensive and expansive. Girls in the ultra-Orthodox Haredi communities have unprecedented access to sacred writings—learning Bible and even Jewish law—and in the Modern Orthodox community, many Jewish girls are exposed to the full range of Jewish sacred texts. Girls are learning Talmud in greater numbers than ever before and some women have begun to teach Talmud in Modern Orthodox day schools and Israeli women's yeshivot. Thousands of Jewish girls attend intensive yeshivot in Israel in post–high school programs, and hundreds of women have studied Jewish texts in rigorous post-college programs at the Drisha Institute and at Stern College.

This high-level engagement with Jewish texts has led to an unprecedented expansion of women's leadership opportunities. In half a dozen Orthodox congregations in the United States women are serving in rabbinic leadership positions as *madrichot ruchaniyot*, spiritual leaders, and congregational interns alongside male rabbinic colleagues—teaching classes, counseling individuals, and offering halakhic insight and advice. In Israel, women serving as *toanot*—advocates in the rabbinic courts—have transformed the experience of women appearing before the *battei din*, the religious courts. Trained to argue the intricacies of halakhah and challenge legal rulings, these women are directing the course of halakhic decision making in revolutionary ways. *Yoazot halakhah* (halakhic advisors) who have been rigorously trained in the laws of *niddah* and *taharat ha mishpacha* (menstrual and ritual purity laws) at the Nishmat Center in Israel have upended the traditional gendered binary that has had women consulting with men over the most intimate aspects of their bodies and lives.

The Challenges

Even as the Orthodox community has made visible and meaningful strides toward greater inclusion of women in Jewish institutional and religious life, there are significant challenges—both halakhic and sociological—that continue to impede the full realization of Orthodox women's covenantal partnership.

While it is unthinkable today for Orthodox Jewish families to educate their sons Jewishly but not their daughters, it is important to consider what it is that these children are learning. Unfortunately, all too often, the way that Jewish studies has been traditionally taught in many Jewish day schools serves to reinforce the centrality of the male biblical figures and issues of Jewish ritual and learning that are less relevant to Jewish girls, such as the emphasis on tzitzit and tefillin and other commandments traditionally assigned to men.[5] The centrality of Jewish men and boys to prayer services can marginalize Jewish girls, making them spectators in the daily worship experience at their schools. In addition, many yeshiva day schools subscribe to a traditional curriculum that does not teach Talmud to girls, continuing to deny them the tools that would allow them to fully engage in the halakhic discourse. The unparalleled role of education in shaping minds requires serious consideration of the gender messages that children's teachers and schools are transmitting, and how Orthodox feminists can drive and shape those messages.

The mechanics of Jewish divorce—with its inequitable distribution of power in favor of the husband—represents a challenge to the ethical system of justice that underpins much of the rest of Jewish life. The situation of *agunot*—women chained to husbands who refuse to grant them their *get* (religious divorce)—fundamentally challenges Orthodox feminists committed to halakhah. Some rabbis have taken a stand to try to end the *agunah* problem through whatever halakhic and social remedies are available. But far too many others have demonstrated a failure of leadership. Thousands of women remain in limbo, denied their *gets* and thus denied their future, with the active and passive complicity of their rabbis and their communities. For Orthodox feminists, the demand for comprehensive solutions to the *agunah* crisis is an obligation, one necessary to protect Jewish women, prevent future *agunot*, and restore the requisite ethics to halakhah.

The most pervasive challenge to Orthodox women achieving covenantal partnership comes less from halakhah and more from the tendencies in contemporary Orthodox life toward conservatism—a conservatism that often manifests itself precisely in opposition to values of equality and opportunity for women.[6] In these circles, feminism or any attempt to reconfigure women's religious opportunities is perceived as a radical movement that will destabilize traditional gender roles and violate the sanctity of the Jewish family. Here, tradition is often wielded as a patriarchal club to maintain the status quo, often at the expense of women's fulfillment.

The conservatism espoused by these elements of Orthodox society relies on distorted notions of *tzniut* (modesty) to buttress their claims that women should not take public roles in religious life. Jewish girls have been advised for centuries *"kol kvudah bat melech pnima,"* that is, "all the glory of the princess is internal" (Ps. 45:14, translation mine). In an egregious misinterpretation of this biblical phrase, the Jewish girl is told that modesty demands that she not seek the public spotlight or enjoy greater visibility. A woman's "true" greatness comes from working behind the scenes, praying behind the *mechitzah*, teaching Torah behind a curtain, and raising her children behind the closed doors of her home.

One specific halakhic expression often used as a means of maintaining traditional practices in the synagogue is *kavod hatzibbur.* Usually translated as "the dignity of the congregation," *kavod hatzibbur* refers to conduct that is unnecessarily bothersome to the congregation or that disturbs the propriety and seriousness of the service. It is a concept that has particular and specific applicability. *Kavod hatzibbur* is not a synonym for *tzniut,* yet they are often used synonymously. It also is not a prohibition against women's participation in the synagogue, yet it is often cited for that express purpose.

When contemporary rabbis and lay leaders explain that women should not take greater roles in synagogue life—whether dancing with a Torah scroll on Simchat Torah, delivering words of Torah from the pulpit in the main sanctuary, or even serving as synagogue president—they often justify their position with reference to *kavod hatzibbur,* claiming that it offends the dignity of the congregation for a woman to do such things. This quickly bleeds into the idea that it is not *tzanua*—modest or appropriate for a woman to do such things. By conflating these two terms, Jewish leaders create and sustain the fantasy that protecting a congregation's dignity lies in its ability to shield itself from immodest women. However, a congregation's dignity would be protected far better by enhancing the dignity of all the congregants, both men and women.

This contemporary conservatism can be traced back to the dictum of the Hatam Sofer. Staggering changes have affected the traditional Orthodox community—and in particular the Modern Orthodox community—as men and women engage daily in the secular world through their access to higher education, through their professions, and in their neighborhoods. By investing traditional gender roles both in the family and in public Judaism with sacrosanct inviolability, Modern Orthodox Judaism points to the role of women and claims that "nothing new is under the sun" and is thus able to buttress Orthodoxy and maintain the illusion of authenticity even as it has profoundly changed.

Where Do We Go from Here?

Despite the striving of some Orthodox women and men, Sarah's promise of covenantal partnership remains unfulfilled. Key to achieving this promise is the recognition that true partnership can only exist where each partner's intrinsic value is recognized.

In the biblical recounting of the love story of Rachel and Jacob, the Torah teaches that even after Jacob was tricked into marrying Leah, "Jacob still loved Rachel more than Leah" (Gen. 29:31, translation mine). Sforno, a sixteenth-century Italian commentator, explains that Jacob loved Rachel not because of her external beauty, or any other particular characteristics, but simply because she was Rachel. Sforno's interpretation offers insight for understanding Jacob's anger a few verses later when Rachel cries out, "Give me children, or else I am dead" (Gen. 30:1, translation mine). Jacob is angry because Rachel does not see herself the way that he sees her. She cannot see that her value is intrinsic—that it lies in her Rachelness; not in what she does, but in who she is.

Intrinsic value certainly coexists with instrumental value. What women contribute to families, communities, and their relationship with God is crucial to women's wholeness as human beings. But for far too long, women in Orthodox Judaism have been celebrated for their instrumental value—the rewards of birthing children, bringing their children to the study hall, and freeing their husbands to observe commandments. It is only the recognition of intrinsic value that compels human beings to seek change and demand fulfillment.

Intrinsic value stems from each and every human being created in the image of God, as it says in Genesis, *b'tzelem elohim*. According to Rabbi Joseph Soloveitchik, God invests every person, both male and female, with *tzelem elohim*—moral sense, free will, and intellect. As bearers of *tzelem elohim*, individuals must strive for autonomy, individual worthiness, uniqueness, and freedom, for it is only as fully actualized humans that Jews can participate in a covenantal relationship with God.[7]

The position of women in Orthodox Judaism today, Rabbi Yitz Greenberg has suggested, does not allow women to realize their potential as *tzelem elohim*.[8] Women are asked to sacrifice their uniqueness and individual worthiness as Jews for the good of the community. According to this reading of Rabbi Soloveitchik, the key to the human realization of the dignity of *tzelem elohim* for both men and women is the human capacity to change the world. A gap exists between halakhah in its ideal form and the real world. Given that the world is imperfect, the Torah moves toward perfection piece by piece, by actualizing an ideal halakhah in the midst of a real world.

Orthodox feminists today live in the gap between the ideal and the real. What defines the Orthodox feminist is the willingness to live amid the struggle and tension of realizing the ideal halakhah, when women will be fully actualized as Jews. Despite the bruises and pain that living in this tenuous space creates, she continues to fight to achieve her place as a full member of her Jewish community. The commitment to struggle comes from a love of Torah and the desire to be a full partner in Torah life.

With the recognition of women's *tzelem elokim*, women's intrinsic value, comes an obligation to nurture, grow, develop, and fully actualize women's potential as covenantal partners. With the recognition of women's *tzelem elokim*, Jews are reminded that Sarah, too, had an independent covenantal relationship with God—one that still demands fulfillment. For Orthodox feminists, women deserve, and indeed must demand, every opportunity available within the bounds of halakhah to achieve these ends.

Rabbi Rachel Sabath Beit-Halachmi is the Shalom Hartman Institute's director of the Center for Lay Leadership Education as well as a member of the institute's faculty. Ordained at the Hebrew Union College in New York in 1995, Rachel is a member of the faculty of Hebrew Union College in Jerusalem. Currently completing a PhD in Jewish theology, she is coauthor of *Preparing Your Heart for the High Holy Days* and *Striving toward Virtue: A Contemporary Guide to Jewish Ethical Behavior*, and has published several articles on theology, gender, and Israel. See www.hartman.org.il. Rachel lives with her husband, Rabbi Ofer Sabath Beit-Halachmi, and their daughter, Tehillah, outside Jerusalem in Tzur Hadassah. See www.ktzh.org.

The Changing Status of Women in Liberal Judaism

A Reflective Critique[1]

RABBI RACHEL SABATH BEIT-HALACHMI

The Changing Status of Women in Modernity

THE AGE OF MODERNITY, the period following the Enlightenment and the emancipation of most Jews from politically imposed restrictions in most of the world, has been a time of great optimism and hope for progress, for people in general and for Jews in particular. As Western societies began to reexamine and expand the freedom and rights exercised by minority groups, Jews and members of other minority religions were great beneficiaries. Throughout the West, women also benefited significantly from an expanded understanding of their rights in public and private spheres. By the early part of the twentieth century, women began to take on public leadership roles and have a more visible impact on society. This move toward greater equality in the public sphere laid the foundation for what later became liberal Judaism's model of a just society in which men and women are equal.

As women gained the right to vote in public elections, many Jews argued that women could no longer be denied the same right within Jewish organizations. The interplay between women's increased equality at large and that within the Jewish community is also apparent in regard to study, whereby just as with modernity women could for the first time study in secular universities, within the Jewish community they could finally access and study previously inaccessible sacred Jewish texts. Jewish women's increased involvement and knowledge led to new understandings of gender and religion, which in turn dramatically affected two main areas of liberal Jewish life: (1) religious law and practice, and (2) leadership in the synagogue and in community organization.

The significant change in the role of Jewish women following the Enlightenment makes modernity a dividing line between two types of intellectual and religious views of Jewish women. The first sees women as primarily responsible for the private sphere characterized by the home and family-centered domain, while the second accords women a full (or nearly full) religious agency in the public domain. This dividing line is especially pronounced in the context of liberal (non-Orthodox) Jewish life. Reform Judaism in particular embraced the expanding role of women by granting women full membership and voting rights in synagogues as early as 1893[2] and by gradually permitting women to perform many public ritual acts previously restricted to men. Reform leaders not only argued that women should be permitted to serve in leadership positions in synagogues, but in 1922 they voted to allow women to be ordained as rabbis[3]—though the first actual ordination did not occur in North America until 1972.

While some may argue that these changes in status provide an answer to the question of the role of women in Jewish life in the modern era, I argue that such changes are in fact only the first two phases of the transformation that is necessary to fulfill modernity's promise of equality for women. In spite of the fact that Jewish women today have multiple possibilities available to them, we have yet to see the full equalization of gender roles and rules in all areas of liberal Jewish communal life. In order to understand the complexities of the "unfinished business" that remains before we can realize women's quest for equality, as well as the possible conceptual and textual bases it may rest upon within Judaism, we must first conduct a critical evaluation of the changes that have already taken place and the various methodologies according to which such changes were made. Taking into account what we might learn from such a critique, as well as the importance of more fully transforming the liberal Jewish community, there is still a need to think about and create a more inclusive, egalitarian, and sustainable Jewish community in the future.

Phase One: Toward Equality through Shifts in Legal Status

There have been many changes in women's role in the liberal Jewish community, and different methods used to achieve them. These changes can be divided into two main phases that parallel, to some degree, various subperiods in modern Jewish history as well as the different waves of feminist history. The first phase, much like the first wave of feminism, focused primarily on achieving equal access to and participation in the public sphere, and equal rights and decision-making power both in private and in public. Embracing the ideas of progress and reason, the arguments made during this first phase (largely from 1870 to 1970) employed the principle, considered radical at the time, that Jewish women should exercise the same rights as Jewish men. Alongside this principle, feminists argued that it would contradict "the spirit of the age" to prevent women from performing the same religious duties or from studying the same religious texts as men.

Justifications for reform in the two main areas of change—in religious law and practice, and in access to leadership in the synagogue and communal organizational life—rested primarily on the prevailing notions of reason and ethics, and on a belief in the supremacy of Judaism's ethical monotheism. Thus, the arguments for change often referred to the "historic veneration of women" and cited Biblical proof texts and precedent models, such as the prophetesses Deborah (Judg. 4:4ff) and Miriam (Exod. 15:20ff), who led the Jewish people in times of crisis and spiritual celebration. While these arguments also made occasional reference to the "exalted spiritual status" of the Jewish woman, the central justification for change was the conviction that Judaism at its core was a progressive and ethical religion "ever striving to be in accord with the postulates of reason," and that it must therefore evolve in accordance with modern notions of ethics and gender equality.[4]

In early discussions regarding the halakhic role of women, Reform thinkers asserted that rabbinic legal literature was no longer absolutely binding, and most argued that it should be used as a source of what some of its leaders referred to as "guidance rather than governance." Adopting the era's emphasis on liberation and equality, these *poskim* (religious lawmakers) believed that they had the right to introduce religious reforms especially with regard to the status of Jewish women. They argued for the full equality of women in four areas in particular: (1) religious commandments, including time-bound ones traditionally restricted to men according to halakhah; (2) the Jewish prayer quorum *(minyan)*; (3) education; and (4) marriage laws (where reforms would work to prevent a woman from becoming an *agunah* [a woman who is prevented from remarrying since her husband refuses to grant her a Jewish divorce] and help create an egalitarian marriage contract).

Some of these initial legal changes were made by employing the halakhic principle, echoed by nonreligious law, of going "beyond the letter of the law" *(lifnim mishurat ha-din);* this principle enabled lawmakers to focus on the ethical underpinnings of Judaism and correct laws from earlier periods that contravene these ethics, such as the full rights of women to participate in all areas of Jewish ritual life or the right for both women and men to initiate divorce. Other changes were made by employing interpretive principles from within rabbinic literature that take into account the influence of different practices among the Jewish people (such as the Talmudic teaching of "Go out and see what the people are doing" to settle any doubt about a prevailing custom) as well as considering the needs of people within the community in instituting change. In some cases, changes were made by taking into account the reality of the ongoing evolution of Jewish practice over the ages together with the extent to which changing contexts demanded accommodation in religious practice.

Traditional halakhic literature itself at times acknowledges the need for change given changing circumstances, even declaring outright: "In other times we did that; now we do this," or simply reasoning that "times have changed." Wherever the halakhic literature read women out of influential roles because of supposed inherent intellectual or psychological limitations, Reform thinkers adopted a very different understanding of women's role based on a different conception of women. By employing such meta-halakhic ethical, historical, and interpretive principles, Reformers sought and still seek to create a Jewish practice that, according to Mark Washofsky, is "more lenient, flexible, affirmative of contemporary values, and morally uplifting" than that of nonliberal Judaism. They saw and continue to see these first-phase changes in women's halakhic status and role as part of an ongoing process of the evolution of halakhah.

While this first phase led to radical changes by significantly expanding the possibilities for women's religious and intellectual activity, including enabling the eventual ordination of women as rabbis, it had its limitations and merits a respectful critique. This phase of change largely created a new reality in which Jewish women who were interested—and who had the necessary skills, training, and opportunity—could live Jewish lives as what some have called

"honorary men." This first phase produced a great ethical achievement, and yet it meant equating women with men and is similar to
what feminists call "formal equality." With significant exceptions,
the extent to which women could be considered and possibly even
valued like men was based on the extent to which women acted,
thought, and communicated like men, as well as the extent to which
they accepted men's interpretations of what were traditionally
halakhic obligations or religious duties. Thus, if women wanted to
take on the halakhic privileges of men, they needed to take on male
obligations. In other words, women were allowed to become rabbis,
but rabbis were hardly allowed to be women. Thus, the achievements of this first-phase, like those of first-wave feminism, largely
assumed male achievements, values, and standards as the norms to
which women should aspire.

Few efforts were made to envision alternative models for fully
integrating women into Judaism. In particular, there was little
understanding of the benefits of encouraging women to retain their
unique perspectives while integrating their experiences of Judaism
in the past and present. Few asked what kind of Jewish life could
occur if women not only had equal access but could also be interpreters, shapers, and leaders from within Jewish culture according to
differently defined parameters, values, and theology. Yet this first
phase is only one of the approaches that modernity enables: ethical
equality based on sameness.

Although the term "honorary men" might carry a negative connotation, in many ways this was a necessary as well as groundbreaking phase in the role of women in Jewish life. In order to not only
expand the previously limited space permitted to Jewish women in
the public sphere but to also allow for women's full equality, it was
first necessary to create the possibility of a near-level playing field. If
Jewish women were previously denied access to central public activities and sources of communal power in part because they did not
have access to the relevant body of knowledge or the possibility of
acquiring necessary skills, then a corrective model in which they

could gain full access and master previously male-only arenas was crucial. Certainly a renegotiation of the role of Jewish women that permits them to serve as witnesses, be counted as members of prayer quorums, receive aliyot, read from the Torah, become b'not mitzvah, and serve as *shlichot tzibbur* (prayer leaders) is radically transformative by all premodern standards. Thus, halakhic status changes and equal access were necessary. Nonetheless, they remain insufficient changes. Moreover, they carry with them potentially negative repercussions. Indeed, while liberal Jewish women ostensibly gained equal access during this phase to previously male-only spheres of knowledge and religious activity, in fact they often became pigeonholed and were expected to represent only women's issues; according to a 2005 report by Ma'yan: The Jewish Women's Project, the few women who were admitted as leaders were often token women and more often than not failed to receive equal salary and benefits. Through this and other related phenomena, Jewish women have remained effectively marginalized in many spheres of liberal Jewish communal life. Looking at this phase and its results after a century of experience, many questions and problems regarding women's role remain. We must, therefore, ask what other modes of transformation may still be implemented and what their implications are for the Jewish community.

Phase Two: Expanding Liturgical-Theological Models

A second phase of change has been possible only since the late 1980s and early 1990s, when a significant number of Jewish women began serving the liberal Jewish community as rabbis, creating prayers and rituals, and writing Jewish feminist theology. With nearly one thousand women rabbis today, it has been the onset of a critical mass of communally authenticated and legitimated female religious leadership with demonstrated capabilities that has produced an impetus toward a methodology beyond formal equality. The second phase of change has brought a number of achievements: a dramatic increase in the creation of alternative blessings, such as those of Marcia Falk in her *Book of Blessings;* a plethora of new prayers and new ways of turning to God, such as those found in the new Reform prayer book *Mishkan Tefillah;* and the recovery and incorporation of previously omitted texts from over the centuries.

This phase has also brought the development of dozens of new life cycle ceremonies designed specifically for liminal or transitional moments in Jewish women's lives, for which there was previously no liturgy and no leadership or religious-spiritual counsel; it has similarly brought about a continual revision of ceremonies and rituals—such as marriage—in which Jewish women and men have only recently established a variety of ways to ensure equal participation. Egalitarian *ketubot* (marriage contracts), rituals for menopause and for healing from traumas such as rape or mastectomy, covenant ceremonies for baby girls, as well as rituals for men and women around marriage and divorce are just a few examples that exemplify this renewed theology. Because of this second phase of change, both women and men in mainstream Jewish communities now turn to God with feminine and feminist language and song, experience how both women and men can lead prayer and creative religious ceremonies, and have access to a greater diversity of models for religious Jewish family and communal life.

A prominent example of Jewish feminist theology from the second phase is *Standing Again at Sinai* (1990) by Judith Plaskow,[5] whose work also appears in this collection. In it Plaskow argues for the reclamation of history and an inclusive creativity that will not only allow for new understandings of divinity but also aim at creating a new and more just religious and social order.[6] She suggests that there will be new possibilities of transformation for the entire Jewish tradition once women are able not only to access but also to interpret Judaism's most sacred concepts.

In some ways the second phase parallels the achievements—and also the problems—of second-wave feminism. There are inherent limitations in achieving equality through rabbinic interpretive methodologies that make it necessary for us to simultaneously seek ways to reshape Jewish tradition by incorporating women's varied and different voices while continuing to work for equality. For example, Plaskow's theology leaves important questions unaddressed. While it widens our liturgical and theological horizons, it leaves us to transform our community without a clear methodology for determining or sustaining the social and interpretive process of creating a Judaism that has fully evolved to embrace the new challenges of gender in modernity. Indeed, this second phase brought liberal women qua women and their particular perspectives more into the mainstream of Jewish religious and communal life, which was only possible following the first stage of equal access.

The Challenges of Moving toward a Third Phase

The full realization of equality within Judaism is in many ways still a work in progress. For instance, despite significant changes in the role of women in liberal Jewish life, women continue to experience inequality in Jewish professional arenas; many halakhic issues remain untouched by the influence of the first and second phases of change; and the underlying hierarchy that privileges men and male-centered frameworks continues to exist within liberal Jewish communities.

Most of the changes that have been made have used male-created and -controlled methods and structures of thought and legal decision making. To a large extent, the worth and authenticity of the contributions of women continue to be evaluated from a prefeminist or early feminist perspective. In communities where halakhah remains central, attempts to continue the work of equality are bound by the supremacy of legal precedent and form. We must even ask whether full equality can ever be created while employing these methods.

The necessary skepticism of our age demands the development of new methodologies for continuing this unfinished two-fold project of fully assimilating women into all arenas of Jewish life and drawing out the ways in which the community can meet men and women's different needs while simultaneously benefiting from their equality.

As theologian Rachel Adler writes, although we have inherited modernity's "egalitarianism, its faith in the human power to remake society and lavish benefits on all its members ... perhaps its optimism, its belief in a harmonious and balanced universe are no longer theologically convincing."[7] Not only do we need models of theology that are more "convincing" in view of the complex and rapidly changing world in which we live, we also need a legal methodology that is constructive and not just deconstructive. We need ways to establish the institutions and environments that will benefit from the achievements of both phases while ensuring that the ethics of the first and the contributions of the second are not sacrificed.

Part of a more constructive methodology at this stage might emerge from seeking to understand the ways in which the two earlier phases can conflict, and yet harnessing their combined insights in order to move forward. Indeed, the first phase's search for equality and the second phase's development of alternative perspectives often produce a conflict, as women's success in the mainstream may currently come at the expense of being able to deepen women's unique contribution, while conversely, developing women's unique voice often comes at the expense of their being able to fully participate in and influence the system. This is not only a theoretical point but an observation of conflicts that Jewish women currently experience. What we need now is a way to live both phases simultaneously. This will require being vigilant about safeguarding the achievement of both earlier phases of change, while at the same time seeking to envision a third.

The Jewish community might respond to this challenge on two levels. First, on the theoretical level, we now have the experience of two centuries of modern integrative thinking in liberal Judaism that prides itself on seeking ways to live in the nexus of two worlds; in fact, this is something on which liberal Judaism has thrived. We should celebrate the challenge and the ways in which living simultaneously in both worlds leads to more creative thinking and experimentation with new models. Liberal Jews succeed in living as committed ethical humanists as well as committed Jews in spite of the fact that some argue that these two modes of existence are irreconcilable.

The relevant parallel is that it is possible for women to be fully accepted and culturally at home within Jewish community organizations, while at the same time retaining and further developing a sophisticated different voice from "the outside." As with modernity and Judaism, an external critical and an internal constructive feminist voice can also be integrated. The teaching institutions of liberal Judaism face this question on a regular basis, and ask how they can teach all the skills necessary to read Talmud and at the same time teach people to read the text with new lenses. Like the challenge facing all new endeavors, we need to devise a way to be sensitive to marginalized voices, while at the same time maintaining rigorous and consistent standards regarding merit. These challenges are palpable in the synagogue, in the academy, and in most Jewish organizations.

A response on the pragmatic level could include the ongoing development of truly pluralistic and heterogeneous religious communities and institutions that facilitate equal access and representation for all, and where women's full participation in all aspects of community life and leadership is ensured. By guaranteeing equality in practice, such a community would have significantly more internal creative power at its disposal to move forward; previously critical voices heard only from the outside would then be understood as calls from among the Jewish people that must be heeded in order to ensure Judaism's ethical and theological survival.

In an ideal vision, such an intensely inclusive pluralistic Jewish community would fully value the unique perspectives and contributions of women, as well as those of other marginalized groups. This kind of community would embody a reciprocal commitment to the general membership on the one hand, and to particular groups that have access to different visions on the other, something characteristic of a postmodern age. After modernity we know that any identity is multilayered and reflective of a particular contemporary context, and so, too, can we understand gender and Jewish identity.

Developing a Third Phase:
Textual Grounding and Ethical Vigilance

Once the lessons of the previous two phases are internalized, we can and should find ourselves working out the reality of a third phase of change. An example of such a move might be Rachel Adler's *Engendering Judaism: An Inclusive Theology and Ethics* (1998),[8] which models the central principles of ethics and theology found in the first and second phases while pointing to a possible transformation in understanding the complexity of gender and Judaism. In a postmodern interweaving of disciplines that uses contemporary legal theory as well as literary theory, theology, and ethics, Adler shows the limitations of the two phases previously discussed and states that a formal shift in Jewish legal and ritual systems together with new liturgies and theology are necessary but not sufficient to provide a full response to the challenge of gender after modernity.

Focusing on the foundational principles of feminist and liberal theology, and building on multiple principles of interpretation offered by rabbinic literature, Adler addresses many of the remaining dilemmas of equality in halakhah and ethics, such as the ethical and legal imbalance between bride and groom in traditional Jewish marriage ceremonies. Adler proposes a new kind of covenant in place of the marriage *ketubah,* a *brit ahuvim* (a lovers' covenant), which exemplifies the methodology of transforming a foundational religious element based on new readings of traditional texts. The reclamation of a discarded practice of a covenant of partnership *(shituf)* in place of the traditional *ketubah,* which many modern sensibilities reject because of its inequality, is an example of the kind of work that a third phase needs to encourage.

A third phase, which can and does operate simultaneously with the previously described phases, continues to seek both halakhic and aggadic (nonlegal) textual grounding and resources in past and present Jewish narratives that can provide new possibilities for the continuing adjustment of Judaism to the constantly shifting roles of men and women after modernity.

We must, however, recognize the potential problems inherent in the work of recovering the teachings of ancient texts and appealing to precedent and continuity. Such legitimizing of past systems may appear to imply acceptance of the entirety of the system. Given the unequivocal ethical and feminist foundations that have taken root in liberal Judaism, I do not believe that we need to be concerned. We are fully capable of engagement with the texts in the fullness of what they represent without sacrificing the perspective we have gained through modernity and the ethics we have come to cherish.

The Talmudic scholar Daniel Boyarin provides a model that shows that our resources for the future are not only the theory of the present but also a new application of the voices of the past. Rather than focusing on misogyny and the traditional lack of Jewish female power and autonomy—a focus that often serves to reproduce it—Boyarin seeks to show how the "recovery of those forces of the past that opposed the dominant androcentrisim can help put us on a trajectory of empowerment for transformation."[9] Instead of only rejecting the negative ways in which women might have been treated in many of the ancient texts, a model such as Boyarin's suggests that we find strategies for the future in the suppressed opposition to male dominance and in the more dormant feminine voices, however sparse, of precisely those narratives.

Through reading texts with a critical but generous eye, we can benefit from the past without being restricted by the limitations of older modes of interpretation. Relying on neither apologetics nor negativity, we can allow for new kinds of understandings that are neither a combination nor an averaging out of these two phases, but a new posture. If we embrace rather than reject or immediately reinterpret the texts with solely our ethical autonomous goals in mind, they might better serve us in our project of constructing a new model for how Jewish life adjusts to the fullness of gender and sexual identity, given what we know to be true in our time. Therefore, the third phase is one of rereading and reinterpreting the ancient texts of Judaism from a new perspective, in ways that preserve and present to us the resources of their creative and spiritual power.

Authority and Authenticity for a Third Phase

Beyond the cultural value of finding textual resources, there is much to be said for rethinking the entire halakhic system, especially where it leads to unjust situations, such as many that exist regarding women's status. At the same time, we must keep in mind that in many circles of liberal Jews, we now witness the playing out of the opposite extreme, namely the failure to achieve Jewish communal norms in a variety of areas of Jewish life, precisely because of our policy of over-privileging individually defined ethics and autonomy. The absence of shared communal norms continues to impact not only women's roles but also questions of Jewish identity altogether, raising new questions about the nature of Jewish peoplehood. A third phase, therefore, must demonstrate how it is possible to seek out a Jewish way of living that has norms and a shared praxis that are morally informed yet based on a serious knowledge of the narrative of our tradition. Part of what will give such a system its authenticity and authority will be precisely its continuity with the past and its ability to participate in a larger nonsectarian communal process of development. At the same time, this third phase must continue to allow for differences in the application of moral and ethical values and in its interpretation and experience of God as a demanding and commanding reality of any Jewish religious life.

Among the specific goals of this next stage are several elements, some of which were absent or lost in the earlier phases of change: (1)

preservation of the most culturally significant and relevant aspects of tradition, especially through the greater activity of women in intensive learning communities, thereby allowing for a greater constructive interweaving of past and future and a greater simultaneous engagement in multiple intellectual and spiritual methodologies; (2) ongoing recovery and creation of rituals and ritual activity for women and men, such as those regarding mikveh (ritual bath) practices; and (3) development of a standard of religious pluralism and transdenominational activity within the Jewish community and among women in particular that will allow for the ritual practice and text learning that is more prevalent in traditional Jewish communities to affect liberal women, and reciprocally to allow for the greater equality and authority that liberal women already experience to affect the same processes of transformation in the more traditional communities. Such a model of pluralism would be redemptive.

The complex task that remains is the harnessing of the richness and multivocality of Jewish tradition, combined with the knowledge of what a completely different approach and experience of it might teach, in order to create new ways of studying Jewish text and living Jewish lives for both men and women. Such a new approach, if carefully and responsibly developed, will surely contribute to the development of Jewish religious and cultural life as a whole and thus ensure that one of modernity's greatest promises—equality for women—will be met with the evolving wisdom and creativity of all of the Jewish people.

Rabbi Haviva Ner-David, PhD, is a writer, teacher, spiritual counselor, and activist. She received her ordination from an Orthodox rabbi in Jerusalem, and her doctorate from Bar Ilan University. She is the founding director of Reut: The Center for Modern Jewish Marriage, where she runs pre-marriage seminars for couples and private counseling sessions. Her first book, *Life on the Fringes: A Feminist Journey Towards Traditional Rabbinic Ordination*, came out in 2000, and her latest book, *Finding Chanah's Voice: A Feminist Rabbi's Challenge to Religious Patriarchy*. Rabbi Dr. Ner-David is on the board of Women of the Wall, in which she has been active for years, and Rabbis for Human Rights. She lives in Jerusalem with her husband and six children.

Feminism and Halakhah

The Jew Who (Still) Isn't There

HAVIVA NER-DAVID

IN 1971 AN ARTICLE by Rachel Adler appeared in Susannah Heschel's groundbreaking anthology, *On Being a Jewish Feminist.*[1] The article, "The Jew Who Wasn't There: Halakhah and the Jewish Woman," initiated the discussion about what the relationship should be between feminism and halakhah, Jewish Law—or, more accurately, the system of oral law that has been, until now, the ongoing interpretation of the Torah by Jewish male (and only male!) rabbinic authorities throughout the ages. This discussion continues to this day, as voices coming from a broad spectrum of communities in the Jewish world—from ultra-Orthodox to Jewish Renewal—contribute to and deepen the debate as to what the goal of religious Jewish feminism should be and how to get there.

A formerly self-proclaimed Orthodox Jewish feminist with *semicha* (rabbinic ordination) from an Orthodox rabbi, I once saw the goal to be equal access for women in Jewish ritual, public life, and halakhic decision making. Today, calling myself a post-denominational rabbi, I see sectarian movements and the hierarchical assumptions built into that communal structure as but one symptom of a Jewish world in serious need of repair. Equal access is merely a first step toward a much deeper transformation that can only take place when women are not willing to settle for the equal right to play by the rules, but rather insist on—together with men—rewriting what the rules should be. Until women are open to being changed by men and men are open to being changed by women, the feminist battle has not been won and the balance between male and female energy needed in the world in order to bring about *tikkun olam,* the repairing of the world, has not been achieved.

When Adler wrote her original article, she was also a self-proclaimed Orthodox Jewish feminist; today she is a Reform theologian. She argued in this bold piece that women "are viewed in Jewish law and practice as peripheral Jews ... Members of this category are exempt from all positive commandments which occur within time limits. These commandments would include hearing the shofar on Rosh Hashanah, eating in the sukkah, praying with a lulav, praying the three daily services, wearing tallit and tefillin, and saying Shema. Members of this category have been 'excused' from most of the positive symbols which, for the male Jew, hallow time, hallow his physical being, and inform both his myth and his philosophy."[2] As peripheral Jews, women have been educated and socialized toward a peripheral commitment, she added. The Jewish woman's role is a supporting one. She is the enabler who makes it possible for the men in her life to perform their sacred duties, such as studying Torah. She further argued that a Jewish woman's main identification with her Judaism is negative, since she is obligated to observe all of the negative commandments but only some of the positive ones. And most of those mitzvot in which she is involved are physical and not spiritual, material and not mental, so that woman becomes associated with *gashmiut* (the material world) rather than *ruchniut* (the spiritual world).

313

At the end of the article, which includes much harsh and deep criticism of the halakhic system and its androcentrism, Adler called upon the rabbinic authorities of her time to solve these problems. And if they could not meet the challenge, she called upon women to agitate for them to do so. And if they still turned a deaf ear, she called upon the most learned women of the time to make halakhic decisions for the rest.

Almost three decades later, in 1998, the anthology *Jewish Legal Writings by women* [sic], edited by Micah Halpern and Chanah Safrai, was published by Urim Publications. Essays in the book cover timely topics, some of which directly address the dissonance between feminism and traditional Judaism, such as "May Women Wear Tefillin," "Artificial Insemination in Single Women," "Hair Distractions: Women and Worship in the Responsa of Rabbi Moshe Feinstein," and "Establishing and Uprooting Menstruation with the Pill." On the surface, it seems Adler's last-resort scenario came true.

Indeed, in the introduction to this anthology, the editors call the book the culmination of "an explosion of women's seminaries in Israel" and "a forging of a new presentation and understanding of accepted law." Yet, in an essay titled, "Women and the Issuing of Halakhic Rulings," Chanah Henkin, founder and dean of Nishmat, the Jerusalem Center for Advanced Jewish Studies for Women, writes:

> So what of women? Will they remain in the category of ... unqualified candidates for *hora'a* who might fell many, or will women reach the level of ... those scholars who should issue rulings lest "great are her fallen"?... Our major concern must be the Halakhah. Not for the purpose of empowering women, but enabling women to observe mitzvoth meticulously, to blossom with the full richness of the fabric of the religious experience.... Today, we are witnessing, before our eyes, with profound emotion and gratitude to

HaKadosh Baruch Hu, the emergence of a first generation of talmudically-literate women who will be able to
advise other women in this field. They are committed
to the Halakhah and devoted to their fellow women. We
must utilize this precious new resource of learned
women to inspire piety and devotion to Torah in other
women.[3]

These are not just words for Henkin. Nishmat, which was
founded in 1990 and produces learned women who answer halakhic
questions in the area of *niddah*, the Jewish menstrual laws, is a huge
success by the measures Henkin lays out in her essay. These women
are committed to and quite literate in the halakhah. But Henkin is
careful to stress that they are not *poskim*, halakhic decisors. Adler
today would not be content with this development. Since writing
her 1971 article, Adler has denounced her former writings on feminism and Judaism and has developed a new and much more radical
approach, which she lays out in her book *Engendering Judaism: An
Inclusive Theology and Ethics.*[4] Today, Adler would argue that these
women are so committed to traditional halakhah that they are simply "honorary men," a title Adler uses to describe all female Torah
scholars who insist that they retain the traditional male-created and
male-enforced rules.

In the same 1971 Heschel anthology where Adler's essay
appeared, Reform theologian Judith Plaskow wrote another pivotal
essay, "The Right Question Is Theological," which she later developed into her famous book *Standing Again at Sinai*. In this essay,
Plaskow argues that changing specific halakhot in order to "alter
women's situation," does not get to the root of the problem that
causes women's inferior status. She writes:

It is specific halakhot that have been questioned and
not the fundamental presuppositions of the legal system. The fact that women are not counted in a minyan,
that we are not called to the Torah, that we are silent in

315

the marriage ceremony and shackled when it comes to divorce—these disabilities have been recognized, deplored, and in non-Orthodox Judaism, somewhat alleviated. The implications of such laws, their essentially nonarbitrary character, has received less attention, however. Underlying specific halakhot, and outlasting their amelioration or rejection, is an assumption of women's Otherness far more basic than the laws in which it finds expression. If women are not part of the congregation, if we stand passively under the chuppah, if, even in the Reform movement, we have become rabbis only in the last ten years, this is because men—and not women with them—define Jewish humanity. Men are the actors in religious and communal life because they are the normative Jews. Women are "other than" the norm; we are less than fully human.[5]

In *Engendering Judaism,* Adler agrees with Plaskow on the point that gender issues run so deep in Jewish theology that "the impact of gender on Judaism ... is not a women's issue; it is an issue for everyone who seeks to understand Judaism."[6] She continues:

Rather than facing these questions head-on, liberal halakhists tend to evade or disarm them through formalist or positivist legal strategies. These strategies make it impossible for the core questions of feminist critique to be articulated. By translating the critique into terms classical halakhah has in its conceptual vocabulary, liberal halakhists distort the questions. The system's own terms and categories are taken as a given. The feminist critique of them is restated as "women's desire for equal access or equal obligation" and pasted onto a basically intact halakhic system, like a Band-Aid covering a superficial cut.[7]

However, Adler argues that Judaism cannot survive without halakhah, because without halakhah, Judaism becomes disembodied. A communal praxis by means of which Jews can live out their communal ideology is an absolute necessity, according to Adler. Yet, she feels that we cannot work within the traditional halakhic system because of its rootedness in old norms and assumptions. She comes up with a new term for the communal praxis she envisions: "a halakhah," "a way for communities of Jews to generate and embody their Jewish moral visions," as opposed to "the halakhah," "a closed system of obsolete and unjust rules."[8]

Adler uses the legal theory of Robert Cover, who describes law as a bridge between the world-maintaining mode and the world-creating mode. With such a vision of halakhah, Jewish legal decisions can be proactive, representing our vision for where we want to be, not simply reactive, preserving tradition and the status quo; but at the same time, we remain rooted in and in dialogue with traditional texts that represent where we have come from as a people.

All of this Adler sees as part of her project of *Engendering Judaism*—that is, reenvisioning Judaism in light of what we now know about gender. Therefore, her halakhic system would be nonhierarchical, nonauthoritarian, nonapologetic, and nonexclusionary. Moreover, it would be multidisciplinary and heuristic: "attentive to potential resources in its immediate environment, imaginative about combinations, and flexible about the structure of the recipe."[9] Adler would not be content if women were to be allowed into the "men's club" of Judaism and the halakhic system, because that would value traditional male methods over nontraditional methods that have been considered feminine and therefore less worthy.

Thus, for her, in order to retain some kind of halakhah within Judaism, it must be a renewed halakhah that women and men create together by first getting to "know one another," rather than women simply learning to "play by the rules" that men have established. For, as Adler writes, if women were to simply learn to master the system: "Women rabbis could also become authorities—as long as they committed themselves not only to the traditional halakhic process but to the stipulated theological underpinnings."[10] What aside from equal access would be gained by this development? Women's true voices would still not have been heard, because women would simply have learned to adapt their voices in order to be accepted by those in power—the male rabbinic authorities.

Henkin concludes her essay on learned women with a plea to these educated women not to abandon their *midat rachamim*—their role as supporters that Adler referred to in her original essay—as examplars of *chesed*, the value of "deferral to others' needs ... which the domestic role has, through the ages, nobly accommodated. The dangers to the delicate balance between din and rachamim, between formalized and spontaneous behavior, that comes not from high Torah learning for women, but from the roles men and women are already playing in an increasingly impersonal and technological society."[11]

"When we create new role models for women's religious leadership, we must ensure that they represent not only great learning but also personal piety, commitment to family and to chesed, and excellence in middot as well," are Henkin's final words. She too is wary of women becoming "honorary men," but for very different reasons than Adler. Henkin is afraid that if women become halakhic authorities and move into the realm of what has been considered until recently the "man's role" in Judaism, the Jewish family will be threatened, and without this stable base for passing on tradition, Judaism as we know it will be at risk of extinction.

Tamar Ross, in her comprehensive and insightful book *Expanding the Palace of Torah: Orthodoxy and Feminism*,[12] recognizes the power of Adler's arguments and therefore devotes a significant portion of her book to explaining and critiquing Adler's position. Ross takes Adler's arguments so seriously that she even admits that were she a Reform Jew, she would agree with them. However, being an Orthodox Jew, Ross is committed to "the halakhah" and therefore cannot allow herself the freedom to believe in the possibility of "a halakhah." She faults Adler for not appealing to "the consensus of the experts," or to "the larger community of the halakhically committed," or to "a dimension of transcendence."[13] In other words, Adler's system, according to Ross, rejects rabbinic authority, will not be accepted by the Orthodox community, and threatens the notion that the Torah is divine.

Adler, I think, would agree with the first two objections, although I think she would take issue with the third. Her definition of transcendent, however, would differ from Ross's, in my opinion, although not in as significant a way as perhaps Ross believes. Ross believes in "cumulative revelation" of God's will through our continuing interpretation and reinterpretation of Torah in light of divine values that are revealed at certain points in history and that are meant to be incorporated into Judaism, while building upon the foundational values of the religion. Adler, however, is not willing to accept those foundational values as more basic to Judaism than values that are revealed at a later time. Both Ross and Adler admit that Judaism can potentially become whatever Jews make it. The possibilities are endless, they both agree. However, Ross seeks value in patriarchy itself. She sees it as the best way proven as of yet to preserve the traditional family unit and thus transmit values from one generation to the next. Adler, on the other hand, sees patriarchy as a value system that has corrupted Judaism and therefore must now be overthrown.

Adler and Ross are not so far from each other theologically, because Adler too sees the only means toward creating a halakhah as being in dialogue with traditional texts, though we bring to the table our own values. Ross would not have a problem with that. The difference between their approaches would be played out more in the balance between foundational values and modern values that, according to Ross's model would be checked by rabbinic authority, and the degree to which the Orthodox community would be willing to accept change. Ross, who is coming from an Orthodox Israeli context, and Adler, who is coming from an American Reform context, are not talking about the same communities, and therefore, it is no wonder that their radical feminist theology can be applied to different degrees. Whereas Adler is free to envision a Judaism that completely reflects her value system, Ross is limited by the boundaries allowed within the Orthodox community. And while Ross would argue that these boundaries makes her Judaism more authentic, Adler would counter that her freedom gives her own Judaism more integrity.

In fact, Rabbi Zalman Schachter-Shalomi, founder of the Jewish Renewal movement, recently came out with a book titled *Integral Halakhah: Transcending and Including*,[14] in which he sets out his recipe for a halakhah that would bring Judaism into the twenty-first century. Like Adler, he sees the current age as belonging to a totally new paradigm in which old categories and methods no longer apply. His approach to halakhah is to look deeply into the traditional sources to understand the root value of the law, and then create new ways to live out those values.

For instance, he states that the reason behind *shechitah* (ritual slaughter) is to minimize the pain to the animal. Today, he argues, since we know more about what causes and can lessen the animal's anxiety, and since we have the technology to tranquilize the animal before slaughter, perhaps we should be doing so. After all, most Western cultures do stun animals before slaughter in order to minimize their pain. This leaves Judaism morally lagging behind in this area, whereas historically, *shechitah* was ahead of its time in terms of concern for the animal's emotional and physical suffering.

In this way, halakhah does not risk becoming a mere shell lacking meaning, a form without content. For Schachter-Shalomi, it is the content that matters and is timeless. The form, however, is transient and is not the essence of God's will. The main difference between Schachter-Shalomi and Adler is that whereas she sees gender as the factor that uproots tradition, he sees gender as but one example of a more general "paradigm shift"[15] we are now experiencing as the natural progression in God's plan for the world. In reality, though, the three theologians Adler, Ross, and Schachter-

Shalomi, from three different denominations—Reform, Orthodox, and Renewal—are quite close in their view of Judaism as being in the midst of a transformative era that must necessarily be reflected in halakhah if Judaism is to survive.

Nevertheless, what seems to separate the Orthodox from the more liberal Jewish feminists is the former's inability to see beyond the parameters and definitions of their own community. Out of fear of losing the religious Jewish status quo, they are forced to abandon a Judaism that reflects a truly redemptive vision of what religion can embody. Without a willingness to let go of patriarchal structures and assumptions, Judaism will always lag behind the general culture in its redemptive possibilities.

While it is true that more radical approaches to halakhah risk losing Judaism as we know it, those, like myself, who espouse these approaches, do not fear this. In fact, that is our desired result. We do not wish to hold on to a Judaism that retains oppressive values from the previous paradigm. Rather, our goal is to bring Judaism into the future without losing what we consider its core redemptive function in the world. In this way, we are actually more committed to the power of transcendence than those who champion more conservative approaches to halakhah.

Perhaps what truly divides our two camps is process more than theology. Whereas feminists who hold on to "the halakhah" fear that without patriarchy Judaism will be lost, feminists like myself who believe in the vision of "a halakhah" believe that it is only by letting go of patriarchy that Judaism can survive. The core question is: Is the patriarchal model such an integral part of Judaism that it must be retained even at the cost of sacrificing the redemptive nature of Judaism? Or is the patriarchal model but one paradigm through which deeper Jewish values have been expressed in the past? Can we also imagine these deeper values being expressed in ways more appropriate to our current reality?

As a woman (now a rabbi with private Orthodox ordination) who has devoted much time and energy to the Jewish feminist cause,

I believe the latter is true. Like Adler, I once carried the banner of Orthodox feminism. However, witnessing and experiencing the sacrifices that the Orthodox feminist movement has been willing to make in order to be "accepted" by the male powers that be, as well as the unwillingness of those same male powers to meet us at least part of the way, I no longer believe in the importance of working "within the system."

For me, a significant aspect of the feminist project is the breaking down of a hierarchical model that places women beneath men and reinforces the power of the already empowered. But this applies not only to a hierarchy of people, but also to a hierarchy of ideas and methods. Even if we succeed in gaining equality for women in Jewish law and ritual (which is so far from the reality even in liberal Orthodox circles today that this is not even a spoken goal of that movement), is that really what our goal should be? I believe not. If women are fighting for the right to say what men have been saying all along, what have we gained? Rather, my vision of a Judaism for our current paradigm is one that equally weighs all voices—male and female, past and present—and is bold enough to sacrifice tradition when necessary in order to retain its power to be a redemptive force in our broken world.

Rabbi Gail Labovitz, PhD, is assistant professor of rabbinic literature at the American Jewish University, where she teaches rabbinic texts and Jewish law, and chairs the department of rabbinics for the Ziegler School of Rabbinic Studies. She received her doctorate from the Jewish Theological Seminary in 2002, where she was also ordained as a Conservative rabbi in 1992. While in rabbinical school, she served as the administrative assistant to the Committee on Jewish Law and Standards of the Rabbinical Assembly. She has also served as a senior research analyst for the Feminist Sexual Ethics Project at Brandeis University and as the coordinator of the Jewish Feminist Research Group, a project of the Jewish Women's Studies Program at The Jewish Theologial Seminary of America.

Feminism and Jewish Law in Conservative Judaism

RABBI GAIL LABOVITZ, PhD

ON MARCH 14, 1972, a group of Jewish women calling themselves Ezrat Nashim—the Hebrew term for the women's section of the synagogue, but also translatable as "women's help"—came to the annual convention of the Rabbinical Assembly (RA), the rabbinic organization of the Conservative movement, and distributed a document titled "Jewish Women Call for Change." The women wrote: "For three thousand years, one-half of the Jewish people have been excluded from full participation in Jewish communal life. We call for an end to the second-class status of women in Jewish life." Among their petitions were:

the counting of women in the minyan
full participation for women in religious observances (aliyot, ba'alot kriah, sh'lihot tzibbur)[1]

the recognition of women as witnesses before Jewish law

the right of women to initiate divorce

permission and indeed encouragement of women to attend
    rabbinical and cantorial schools, and to perform rabbinical
    and cantorial functions in synagogues

the consideration of women as bound to fulfill all mitzvot
    equally with men

In October of 1983, after the faculty of the Jewish Theological Seminary (JTS) voted to admit women to the rabbinical program, members of Ezrat Nashim (including two who by then served on the faculty of JTS) issued a press release, in which they declared of the decision:

> It is consonant with Conservative interpretations of the development of halakhah (Jewish law). It also follows logically from earlier decisions of the Conservative movement to reject the sexual segregation characteristic of the Jewish past by providing equal education for Jewish daughters, introducing mixed seating in the synagogue, counting women in the *minyan* (prayer quorum), and calling them to the Torah.

Paula Hyman, one of the group members (and one of the women who voted as members of the JTS faculty), has since written, "For Ezrat Nashim, the vote marked the culmination of achievement of almost all that we had lobbied for over the course of more than a decade."[2]

These sources demonstrate that questions and concerns about the place of women in Conservative Judaism have always been intimately (though not exclusively) tied to questions and concerns about the place of halakhah in Conservative Judaism. As Rabbi Robert Gordis wrote in his introduction to *Emet v'Emunah,* the movement's statement of its principles and beliefs, among the "fundamentals of the philosophy of the Conservative

Movement" is that "we recognize the authority of the Halakhah which has never been monolithic or immovable."[3] That is, the ideology of the Conservative movement holds that Jewish law is an essential part of Jewish life and is binding on Jews, though Conservative Jews may and do disagree about the theological underpinnings of why, and how, it is binding. At the same time, the movement also holds that Jewish law is not static and never has been, that it grows and changes and is adaptable to changing times, changing social situations, and changing ideas about what is moral and right. Feminism, of course, represents just such a revolution in the popular understanding, a claim that discrimination based on gender is a moral wrong. When these factors come together, then, it is perhaps not surprising that the majority of the goals (those cited above being six out of eight listed by Ezrat Nashim) of a group of women addressing the Conservative movement and its rabbis would be items seeking a change in women's ritual and legal status.

The list presented by Ezrat Nashim suggests three areas in particular in which it has been especially important for the Conservative movement to address feminist concerns from a halakhic perspective (the first two of which are especially interrelated): women's participation in prayer and ritual, allowing women to serve as religious authorities, and inequities in the Jewish law of marriage.[4] By looking at how these issues have been addressed, we can see some important patterns emerge regarding the Conservative approach to bridging feminism and halakhic process. First, however, it is necessary to explain some details about the means by which halakhic decision making takes place within the Conservative movement.

Most halakhic issues are addressed by the Committee on Jewish Law and Standards (CJLS) of the Rabbinical Assembly. This body is made of twenty-five rabbis who are voting members, as well as five lay members and a representative of the Cantors' Assembly who participate in debate but do not vote. When a question or issue is raised in the movement, rabbis (usually but not exclusively members of the CJLS) write *teshuvot*—legal responsa— which are then debated and voted on. At different times, different rules have prevailed as to the number of votes needed to validate an opinion; at the current time, any *teshuvah* that receives six or more positive votes becomes a legitimate option within the movement. A crucial additional point to understand about Conservative Judaism, however, is that alongside its commitment to an evolving and adaptable halakhah, the movement also holds "pluralism" as one of its highest values. In practice, what this means is the recognized validity within the movement of differences—between rabbis and/or between communities—in halakhic interpretation and practice. This occurs in (at least) two ways within the official structure of the movement. First, as might be evident from current CJLS procedure as already described, it is quite possible that on a given issue, more than one *teshuvah,* each taking different approaches or coming to different conclusions about the issue at hand, might each receive six votes, making different opinions legitimate options for Conservative Jews. This then couples with another important principle in Conservative Judaism, the commitment to the role of the individual rabbi as the *mara d'atra* (Aramaic for "master of the place"), meaning that the local rabbi is recognized as the ultimate authority for all halakhic decision making in his or her community. Thus, the *mara d'atra* may follow any legitimate opinion issued by the CJLS, or may even choose to act and rule on his or her own authority without reference to the committee's rulings.[5]

Women's Participation in Prayer and Ritual

Some of the issues raised by Ezrat Nashim in 1972 had, in fact, already been raised in Conservative circles. As early as 1955, a minority opinion allowed women to receive an aliyah (be called to the Torah) on an equal basis with men, while the majority opinion admitted the possibility of calling a woman for an extra aliyah on a special occasion. In 1973, just after the appearance by Ezrat Nashim, the CJLS decided by a vote of 9-4 that women may be counted in a minyan without adopting a specific responsum to provide the underlying rationale (more than one had been offered to the committee). Subsequent committee correspondence confirmed that this ruling could be interpreted to allow women full participation, including as prayer leaders, in those minyanim. Other new issues that flow from these decisions have also been raised to and addressed by the CJLS: For example, if women are being called to the Torah, may a married couple be called together? Should a woman be called as a Cohen (priest) or Levite, if that is her lineage? In addition, in recent years the CJLS has undertaken a broad project of revisiting some of its earlier decisions in order to ground them in more rigorous halakhic argumentation; thus, in 2002, the CJLS adopted, by a vote of 15-0 (and 2 abstentions), a *teshuvah* by Rabbi David J. Fine reaffirming that women may count in the minyan and serve as leaders of prayer.[6]

Crucial here, however, is the word *may*. Given the movement's ideological commitment to pluralism, a decision that it is permissible to count women in the minyan does not, from the Conservative perspective, negate the halakhic validity of the classical ruling that a minyan is made up of ten adult males. Although the Conservative movement has done much toward making full egalitarianism a viable option in Conservative prayer communities—and although egalitarian worship is by far the more common practice in those communities—the movement does not have an institutional commitment to promoting egalitarianism as the preferred model for Jewish community. Thus, at many Conservative events (such as the annual conventions of the RA or United Synagogue for Conservative Judaism) and institutions (such as camps in the Ramah system), there will be two prayer services offered at any given time, one in which men and women count and participate equally, and one in which only men are part of the quorum and lead prayer.

Women as Religious Authorities

As mentioned above, the decision to ordain women as rabbis was made by the faculty of JTS in 1983, rather than by a vote of the CJLS, a somewhat anomalous procedure in movement history (women were similarly admitted to the cantorial school shortly thereafter). Nonetheless, CJLS decisions regarding women's status did have an important impact on the process that led to that historic vote in 1983. Notably, at its 1977 convention, the RA passed a resolution calling on the various arms of the movement to together establish a commission to study the question of ordaining women, which they did later that year. The members of the Commission for the Study of the Ordination of Women as Rabbis submitted its report to the RA at its 1979 convention. Not surprisingly, the commission noted that "the demands of *halakhah* led the list of matters to be resolved."[7] The commission further observed that while there is no strict set of halakhic guidelines dictating that a modern rabbi must perform a certain set of tasks, such as leading prayer or officiating at weddings, it might nonetheless be the case that "granted that the religious functions in question are logically distinct from the role of the rabbi, they are certainly connected closely enough in practice to be a serious cause for concern."[8] To answer this concern, the commission pointed to the CJLS decisions allowing women to count in the minyan and participate in services by being called to the Torah and leading prayer, already discussed above. The commission further noted that another vote in 1974 produced a minority position of sufficient numbers (by the rules of the time) to allow women to serve as witnesses to religious acts and as signatories on religious documents (such as the marriage contract). This latter decision is also one that was more recently revisited by the CJLS, in 2001, at which time two *teshuvot* advocating for women's full rights in this area each received sufficient votes to be adopted.[9]

As in the case of women's participation in prayer and ritual, here, too, members of Conservative communities, including rabbis, may take a variety of stances regarding women's religious leadership. The question of women serving as witnesses has been a particularly complicated one, in that it also potentially affects matters of personal status, such as the validity of conversions, marriages, and divorces. Female rabbis (and cantors) in the movement make their own individual choices in this area, tempered by local conditions in which they may find themselves (for example, a woman might agree to refrain from serving as a member of the court that validates a conversion in order to foster an interdenominational program). Some choose not to serve as witnesses at all, while others might take an approach of "informed consent" from those on whose behalf they sign marriage or conversion documents. At this time, however, the movement-wide Joint Bet Din (religious court) that oversees divorces and annulments of marriages (discussed below) does not use women as witnesses, out of concern that such divorces would then be automatically rendered null among those who do not accept the legitimacy of women's testimony, leading to a variety of problems when one or the other spouse seeks to remarry or has children from a subsequent relationship.[10]

While discussing the topic of Jewish law and women as religious leaders, it is also worth considering how women in the Conservative movement have started to themselves become participants in the process of halakhic decision making. Records of the CJLS show that even before the ordination of women, at least one woman served as the coauthor of a responsum presented to the committee.[11] Eight women have served or are currently serving as full-voting rabbinic members of the CJLS in North America, while several more have served on the Israeli Va'ad Ha'Halakhah (Law Committee); nine *teshuvot* authored or coauthored by a woman have been adopted by the CJLS. It is perhaps too soon to tell, then, whether— or how—the presence of women might change the nature of either the questions that will be raised in the movement or the answers that will be given (not to mention the means by which those answers will be reached). So far, women's *teshuvot* have addressed issues directly related to gender (whether or not may women tie the ritual fringes on a tallit or serve as witnesses), questions that touch on matters of gender and gender relations that affect both men and women (mourning for miscarriage and still-birth, how traditional laws about sexual abstinence during menstruation should be observed by Conservative couples), and matters that do not relate to gender (details of reading the Torah on a triennial, three-year cycle). Relatedly, although women do not at this time serve as participants in the process of overseeing divorces, a number of women have participated in an RA program to train *mesadrei gittin*, as the authorities handling divorces are known in Hebrew. At the time of this writing, two have passed the qualifying examinations and are now listed with the RA, while several more are poised to do so; it remains to be seen what role these women will eventually take in the movement in this area.

Marriage and Divorce

Finally, marriage—and divorce—is the topic that has the longest history of discussion in the Conservative movement. This issue arises because of the way in which a marriage is created in Jewish law. At the heart of a Jewish marriage is the act of *kiddushin*, betrothal, also known as *kinyan*, acquisition. The man gives the woman an item of value (a ring is the standard item used) and declares, "With this ring you are betrothed to me according to the law of Moses and Israel." The woman's tacit acceptance of the ring as the man places it on her finger is deemed to be her consent. There is nothing she needs to say, or traditionally does say, as part of the legal act; she does not acquire him. In fact, some Conservative rabbis do not allow a double ring ceremony, or at least do not allow the woman to say a complementary formula when giving a ring to the groom, because this could make the ceremony appear to be an exchange rather than the unilateral act that it is legally supposed to be (even those who do permit the complementary formula often justify doing so because once the man's acquisition of the woman as his wife has taken place, her declaration is legally meaningless). Moreover, since the marriage is unilaterally created by an act of the husband, so too it must be dissolved by a unilateral act of the husband, the giving of a divorce document known as the *get*.

Thus, some of the earliest records of a halakhic issue being addressed by Conservative authorities relate to the problem of the *agunah*, the chained wife whose husband has not granted her a divorce. Such a woman cannot remarry under Jewish law; any relationship with another man is legally adulterous and any children born would be considered *mamzerim* (illegitimate children), who are forbidden to marry other Jews of "ordinary" lineage.[12] There are grounds for a wife to petition for a divorce, but a court cannot grant the divorce on the husband's behalf; he must commission the writing of the *get* of his own free will. Therefore, it is possible for a man to use the threat of withholding the divorce as a form of blackmail over his wife, or to refuse to grant it altogether. A proposal for the husband to sign a legal instrument at the time of the wedding to grant power to a court to write a divorce on his behalf appeared in the *Proceedings of the Rabbinical Assembly* of 1930–32. Numerous additional proposals were discussed and adopted between then and 1968. Three basic approaches are used in the movement now: (1) conditional marriage, such that if a *get* is not granted within a set time after a civil divorce decree, the Jewish marriage becomes retroactively null and void;[13] (2) the "Lieberman clause," whereby the classic marriage contract known as the *ketubah* includes a commitment from each member of the couple to appear before the Joint Bet Din if summoned by the other and to abide by its dictates; this clause is meant to be enforceable as a civil contract;[14] (3) allowing for the power of the court to retroactively annul marriages when all other means of securing a divorce have been exhausted.[15]

Here, then, we come to one of the Ezrat Nashim proposals that has not been met by the Conservative movement. No proposed solution to the problem of the *agunah* challenges the fundamental inequity at the heart of Jewish marriage. A woman may not give her husband a divorce. Even the (at the moment, all-male) court cannot grant a divorce, but rather must uproot the marriage altogether, and only after exhausting other avenues to persuade the husband to give the *get* himself. Indeed, it is intriguing that within the Conservative movement's recent decision to recognize homosexual relationships, one can detect a desire to "protect" *kiddushin* as a "privileged" right/rite reserved for heterosexual couples. In the *teshuvah* that was adopted by the CJLS, the authors write in their conclusion:

> We are not prepared at this juncture to rule upon the halakhic status of gay and lesbian relationships. To do so would require establishing an entirely new institution in Jewish law that treats not only the ceremonies and legal instruments appropriate for creating homosexual unions but also the norms for the dissolution of such unions. This responsum does not provide *kiddushin* for same-sex couples.[16]

A "Summary" on the Rabbinical Assembly website is even clearer: "Commitment ceremonies that avoid the legal mechanisms of *kiddushin* may be designed for gay and lesbian couples."[17] The very next sentence reads: "There is to be no discrimination against gay and lesbian Jews," but the true irony may be that we soon see a situation in the Conservative movement in which a woman who makes a life commitment to another woman will be a more equal partner in her ceremony (and the underlying nature of the legal bond between them) than her sister who marries a man.

The nature of the halakhic process within Conservative Judaism has particular implications for the ways in which the movement has addressed the status and roles of women. On the one hand, the ideological commitment of the movement to Jewish law's flexibility and ability to meet changing social conditions has allowed the movement to develop legal opinions and take stands that ameliorate most of the outstanding disabilities that women have historically faced in Jewish practice. Conservative interpretations allow women to participate as equals in religious services and rites, and to serve as religious authorities. On the other hand, the movement's equal commitment to religious pluralism and the possibility for multiple interpretations of Jewish law means that more traditionalist forms that exclude women remain legitimate options for Conservative communities. Moreover, as is most evident in the area of marriage law, it has often been easier within the interpretive methods used by Conservative authorities to address the symptoms of gender discrimination—such as chained wives—than to uproot the underlying assumptions and legal structures that create inequity. How the presence of women—and men who have been sensitized to the effects of sexism in Jewish law—as interpreters of halakhah within Conservative Judaism will affect how the movement addresses these larger challenges remains to be seen.

Rabbi Barbara Penzner currently serves as spiritual leader of Temple Hillel B'nai Torah in Boston. She was among the first two hundred women to be ordained as a rabbi. She is a past president of both the Massachusetts Board of Rabbis and the Reconstructionist Rabbinical Association. She is also a founder of Mayyim Hayyim Mikveh and Education Center in Newton, Massachusetts. Rabbi Penzner is married to Brian Rosman. They have two children.

Women and the Reconstructionist Movement

RABBI BARBARA PENZNER

IT IS OFTEN SAID that Rabbi Mordecai Kaplan had four reasons for introducing the bat mitzvah ceremony for girls in 1922: his daughters Judith, Hadassah, Naomi, and Selma. Over eighty years later, the quiet revolution that Kaplan began in the height of the women's suffrage movement has grown and flourished into what Kaplan founded in the mid-twentieth century: Reconstructionist Judaism. Reconstructionist Judaism, the fourth major Jewish movement of our day and the only home-grown North American movement, was built on and thrives in an environment of equality for women. But equality was actually only the starting point for Reconstructionist ideology and practice regarding women. Since Kaplan's time, Reconstructionist Judaism embraced the transformational aspects of feminism. Today, the Reconstructionist movement may be said to be at the forefront of access for women to leadership and ritual practice, feminist scholarship, and creative applications of feminist thinking in Jewish life. Reconstructionist rabbis and congregations have led the way toward inclusive policies and innovative practices, and the rest of North American Judaism has followed, often unaware of the pivotal role of this small, yet pioneering movement.

Kaplan's Reconstructionist approach infused Jewish life in America and Canada long before he agreed to found a separate movement. Institutions that are commonplace today, such as the synagogue as a Jewish center (as opposed to a strictly religious institution), "new" Haggadot, the bat mitzvah ceremony, and even support for Israel, were adopted early on by Kaplan and his followers. Rabbi Kaplan taught at The Jewish Theological Seminary of America (JTS), the rabbinical school of the Conservative movement, from 1909 to 1963, influencing a generation of Conservative rabbis. His eagerness to adapt Judaism to modern democratic ideals, to experiment with religious ritual, and to promote action in the world on ethical principles created fertile ground for women's rights and feminism to take hold.

The nineteenth amendment to the U.S. Constitution, which granted women the right to vote, was ratified in 1920. But in 1918, inspired by the suffrage movement, Kaplan had already raised the question of equality for women in Jewish life at the annual convention of United Synagogue, a group of twenty-two synagogues that Kaplan helped found with Solomon Schechter in 1913 that were not part of the Union of American Hebrew Congregations. While the discussion had no apparent immediate impact, in 1922, shortly after Kaplan established and became the rabbi of the Society for the Advancement of Judaism (SAJ) in New York City, he introduced mixed seating at High Holy Day services. At that time, outside of Reform synagogues, separate seating for men and women was the norm. Kaplan also spoke vigorously from the pulpit in support of equality for women. Within that context, he invited his oldest daughter, Judith, to be called to the Torah at age twelve as a bat mitzvah. It was a small and impromptu ceremony by today's standards. Judith chanted the Torah blessings and read a portion of the Torah in Hebrew and in English. Gradually, other girls began to follow the precedent, though it took another twenty years before adult women were called to the Torah at the SAJ on a regular basis. In 1950, the SAJ voted to grant full religious equality to women, and in 1953 voted to include women in the synagogue board. As a result, women in Reconstructionist circles took active part in Jewish ritual and leadership a generation before it became widespread in the North American Jewish community.

In 1968, Ira Eisenstein, Kaplan's closest follower and Judith's husband, finally convinced his father-in-law to break away from the Conservative movement and begin training Reconstructionist rabbis independently from JTS. That year, Sandy Eisenberg Sasso applied and was accepted to the Reconstructionist Rabbinical College (RRC) and became its first woman graduate in 1974. By the mid-1970s, half of each entering class at RRC was made up of women. RRC welcomed women equally as students, professors, and administrators, and today most of the senior staff of RRC is comprised of women.

When I first explored applying to rabbinical school in 1979, I had never met a female rabbi. No one had ever suggested this career path to me. At first, I sent a query to the Conservative movement in which I was raised and educated and was told that they would ordain women "eventually." After that disappointing response, I learned about Reconstructionist Judaism and applied to RRC. There I met women and men who introduced an approach to Judaism that spoke to my heart and to my head. The writings of Mordecai Kaplan resonated with my Jewish experience and answered many questions I had about why Judaism should be an important part of my life and the life of the Jewish people. As part of a young movement that believed in empowering Jews to discover their true path, rather than follow the rabbis' dictates, I enjoyed the excitement of RRC's creative and experimental atmosphere. I also found at the college a commitment to creating supportive communities. In the class with which I was admitted, there were four men and six women, so I always felt that my voice was heard and that women's issues were taken seriously. This has held true in my experience as a congregational rabbi as well as a movement leader.

A Program of "Firsts"

Riding the waves of feminism and activism of the 1970s and 1980s, the growing movement and its nascent rabbinical college offered women many opportunities to be the "first." In 1979, Rabbi Linda Holtzman became the first woman to serve a Conservative congregation, well before JTS ordained its own women rabbis. In 1984, the lay arm of the movement, then known as the Federation of Reconstructionist Congregations and Havurot (FRCH), chose Lillian Kaplan to become its president, making Kaplan the first woman to lead any major Jewish synagogue organization. The first woman to head a rabbinical association was Sandy Eisenberg Sasso, who served as president of the Reconstructionist Rabbinical Association (RRA). (Earlier I noted that Sandy was the first woman graduate of the RRC. Later, Sandy and her husband, Dennis Sasso, were the first rabbinic couple, and she was the first rabbi to become a mother.) Sandy's leadership was followed by Rabbis Joy Levitt, Barbara Penzner, Nancy Fuchs-Kreimer, and Amy Small. In 2007, Rabbi Toba Spitzer became the first openly lesbian rabbi to lead a rabbinical association.

The influx of women rabbis led to important changes in Jewish life broadly, spearheaded in the Reconstructionist movement and moving outward from there. Women rabbis enthusiastically experimented with ceremonies for welcoming baby girls into the covenant. Sandy and Dennis Sasso published their original *b'rit banot yisrael* ceremony in 1974. Rabbis Linda Holtzman, Nancy Fuchs-Kreimer, and Rebecca Alpert joined with several Reform women rabbis to create the *brit rehitzah*, a welcoming ceremony for girls based on biblical texts and women's connection to water. Women rabbis developed a host of innovative ceremonies that involved water, candles, creative readings, and new blessings. These were passed down from one rabbi's files to the next, back in the days before e-mail and computers, and long before the mainstream Jewish press began to collect and publish them. RRC maintained a "Creative Liturgy Library" to disseminate these and other original ceremonies that seemed to appear on a daily basis as women encountered life events that had no existing Jewish blessings or celebrations.

Within this laboratory of Jewish ritual life, my colleague Rabbi Amy Small and I developed a new ritual for brides to immerse at the mikveh. Along with a few others, we rediscovered the power of mikveh and hoped to promote it more widely, seeking to overcome the negative images associated with mikveh in our time. While some "classical" Reconstructionists found these forays into traditional Judaism off-putting and non-rational, we continue to promote Jewish rituals, even seemingly antiquated ones, within the Reconstructionist context. As a movement that is not tied to practice through halakhah (Jewish law), rabbis and lay people enjoy the liberty to invent new rituals and liturgy, and to revalue traditional practices. Our emphasis on peoplehood and our commitment to remain connected to the Jewish people permits us to experiment in ways that foster Jewish life that is authentically grounded in our past.

Feminist creativity at the college brought some criticism from outside the movement in the 1980s. There were articles in major Jewish publications claiming that the Reconstructionist movement was practicing paganism because some rabbinical students had developed rituals invoking the goddess as a means to access the feminine aspects of divinity. Even today, criticism is leveled at the movement for its openness to non-traditional liturgical and ritual expressions, and its complete acceptance of women's leadership.

An important aspect of developing an authentic and yet novel approach in the Reconstructionist movement arose from uncovering women's experience. The RRC introduced and supported feminist scholarship and has had wide influence in our movement and beyond. The RRC established women's studies as part of the curriculum in the 1980s, expanded the program into the Jewish Women's Studies Project in 1990, and in 1997 established Kolot: the

Center for Jewish Women and Gender Studies. This feminist center at RRC trains Jewish leaders; promotes research; and provides programs and material on Judaism, women, and gender to the general Jewish community. Today, its on-line resource, *Ritualwell.org* (developed with Ma'yan: The Jewish Women's Project of the JCC in Manhattan), carries on the tradition of RRC's "Creative Liturgy Library" with its treasure trove of thousands of readings, rituals, and music to download or use as the basis for one's own creation. Kolot also created and pioneered Rosh Hodesh: It's a Girl Thing, a popular educational program to help teenage girls develop identity and self-esteem in a Jewish context. In 2001, Lori Lefkovitz, the director of Kolot, was appointed to the Gottesman Chair, the first-ever chaired professorship in gender and Judaism. Kolot's presence at RRC ensures that both scholarly and practical applications of feminism will continue to infuse the movement's leadership and thinking.

Polices for Equality

One of the first policies established by the Reconstructionist Rabbinical Association (RRA) was the egalitarian *get* (divorce document). The association created procedures and documents permitting women to initiate Jewish divorce for the first time, abandoning the notion that a woman needs to be released by her husband or else become an *agunah*, "chained woman," who may not remarry. This effort was among the RRA's first attempts to create innovative policy and has engendered lively debate ever since. Some argue that the notions of the *get* and the *agunah* are inherently sexist and no longer necessary, while others claim that we should not be using traditional language for non-traditional practices. Individual rabbis today choose their own practice, although many have adopted "divorce ceremonies" to add spiritual closure to a marriage, with or without a *get*. The egalitarian *get* demonstrated a commitment to an activist inclusivity and to mutual respect between men and women in the early days of the RRA.

The prayer book is perhaps a movement's most visible illustration of its principles. As the Reconstructionist movement developed its prayer book series, *Kol Haneshamah*, in the early 1990s, it was understood that feminist principles of egalitarianism would lead to liturgical innovation. The series was developed through the pioneering establishment of a prayer book commission comprised of men and women, lay leaders and rabbis. English readings and commentaries were authored by an array of male and female contributors. From the outset, there was no question that the English translations for the names of God would be gender-neutral; this decision came before any other movement had taken this step. *Kol Haneshamah* also brought feminist thinking into the Hebrew text. Wherever the patriarchs Abraham, Isaac, and Jacob were mentioned, the matriarchs Sarah, Rebecca, Rachel, and Leah were included; and the Hebrew for "our mothers" stood beside "our fathers." In addition, the prayer book includes options for changing the Hebrew blessing formula itself, including Marcia Falk's poetic reinterpretation *nevarech et eyn hahayim* ("Let us bless the Source of Life") as a possible substitute for the standard *Baruch atah Adonai* ("Blessed are you, Lord"). *Kol Haneshamah* was the first siddur to deliberately include women's voices in a variety of ways. For many Reconstructionist affiliates, it provided a place to raise questions about liturgy and theology, and enabled more congregants to take charge of services.

Feminist ideals of inclusion transformed Jewish life beyond equal access for women. As Rebecca Alpert wrote, "feminist consciousness ... brings to the foreground the way Judaism has defined and limited people based on gender."[1] Therefore, the inclusion of gay, lesbian, bisexual, and transgender (GLBT) Jews is another hallmark of the Reconstructionist movement. In 1984, the RRC faculty was the first to admit openly gay and lesbian rabbinical students, and the rest of the movement followed in time. After years of debate within the rabbinic community, both the RRA and JRF (Jewish Reconstructionist Federation, formerly FRCH) recognized the importance of welcoming gays and lesbians openly, well before other synagogue movements. Yet some rabbis serving congregations outside of the Reconstructionist heartland of Philadelphia felt threatened by the idea of educating lay people to become more open to gays and lesbians. For many years, gay and lesbian rabbis who had been open at RRC debated whether to be "out" in job interviews. Some suffered rejection when they came out to their congregations.

The Joint Reconstructionist Commission on Homosexuality, which included representatives from the three arms of the movement—RRC, RRA, and JRF—published its report in 1992 supporting gay men and lesbians as rabbis and members of congregations. The movement published a six-part workshop series to help congregations become welcoming communities. The RRA pioneered same-sex commitment ceremonies, including a model in the first RRA Rabbis' Manual published in 1997. The Reconstructionist movement provided leadership for other movements and Jewish organizations to welcome GLBT Jews fully.

Likewise, women's involvement in the rabbinate helped shape new models for both male and female rabbis. It is important to note that the Reconstructionist movement has always aimed to train rabbis who are teachers, rather than halachic authorities or preachers. Reconstructionist rabbis seek to provide Jews with the tools of Jewish learning and practice as well as an understanding of their historical context and contemporary meaning, to empower individuals to develop their own Jewish path. Reconstructionist rabbis are also trained as organizers, to develop caring communities that live the values that they espouse. In this way, the feminist goals of participatory leadership, consensus, and team building are made manifest in rabbinic models, and there is much less "priestly" public function for rabbis than in other movements.

Finally, the experience of women as rabbis led to concerted efforts to balance the demands of professional life with an intrinsic respect for family life. As a result, both men and women rabbis strive to model that balance for their congregants. In 2001, the Reconstructionist

341

movement's Commission on the Role of the Rabbi published a groundbreaking report, *The Rabbi-Congregation Relationship: A Vision for the 21st Century*. The report describes the rabbi's role as part of a system, with attention to the rabbi's spiritual, personal, and family life as well as the rabbi's responsibilities to the congregation or other workplaces. The role of the rabbi continues to evolve, with important input from women in the field, some of whom are nearing the age of retirement.

Call to Action

The Reconstructionist movement is built on the notion of Judaism as the evolving civilization of the Jewish people; therefore we expect that the impact of women and feminism in the Reconstructionist movement will continue to evolve in ways we cannot envision today. If feminism is a movement concerned with giving women equal access and advancing women to positions of power and influence, then the Reconstructionist movement has fulfilled those goals. Every arm of the movement has had significant female leadership. Women serve in a variety of rabbinic roles, including large and small congregations, chaplaincy, education, campus life, and the military. There are no "glass ceilings" to be broken within the Reconstructionist movement. Ritual life and decision making in Reconstructionist congregations are unabashedly egalitarian. In the wider Jewish world, women's rights and issues require continued attention and Reconstructionist men and women will most certainly be involved in those struggles, if not leading the way.

It could be, then, that the work of Jewish feminism, as experienced in the rest of the Jewish community, simply does not carry the same weight of angst in the Reconstructionist movement. We are now debating the fine points of gender and inclusivity with an overriding assumption that feminist gains have been won.

Ironically, though, the Reconstructionist movement today is most concerned about the overwhelming number of women leaders and the simultaneous loss of male leadership. The mystery of the vanishing Jewish male has become quite noticeable in both Reconstructionist congregations and movement institutions. The next major feminist issue for Reconstructionists to confront, consider, and change is the role of men and boys in Jewish life. Have we included women to the exclusion of men? Has spiritual life become a new "women's domain"? Have men lost interest in Jewish leadership because of the presence of Jewish women? Are there aspects of Jewish life that appeal to men that we have somehow lost or forgotten?

Most important is to craft a new balance that reinvests the movement with male leaders while retaining and supporting women as full and equal participants in our community. Reconstructionist Judaism, by definition, should offer multiple doorways to Jewish life. Just as women have flourished in Rosh Hodesh groups and consciousness-raising groups that are single-sex, perhaps we can once again welcome all-men's groups in a Jewish context while maintaining principles of egalitarianism. In this next phase of feminism, we are called to embrace and celebrate differences, including differences between men and women. Having created a movement that accepts diversity, it is time to encourage flexibility in talking to boys about what Jewish men do, to provide strong positive Jewish role models for boys, and to create environments that support boys' development. Programs akin to Rosh Hodesh: It's a Girl Thing are urgently needed for Jewish boys today. In classrooms, youth groups, and camping outings, educators need to become more attuned to the different intelligences, needs, and interests of boys and young men. Having learned to create communities of mutual respect, the ultimate goal of feminism would be to advance the interests of Jewish males without giving up our commitment to women's voices and women's issues. A true vision of a feminist Reconstructionist Judaism will become reality when gender is not only a women's concern, when we stop counting how many men or how many women are on the bimah, when our children no longer worry whether God is a "he" or a "she," but instead we all see God in each other's faces.

PART VII

Leadership and Social Justice

IF JEWISH FEMINISM WERE just about my right to wear a tallit, it would have been an easy decade. I can wear a tallit, I do, and lots of other women do, too. So much has happened for women in the synagogue: prayer books have been rewritten, feminist commentaries are not only in the Sisterhood bookshop but in the pews, women's ritual art abounds, and most rabbis, if not all, are aware of women in the biblical narratives about which they are preaching or teaching each week.

It is outside the synagogue walls that we as Jewish feminists now must look and see what is to be done. The Talmud teaches that a synagogue must have windows so that we can see outside: "A person should always pray in a house where there are windows" (Berachot 31a, 34b), because our prayers must lead to action. We can't sequester ourselves in our safe haven of spirituality unless, as it says in the morning prayers, "we learn in order to do." And so violence against women, civil rights, politics are all "Jewish feminist" issues; and are all issues that call for our immediate involvement.

It would be easier, of course, to bring more "women's issues" to the fore if more of our leaders—in government, organizations, religious institutions—were women, or were men attuned to the fact that "women's issues" are human issues. But women still are not represented in the upper echelons of Jewish organizations, or in the decision-making cabinets of venerable and well-known Jewish institutions. While women constitute the majority of participants in many of these organizations, they aren't yet the movers and shakers. Is that just because of the sociological fear of women "on the top"? Is it deeper, touching upon the feeling, often unspoken, that power and authority are ultimately masculine? Or will it be that women in power change the very definition of power?

What do we see as women when we look outside those windows? Is *tikkun olam*—the repair of the world—a Jewish feminist imperative? As those who bring life into the world, do we women have both a special burden and a special blessing in the preservation of that life, indeed of the whole planet?

Shifra Bronznick is a consultant who specializes in creating new initiatives and helping nonprofit organizations navigate change. The founding president of Advancing Women Professionals and the Jewish Community, she is coauthor with Didi Goldenhar and Marty Linsky of *Leveling the Playing Field*. Shifra also designed the program for the White House Project's National Women's Leadership Summits. Her newest initiative for the White House Project, "Women Rule," is a groundbreaking leadership program for women, launched in partnership with *O*, the Oprah magazine.

Jewish Women's Leadership for the Twenty-first Century

SHIFRA BRONZNICK

MY COMMITMENT TO advancing women's leadership emerged from two different sources. One was anger that women were prevented from exercising their potential and were absent from so many important places—from the White House to the bimah, from the platforms of public intellectuals to the corner offices of Jewish organizations. The second was my passionate belief that the world needed transformation, and that women were best suited to be agents of that change because they had the most to gain from the change and the least to benefit from the status quo.

Over the lurching years of trying to make change in the Jewish community and in the larger society, I've come to understand that the challenges for women exist on two levels: first, on the level of perception, in the way that leadership is defined and how women are viewed in that frame, and second, on the practical level, in the way that professional and personal lives are structured. Unless we change both—our beliefs about what leaders look like and how leaders behave, and our assumptions about how work is structured and caregiving commitments are met—we will not create equity in leadership in the Jewish world.

Jewish Feminism in the 1970s: When the Personal Was Political

In August 1970, when I marched on Fifth Avenue for New York's first rally for women's liberation, I was a high school student at an Orthodox Jewish day school. The speeches and conversations swirling around me struck a deep chord. The personal was political. Just eighteen months later, I joined dozens of other women to plan the first National Conference of Jewish Women, sponsored by the North American Jewish Student's Network.

Throughout the 1970s, as the second wave of feminism swept in the movement of Jewish feminism, personal liberation was inextricably linked to societal change. No aspect of personal life, no matter how intimate, was exempt from political interpretation. For a brief shining decade, the structures of sexuality, family, child rearing, friendship, and partnership were subject to the same transformative analysis that was applied to workplaces, religion, community, and formal institutions of every kind.

As Jewish feminists, we challenged the reigning stereotypes—the overbearing Jewish mother, the spoiled Jewish American Princess, and the castrating materialistic Jewish wife. We pushed back on the conventional assumptions that closed options for women: Why should marriage be the norm? Must children occupy the exclusive center of a woman's life? Why was heterosexual partnership privileged over homosexuality and singleness? What might be the alternatives, so that women would have the freedom to pursue a wider spectrum of choices in their lives?

Simultaneously, we took on the religious community, calling for the ordination of women rabbis, equality of participation in ritual, new life cycle events to mark women's milestones, and a fierce commitment to women's Jewish literacy and scholarship that would prepare them to assume spiritual and intellectual leadership.

In Jewish communal life, we started to advocate for the inclusion of women as board members and top professionals. We publicly raised the issue of the many talented women volunteers who were relegated to the sidelines of leadership. We also critiqued our own organizations—in the student movement, in the counterculture, and in the *chavurah* (fellowship)—fighting with our male friends to achieve equity in our own backyard.

Over the next decade, we enjoyed victories—the ordination of women rabbis in the Reform, Reconstructionist, and Conservative movements; the accomplishments of women academics in Jewish studies; the growing influence of women as student leaders on campus; the emergence of women's voices as writers and public intellectuals; and more visibility for women volunteers in Jewish organizations. But we also struggled with the challenge of moving feminism forward without the financial resources that would institutionalize our ideas and embed them in Jewish communal life.

Thirty Years Later: Leadership in Jewish Life and Corporate America

Thirty years later, we still live in a Jewish community characterized by predominantly male leadership. What makes this phenomenon even more striking is the fact that, in society at large, Jewish women are succeeding in significant leadership roles—legislating in the Senate, presiding on the Supreme Court, serving as presidents of Ivy League universities, and directing several of the nation's largest philanthropies.

By contrast, the Jewish community insists on lagging behind the times. The most prominent Jewish organizations, though overwhelmingly staffed by women, are still led by men—from the twenty largest federations to the major institutions focused on Jewish education, community relations, social service, public policy, and Israel advocacy. The few exceptions include Jewish women's groups and a sprinkling of general organizations such as the American Jewish World Service, the Foundation for Jewish Culture, and the Israel Project. As even a cursory search of the Internet will show, every other national Jewish organization, and every religious institution, is directed by a man.[1]

It was because of these glaring inequities that, in the year 2000, I brought together a team of women and men to launch Advancing Women Professionals and the Jewish Community (AWP), made possible by the extraordinary support of philanthropist Barbara Dobkin. AWP was created to promote gender equity in the Jewish community through research, education, and advocacy.

AWP's early research identified gender bias as the chief obstacle for women who seek leadership positions in the Jewish community. Our conversations with many federation executives and board presidents revealed the main assumptions that drive decisions around hiring, promotions, and executive searches, including the perception that women lack the "toughness" to direct major institutions, that they will not be as successful in raising mega-funds from mega-donors, and that their career ambitions will take second place to their family commitments.

Gender bias affects women in every professional environment, not just the Jewish community. The progress of women into CEO positions has been glacial, especially where large amounts of money and power are at stake. For all the rhetoric about celebrating diversity, most Fortune 500 companies claim that the glass ceiling is the consequence of women's lack of experience or ineffective leadership styles. Moreover, rather than acknowledging their own failure to create equitable work environments, many corporate leaders still cite individual family choices as justification for the gender gap.

That most corporations continue to sidestep the gender gap is puzzling given recent studies by Catalyst, the premier research organization for women and business, that show a direct correlation between diversity in leadership and positive financial results.[2] However, some corporations are experimenting with new initiatives for attracting, retaining, and cultivating talented women. By contrast, what distinguishes the Jewish community is its inertia around gender discrimination, and that so little has been done to improve the likelihood that women professionals have equal opportunity to aim for the top positions.

Leadership and the Power of Perception

Women are most frequently derailed from their career aspirations by gender-based perceptions of leadership. They are considered not "tough enough" for the corner office, and they are not valued for their use of "soft power." The irony is that, in the Jewish community and in the corporate world, CEOs and management gurus extol the virtues of emotional intelligence and consensus building as critical leadership tools, and executive coaching has become extremely popular as a way to develop stronger "people skills." Nevertheless, the emotional intelligence and people skills that are so valued when practiced by men rarely translate into recognition or promotions for women.

Joyce K. Fletcher, a distinguished professor at the Simmons School of Management, offers insight into this paradox. Her ethnographic study, *Disappearing Acts,* followed women in a male-dominated engineering firm. She found that the firm's success depended on the women who developed the "connective tissue" for effective teamwork. However, these efforts were neither recognized nor rewarded.[3] In subsequent research, Fletcher concluded that caring, supportive behavior is seen as "motherly" and becomes invisible when demonstrated by women. The same behaviors are celebrated as "post-heroic" collaborative leadership when practiced by men.[4]

This paradox presents a particular problem in the Jewish community. Because many professionals and volunteers choose these organizations as a place to pursue their Jewish identities, the work

351

environment becomes highly personalized. But the warm family feeling of our Jewish workplaces results in negative outcomes for women that are entirely consistent with Fletcher's findings. Women professionals in Jewish organizations are easily stereotyped as loving mothers and good daughters whose collaborative skills are expected but not valued. Alternatively, when women take on the assertive behaviors that are prized for leadership advancement by men, they are dismissed as too abrasive for the relationship building that is so essential to Jewish communal life. Thus, they are caught in a vise-like paralysis between being too soft and being too hard.

Leadership and the Structure of the Workplace

The Jewish community holds aloft the values of family, community, and spirituality. Nonetheless, the Jewish community places massive demands on its organizational leaders—as visionaries, ambassadors, strategists, fund-raisers, and managers. The risk is that, by limiting leadership to those who are willing to work 24/6 (and often even 24/7) and to sacrifice their personal lives, the Jewish community diminishes its own talent pool. We hear Jewish pundits, funders, and lay leaders bemoan the fact that there are so few top-notch candidates for important jobs, and yet little effort has been made to structure work environments that would support people in advancing to leadership while fulfilling personal commitments and building the kinds of Jewish families the community so desperately wants.

AWP's most recent study, "Cultivating the Talent," looks at the career aspirations of women professionals in the Jewish federation system. Didi Goldenhar, the study's lead author, analyzed the results of interviews with 135 women professionals and found that even though most of these women aspire to senior executive posts, they struggle with the bifurcation between ambition and caregiving that permeates the federation culture. At first glance, this split is hard to detect, for in fact, many women chose federations because they appear to be "family-friendly"—for example, closing early on Shabbat and Jewish holidays.[5] However, while some federations offer informal workplace flexibility, most senior managers shift their women professionals to the "mommy track" if they request part-time schedules during the early child-rearing years; similarly, older women with many years' tenure are switched to the "daughter track" when they ask for alternative arrangements to care for aging relatives.

Inside and outside the Jewish community, many professional women will need flexible work arrangements at some point in their careers. Given the reality that women still shoulder two-thirds of all family and household responsibilities, this should come as no surprise. However, contrary to popular opinion, most women professionals do want to return to work and advance in their chosen professions. What they find is that even a temporary leave is enough to permanently downgrade their pay scales and sideline their careers. These organizational norms have an impact beyond the particular individuals involved. Over time, managers project these assumptions onto all women hires, assuming that they are not worth significant career investments, as they will eventually leave.

Jewish Women and Leadership: Making New Choices

The obvious recommendation to solve these problems is that women need to transform their Jewish organizations from within. But this task is mined with risks since advocacy on behalf of women is often seen as a diversion from the communal mission—saving Jewish people, caring for vulnerable populations, fighting anti-Semitism, supporting Israel, and ensuring the continuity of the Jewish people. As a result, women are reluctant to demand equal pay for equal work, paid maternity leave, flexible work arrangements, or equitable representation in the leadership of their organizations, and are frightened to appear too determined to push "women's issues."

Women who want to build their careers in the Jewish community have choices about where and how they choose to lead. In the corporate world, there has been a trend of record numbers of women leaving mainstream jobs to start their own businesses. In the Jewish world, too, some women are choosing to start their own organizations, to create meaningful lives that make sense, professionally and personally. Some of the most vibrant new spiritual communities are founded by women, as are several leading-edge organizations devoted to fostering connection and community, from the engagement of gay, lesbian, and transgender Jews to building relationships among Israelis and Palestinians, to building support groups for Jewish women with breast cancer. Simultaneously, feminist philanthropy has supported the emergence of several major organizations devoted to gender leadership and change in the Jewish community.

Women are also entering the Jewish community from other fields, with credentials from major corporations, politics, and cultural organizations. These women are applying their expertise to Jewish life with impressive results, both on the global stage and internally, by developing personnel policies around paid maternity leave that truly support Jewish families and continuity. These leaders are transforming the Jewish landscape and also changing our ideas about women's leadership in the Jewish community.

The Personal Is Political, Now

We need to start telling a new story about leadership in the Jewish community. The stories of women leaders need to be shared if we want the next generation of women to aspire to leadership in Jewish life.

We also need to tell the truth: no leader does it alone. Most accomplishments are collective, not singular. Being straightforward about all the players—alongside the leader and behind the scenes—would shatter the perception that one person has to have every attribute and be able to handle every single responsibility to be accepted as a leader. This acknowledgment would help many women and men in the next generation to see themselves as capable of leadership in a collaborative context.

We need to be honest about the struggles that everyone faces—especially women—in balancing life and work. When we dismantle the notion that a 24/6 (or 24/7) work schedule equals excellence, we will create the kind of work environments where Jewish professionals are working smarter, not harder.

Finally, we need to persuade our Jewish organizations to end the bifurcation between the personal and the political. You can't celebrate children and not support child care. You can't make speeches about continuity yet fail to provide conditions that permit professionals—women and men—to do good work and lead good lives. You can't advocate for the presence and influence of Jews in every sphere of public life and then fail to recognize the contributions of women, who represent half of the talent pool. It is time to "walk the talk."

Feminism started with the radical notion that the "personal is political." This is still true, perhaps now more than ever. The "personal" values that Jews hold dear as a community, for which we advocate so vigorously, must be reflected in every aspect of organizational policy and behavior. We must find a way to create lives, workplaces, institutions, and communities that allow us to be both fiercely ambitious and deeply caring about the way we live and the way we lead.

Rabbi Jill Jacobs is the rabbi-in-residence at the Jewish Funds for Justice. She writes and speaks frequently about Jewish perspectives on contemporary economic and social concerns; her writings on issues such as housing, *tzedakah* (charity), living wage, and unions have appeared in more than two dozen books, journals, and magazines. Rabbi Jacobs received rabbinic ordination and an MA in Talmud from the Jewish Theological Seminary, an MS in urban affairs from Hunter College, and a BA in comparative literature from Columbia University. She lives in Manhattan with her husband, Guy Austrian.

Bread, Roses, and Chutzpah

Jewish Women in American Social Movements

RABBI JILL JACOBS

THE STORY OF the major American social movements of the last hundred years can be read as the story of Jewish women's emerging leadership in the United States. Not only do Jewish women appear in disproportionate number among the leadership of the labor, feminist, and civil rights movements, but Jewish women's organizations, such as Hadassah and the National Council of Jewish Women, have engaged in struggles for universal suffrage, reproductive rights, health care, and immigration reform.[1]

Is it just a coincidence that Jewish women have played such prominent roles in major social movements? Is doing social justice work as a Jewish woman fundamentally different from doing social justice work as a man, or as a non-Jewish woman? And should this historical phenomenon have any effect on how contemporary Jewish women think about our own commitments?

To answer these questions, we will explore how three historical Jewish women, involved in three different American social movements, have spoken about the intersection of their female, Jewish, and activist identities. Since feminism has taught us that the personal is political, I will also reflect on my own experiences doing social justice work, with attention to what it means for me to do this work as a Jewish woman. Through these examples, we will explore potential means of constructing a specifically Jewish, female, and justice-centered identity.

The Labor Organizer

In 1909, tens of thousands of young, mostly Jewish, women stunned New York by striking for three months to protest the dangerous working conditions and low wages of the garment factories that employed many immigrant women. This strike, the culmination of several years of organizing, was notable on at least three accounts. First, women, who had been dismissed by the male union establishment as "unorganizable," thrust themselves into the center of the labor movement. Second, the struggle was primarily an internal Jewish one, with young Jewish women organizing against older Jewish male factory owners. Finally, the strike generated cross-class alliances, as wealthier women stepped in to support the strikers.[2]

Rose Schneiderman was one of the young women who stepped into the limelight during "the Uprising of the Twenty Thousand," as the strike came to be called. She would go on to devote her life to being a professional labor leader. While Schneiderman studiously avoids personal reflection in her autobiography, she does offer a few scattered hints about her self-perception as a Jewish woman.

In recalling her childhood in Russian-occupied Poland, Schneiderman points to a love of learning that will become a constant theme in her life:

> I started going to Hebrew school when I was four. Though it was somewhat unusual for girls to study in these primitive schools which were almost always in the home of the *Melamed* or teacher, Mother was determined that I learn Hebrew so I could read and understand the prayers recited at home and in the synagogue.[3]

This ability to read would later serve Schneiderman well when economic pressures forced her into the workforce. Not long after her family immigrated to America, her father died, and the teenage Schneiderman dropped out of school to work in a factory. Determined to continue her education, Schneiderman enrolled in night school, only to find that the teacher was more interested in chatting with students than in educating them. In frustration, she quit night school and began to read at home with her mother:

> To my great joy I found there were other ways of acquiring knowledge. Mother, who had always loved books, (although she could read only the Hebrew prayer book), asked me to read the Bible stories in Yiddish to her. We started with the story of Joseph and his brothers which Father had dramatized years before, and we had a wonderful time as I tearfully read about the inhumanity of Joseph's brothers.... Later on I began reading English novels in the ten-cent paperback editions of the day that I somehow managed to buy.... I devoured everything I could lay hands on.[4]

For Schneiderman, biblical text became a gateway to the world of learning and a means of accessing a new world of possibility. Perhaps her tears over the inhumanity of Joseph's brothers reflect her pain at the cruelty of her own "brothers"—the Jewish men who ran the factory in which Schneiderman worked as a cap maker, and who seemed similarly willing to sell their siblings for a small profit. In reading with her mother after her father's death, Schneiderman also began to develop a sense of herself as a member of a community of Jewish women. Indeed, few men play more than cameo roles in her book.

Schneiderman's introduction to biblical justice and injustice gave way to more practical lessons as she discovered the world of labor organizing, also through a community of Jewish women:

> Early in 1903, a young woman named Bessie Braut came to work with us.... She wasted no time in giving us the facts of life—that the men in our trade belonged to a union and were therefore able to better their conditions.... As her words began to sink in, we formed of a committee.... bravely, we ventured into the office of the United Cloth Hat and Cap Makers Union and told the man in charge that we would like to be organized.... A new life opened up for me. All of a sudden I was not lonely anymore.[5]

Schneiderman rarely reflects on her place as a Jewish woman. From time to time, she does acknowledge the social service infrastructure of the Jewish community, commenting at one point that United Hebrew Charities helped her to get her first job, and that "in those days poor Jews looked to them for everything."[6] For the most part, though, Schneiderman identifies with other members of her class, most of whom, given the Lower East Side milieu, happen to be Jewish. Unlike later activists, she did not choose to affiliate with a women's movement; the exclusion of women from the mainstream trade unions left her no other real option. Later, Schneiderman would reach out to women of other class backgrounds, but her early efforts took place within the context of her immediate community.

A few elements of her Jewish background did, however, inform Schneiderman's activism. First of all, her immigration experience gave Schneiderman an early taste of struggle and survival. Later generations of Jews, both men and women, claim their parents' and grandparents' immigration stories as the inspiration for their own activism; Schneiderman and others of her generation needed no help in imagining the experience of being an outsider. Second, Schneiderman's early Jewish education ultimately offered her the possibility of escaping the harsh reality of the factory. In the biblical narrative, she could find models of justice and injustice, and in reading other books, she could envision a different life.

The Freedom Rider[7]

In a 1962 issue of the *Reconstructionist,* Betty Alschuler reflects on her experience traveling to Albany, Georgia, with a group of ministers in an attempt to desegregate the city:

> A Jew, as I am, heading south, led by a Christian minister on a Christian mission, has a crowd of memories. My head was teeming: "And the Egyptians dealt ill with us," "And a stranger shalt thou not oppress for ye know the heart of a stranger seeing ye were strangers in the land of Egypt."...
>
> The Unitarian is glad there is a Jew with the party. He feels less like an outsider. The Catholics are glad; they feel less like outsiders, too. The Negro is glad there is a Jew; we have been slaves. The Protestants are glad, I don't know why....
>
> Freedom songs sung by beautiful rich colored voices. Clapping, rhythmic melody. "We are Climbing Jacob's Ladder," Gospel songs. But I am not a soldier of the cross. I close my mouth, for I can't sing this. As I do, I think some part of me is shut off from this war. I can't be wholehearted about it. How can I fight a war which does not engage my whole self? Because I am Jewish?...
>
> My daughter and I speak with two members of the Jewish Congregation in Albany. Two men of dignity and status. My daughter tries to convince them that

integration is a must. I listen. We hear frightened men,
confused men, say "This is not a Jewish problem. This
is not for outsiders...." They are charming, gallant, well-
assimilated southerners who know the art of speaking
to women.... I see these gentlemen, Jews, under their
southern manners, trapped. If the Klan marches, and
they are gathering, if violence breaks, they know they
will get it.... My sympathy goes to them, even though
their speeches are absurd.[8]

Alschuler simultaneously struggles to understand how she, as a
Jew, fits into the integration struggle, and how she, as an integrationist, can relate to the Albany Jewish community. She finds precedent for her own involvement in the biblical story of the Exodus
from Egypt, but also is confused by the juxtaposition of the Torah's
image of Jacob's ladder with lyrics celebrating soldiers of the cross.
She sympathizes with the Jewish "gentlemen," whom she knows to
be as vulnerable to anti-Semitism as she herself is, but cannot sym-
pathize with a viewpoint that does not consider integration to be a
"Jewish problem." Alschuler searches for a way to "engage [her]
whole self" in the effort, but finds no place for her whole self among
either Jews or Christians.

In the South, Alschuler is an outsider on multiple levels: she is a
Jew among Christians, a northern integrationist among southern
Jews committed to the status quo, and a Jewish woman arguing with
"men of dignity and status" in a time before women occupied positions of Jewish communal leadership. Alschuler's apparent lack of
anger at the Jewish men who condescend to her and her daughter
may emanate from her awareness of herself as a triple outsider. She
recognizes the men as fellow outsiders, but also realizes that they are
not quite sufficiently outside to see the ways in which their own fate
is tied to that of southern African Americans.

Unlike Schneiderman, Alschuler did not organize around an
issue that primarily affected her own community. While the civil

rights movement would result in tangible benefits for the Jewish community, Alschuler went south to champion integration, not principally to benefit herself or other Jews. At the same time, she appreciated the history of oppression and the threat of discrimination that she shared with the African American communities at the center of the struggle.

The twin themes of biblical inspiration and identification with the outsider recur throughout the history of American Jewish activism in general, and of Jewish women's activism in particular. Judith Rosenbaum comments, "The otherness that many Jewish women felt as Jews in postwar America dovetailed with their experiences of otherness as women. Though often painful, the parallelism of these experiences bolstered their determination to fight for inclusion and equality."[9] Alschuler's own experience of being an outsider enabled her and others like her to identify with the marginalized, and inspired these women to fight for equality.

The Feminist

Betty Friedan had already well established herself as a feminist leader when she began to speak also as a Jew. In a 1988 interview with *Tikkun* magazine, she reflects on the ways that her Jewish upbringing and later Jewish encounters guided her feminism:

> I remember very distinctly that [being Jewish] was first oppressive to me when I was in high school. Sororities and fraternities dominated social life in this Midwestern town. All my friends got into sororities and fraternities and I didn't because I was Jewish.... So being Jewish made me an observer, a marginal person, and I made one of those unconscious vows to myself: "they may not *like* me but they're going to look up to me." Although it was many years before I identified in any way with feminism, I think my passion against injustice came from my experience of being a Jew in Peoria....

Traditionally Jewish women received their self-definition solely in terms of the family. And yet, the little girls, like the little boys, are brought up to respect the culture of the book and get all A's.... But once we broke through to authenticity as women, which our generation began to do, we said we would not buy someone else's definition of what being a woman is. I am a person, and what I am as a woman is all of me, not just the part of me that will give birth.... We didn't have that sense of authenticity from our Jewish experience if we grew up as I did in an assimilated, almost anti-Jewish community. There was the fixing of noses, the changing of names....

My experience as a Jew informed, though unconsciously, a lot of the insights that I applied to women, and the passion that I applied to the situation of women. But then, conversely, the sense of breaking through to your authentic self as a woman prepared me when I began to experience the new form of anti-Semitism in the international women's conferences.... I began to make the links with my Jewish experience and my own identity, and I began to get more interested even in theology.... My feminism has led me to an unabashed sense of the unity of spirit and political values.[10]

Friedan, like Schneiderman and Alschuler, sees herself as an outsider, both within the male-dominated Jewish community and within the white Christian Midwest. As a Jewish woman, she received mixed messages about whether to aspire to motherhood or to academic achievement. Growing up in a secular family, with a mother she describes later as "an anti-Semitic Jew," Friedan experienced Judaism primarily as a social handicap and a cause for embarrassment. In a community in which nose jobs are the norm for teenage girls, one could not even be "out" as a Jew to oneself.

Her childhood as an outsider instilled in Friedan a passion for bringing the margins into the mainstream. This commitment led her first to feminism, where she helped to change the place of women in American life. Later, the same experience of being an outsider led Friedan to reclaim her Judaism, as she encountered anti-Semitism in the women's movement. As of this 1988 interview, parts of the Jewish community remained closed to women, and the women's movement had not fully grappled with anti-Semitism. Friedan remained an outsider, in important ways, to both communities, but recognized that only an integration of both parts of her identity would allow her to lead an authentic life.

My Own Story

My own Jewish feminist social justice awakening came in two stages. As a teenager, I became enraged when my high school principal declared to the local newspaper that teen pregnancy was not an issue at Framingham High School. Walking the halls every day, I saw quite a different reality. With a bit of research, I learned that my school in fact had one of the highest rates of teen pregnancy and venereal disease in the state. Several friends and I began a campaign to persuade the school board to implement a sex education program, and to allow the distribution of free condoms. Needless to say, this proposal did not go over well in our predominantly Catholic suburb of Boston. More surprising to me, my non-Jewish friends slowly started dropping off the campaign, under pressure from parents and priests.

I did not know then how many Jewish women had preceded me in fighting for birth control, nor did I quite perceive the issue as a feminist one, even though few boys chose to get involved. It was not, however, lost on me that the Jewish parents and the local rabbis chose either to support the movement or to stay quiet. Though I could not have articulated why, I knew that my activism was somehow Jewish.

In college, I got my first taste of community organizing through a different group of Jewish women. Frustrated with the Orthodox- and male-dominated life on campus, I found my way to Lights In Action (LIA), a national Jewish student organization that was creating pluralist materials and experiences for Jewish college students. This organization, which disbanded in 2001, was one of the last vestiges of the American Jewish student movement. Like all good student movements, it assumed that students should do for students, rather than let older adults determine our Jewish experiences. We challenged the boundaries of acceptability within the Jewish world of the 1990s by running conferences and leadership-training workshops for Jewish gay, lesbian, bisexual, and transgender (GLBT) students, children of intermarriage, and campus social justice activists. We also mailed provocative materials to one hundred thousand college students, protested at the United Jewish Communities General Assembly, and ran programs about Israel that considered all sides of the Israeli-Palestinian conflict.

Though LIA was not, by design, a women's group, the core activists were always women. I do not think that it is accidental that this female-dominated group, whose members ran the gamut from traditionalist Orthodox to avowedly secular, grappled more successfully with controversial issues than any Jewish group I have since encountered. For us, the personal was absolutely political. Our cardinal rule was that we could not make a decision that would force someone to leave the group. From within this context, we debated gender and sexuality, intermarriage, politics, and Israel. While our politics differed, our commitments to one another remained primary. This group of women remains my closest community. Many of us still have professional relationships with one another, and we continue to collaborate on writing projects, educational materials, and programming. This group of women has also come back together to celebrate marriages, babies, and multiple graduate degrees, as well as to support one another in divorce, the death of a parent, and most tragically, the untimely loss of one of our own circle to breast cancer. The fluidity between the personal and the political has enabled close personal relationships, difficult ideological conversations, and ultimately groundbreaking work.

What Is Jewish and Feminist about Jewish Women's Activism?

Rose Schneiderman, Betty Alschuler, Betty Friedan, and I came to activism out of different combinations of need, responsibility, anger, and hope. For all of us, Judaism offered inspiration, community, and a glimpse of possibility. The accident of being born a Jewish woman forced on all of us the experience of being an outsider several times over. All of us found in activism a chance to integrate the different parts of ourselves, while also creating a different reality for the future.

Today, many Jews—men and women—who devote themselves to social justice work explain their commitment to justice work in terms of their Jewish textual and historical heritage. We plumb the Jewish textual tradition for passages that will inspire and inform our work. We remember our families' immigration journeys, and appreciate their struggles to make it in America. We speak proudly of earlier generations of Jews who risked their reputations and sometimes their lives in the pursuit of justice.

While many of us can name women such as Schneiderman, Alschuler, and Friedan as our heroes, we rarely speak of economic or social justice work as a feminist endeavor. We often define "women's issues" as limited to reproductive choice, breast and ovarian cancer, and equal rights. And we tend to define "Jewish issues" as those relating to Israel, school vouchers, hate crimes, and other policies that directly affect the Jewish community.

What, then, does it mean to do social justice work as a Jewish woman?

Rose Schneiderman knew that without a union of their own, women would continue to be paid less than men and to work under unsafe conditions. She also knew that working-class women alone would not garner the attention that a cross-class women's alliance would attract; she therefore cultivated relationships with upper-class women, including Eleanor Roosevelt, with whom Schneiderman grew extremely close. Today, women are still paid less than men for equal work, and low-income women fare worst of all. From Schneiderman, we can learn to build alliances across class boundaries and to ground these alliances in the recognition that women of weaker economic and educational backgrounds remain vulnerable to workplace discrimination.

From Alschuler, we learn that the experience of being an outsider multiple times over can and should lead us to greater compassion, both for those who recognize themselves—and are recognized by society—to be outsiders, and for those whose outsider status is not yet apparent. We also learn from her that social justice work should begin not with a desire to do for others, but with an understanding of the extent to which our well-being is entwined with that of others.

Betty Friedan challenges us to reclaim Jewish text and history as a means of reclaiming power. Whereas men previously controlled definitions of and access to "authentic" Judaism, women can now reinterpret and reimagine texts and tradition, thereby creating a new narrative of Jewish social change in which women play a central role. Through interpretation, the outsider becomes an insider and begins to be able to use texts and traditions as a means of promoting social change, rather than as tools for maintaining the status quo.

From my own experience, I have learned the importance of developing relationships strong enough to allow individuals to transcend ideological, cultural, and religious boundaries. Women's socialization into a culture of relationships may contribute to the willingness of Jewish women's organizations to take positions and to form alliances that many male-dominated organizations would find too radical.

Finally, all of the women discussed in these pages teach us that the personal is profoundly political. Our various relationships with Judaism, experiences of power or disempowerment, and commitments to others color our understanding of the world and instill in us the passion and the ability to make change.

Rabbi Lynn Gottlieb currently serves as program associate of American Friends Service Committee (AFSC) in San Francisco. She is also rabbi of the Danforth Circle in Toronto. She is rabbi emeritus of Congregation Nahalat Shalom and cofounder of Shomer Shalom Institute for Jewish Nonviolence as well as the Muslim Jewish PeaceWalk for Interfaith Solidarity. She is author of *She Who Dwells Within: A Feminist View of Renewed Judaism* and contributing editor of *Fellowship* magazine. Lynn is a performing artist, klezmer dancer, and peace activist. She has been a pulpit rabbi for more than thirty-six years.

Women's Right to a World Free of Violence

RABBI LYNN GOTTLIEB

I hope a time will come for all of us in which there will be no more questions on the subject of "women": for as long as there are questions, something is wrong.
—RABBINER REGINA JONAS, FIRST ORDAINED WOMAN RABBI[1]

I shall not lie below you because we are both equal, we are both created from the soil of the earth.
—THE VOICE OF LILITH IN THE ALPHABET OF BEN SIRACH,
EIGHTH CENTURY CE

AFTER TWO HUNDRED YEARS of struggling for women's rights in Judaism, is the Jewish community still weighted down by sexism? Is the work of Jewish feminism complete? One way to measure the answer to those questions is through the lens of violence against women. To the degree that women are still vulnerable to male-initiated violence against them, we have not completed the feminist task. Even as Lilith's daughters construct new visions of paradise, disgruntled sons of Adam, fearful of loss of control, stalk female independence in the most intimate of situations. The following appalling information applies to the Jewish community as well the general populations where Jews live. Information regarding the existence of domestic violence, dating violence, and sexual abuse is available on the Jewish Women's International website, which is the best source regarding domestic violence and sexual abuse in the Jewish community. Each one of these informational statements represents the lives of women and children we know as our close friends, coworkers, members of our congregations, and children in the circle of our communal life:

- The sphere of gender-based oppression that privileges men and disadvantages women includes sexual, physical, emotional, economic, and spiritual abuse.
- One out of three women will be sexually assaulted in her lifetime.
- At least one in four women will experience domestic violence in her lifetime.
- In 85 percent of the cases of domestic violence, the abuser is male.
- Women are victims of family violence across race, class, age, and religion.
- Male survivors, both gay and heterosexual, and women abused in lesbian relationships often face additional barriers seeking help.
- Women and children whose male family members serve in military, police, and security professions are more likely to experience violence at home.
- Children who live in a home where domestic violence occurs are at least seven times more likely to be physically and/or sexually abused.

- Teens between the ages of sixteen and nineteen are three and a half times more likely to be sexually assaulted than the general population.
- Domestic violence, sexual abuse, sexual trafficking, exploitation of women in the work place, child pornography, and date rape profoundly affect the lives of women and their circles of relationships in the Jewish community.

How should we respond to the reality these facts present? That one out of three women will be sexually assaulted at some point is not an insignificant statement. That means each of us is acquainted with dozens of women who have experienced or will experience male violence.

In order to engage in the work of prevention of violence against women, humanity must confront the gendered nature of violence. The following statistics have been collected by the National Conference for Community and Justice and are also available online:

- 85 percent of people who commit murder are men.
- 90 percent of people who commit violent assault are men.
- 85 percent of child sexual abuse against both males and females is committed by men.
- 99.8 percent of people in prison convicted of rape are men.[2]

When we speak about gender equality as a goal of feminism, we cannot ignore the overwhelming problem of male violence. The climate that creates the possibility of male violence stems from attitudes, beliefs, and behaviors that are learned through observation and experiences, reinforced by family, community, school, peer group, cultural, and national ethos.[3] Gender-based oppression is embedded in the social fabric of Jewish lives. It is found equally among Orthodox and Reform Jews. There is no kind of Jewish religious practice that, in and of itself, protects women from male violence if it is not accompanied by a proactive effort to set up institutional structures that respond effectively to domestic violence, sexual abuse, and the attitudes and beliefs that stem from sexism.

Violence and the threat of violence is a key instrument in the oppression of women on the basis of gender. Whether personal or structural, violence and the threat of violence advantages men in the distribution of material resources and economic, political, religious, and social power. The threat of violence infuses institutions that privilege men, reinforcing male attitudes of superiority, entitlement, authority, and the expectation to be served. Male-bodied individuals are socialized to see themselves as decisive, strong, independent, competitive, powerful, tough, and helpful as providers of goodness, security, and oversight. The targets of oppression are viewed as inferior. Their thoughts, feelings, and opinions are dismissed, ignored, or intentionally resisted. These attitudes help enable the widespread occurrence of male violence against women that exists in the world today.

The difficulty of preventing and eradicating violence against women in the Jewish community is compounded by many degrees of denial. The first level of denial is the refusal to admit that the problem exists in the Jewish community, as if we are immune. As long as this level of denial persists, those who suffer domestic violence and sexual abuse remain invisible to the people and institutions who might otherwise be able to intervene or work toward prevention. Once communities and rabbinic leadership accept the reality of the problem, the next step is implementing procedures and programs that represent best prevention and intervention practices. This means moving through the second stage of denial, where we admit the problem exists, but decide we can't do anything about it, or that we are already doing enough. This phase of response needs the input and partnership of rabbinic and lay Jewish leadership, domestic violence prevention and intervention advocates, and most important, the input of victims themselves. The sheer number of community demands often overwhelms rabbis. Unless domestic violence prevention and intervention is viewed as a priority, rabbis may not provide their communities with the leadership necessary to properly respond to domestic violence. Domestic violence prevention and intervention training must become a standard part of rabbinic learning in every seminary and deserves more than a few token hours. The fact that women are becoming one half of the rabbinate is not a guarantee that such measures will be put in place. Women in leadership are not immune to ignorance, confusion, or fear concerning this subject. The only way to overcome domestic violence is to institutionalize prevention and intervention within all our communal structures.

A particularly difficult type of denial may arise through the confusion rabbis and congregants feel when one of their own is involved in sexual misconduct, domestic violence, or sexual abuse. Without clear standards and oversight by rabbinic institutions and lay leadership, such situations can persist for decades while victims go untreated and unprotected. Finding out that an esteemed rabbi may be an abuser is such a terrible revelation that the community may turn against the victims in order to preserve the reputation of the rabbi. This denial can take the form of minimization of the act. In response to one such revelation in a community, another rabbi tried to explain years of predatory behavior on the part of a colleague by framing it as an overload of uncontrollable kabbalistic love! Denial is at the root of justifications such as "it never happened," "it only happened once," "it was the victim's fault," or "it only happens when he drinks." Another form of denial is the dismissal of the act in light of all "the good" that a religious leader has done on behalf of his or her community. Thus, some victims are subjected to widespread honoring of their abusers while their own needs are not considered.

The persistence of these types of denial points to the need for formal training and education for rabbis, lay leaders, and community members so that denial no longer inhibits the kind of prevention, intervention, and treatment necessary for the creation of safe families and communities. Anyone who is involved in healing from sexual abuse or domestic violence knows that it is difficult to forgive those whom you suspect may inflict harm again. That is why public exposure of crimes is important; it diminishes the stature of those committing the crimes. This diminishment, in turn, generates an environment in which healing can more easily occur. Exposure cannot happen if the status quo is heavily invested in protecting the perpetrators rather than the victims of abuse. Clear codes of ethics and fair consideration of any charges must also be part of domestic violence and sexual abuse prevention and intervention.

Violence against women and children as well as other targeted groups, such as individuals who identify as gay, lesbian, bisexual, or transgender, thrives in an atmosphere of social intimidation and psychological acceptance of the status quo. Hannah Arendt observed that, in the relationship of the abuser to the abused:

> Simple compliance rarely satisfies him. He appears to have a psychological need to justify his crimes and for this he needs the victim's affirmation. Thus he relentlessly demands from his victim professions of respect, gratitude, or even love. His ultimate goal: the creation of a willing victim. Hostages, political prisoners, battered women and slaves have all remarked upon the captor's curious psychological dependence on his victim.[4]

Ultimately, male gender privilege depends on a lack of female autonomy and perceived female dependence on male power for safety and security. A range of female self-destructive behaviors point to Hannah Arendt's notion of the willing victim. Eating disorders, suicide, depression, addictive behaviors, living silently with abuse are all indicators of internalized oppression. Feelings of inferiority, powerlessness, subordination, passivity, and the internalized expectation that goodness is linked to providing services are part of the negative complex of oppression. Gender privilege allows men to dismiss, discount, minimize the experience and knowledge of women. This is another form of denial. It causes women and children to self-silence in the belief that the burden of guilt rests on them and not on their abuser.

Male gender privilege is reinforced by so many of the basic stories that are told within a Jewish context. Even though feminism has wrought many gains, women's stories are often compartmentalized apart from the usual rendering of Jewish teachings by professionals on a weekly basis. From the story of Eve's punishment for eating the forbidden fruit to Miriam's punishment inflicted by God in the form of skin disease for the sin of challenging Moses's authority, there remains an overwhelming lack of female stories and a preponderance of male rabbi stories that compose the bulk of traditional teaching. Men are still raised up as the ultimate containers of Jewish wisdom. Until we transform the way we convey the past, we will continue to come up against the privileging of men's voices over women's voices.

The first step in healing from male gender violence, domestic violence, and sexual abuse is to affirm our voices and our stories by creating environments where such stories can be told, received, and responded to in a way that protects the safety of victims. Finding counselors and communities that provide a safe and nurturing atmosphere for women to share their experiences and connect with other women, men, and transgender individuals going through the same healing process is necessary for healing to occur. Many healing resources already exist. The key for activists who support ending the existence of domestic violence, dating violence, and other forms of intimate and social violence is to make these resources available to our communities by creating networks of awareness in every Jewish institution that serves families and youth. In addition, the exploration of the meaning of *gender* has to begin at an early age. What does it mean to be a Jewish man, a Jewish woman, a Jewish transgender person? There are many resources designed for a spectrum of ages that help young people consider the cultural, religious, and familial values that they carry about gender. Use of theater poetry, and other creative forms of interaction can be very helpful in this process.

What is missing from society's efforts to end domestic violence is a comprehensive, nationwide effort to take the next steps in the battle. Preventing violence against women requires ongoing activism, even when prevention and intervention programs have been introduced to synagogues and institutions of Jewish learning and social service. The effectiveness of instituted prevention and intervention programs has to be evaluated on a yearly basis according to best practices. Are we set up for such evaluations? Do we survey our communities? What do we have in place and how do we know it is enough? What is the next step? You only need to consult with the groundbreaking work of Jewish Women's International to plug in to a national and international network of people engaged in multisector collaboration that includes strengthening individual knowledge and skills, community education, forging networks between domestic violence prevention and intervention providers and religious leadership, influencing policy and legislation, and changing organizational practices.

Another key to ending violence against women is to capitalize on our capacity to network with each other across denominational, class, ethnic, and national boundaries. Jewish feminism must acknowledge the many varieties of feminism and Judaism that exist within our communities to effect lasting change. In this context, we have to keep in mind the intersection of male gender privilege with systems of heterosexual, upper-class, and white privilege. People hold multiple identities. A person can be privileged in one identity category and targeted in another. Systems that grant privilege on the basis of class, race, religion, age, gender, sexual preference, physical or mental ability while disadvantaging others are forms of structural violence. Being a feminist means examining our own place in intersecting systems of privilege so that we do not perpetuate the very forms of oppression we are trying to overcome. Only by identifying our place can we take responsibility for our role in perpetuating male gender privilege and other forms of oppression.

Privilege constructs bubbles of protection that often make oppression invisible to those who possess it, while oppressing those who do not share this privileged status. We may think we see what is going on, but we do not. Oppressive groups make the other invisible in order to conceal and repress the power of targeted groups. For instance, referring to feminists in the past tense, romanticizing love, appropriating women's cultural knowledge and attributing it to men, and retelling the story of Jewish history as if women played minor roles are elements of violence that are part of the structure that maintains the status quo of those who possess privilege and power. Analyzing the structures of male gender privilege continues to be crucial to the feminist project, so that we can dismantle those structures and create healthy environments that are violence free.

This process will not be seamless. Another form of denial arises when the status quo is challenged by targeted groups in an attempt to make their oppression visible to those who hold the reigns of power and to those who draw sustenance from that power. Inevitably, those with power find ways to push back in order to preserve their power, which resides in the status quo. Push-back can occur in many ways. Character assassination, economic and social marginalization, imprisonment, and even sanctioned physical retaliation are all forms of violent push-back. To the degree that male gender privilege ultimately rests on a notion of the just use of force to subdue opponents, challenging structures that perpetuate a climate of impunity for male violence can be deadly. When a woman summons the support to leave an abusive situation, for instance, she is vulnerable to immediate loss of income, homelessness, social blame, and the likelihood that the abuser will retaliate in the form of physical violence. How do we respond to this likely eventuality? Do we have in place the community structures that enable those who suffer from abuse to successfully leave?

On a macro level, the whole notion of male gendered violence as a legitimate form of self-defense deserves our attention. I believe this—the idea that male violence can redeem us and keep us safe from other male enemies—is the hard heart of sexism. This under-lying belief is so pervasive in North America and throughout the world that it remains largely unchallenged. Mass entertainment is mostly the story of male heroism in the face of danger through use of violence and goodness together. Traditionally, Jewish culture per-ceived itself differently. In fact, Jewish manhood was valued for scholarship, verbal skill, and avoidance of causing harm. Statements such as, "Not by military might, nor force of arms, only by Spirit," or "Once an arrow leaves the bow, not even the strongest warrior can bring it back," reflect the core Jewish value that violence used with the intent to cause harm is un-Jewish. However, this view of Jewish manhood has been seriously challenged by the events of the Holo-caust and the rise of the State of Israel.

While traditional Judaism preferred the book over the sword, the creation of the State of Israel in 1948 led to the normalization of the military as an acceptable agency for the sustenance and security of the Jewish people. Jewish soldiers, with kippot on their heads, pray at the Western Wall, machine gun in hand. Radical redefini-tions of Jewish masculinity have followed a perception that only by might and military power can we ensure the survival of the Jewish people in history. In the spirit of working to prevent violence toward women, I want to address the intersection of Israeli mili-tarism and it's impact upon the Jewish community, definitions of Jewish masculinity, and the resulting increase in violence against women.

The right to defend oneself against harm has become the blanket under which pervasive abuse takes place. Researchers working with the Haifa feminist center Isha L'isha (Woman to Woman) reported that, between 2000 and 2005, 47 percent of Israeli women who suf-fered homicide were murdered by partners or relatives who served as security guards, soldiers, or police officers. In the army itself, 81 percent of women in the army, 2 percent of whom are in combat units, experience sexual harassment that can include humiliating innuendo, unwanted sexual proposals, and individual and gang rape.[5] Beyond the existence of physical, sexual, and emotional abuse, Orna Sasson-Levy of Bar Ilan University found no benefits to women in the army. Her research challenges the widely held assumption that the army results in equal achievement in civil society. Israeli culture is so gendered that women have no success unless they reproduce chauvinistic behavior toward other women.[6]

In the fall of 2002, while addressing Congregation Nahalat Shalom during a program called Creating a Culture of Peace, Marty Rafferty, a Quaker from Northern Ireland who works tirelessly to support Protestant-Catholic reconciliation, remarked that the loss of previously cherished values and the increase of violence as a tool for control is a step-by-step process that changes the heart and soul of an entire population. Unthinkable things become normal. Testimonies from an Israeli project called Breaking the Silence reveal that male soldiers express apathy toward human life, increase of aggression, and loss of moral sensitivity. We are educating Jewish children to have faith in the power of the military response to save us from violence. However, male violence does not protect women. The opposite is true. Idan Halili, a young female Jewish high school student in Israel, came to the same conclusion.[7] Halili successfully refused military service on the basis of her feminism. She states that military service is incompatible with feminist ideology on several levels: "because of a hierarchal, male-favoring army structure; because the army distorts gender roles; because of sexual harassment within the army; and because of an equation between military and domestic violence." In Halili's case—as tends to happen—she was originally refused a hearing before a conscience committee and was sent to military prison when she refused to enlist. That decision was later reversed. "We argued that, although Halili's case against serving was 100 percent feminism, her ideology of feminism also meant she was a pacifist, objecting to any military system," says her solicitor, Smadar Ben-Natan.

The committee did not grant Halili exemption on the basis of conscientious objection. But the outcome was nonetheless some form of an indirect admission. "The committee said that her feminism, not pacifism, seemed more dominant and that, on the basis of holding such views, she would be unfit to serve," explains Ben-Natan.

Women are not safer as the result of male definitions of security, and they are not safe from the aggressive character that must be stimulated in men in order for men to be able to kill. Even as we embrace the right of Israel to security, we cannot ignore the tremendous toll that male military violence imposes on the internal population of Israeli Jewish women, and even more so on the non-Jewish populations of Palestinians who live under Israeli military rule. Jewish male identity now embraces the right of men to be violent if it can be justified as a "security" measure. This is not a positive development for women, and is why we must choose nonviolence and feminism as the foundational ethics for the expression of Judaism.

Part of the ongoing work of feminism is to research the kind of environments that successfully reduce and end violence against women. Feminist environments can provide the kind of safety that women need to heal from trauma, remember and mourn, break out of helplessness, reestablish relationships based in mutuality and trust, and create a positive future. As men fight, flee, or freeze in order to access testosterone to prepare them for conflict, women have a different reaction: nesting and cooperative action in the form of networking with other women and plotting with other women for safety and security. The more isolated women are, the more they are susceptible to violence. The more we come together across our diversities, the more chance we have to create a better future.

Jewish tradition demonstrates sensitivity to groups of people who are targets of discrimination on the basis of economic status, ethnic and religious identification, and more recently, gender, race, sexual preference, age, and physical or mental condition. The historic oppression of Jews forms a primary point of reference for anti-oppression work among Jewish people; for Jewish feminists, however, the issue of gender equality remains a central concern.

Within that context, feminists must continue to advocate for serious study of those attitudes, beliefs, and behaviors that create a climate that tolerates violence against women. As long as one out of three women experiences abuse, we have a long way to go before we've reached safe haven.[8]

Rabbi Valerie Joseph, a Wexner Heritage Fellow, has served as a resident chaplain at both the Veterans Hospital and Stanford University Hospital and Clinics. She is the author of *Abigail to Zechariah: A Treasury of Biblical Names,* and is currently executive producer of the documentary film *Joann Sfar Draws from Memory,* in production with the Franco-German public broadcasting corporation ARTE. She was ordained at the Ziegler School of Rabbinic Studies in 2007.

Rabbi Alana Suskin is a writer and educator. She has published dozens of articles and essays on the subjects of feminism and Judaism, Jewish sexuality, Jewish liturgy, the cutting edge of Judaism, and ethics and social justice in Judaism. She serves as managing editor for Jewschool, called "The most important thing happening online in the Jewish community today" by the noted Jewish sociologists Ari Kelman and Steven M. Cohen. She was ordained at the Ziegler School of rabbinic studies in 2003.

Servants before the King

Raising Up the Healer to Leadership

RABBI VALERIE JOSEPH AND RABBI ALANA SUSKIN

"*EL NA REFAH NA LAH*" (Please God, heal her). These words from Numbers 12:13 are often quoted as the shortest prayer in the Hebrew scriptures. When Moses's sister Miriam is struck by disease, Moses offers this prayer for her. From here we learn that the Jewish healer is one who responds to pain with alacrity. Pain and fear, whether spiritual, physical, or mental, are an opportunity for human beings to serve as God's hands in the world. Unlike law, which is the subject and object of extensive debate, interpretation, and haggling, Jewish tradition understands pain and fear as something to be addressed immediately. We do not wait. We act quickly, even tersely: *El na refah na lah.* Please, God, heal her. There is no time to waste.

These words are possibly the first healing blessing in the Tanakh. They are important for their message of compassion, showing us the importance of truly understanding what someone needs. As women and Jewish healers, however, we must work to find more than just words of healing; we must find Jewish role models for healing that do not exclude women but are instead easily relatable. In studying the classical texts of Judaism, we have come to see that the prophet Deborah offers us a model for healers that can, itself, heal the unbalanced approach to healing that Judaism takes. We see that the Jewish healing movement, a movement created largely by women, has transformed the landscape of Jewish healing. This is a feminist message: healing women heal Judaism. This chapter explores some of the role models of healing that we have studied, and resolves with Deborah the prophet.

The Jewish healing movement in the United States started in the 1980s, no doubt influenced by the ordination of women as rabbis. Rabbi Amy Eilberg says, "As women became rabbis, the interest in spirituality increased." Over time, we have come to see that not all rabbis are pulpit rabbis; and indeed, over time, both men and women have been transformed by women in the rabbinate, not least by both men and women choosing to serve the people Israel through chaplaincy, teaching, and other non-pulpit positions.

It is part of the Jewish tradition to immerse oneself in "the conversation," the give and take of humans with God through the medium of holy texts, meditation, and prayer. Although Jewish tradition does indeed recognize the importance of healing and emphasize the intimate nature of one who heals with the Holy One, over time, the intimacy and holiness have been downplayed in the American Jewish community. But whether through chaplaincy or teaching, the unfolding of what is hurting a person through the art of active listening is an essential piece of our tradition that it took feminist healers to recover.

There are three major innovations that feminism brings to healing. The first, personalization of spiritual experience, is that when the Jewish community absorbed from the society around us the idea that technology would save us from all evils, it took the inspiration of a group of Jewish women, mainly rabbis, to bring us back to the Jewish teachings that have always sustained us. These leaders demonstrated that healing is inextricable from our spiritual lives, through *bikkur cholim* (visiting the sick), through spiritual guidance by rabbis and chaplains, through innovative views of spiritual support and healing by rabbinic doulas, through healing centers and innovative use of the mikveh and other rituals.

The second is that healing is not simply a matter of individuals. Our communities need healing as well, and feminist leaders have used tradition to bring healing to our communities in the past—through rituals such as the *misheberach* (prayer for the ill)—and will need to continue to do so in the future.

The third is the challenging of divisions in Jewish society and Jewish life. While healing is not a feminist matter in itself, the bifurcation of the world into scholar and healer is an unhealthy one, and has paralleled the bifurcation of roles of men and women in both our religious and secular worlds. Leaders in Jewish healing are showing us ways to heal that false dichotomy as well. The Jewish people ought not to be divided into categories of minister and servant, scholar and congregant. Instead, we all need to engage in each role in our own way. Men are not only minds, and women are not only bodies; both men and women need to rebuild Judaism to become whole people who are engaged in both study and prayer.

Judaism does not view us as souls in bodies, but as a totality. The Shema, one of the two central prayers of Judaism, declares in its second verse (Deut. 6:5), "And you shall love the Lord your God, with all your heart, with all your soul, and with all your might." Psalms 35:10 says, "All my bones shall declare, God, who is like unto you?" The Hasidim understood this as a command to use their totality in

God's service, body and soul. It is a command upon every Jew to do *bikkur cholim.* Ideally, feminism brings change through a woman bringing her perspectives as someone who experiences a different social reality and leading innovations that spread throughout the community. Feminism changes the social and communal milieu not just for women, but for the entire community. The community cannot fulfill the commandment to love God with all that it has until both men and women can give all they have to offer, equally.

Judaism's View of a Healer

Judaism traditionally views doctors with great respect. In fact, the Talmud says that God authorizes doctors to heal. Berachot 60a says, "It was taught in the school of Rabbi Yishmael: [It is written], He shall cause him to be thoroughly healed (Exod. 21:19). From this we learn that permission has been given to the physician to heal."

Judaism did not ever suggest that we should forgo healing as a sign of trust in God. The doctor is God's messenger, and not above God. Human healing is important, but it cannot be divorced from the spiritual. Thus, Judaism does not view doctors as the only healers. In Baba Batra 116a, the Talmud states plainly, "Whosoever has a sick person in his house should go to a Sage who will invoke [heavenly] mercy for him; as it is said: The wrath of a king [i.e., God] is as messengers of death,' but a wise man will pacify it."

The Role of the Healer

Our tradition teaches that the one who visits the sick eases their illness. The Rabbis viewed this obligation to visit the sick as part of the healing process. Those who are ill need not just medical care, but the care of the community to heal them. Even God participates in this mitzvah (commandment). In tractate Sotah 14a, the Rabbis interpret the verse found in Deuteronomy 13:5, "You shall walk after the Lord your God," as a commandment:

> The Holy One, visited the sick, for it is written: And the Lord appeared unto him by the oaks of Mamre [Genesis 18:1, the previous verses were concerning Abraham's circumcision; the Rabbis took this to mean that God was visiting Abraham after his surgery], so do thou also visit the sick.

In our visits to the sick, however, there are appropriate ways to behave. In tractate Shabbat 12b we learn:

> The one who enters to visit the sick should not sit on top of the bed, nor on top of the chair, but rather should wrap themself and sit before [the patient] because the Shekhinah [the indwelling presence of God] is above the headboard of the sick one.

This is why we should not sit on the bed when making a pastoral visit; we must sit a bit lower than the patient. Rabbi Carla Howard offers this insight: "The reason we sit lower is to allow the divine presence of God as the Shekhinah, which sits at the headboard of the bed, to be reflected in our eyes, so that the patient who is not able to see the Shekhinah atop the bed can have this reflected for him or her."[1] In sitting below the patient, we serve them by lowering ourselves, literally, at their feet. When we do this, we become a vessel for the Holy One, in which the Divine can be seen by someone who might not otherwise be able to see the Divine. Through our *bikkur cholim*, we bring God's presence. Together, God, the visitor, and the doctor build a circuit of healing that draws completeness into the room when they all work together to reflect one another.

Feminist Role Models for Spiritual Care Providers

In the Talmud, as in the Torah, there is no clear distinction drawn between healing the body and healing the soul. The clearest model of a healer that we have in the Talmud is found in the person of

Rabbi Hanina ben Dosa, who appears in two stories about healing in tractate Berachot 34b:

> Our Rabbis taught: Once the son of Rabban Gamaliel fell ill. He sent two scholars to R. Hanina b. Dosa to ask him to pray for him. When he saw them he went up to an upper chamber and prayed for him. When he came down he said to them: Go, the fever has left him; they said to him: Are you a prophet? He replied: I am neither a prophet nor the son of a prophet, but I learnt this from experience. If my prayer is fluent in my mouth, I know that he is accepted: but if not, I know that he is rejected. They sat down and made a note of the exact moment. When they came to Rabban Gamaliel, he said to them: By the temple service! You have not been a moment too soon or too late, but so it happened: at that very moment the fever left him and he asked for water to drink.

In this story, the role as a healer stems directly from the Rabbi's ability to enter wholly into the prayer. We might initially think that this is simply another way of showing Rabbi Hanina ben Dosa's skill as a learned man, but upon closer reflection, we see something rather unusual. Unlike the usual emphasis on textual skill, it is Rabbi Hanina's emotion that underlies his efficacy as a healer. When he enters into communion with God unselfconsciously, entirely absorbed by his prayer, he knows that his prayer has been accepted. This emotional aspect to prayer is something with which many women can identify, as part of an assigned cultural role and closely tied to our assigned role as caretaker of the bodies of the household as well as our status as "servant" in the home and society. In the story of Rabbi Hanina ben Dosa, where a man takes on the role of servant-healer, serving becomes elevated, and thus reveals a path that we, as women, can develop toward a new role for ourselves in society. In reformulating the role of healer to one in which the emotional is lauded for both men and women, and one in which service is to God rather than because of an innately different role, perhaps we can use the position of healer to overcome the limitations imposed upon us.

The second story about Rabbi Hanina ben Dosa gives us an additional insight:

> On another occasion it happened that Rabbi Hanina b. Dosa went to study Torah with Rabban Yohanan ben Zakkai. The son of Rabban Yohanan ben Zakkai fell ill. He said to him: Hanina my son, pray for him that he may live. He put his head between his knees and prayed for him and he lived. Said Rabban Yohanan ben Zakkai: If Ben Zakkai had stuck his head between his knees for the whole day, no notice would have been taken of him. Said his wife to him: Is Hanina greater than you are? He replied to her: No; but he is like a servant before the king, and I am like a nobleman before a king.

This story shows us precisely how the subservient role is the one that makes a healer effective. Rashi, in his comment on this page of Talmud, says that the explanation of Rabban Yohanan ben Zakkai's statement to his wife is that the servant has regular and unimpeded access to the king, and so is on intimate terms with him, and thus can approach him at any time. In contrast, the minister, who is more important, can only come before the king at the king's will, and so cannot make requests at any time.

In both of these schemas, it is the modest servant, the more lowly Rabbi Hanina, with whom God is on more intimate terms, and to whom God is more inclined to grant requests. In terms of healing, it is the one who serves others who is granted an intimacy that allows the healer to serve those in need most effectively. We must be extremely careful, however, when applying a model that emphasizes submission to the role of women as healers and leaders, given the historical stereotype of women as the more submissive gender.

Healing is a human endeavor, not just a women's endeavor. Men have been healers as long as women. We can see from the texts discussed, as well as many others, that in Judaism, healing is part and parcel of a particular approach to God. There are two basic ways that Jews relate to God, both of which are usually considered necessary for a full relationship, though many people are better at one way than the other: as the scholar, the one who excels in the making of legal decisions, and as the *ba'al tefilah*, the one who excels at prayer. The first role is intellectual, and the second, emotive.

In the Talmud, the role of scholar is explained as a superior approach. It is the approach of the minister, the official, the one who is on a more even footing with God. The healer is master of the heart. He or she is humble, not even close to being able to stand before God and discuss. But the *ba'al tefilah*, the master of prayer, has the run of the house and is on intimate terms with God. So even though he or she is less honored than the scholar, the master of prayer has access that the scholar lacks. If we can collapse the two models and make the healer eradicate the dualism of these two roles, instead showing how they are linked, we can offer redemption to the healing role already often assigned to women. In doing so, we can take as a model Rabbi Hanina ben Dosa. Although he is portrayed as a servant and inferior to Rabban Yohanan ben Zakkai, in truth he was a scholar as well. He chose to take on the servant role, rather than one in which he was a law-interpreter, in which he had authority over others. If we view Rabbi Hanina as the healers' forebear, we can create models that not only female healers, but male healers as well, will follow, creating new leadership roles for all.

When we speak of healing, we do not necessarily mean only the literal healing of the body. The goal is not to cure the disease, but to help afflicted people change their approach to their situation, to give strength to face with courage whatever is required, and to connect individuals with God and the community. The goal is to give life to the soul. Prayer verbally says aloud that which was formerly hidden and private, releasing it into God's receptive universe. The Hebrew word for prayer, *tefilah,* comes from a reflexive verb that means "plead," "think," or "judge." Thus, prayer is to judge yourself, or introspect. Rabbis as healers voice people's concerns and release into the public domain that which was cried in the dark, alone.

Another role model of women healers is Hannah, one of the seven women listed in the Talmud as a prophet. She is the exemplar par excellence of healing and prayer. In 1 Samuel 2, we read that the sons of Eli the priest were "worthless men" who did not know God and spent their days in sin. Hannah, who makes yearly trips to worship in Shiloh, would surely have known this. Hannah cries out to be a mother and carry the son that will put in order the house of this unworthy priesthood.

The Talmud recognizes Hannah as a model for prayer not simply for women but for all people. Tractate Berachot 31a notes that Hannah spoke from her heart, moving her lips while she prayed, and directed her heart to God. The Rabbis instruct us that we, too, must direct our heart and speak our prayers with our lips. More than that, Hannah is not simply content to weep and pray. She actually uses her knowledge of Jewish law to force God to give her a child. Berachot 31b states:

> R. Eleazar said: Hannah said before the Holy One, blessed be He: Sovereign of the Universe, if Thou wilt look, it is well, and if Thou wilt not look, I will go and shut myself up with someone else in the knowledge of my husband Elkanah, and as I shall have been alone they will make me drink the water of the suspected wife, and Thou canst not falsify Thy law, which says, She shall be cleared and shall conceive seed.... As it has been taught: "She shall be cleared and shall conceive seed": this teaches that if she was barren she is visited.

Hannah storms the gates of heaven to get her desire. Here we see a connection between how the Rabbis viewed knowledge of Jewish law and healing. If we know the law well enough, we can force God to bring healing. This is almost diametrically opposite the model of Rabbi Hanina ben Dosa, the humble servant. Here, Hannah is no humble maiden, but a smart knowledgeable woman who uses every trick she has to heal herself—and in doing so brings healing to her community as well. The implication here is that there is a connection between healing of ourselves and healing our communities. Moreover, it is *not* only the servant who has the king's ear, but also the scholar—and here the scholar is a woman.

Deborah was recognized by authority figures as herself having power and being an authority figure. A judge of Israel, Deborah sends for the military leader Barak to come to her—a mark of her authority (Judg. 4:6). She escorts Barak, not for ornamentation, but rather for national deliverance in the name of God. Deborah accompanies Barak, marching along with him, to bring the presence of God into his victorious battle and serve as an advisor. Deborah is the first army chaplain, going into battle with Barak.

How Jewish Women Have Taken Up the Role of Healer

The innovation of the woman as healer is not only to reopen our communities to the ancient traditions that look beyond simple physical healing to the needs of the soul, but to open the community to the voices of the isolated, those who are pushed aside or silent—the childless by intent or despite their desires, the single woman, the ill child, man, or woman—and to include in the community those who were once considered outsiders, those whose voices were traditionally silenced, and those whose lives were hidden in the cracks by shame—women, gay men, lesbians, bisexuals, transgender individuals.

As Jewish women who have finally claimed prominent roles in the Jewish community as rabbis, spiritual directors, and chaplains, we are broadening what is considered to be a leadership role for both men and women. We are expanding the view of what

391

leadership is by bringing healing—not just personal, physical healing, but also public and even political healing of ourselves, our families, our communities, our people, and the world.

Healers are not just doctors who literally heal the body, or rabbis who serve the spirit and soul of the troubled and ill. Women have become leaders in bringing healing to many arenas of Jewish and public life. In particular, many women have been at the forefront of the Jewish healing movement. These women paved a new path for what is now seen as a legitimate role—that of being a spiritual care provider, a chaplain, a rabbi/healer. As Rabbi Rachel Cowan states in the Jewish Women's Archive, "I believe that it took a group of women—including rabbis—to break through the Jewish cultural barrier that saw medical treatment as the only response to illness. We understood that even though illness might not be curable, there were many ways to relieve the suffering. Rituals could restore a sense of calm and order to the emotional and physical chaos of the experience of illness. We knew that relationships and community were the key to healing."[2]

Rabbi Lori Klein, cancer-care chaplain at Stanford University Hospital has another perspective on why so many Jewish women were involved in the creation of this movement. "Women may have been inspired to start the Jewish healing movement because they have always been the caretakers for their families and communities throughout the life cycle from birth to death. During the most virulent years of the AIDS epidemic in the United States in the 1980s and early 1990s, gay, lesbian and community health activists created new models of physical, emotional and spiritual caretaking so that friendship circles and communities could care for the large numbers of sick and dying young and middle-aged adults, some of whom were estranged from their families of origin. Lessons learned there carried over into other contexts, including care for cancer patients and (I think) the Jewish healing movement."[3]

There is a perception that Judaism accepts only medical intervention as a response to illness, but there is a strong tradition of respecting the healer as an extension of God's hands. As Jews were accepted into the mainstream of American society, during a period in which technology was seen as the ultimate salvation for all the ills of humanity, many of us adopted the notion that "technology is the great savior" as part of our religious values as well. But today we recognize that, while science gives us many worthy tools, it does not address the totality of human experience. Judaism, of course, has always taught this, but it took a group of knowledgable Jewish women to bring us back to this Jewish idea.

Healing centers revitalized these traditions—some consciously, some by borrowing from other non-Jewish sources. The new ways of accessing our traditions of healing spread and are now nearly universal in the larger urban centers. The Jewish healing centers begun by innovative women spawned a movement, and now more than forty such centers exist.

Since the first healing service in 1991, these services have also proliferated. Regular healing services are now held throughout the Jewish community, some led by relatively traditional rabbis. And now nearly every synagogue does the *misheberach* on Shabbat, to the extent that, in just over fifteen years, it has come to be considered the norm and few know that it is not an ancient custom.

In reality, the custom of saying *misheberach*s as a regular part of the Torah service on Shabbat morning is a relatively recent innovation. Traditionally, *misheberach*s were said, in a very quiet, informal way during Torah services, generally during the week (when one makes *bakashot*, requests of God) or during Shabbat Mincha—the very short afternoon service on Shabbat, which is quieter and shorter than the long Shabbat morning service. The current practice is to have *misheberach*s at Shabbat Shacharit, the Torah service between Shacharit and Mincha. In addition to moving the *misheberach* to a more prominent service, the blessing itself has come to be more public and more prominent within the service.

Moreover, the *misheberach* was traditionally only recited in life-or-death situations, not as it has developed into its current use—to include even relatively minor ailments, or even, in some cases, spiritual or emotional struggles. The expansion of prayers such as the *misheberach* has come about largely because of social factors: in most non-Orthodox communities today, people no longer live embedded in the close network of synagogue community. Many people drive to synagogue, and so may only see the other members of their community on Shabbat or holidays. The everyday interactions that derive from proximity have thus been disrupted, often leaving the community's members—especially the more vulnerable elderly or ill—feeling excluded or distanced.

The rabbi thus has become—among her or his other roles—one who must heal the broken community. The mention of the names of those who are not present because of illness has become extremely important, as the isolated individual can be both spiritually and emotionally drawn into the community network at a time when a larger number of community members are there to hear. The logic of this new custom is much like the ancient Sages assigning Monday and Thursday as Torah-reading days because those days were market days, and so more people were present to hear God's word.

An outgrowth of the Jewish healing centers are the many organizations that strive to offer Jewish spiritual direction, such as the Yedidya Center for Jewish Spiritual Direction, codirected by Rabbi Amy Eilberg, one of the founders of the healing movement. Many of these organizations were begun by founders who got their start as leaders in the creation of healing rituals and learning, such as Nan Fink Gefen and Bobbi Breitman.

There are other kinds of Jewish healing as well. Rabbi Carrie Benveniste is creating a new model for Jewish women bearing children. Trained as a doula, she is working to create a birth experience in which the focus is not on the technological instruments upon which many doctors depend, but on options that are safe, healthy, and Jewish. Birth ceases to be a medical experience and returns to the realm of a holy process. The importance of the woman who assists at birth is supported by Jewish tradition. In at least two places, Eruvin 45a and Rosh Hashanah 23b, the Talmud mentions that midwives are exempted from the boundaries beyond which we are not permitted to travel on Shabbat. The need to assist at a birth overrules these restrictions, as indeed all lifesaving activities overrule the restrictions of Shabbat.

Chaplains are among those who serve as healers in the most urgent of circumstances. Whether at civilian or military hospitals, or on the battlefield, women are becoming part of that picture, though there are still very few women serving as military chaplains. Women were, of course, only recently introduced into the rabbinate, and when women were first ordained, the Orthodox members of the Jewish Chaplains Board opposed the inclusion of women rabbis as chaplains. In 1986 the Jewish Welfare Board (JWB) split over this issue—specifically over including a Reform female chaplain, Rabbi Julie Schwartz—though women were eventually included.[4] In discussing the matter with one of the few current female Jewish chaplains, we were curious about what she thought were the reasons behind so few female chaplains. She believes that since the inclusion of women is such a recent occurrence, not many women have yet begun to serve.

Another example of a broad change brought about by innovations in the milieu of Jewish healing, is the mikveh, or ritual bath of living waters. Over the past two decades, there has been a reclamation of the use of the mikveh. Traditionally used for women after the cessation of their monthly cycle, after the birth of a child, for conversion, and prior to a wedding (for both men and women), the ancient tradition has been for some time expanding into use for healing rituals—such as for survivors of sexual or physical trauma, for cancer survivors, and for those struggling with infertility. The new Boston mikveh Mayyim Hayyim opened in May of 2004. In addition to standard mikveh uses, Mayyim Hayyim hosts many of the innovative rituals mentioned above and functions as a community center.

Healers need to be both public and private figures. At one time, being a private figure of healing meant being the mother or sister who acted as nurse to the household sick. Today, though, our privacy is of a larger sphere. We are doctors or rabbis who tend to our congregations, visit the sick, or literally heal their bodies. As public figures, we heal not simply individuals, but communities—perhaps even nations.

Today, prayer takes not only its traditional forms, but new forms—through new rituals, new venues, and new technologies, such as e-mail lists for healing requests. We are the descendants of the seven prophetesses from whom we inherited a spiritual "medical bag" of healing techniques. We are the descendants of the author of the Psalms, whose poetry and song are used today, three thousand years later, to bring comfort to those in need of healing. We are the descendants of the Talmudic rabbis who noted the differences in the ability of a rabbi to be a legal decisor and the ability to be a "healer" like Rabbi Hanina ben Dosa. And we are the descendants of those physician-rabbis like Rabbi Moshe ben Maimon (Maimonides), who recognized that the body and the soul are two parts of the whole. We are the descendants of a people long immersed in a tradition of healing body and soul together, community and individual, and today we continue this tradition, and bear it again, full of new life.

Rosie Rosenzweig, who calls herself a "post-triumphal Jew," is a resident scholar in women's studies at Brandeis University, and the author of *A Jewish Mother in Shangri-la*, which narrates her Asian travels with her son to meet his Buddhist teachers. Her present work includes examining what she has coined as the New Haskalah, a new Zeitgeist wherein Jewish women are transforming spirituality in Buddhism and Judaism.

Post-Triumphalism and the New *Haskalah*

ROSIE ROSENZWEIG

SOME YEARS AGO I began a workshop with a soulful recording of a wordless Hasidic tune, a *niggun,* sung by a male cantor. Upon hearing this, a female colleague admonished me: "That should be sung by a woman!" Afraid to be politically incorrect, I found a spirited female cantor to record it. She imbued the melody with a forceful joyousness; it didn't work. And all the other female cantors that I knew, by happenstance, couldn't intone that tearful catch in the throat so important to the teaching. Perhaps my friends channeled Miriam, happy and dancing, at the Red Sea, and not the suffering of our biblical foremothers.

My colleague's ardently impassioned feminism led me to make a choice that was wrong both musically and ritually due to my fear of being labeled a weak feminist. Unfortunately, this incident demonstrates a disturbingly prevalent phenomenon: when a war has won some major battles, the combatants don't move on, and minor skirmishes get mistaken for weapons of mass chauvinism.

Rigidity has, in some quarters, enslaved a liberating movement with fixated paradigms. Drunk with the exhilaration of achievement, it seems that some Jewish feminists erected a new *mechitzah* and called it "Jewish feminism."

We have to guard against losing the flexibility and feminist receptivity that has inspirited Judaism with new rabbinical models, new rituals that speak to women with fresh insights about our foremothers, our liturgy, and our history. We must save ourselves for newer, less petty, and more expansive efforts. What will be those efforts?

Jewish and Secular Feminism: Four Waves

Jewish women have been in the foreground of each wave of the feminist movement since its inception. Ernestine Rose, a Polish Hasidic rabbi's daughter, was a prominent first-wave Jewish feminist, with her stirring speech at the Seneca Falls convention for women's rights. Jewish women also led the second-wave movement with its economic, sociological, and legal stance against other people's expectations. To name only a few, Betty Friedan's exposure of the *Feminine Mystique;* Tillie Olsen's classical description of limited drudgery of women in "I Stand Here Ironing"; the Jewish founding editors of *Ms.* magazine; and the political clout of Bella Abzug.

In second-wave Jewish feminism, we saw the launch of a Jewish feminist magazine called *Lilith;* the establishment of New York's Drisha Institute, where women can study advanced classical texts; Blu Greenberg's founding of the Jewish Orthodox Feminist Alliance (JOFA); and, according to Jonathan Sarna, "By the year 2000 ... [half] or more of both [Reform and Reconstructionist] ... ordination classes every year consisted of women."[1]

The secular third wave, born into awareness by Anita Hill's sexual harassment case in the United States in the 1990s, is the youthful advocacy of openness in sex; acceptance of alternative lifestyles; opposition to race discrimination; political activism; reproductive rights; a focus away from upper-class white women; cyberspace usage; emphasis on each woman's unique personal experience; and a celebration and ownership of the female body.[2]

Third-wave Jewish feminists include Helene Aylone, whose exhibit "The Liberation of God" highlighted, in pink, parts of the Torah that were patriarchal, misogynistic, violent, and cruel; Eve Ensler and her play *The Vagina Monologues;* and Judy Chicago and her art installation that used menstrual blood. Since third-wave feminism includes the acceptance of alternative lifestyles, the entry of gay, lesbian, transgender, and bisexual people into the ranks of rabbinical leadership in Reform, Reconstructionist, and Conservative movements exemplifies it as well.

Author Pythia Peay describes a fourth wave of mainstream feminism in an article in the *Utne Reader:*

> At its heart lies a new kind of political activism that's guided and sustained by spirituality. Some are calling it the long-awaited "fourth wave" of feminism—a fusion of spirituality and social justice reminiscent of the American civil rights movement and Gandhi's call for nonviolent change.[3]

The New *Haskalah*

The factors of *tikkun olam* (repair of the world), a spirituality based on social action, have always been at the core of Jewish feminism. Jewish women's spiritual paths may be beyond definitions because they embrace the source that commands all religious forces. Jewish feminists, either in the secular or spiritual realm, have always thought "out of the box." The commitments of fourth-wave feminism may most accurately define the latest ventures for Jewish feminists, who are crossing denominational borders to bond with Jewish women of other movements, and also beginning to include women from other religious traditions. By this expansion, we can understand how universal the enlivening urge is, and how the divine experience for all is the same ineffable merging. This expansion has motivated a new religious broadening championed by Jewish feminists who explore how other religions can inform our own Jewish experience of divinity. When we reenter the religion of our practice, we take on paradigms with which we are comfortable: Shekhinah for Jewish women; Gaia for Hindu women; Avalokitesvara, bodhisattva of compassion, for Buddhists. The latest pathfinders use these sister experiences not to fully emulate non-Jewish experiences, but to inform their own Jewish feminist path.

There are many women operating in this dimension who are part of an emerging consciousness, which I call the New *Haskalah*. The eighteenth-century European Enlightenment, which seeded the first *haskalah* (a word whose root is *saychel*, meaning "common sense, reason, or intelligence"), was characterized by "the rise of the bourgeoisie and the influence of modern science; it promoted the values of intellectual and material progress, toleration, and critical reason as opposed to authority and tradition in matters of politics and religion."[4]

Moses Mendelssohn, a German Jew known as "the Jewish Socrates," epitomized the "Jewish community's knocking at the gate of the modern world."[5] With more exposure to the secular scientific and humanistic education of the 1800s,[6] the *haskalah* was set against blind faith, rigid parochial superstitions, and the mysteries of the kabbalah. This movement advocated more integrative education in secular studies and the rejection of Yiddish. Expanding Jewish presence in realms formerly restricted to Jews, it influenced nineteenth-century Zionism, as well as some twentieth-century secular movements. Now, with the twenty-first century of spiritual expansion, we can define a New *Haskalah*, a product of the interdependent global village that we inhabit. This historical junction is marked by the exponential growth of ideas, spreading democratization, and a global village that influences the political, religious, and spiritual lives of women. Global feminism is being transformed by sister liberation movements throughout the planet; Jewish feminism is likewise expanding to see the commonalities in other religions. The contemporary word *enlightenment* is assuming a meaning derived from Eastern spirituality and is usually associated with Buddhism. With over 500 million followers,[7] Buddhism has found its way into countless avenues of life. According to Mircea Eliade's *Encyclopedia of Religion,* in the Asian context, *enlightenment* "typically refers to that existentially transformative experience in which one reaches complete and thorough understanding of the nature of reality."[8] Going beyond the material objects of mind and body, the path of enlightenment fosters spiritual emptiness that opens a compassionate doorway for all living beings.

In Judaism, the enlightenment of Eastern spirituality can be likened to a Jewish state called *devekut,* a *unio mystico* with the Divine, a state that has influenced the Jewish Renewal movement and Jewish feminism in particular. Buddhism has already affected Judaism in the later twentieth century; many, if not a majority, of the new Buddhist teachers in the West are Jewish. It is not uncommon to hear the term *JuBu* used to describe a Jewish Buddhist, and many of these JuBus are women. So boundaries are being pushed into the area of blended religious approaches, influenced by a break from triumphalism and a corresponding acceptance of multiple truths. This is a characteristic of the consciousness that permeates the New *Haskalah:* a phenomenon wherein all theological approaches are considered to be of equal merit. No theological viewpoint is triumphant over any other. Jewish Renewal rabbi Rolando Matalon of the B'nai Jeshrun Synagogue in New York describes post-triumphalism as follows: "We all have pieces of the complicated truth. Who can deny someone else's connection to God? God is not a follower of any of the religions created by his followers."[9]

Consequently, the New *Haskalah,* as a post-triumphal expansion of the original *haskalah,* seeks to embrace more than a narrow Judaism of fixed rules, superstitions, and beliefs based on male authoritarianism. In this contemporary Jewish Zeitgeist, the expansion is not toward a secular knowledge and away from Jewish tradition, but is a renewal of the old tradition enlightened by other viewpoints. The New *Haskalah* has enormous implications for

401

Jewish feminists, in that the philosophy courts, honors, and uses the female point of view.

The New *Haskalah*'s embrace of non-Jewish spiritual experiences where the divine experience is the common factor among seekers parallels the paradigmatic expansion of the first *haskalah*, with Jewish ideas being assimilated into the secular world. The differences occur when different faiths use familiar paradigms to describe divine experiences. The New *Haskalah*'s essential prerequisite is a flexible mindset. Creative Jewish feminists understand that these other paradigms are metaphors approximating *devekut*, the inward, basically individual experience involving the body and soul.

As a Jewish mother with a Buddhist son, my personal experience is not so unique among Jewish mothers with children who haven't found what they need in the Jewish religion. Receiving a consciousness-changing transmission from a Tibetan Rinpoche motivated me to enroll in the Jewish meditation teacher's ordination program in Berkeley. I believe that we are at the new dawning of "the Age of Aquarius," in which the New *Haskalah*, with Jewish feminism at its heart, will help to find the commonality in all religions. The Enlightenment, by the very word embedded in its center, means to lighten yourself internally, by the flexible freedom of your heart and mind, by education, and by allowing these to spiritually expand in a Jewish context. The New *Haskalah*, as I am defining it, has Jewish feminism as an integral part of world religions.

Additionally, this new consciousness of our twenty-first-century global village seeks a sisterhood in all things spiritual. It is a guard against rigid paradigms; it is essential in this new post-triumphal world of spirituality to help us learn from one another about enlivening the spirit. Sandra Lubarsky, of the Department of Religious Studies at Northern Arizona University, has invented the term "veridical pluralism, the position that there is a multiplicity of traditions that 'speak truth,' that are legitimate forms of truth-bearing ways."[10] When delving into other traditions to cross-pollinate with our own flowerings, grounded feminists assert that no one is leaving

Judaism; we are only informing our own tradition of *devekut*. Jewish feminists can create and adapt ritual, learning, and Torah to embody mysticism with enhancement, self-improvement, movement, and feminine meaning.

Author Carol Lee Flinders, who has included in her writings women mystics such as Saint Teresa of Avila, and Jewish women such as Etty Hillesum, declares that: "Feminism catches fire when it draws on its inherent spirituality." At a Women and Power Conference with a meeting place called the "Red Tent," she added: "When you get Jewish, Catholic, Buddhist, Hindu, and Sufi women all practicing their faith in the same room, another religion emerges, which is feminine spirituality."[11]

With this idea in mind, we can progress toward a true "Age of Aquarius," when these past struggles will all be viewed as antiquated. We can strive toward an era when even the word *feminism* will become obsolete. Then, maybe, the paradigm that Judaism has named the Messiah will actually arrive.

NOTES

Women and Theology

Calling All Theologians

JUDITH PLASKOW, PhD

1. Rita Gross, "Female God Language in a Jewish Context," in *Womanspirit Rising: A Feminist Reader in Religion,* ed. Carol P. Christ and Judith Plaskow (San Francisco: Harper SanFrancisco, 1979), 167–73.
2. Marcia Falk, "Notes on Composing New Blessings," *Journal of Feminist Studies in Religion* 3, no. 1 (Spring 1987): 41.
3. T. Drorah Setel, "Feminist Reflections on Separation and Unity in Jewish Theology," *Journal of Feminist Studies in Religion* 2, no. 1 (Spring 1986): 113–18; Rachel Adler, "'I've Had Nothing Yet So I Can't Take More,'" *Moment* 8 (September 1983): 22; Ellen M. Umansky, "Creating a Jewish Feminist Theology: Possibilities and Problems," in *Weaving the Visions: New Patterns in Feminist Spirituality,* ed. Judith Plaskow and Carol P. Christ (San Francisco: Harper SanFrancisco, 1989), 194.
4. Judith Plaskow, *Standing Again at Sinai: Judaism from a Feminist Perspective* (San Francisco: HarperSanFrancisco, 1990), chaps. 1–4, esp. pp. 9–10.
5. Rachel Adler, *Engendering Judaism: An Inclusive Theology and Ethics* (Philadelphia: Jewish Publication Society, 1998), xxii–xxvi, and chaps. 2 and 5.
6. Tamar Ross, *Expanding the Palace of Torah: Orthodoxy and Feminism* (Waltham, MA: Brandeis University Press, 2004), xvi, 197–98, and chap. 10.
7. Melissa Raphael, *The Female Face of God in Auschwitz: A Jewish Feminist Theology of the Holocaust* (London and New York: Routledge, 2003), 54. See also chaps. 1 and 3, pp. 22 and 60.
8. Lynn Gottlieb, *She Who Dwells Within: A Feminist Vision of a Renewed Judaism* (San Francisco: Harper SanFrancisco, 1995), 6, 7, and passim.
9. Rebecca Alpert, *Like Bread on the Seder Plate: Jewish Lesbians and the Transformation of Tradition* (New York: Columbia University Press, 1997).
10. Naomi Janowitz and Maggie Wenig, *Siddur Nashim: A Sabbath Prayerbook for Women* (privately circulated for the women's minyan at Brown University, 1976).
11. Marcia Falk, *The Book of Blessings: New Jewish Prayers for Daily Life, the Sabbath, and the New Moon Festival* (San Francisco: Harper SanFrancisco, 1996).
12. See, for example, Ellen Frankel, *The Five Books of Miriam: A Woman's Commentary on the Torah* (New York: G. P. Putnam, 1996); Elyse Goldstein, ed., *The Women's Torah Commentary: New Insights from Women Rabbis on the 54 Weekly Torah Por-*

tions (Woodstock, VT: Jewish Lights, 2000); Elyse Goldstein, ed., *The Women's Haftarah Commentary: New Insights from Women Rabbis on the 54 Weekly Haftarah Portions, the 5 Megillot and Special Shabbatot* (Woodstock, VT: Jewish Lights, 2004); Judith A. Kates and Gail Twersky Reimer, *Reading Ruth: Contemporary Women Reclaim a Sacred Story* (New York: Ballantine Books, 1994); Gail Twersky Reimer and Judith A. Kates, *Beginning Anew: A Woman's Companion to the High Holy Days* (New York: Simon and Schuster, 1997); and Tamara Eskenazi and Andrea L. Weiss, eds., *The Torah: A Women's Commentary* (New York: URJ Press, 2008).

13. Published examples include Jane Sprague Zones, ed., *Taking the Fruit: Modern Women's Tales of the Bible* (San Diego: Women's Institute for Continuing Jewish Education, 1989); Alicia Suskin Ostriker, *The Nakedness of the Fathers: Biblical Visions and Revisions* (New Brunswick, NJ: Rutgers University Press, 1994); as well as poetry such as Eleanor Wilner's *Sarah's Choice* (Chicago: University of Chicago Press, 1990).

14. I have in mind books such as Evelyn Torten Beck, ed., *Nice Jewish Girls: A Lesbian Anthology*, rev. ed. (Boston: Beacon Press, 1989); *The Tribe of Dina: A Jewish Women's Anthology*, Melanie Kaye/Kantrowitz and Irena Klepfisz, eds., rev. ed. (Boston: Beacon Press, 1989); Marla Brettschneider and Dawn Robinson Rose, eds., "Meeting at the Well: Multiculturalism and Jewish Feminism," a special section of the *Journal of Feminist Studies in Religion* 19, no. 1 (Spring 2003): 82–128; Melanie Kaye/Kantrowitz, *The Color of Jews: Racial Politics and Radical Diasporism* (Indianapolis and Bloomington: Indiana University Press, 2007).

15. My contributions to "Gender Theory and Gendered Realities—An Exchange between Tamar Ross and Judith Plaskow," *Nashim: A Journal of Jewish Women's Studies and Gender Issues* 13 (2007): 207–51, develop this issue more fully.

16. Apart from Raphael's book, the problem of evil has received little attention from feminists. See Catherine Madsen et. al., "'If God Is God She Is Not Nice,'" *Journal of Feminist Studies in Religion* 5 (Spring 1989): 103–17; and my "Facing the Ambiguity of God," in *The Coming of Lilith: Essays in Feminism, Judaism, and Sexual Ethics, 1973–2003* (Boston: Beacon Press, 2005), 134–37. On the presence of God in human love, see Raphael, *The Female Face of God*, 39.

17. Abraham Joshua Heschel was the first theologian to make these links explicit. See, for example, *The Insecurity of Freedom: Essays on Human Existence* (New York: Schocken Books, 1966). But I also have in mind the works of Michael Lerner, such as *Jewish Renewal: A Path to Healing and Transformation* (New York: G. P. Putnam's Sons, 1994) and Arthur Waskow, such as *Down-to-Earth Judaism: Food, Money, Sex, and the Rest of Life* (New York: William Morrow and Company, 1995).

Major Trends in Jewish Feminist Theology: The Work of Rachel Adler, Judith Plaskow, and Rebecca Alpert

RABBI DONNA BERMAN, PhD

1. As Elizabeth Kamarck Minnich writes, "That which does not carry a prefix seems to be, is assumed to be, universal: literature as it has been taught by professional scholars is the thing-itself, while women's literature is a kind of literature.... The more prefixes, the further from the real, the significant, the best.... A picture of a

white male physician will be called 'a picture of a doctor' by most; a picture of a Black female physician will be noted to be not just a picture of an *unusual* doctor but of a *kind* of doctor, a Black female one." Elizabeth Kamarck Minnich, *Transforming Knowledge* (Philadelphia: Temple University Press, 1990), 43.

2. Throughout this chapter, despite the fact that it is admittedly sometimes cumbersome, I will refer to the women I cite by both their first and last names, never by their last names alone. I have chosen to do this because, as Claudia Card argues, "This practice maintains a lively sense of gender ... as well as avoiding identifying women solely by naming practices that have subordinated us as women."

3. Rachel Adler, "'I've Had Nothing Yet So I Can't Take More,'" in *Jewish Possibilities: The Best of* Moment *Magazine,* ed. Leonard Fine (Northville, NJ: Jason Aronson, 1987), 201–202.

4. Rachel Adler, *Engendering Judaism: An Inclusive Theology and Ethics* (Philadelphia: Jewish Publication Society, 1998), xiv.

5. Ibid., xxv.

6. Ibid., 35.

7. Ibid., 37.

8. Ibid., 58.

9. Judith Plaskow, "The Right Question Is Theological," in Susannah Heschel, ed., *On Being a Jewish Feminist: A Reader* (New York: Schocken Books, 1995), 224.

10. Judith Plaskow, *Standing Again at Sinai: Judaism from a Feminist Perspective* (New York: HarperCollins, 1991), 1.

11. Ibid., 226.

12. Plaskow, "The Right Question Is Theological," 231.

13. Plaskow, *Standing Again at Sinai,* 29.

14. Ibid., 56.

15. Ibid., 76.

16. Ibid., 95.

17. Ibid., 102.

18. Ibid., 107.

19. Ibid., 109.

20. Ibid., 167.

21. Rebecca Alpert, *Like Bread on the Seder Plate: Jewish Lesbians and the Transformation of Tradition* (New York: Columbia University Press, 1997), 7.

22. Ibid., 8.

23. Ibid.

24. Ibid.

25. Ibid., 44.

26. Ibid., 46–47.

27. Ibid., 114.

28. Ibid., 151.

29. Ibid., 152.

30. Ibid., 161.

31. Ibid., 165.

32. Plaskow, "The Right Question Is Theological," 223.

To Her We Shall Return: Jews Turning to the Goddess, the Goddess Turning to Jews

RABBI JILL HAMMER, PhD

1. The title of this essay comes from Z. Budapest's chant: "We all come from the Goddess, and to Her we shall return, like a drop of rain flowing to the ocean."
2. Daniel Dever, *Did God Have a Wife? Archaeology and Folk Religion in Ancient Israel* (Grand Rapids, MI: Wm. B. Eerdmans, 2005); Susan Ackerman, "The Queen Mother and the Cult in Ancient Israel," *Journal of Biblical Literature* 112, no. 3 (1993): 385–401
3. Raphael Patai, *The Hebrew Goddess* (Detroit: Wayne State University Press, 1990); Lynn Gottlieb, *She Who Dwells Within: A Feminist Vision of a Renewed Judaism* (San Francisco: HarperSanFrancisco, 1995); Jenny Kien, *Reinstating the Divine Woman in Judaism* (Parkland, FL: Universal Publishers, 2000).
4. For example, the Asherah discussion list facilitated by Judith Laura, and the Mishkan Shekhinah community led by Deborah Grenn (www.mishkanshekhinah. org).
5. Jay Michaelson, "The Jewish Goddess Past and Present, *The Forward,* May 5, 2006.
6. See www.kohenet.org.
7. That is, not easily divided into good/bad, dark/light, active/passive, Jewish/not-Jewish, or other dichotomies.
8. Belser, Julia, "Making Room for the Divine She," in *Zeek* magazine, August 2007; http://www.zeek.net/708she/.
9. Kim Chernin, "God's Bride on Pesach," in *The Women's Passover Companion: Women's Reflections on the Festival of Freedom* (Woodstock, VT: Jewish Lights Publishing, 2003), 189.
10. Lynn Gottlieb, *She Who Dwells Within: A Feminist Vision of a Renewed Judaism* (San Francisco: HarperSanFrancisco, 1995), 16.
11. Rita M. Gross, "Steps toward Feminine Imagery of Deity in Jewish Theology," in Susannah Heschel, ed., *On Being a Jewish Feminist: A Reader* (New York: Schocken, 1983), 243.
12. Marcia Falk, *The Book of Blessings: New Jewish Prayers for Daily Life, the Sabbath, and the New Moon* (Boston: Beacon Press, 1999), 471.
13. Alicia Ostriker, *The Volcano Sequence* (Pittsburgh: University of Pittsburgh Press, 2002), 64.
14. Daniel Matt, "Beyond the Personal God," in *God and the Big Bang: Discovering Harmony between Science and Spirituality* (Woodstock, VT: Jewish Lights Publishing, 1998), 51–53.
15. Cynthia Ozick, "Notes toward Finding the Right Question," in Heschel, *On Being a Jewish Feminist,* 121.
16. Dever, *Did God Have a Wife?*
17. "Archaeologists Discover Ancient Beehives in Israel," Fox News, Thursday, Sept. 6, 2007, www.foxnews.com/story/0,2933,295757,00.html. Bees were a symbol of the Divine Feminine throughout the Ancient Near East.
18. This is clear from 2 Kings 23:1–14, where the Asherah is removed from the Temple late in the Judean monarchy. See Susan Ackerman, "The Queen Mother and the Cult

in Ancient Israel," *Journal of Biblical Literature*, 112/3(1993), 385–401; D. N. Freedman, "Yahweh of Samaria and His Asherah," *Biblical Archaeology*, 50 (1987), 241–249.

19. Freedman D. N., "Yahweh of Samaria and His Asherah," *Biblical Archaeology*, 50 (1987): 241–249.
20. Jeremiah 7:18.
21. Proverbs 3:18.
22. Justin Lewis, "The Jewish Goddess(es)," http://telshemesh.org/fire/the_jewish_ goddesses_justin_lewis.html; Jeremiah 31:15.
23. Patai, *The Hebrew Goddess*.
24. Amichai Lau-Lavie, quoted in Michaelson, "The Jewish Goddess Past and Present."
25. Zohar I, 49a.
26. Ellen Umansky, "Re-imagining the Divine," cited in Sylvia Barack Fishman, *A Breath of Life: Feminism in the American Jewish Community* (New York: Free Press, 1993), 239.
27. Elyse Goldstein, *ReVisions: Seeing Torah through a Feminist Lens* (Woodstock, VT: Jewish Lights Publishing, 1998), 170.
28. *Thealogy* refers to a theory of the Divine Feminine.
29. Judith Plaskow, "Jewish Anti-Paganism," in *The Coming of Lilith: Essays on Feminism, Judaism, and Sexual Ethics, 1972–2003* (Boston: Beacon Press, 2004).
30. Ecclesiastes 3:1; Proverbs 8:1; Babylonian Talmud, Berachot 6a; Zohar I, 49a; Zohar I, 223 a–b.

Women, Ritual, and Torah
The Hermeneutics of Curiosity: On Reclamation
RABBI DANYA RUTTENBERG

1. For more on this, see Tirzah Menacham (LeBeit Yoreh), "An Abbreviated History of the Development of the Jewish Menstrual Laws," and Charlotte Elishava Fonrobert, "*Yalta's* Ruse: Resistance Against Rabbinic Menstrual Authority in Talmudic Literature," in *Women and Water*, ed. Rahel R. Wasserfall (Waltham, MA: Brandeis University Press, 1997) and Haviva Ner-David, "Reclaiming Niddah Through Ideological and Practical Reinterpretation," in *Sex and Judaism*, ed. Danya Ruttenberg (New York: NYU Press, 2009), as well as Susan Grossman, "Mikveh and the Sanctity of Being Created Human," available on the Rabbinical Assembly website, www.rabbinicalassembly.org/docs/Grossman-Niddah.pdf.
2. Catherine Bell, *Ritual Theory, Ritual Practice* (New York: Oxford University Press, 1992), 184.
3. This term was evidently initially coined by Paul Ricoeur in *Freud and Philosophy: An Essay on Interpretation*, trans. Denis Savage (New Haven: Yale University Press, 1970). It was applied to religious feminist thought by Elizabeth Schüssler Fiorenza in *Bread Not Stone: The Challenge of Feminist Biblical Interpretation* (Boston: Beacon Press, 1984) and *But She Said: Feminist Practices of Biblical Interpretation* (Boston: Beacon Press, 1992), and applied beautifully to Jewish feminist thought by Ellen Umansky in "Jewish Feminist Theology," in *Choices in Modern Jewish Thought*, ed. Eugene Borowitz (New York: Behrman House, 1995).

4. I'm looking specifically at Mishneh Torah, Hilchot Deot 5:6–9. Only 28 percent of the Rambam's use of the word *tzniut* is in any way related to female behavior. Certainly, the Rambam does discuss proper norms of female dress and behavior (noting, in Hilchot Ishut 13:11, that at the very least norms of head coverings are culturally relative), but my point here is that he—as others before him and since—understood *tzniut* as more of a global issue.

The Politics and Aesthetics of Women's Spirituality
LORI HOPE LEFKOVITZ, PhD, AND RABBI RONA SHAPIRO

1. Ritualwell.org was cocreated by Kolot: The Center for Jewish Women's and Gender Studies at RRC and Ma'yan: The Jewish Women's Project of the JCC of Manhattan, and is now sponsored and managed by Kolot. A more extended version of this essay appeared in *Nashim: A Journal of Jewish Women's and Gender Studies* as "Ritualwell.org—Loading the Virtual Canon, or: The Politics and Aesthetics of Jewish Women's Spirituality" (2005): 101–25.
2. As famously articulated by Betty Friedan in *The Feminine Mystique* (New York: Norton), 1963; to combat this isolation, she founded the National Organization of Women (NOW) in 1966.
3. E. M. Broner, *A Weave of Women* (New York: Holt, Rinehart, and Winston, 1978). Arlene Agus dates the first such Rosh Chodesh group to 1972; see her article, "Examining Rosh Chodesh: An Analysis of the Holiday and Its Textual Sources," in *Celebrating the New Moon: A Rosh Chodesh Anthology,* ed. Susan Berin (Northvale, NJ: Jason Aronson, 1996), 3. Penina V. Adelman describes the beginnings of her Rosh Chodesh group in 1978 in her book *Miriam's Well: Rituals for Jewish Women around the Year* (New York: Biblio Press, 1986).
4. See Adelman, *Miriam's Well.*
5. Claire R. Satlof, "History, Fiction, and the Tradition: Creating a Jewish Feminist Poetic," in *On Being a Jewish Feminist: A Reader,* ed. Susannah Heschel (New York: Schocken Books, 1983), 187.
6. Ibid., 189.
7. Ibid., 188–89.
8. Feminist writers in the biological sciences were the first to point out how the female was peculiarly chained to her biology. See Sarah Blaffer Hardy, *The Woman That Never Evolved* (Cambridge: Harvard University Press, 1981); Carolyn Merchant, *The Death of Nature: Women, Ecology and the Scientific Revolution* (New York: Harper and Row, 1980); Susan Griffin, *Woman and Nature: The Roaring Inside Her* (New York: Harper and Row, 1978). We have observed a comparable gender imbalance in Jewish workshop programs, in which men tend to teach texts, and any physical sessions that may be offered (such as "Torah Yoga") are led by women.
9. Cf. Denise Riley, *"Am I That Name?" Feminism and the Category of "Women" in History* (Minneapolis: University of Minnesota Press, 1988).
10. Margaret Wenig and Naomi Janowitz, eds., *Siddur Nashim: A Sabbath Prayer Book for Women* (self-published, 1976).
11. Some of our friends' daughters have agreed to recognize this intimate moment in women's community, but given the self-consciousness of most girls, these puberty

celebrations are not widely practiced and do not command the attention that would be accorded a religious requirement.

12. Lori Lefkovitz, "Sacred Screaming: Childbirth in Judaism," in *Lifecycles,* vol. 1, ed. Debra Orenstein (Woodstock, VT: Jewish Lights Publishing,1998), 5–15.

13. Books such as Irwin Kula and Vanessa Ochs, eds., *The Book of Jewish Sacred Practices: CLAL's Guide to Everyday Holiday Rituals and Blessings* (Woodstock, VT: Jewish Lights Publishing, 2001), while not explicitly feminist, reflect what we are here calling feminist values and were made possible in part by the openness created by the women's spirituality movement and the more recent flourishing of works that present ritual creativity.

14. No matter when interpretations or practices have historically been instituted in Judaism, many Jews view them as being implicit in the Torah. This principle is famously expressed in the legend that imagines Moses, mystified, at the back of Rabbi Akiva's classroom. Although Moses does not understand the later teacher's lesson, he is reassured by Akiva's attribution of it to the "Torah of Moses" (Babylonian Talmud, Menahot 29b).

15. Nina Beth Cardin, ed. and trans., *Out of the Depths I Call to You: A Book of Prayers for the Married Jewish Woman* (Northvale, NJ: Jason Aronson, 1992); Chava Weissler, *Voices of the Matriarchs: Listening to the Prayers of Early Modern Jewish Women* (Boston: Beacon Press, 1998).

16. Cynthia Ozick, "Notes toward Finding the Right Question," and Judith Plaskow, "The Right Question Is Theological," both in *On Being a Jewish Feminist,* ed. Heschel.

17. Lois Dubin, "Who's Blessing Whom? Transcendence, Agency, and Gender in Jewish Prayer," *CrossCurrents* 52, no. 2 (Summer 2002).

18. See Sally Gottesman, "God-Thoughts He-Thoughts She-Thoughts," *Journey* (Spring 2004): 20–23.

19. Marge Piercy, from "The Ram's Horn Sounding," in *The Art of Blessing the Day: Poems with a Jewish Theme* (New York: Knopf, 1999), 174.

20. Debra Nussbaum Cohen, *Celebrating Your New Jewish Daughter: Creating Jewish Ways to Welcome Baby Girls into the Covenant* (Woodstock, VT: Jewish Lights Publishing, 2001).

21. Richard Siegel, Michael Strassfeld, and Sharon Strassfeld, *The First Jewish Catalog: A Do-It-Yourself Kit* (Philadelphia, PA: Jewish Publication Society, 1973).

From Ancient Times to Modern Meaning: Jewish Women Claim Their Ritual Power

RABBI GEELA RAYZEL RAPHAEL

1. See Chava Weissler, *Voices of the Matriarchs* (Boston: Beacon Press, 1998).

2. See www.ritualwell.org for more information about many of the new rituals described in this chapter.

3. Boston Women's Health Collective, *Our Bodies, Ourselves* (New York: Simon and Schuster, 1969).

4. Joshua Trachtenberg, *Jewish Magic and Superstition* (New York: Athenum, 1977), 133–69.

5. See Goldie Milgram, *Living Jewish Life Cycle: How to Create Meaningful Jewish Rites of Passage at Every Stage of Life* (Woodstock, VT: Jewish Lights Publishing, 2008), 190–91.

6. The text of my ritual can be found at www.simcharaphael.com/lrf6.html.

7. Nina Beth Cardin, *Tears of Sorrow, Seeds of Hope* (Woodstock, VT: Jewish Lights Publishing,1999).

8. See Lia Rosen's website, www.claykodesh.com.

9. Penina Adelman, ed., *Praise Her Works: Conversations with Biblical Women* (Philadelphia: Jewish Publication Society, 2005).

10. Rachel Adler, *Engendering Judaism: An Inclusive Theology and Ethics* (Boston: Beacon Press Books, 1998), 169–207.

11. See Sharon Cohen Anisfeld, Tara Mohr, and Catherine Spector, eds., *The Women's Seder Sourcebook: Rituals and Readings for Use at the Passover Seder* (Woodstock, VT: Jewish Lights Publishing, 2003).

12. Arlene Agus, "This Month for You: Observing Rosh Chodesh as a Women's Holiday," in *The Jewish Woman: New Perspectives*, ed. Elizabeth Koltun (New York: Schocken Books, 1976).

13. Marty Cohen Spiegel, "Creating Rituals for Relational Healing," *The Rabbi as Relational Caregiver*, ed. Rabbi Jack Bloom (Philadelphia: Haworth Press, 2005).

14. Chava Neissler, "Women of Vision in the Jewish Renewal Movement: The *Eshet Hazon* [Woman of Vision] Ceremony," in *Jewish Culture and History* 8, no. 3 (Winter 2006 [pub. 2008]): 62–86.

Torah Study "For Women"

WENDY ZIERLER, PhD

1. Vanessa Ochs, *Words on Fire* (San Diego: Harcourt Brace Jovanovich, 1999), 211.

2. Cynthia Ozick, "Ruth," in *Metaphor and Memory* (New York: Knopf, 1989), 240–64.

3. Vanessa Ochs, *Words on Fire*, 340–41.

4. Judith Plaskow, *Standing Again at Sinai* (San Francisco: HarperSanFrancisco, 1991), xv.

Transforming Our Stories through Midrash

RABBI TIRZAH FIRESTONE

1. Barry Holtz, *Back to the Sources: Reading the Classic Jewish Texts* (New York: Summit Books, 1984), 180.

2. Leila Gal Berner, "Isaac and Ishmael," in *Ohr Chadash Prayerbook* (Philadelphia: Aleph Alliance for Jewish Renewal, 1987).

3. Linda Hirshhorn, "Sarah and Hagar," *Heart Beat,* compact disc, Vocolot, 2005.

4. Judith Plaskow, "The Coming of Lillith: Toward a Feminist Theology," in *Womanspirit Rising: A Feminist Reader in Religion,* ed. Judith Plaskow and Carol Christ (New York: Harper and Row, 1979).

5. In a nationwide Harris poll taken in November 2006, only 30 percent of Jews polled said they were "absolutely certain" there was a God.

Women and the Synagogue

1. See Bernadette Brooten, *Women Leaders in the Ancient Synagogue: Inscriptional Evidence and Background Issues* (Chico, CA: Scholars Press, 1982).

The Ascent of the Woman Cantor: *Shira Hamaalot*

CANTOR BARBARA OSTFELD

1. Marcia Falk, *The Song of Songs: A New Translation* (San Francisco: HarperSanFrancisco, 1993), 10.
2. Ibid., xv.
3. Dana Evan Kaplan, "Reform Judaism," in *Encyclopedia Judaica,* 2nd rev. ed. (New York: MacMillan, 2006), 166.
4. "Letters to Sally Priesand from Hebrew Union College–Jewish Institute of Religion," at Jewish Women's Archive: Jewish Women and the Feminist Revolution, www.jwa.org/feminism.
5. Mark Slobin, *Chosen Voices: The Story of the American Cantorate* (Urbana: University of Illinois Press, 1989), 6.
6. "Beloved, Come to Greet the Sabbath Bride," by the sixteenth-century rabbi Shlomo Halevi Alkabetz, a Safed kabbalist. In Ismar Elbogen, *Jewish Liturgy: A Comprehensive History* (Philadelphia: Jewish Publication Society, 1993), 92.
7. "We Have Sinned," Elbogen, *Jewish Liturgy,* 125.
8. Falk, *The Song of Songs,* 31.
9. Lawrence A. Hoffman, ed., *My People's Prayer Book,* vol. 2, *The Amidah* (Woodstock, VT: Jewish Lights Publishing, 1998), 27. This is a meditation on the Amidah that was in use in Palestine in 1096.

Orthodox Women in Rabbinic Roles

SARA HURWITZ, *MADRICHA RUCHANIT* (RELIGIOUS MENTOR)

1. There are several minyanim that do allow women to lead parts of the service, but these minyanim are not yet considered mainstream within the Orthodox movement. Women are prohibited from acting as witnesses, as cited in Sifrei Shoftim 19:17, Talmud Bavli Baba Kama 88a, and Rambam Laws of Witness 9:1
2. Only men have a positive commandment to study Torah. See Tur Yoreh De'ah 245:1 "Talmud Torah" and Rambam Talmud Torah 1:1.
3. See Haym Soleveitchik, "Rupture and Reconstruction: The Transformation of Contemporary Orthodoxy," *Tradition* 28, no. 4 (1994).
4. For example, Nishmat's *Yoetzot Halakhah* Program trains women in the laws of *niddah.* See www.nishmat.net.
5. Talmud Bavli Niddah 49b, Talmud Yerushalmi Yomah 6:1.
6. Shulchan Aruch, Choshen Mishpat 7:4.
7. See also Sefer Hachinuch Shmini 152.
8. See Rashi commentary on Micah 6:4, in which he states that Miriam taught Torah to the women of her generation.

9. See Rambam Laws of Kings 1:5: "Do not appoint a woman to reign, since the verse [Deuteronomy 17:15] states, 'a king and not a queen.' And so too, all positions in Israel—do not appoint anyone but a man."
10. Maimonides' Laws of Women 13:11, citing Psalm 45:14.
11. See Eliezer Berkovits, *Jewish Women in Time and Torah* (Hoboken, NJ: KTAV Publishing House, 1990), 59–68.
12. Shulchan Aruch, Orah Hayyim 46:4.
13. Blu Greenberg wrote, "'The honor of the daughter of the king is within (Psalms 45:15) was applied by Rabbis of every generation to explain the exemption or release for women from duties that would propel her into the public space…. this set women far-back from the public eye in mattress of religious ritual, community participation and spiritual leadership. Today, all this is changing." *JOFA Journal,* (Winter 2004): 2.
14. See Iggrot Moshe, Orah Hayyim 5:12. This, however, does not imply that Rav Moshe would have allowed women to address the congregation publically on Shabbat.
15. See R. Yehuda Herzl Henkin, *Bnei Banim* (Jerusalem: self published), 16. He permits a small number of women in the men's section. See Mendel Shapiro, "Qeri'at Torah by Women: A Halakhic Analysis," *Edah Journal* (2001): 41.
16. See Simon Greenberg, ed., *The Ordination of Women as Rabbis: Studies and Response* (New York: The Jewish Theological Seminary of America, 1988). The ordination of women as rabbis became the defining issue for the Conservative movement at JTS.
17. Rabbis Marc Angel and Avi Weiss have recently founded an organization called the Rabbinic Fellowship, which will provide a safe space for rabbis who are frozen out of other established Orthodox institutions to dialogue without fear of repercussion. It is alleged that women will be equal participants in the Rabbinic Fellowship.

Feminism and the Transformation of the Synagogue

RABBI SUE LEVI ELWELL, PhD

1. Karla Goldman, *Beyond the Synagogue Gallery: Finding a Place for Women in American Judaism* (Cambridge, MA: Harvard University Press, 2000).
2. Susan Faludi, *Backlash: The Undeclared War against American Women* (New York: Doubleday, 1991).
3. Goldman, *Beyond the Synagogue Gallery*, 215.

Where Are the Jewish Men? The Absence of Men from Liberal Synagogue Life

RABBI JOSEPH B. MESZLER

1. Doug Barden, *Wrestling with Jacob and Esau, Fighting the Flight of Men: A Modern Day Crisis for the Reform Movement* (New York: North American Federation of Temple Brotherhood, 2005), 13.
2. Barden, 11–13.
3. David Murrow, *Why Men Hate Going to Church* (Nashville: Thomas Nelson, Inc., 2005), 53.

4. James B. Twitchell, *Where Men Hide* (New York: Columbia University Press, 2006), 241.
5. U.S. Department of Labor Women's Bureau, "Employment Status of Women and Men in 2005," http://www.dol.gov/wb/factsheets/Qf-ESWM05.htm.
6. U.S. Department of Labor Bureau of Labor Statistics, "Men's and women's work hours, 2005," http://www.bls.gov/opub/ted/2006/oct/wk1/art03.thm.
7. The number of hours in the work week has seen an overall increase of 14.4 percent among top wage earners since the 1970s. See Peter Kuhn and Fernanco Lozano, "The Expanding Workweek? Understanding Trends in Long Work Hours Among U.S. Men, 1979–2004," *National Bureau of Economic Research*, Working Paper No. 11895, December 2005, http://papers.nber.org/papers/w11895.) In addition, according to the United States 2000 Census, the number of commuters traveling ninety minutes or more to and from work has doubled in the last decade, and many commute not just from a suburb to a city but from suburb to suburb as well. See Alan E. Pisarski, *Commuting in America III: The Third National Report on Commuting Patterns and Trends* (Washington, DC: Transportation Research Board, 2006).
8. L.A. McKeown, "Breadwinner Anxiety: Man's New Worry," *WebMD Medical News* 2001, http://www.webmd.com/content/article/33/1728_82401.htm.
9. Esther Dermott, "Dads Want Flexibility, Not Shorter Worker Hours," *Medical News Today*, August 25, 2006, http://www.medicalnewstoday.com/medicalnews.php?newsid=50384.
10. Steven E. Rhoads, *Taking Sex Differences Seriously* (San Francisco: Encounter Books, 2004), 150.
11. W. Gunther Plaut, *The Torah: A Modern Commentary Revised Edition* (New York: Union of Reform Judaism Press. 2005), 142.
12. Willie Oliver, *A Few Good Men: What Men's Ministries Can Do for Your Church*, emale.org/article, cited in Barden, 45.
13. Nelson Mandela, *Long Walk to Freedom* (Boston: Little Brown, 1995), 544.

Women in Israel

Gender in Israeli Liberal Liturgy

RABBI DALIA MARX, PhD

1. Regarding gender language in Jewish liturgy, see: R. Adler, *Engendering Judaism: An Inclusive Theology and Ethics* (Philadelphia: Jewish Publication Society, 1998), 61–103; E. Caplan, *From Ideology to Liturgy: Reconstructionist Worship and American Liberal Judaism* (Cincinnati: HUC Press, 2002), 151–54, 220–33; A. Daum, "Language and Prayer," in *Daughters of the King*, ed. S. Grossman and R. Haut (Philadelphia: Jewish Publication Soceity, 1992), 183–202; L. Dubin, "Who's Blessing Whom? Transcendence, Agency, and Gender in Jewish Prayer," *Cross Currents* 52, no. 2 (2002): 165–77 ; M. Falk, "Notes on Composing New Blessings: Toward a Feminist-Jewish Reconstruction of Prayer," *Journal of Feminist Studies in Religion* 3 (1987): 39–53; N. Ophir (Offenbacher), "Liturgical Innovations of God Language in Jewish Feminist Theology," *Lihiyot Isha Yehudia*, 2, ed., M. Shilo (Jerusalem, 2003), pp. 55–75.
2. I will use the term "liberal Judaism" to refer to non-Orthodox Jewish movements broadly.

3. The special characteristics and problems that have to do with women's prayer became more present in the Israeli religious discussion since the publication of Aliza Lavi's book on women's prayers, *T'filat Nashim: Psifas Nashi shel T'filot v'Sipurim* (Tel Aviv, 2005). Although it contains only Orthodox prayers and does not deal with gender issues in a direct form, it serves as a catalyst for the discussion of the liturgical language in wider circles.
4. Some mark the rabbinic ordination of the first woman by Hebrew Union College–Jewish Institute of Religion as the starting point of this discussion (see Daum, "Language and Prayer," 188–96). It seems that until the mid-seventies, gender wasn't a very dominant topic in North America, reflected in the fact that the gender issue does not appear in the list of characters of Reform liturgy that Jacob Petuchowski, the liturgy scholar, composed. J. Petuchowski, *Guide to the Prayerbook* (Cincinnati: HUC Press, 1967), 54–55.
5. E. Friedland, *Were Our Mouths Filled with Song: Studies in Liberal Jewish Liturgy* (Cincinnati: HUC Press, 1997), 261.
6. Tamar Ross suggests a different division. See: *"Ha'od m'sugalot Anu l'hitpalel l'Avinu sh'Bashamayim,"* ed. N. Illan, *Ayin Tova: Du-Siakh b'tarbut Israel* (Tel Aviv, 1991), 264–77.
7. D. Marx, *The Early Morning Ritual in Jewish Liturgy: Textual, Historical and Theological discussion in Birkhot Hashakhar (The Morning Blessings) and an Examination of Their Performative Aspects* (doctoral dissertation written under the supervision of Prof. A. Shinan at the Hebrew University, Jerusalem, 2005), 345–63.
8. It is so in *Ha-Avodah Shebalev*, for example, but in the supplication that appears in the beginning of the bedtime Shema prayer that begins with a male address, *"Hareini mokhel"* ("I hereby forgive").
9. The Response was published on the Schechter Institute website, www.schechter.edu/responsa/0702.htm.
10. See: V. Ochs, *Inventing Jewish Ritual* (Philadelphia: Jewish Publication Society, 2007), 47–56.
11. Ed. I. Lev, *Seder Hagadat Nashim* (Jerusalem, 2004).
12. Ibid. The text was composed by the Conservative rabbi Einat Ramon. Another Hebrew text of "four daughters" was composed by the Reform rabbis Tamar Duvdevany and Dalia Marx. It can be found, along with many other such texts in Hebrew and English, at www.ritualwell.org.
13. There are a few other Israeli prayers for rain that are written according to the traditional structure but add the merit of the matriarchs. Among them are prayers written by Rabbi Yehoram Mazor, Leah Shakdiel, and Mark Frydenberg.
14. For example, the phrase *"banim heinika"* is taken from Sarah's grateful response to the birth of Isaac at her old age (Gen. 21:7). The English "she nursed" does not refer directly to the joyous event at Sarah's tent.
15. Ben-Sason's quote appeared on the website for Kolech, an Israeli Orthodox women's organization: www.kolech.org.il/show.asp?id=22304.
16. In her book *The Book of Blessings* (San Francisco: HarperSanFrancisco, 1996), Falk changes the blessing formula from "Blessed are you Adonai, King of the universe," to "Let us acknowledge the source of life".
17. D. Marx, "No More 'Avinu'? No More 'Malkenu'?" *Kescher* 3/4 (Winter 2005–2006): 19.

Masorti (Conservative Israeli) Women

RABBI EINAT RAMON, PhD

1. Lee Israel Levine, "*Masorti* Judaism in Israel: Challenge, Vision and Program," *The Seminary at 100: Reflections on the Jewish Theological Seminary and the Conservative Movement*, ed. Nina Beth Cardin and David Wolf Silverman (New York: Rabbinical Assembly and JTS, 1987), 381–89; David Golinkin, "The Current Situation: Visions for Strengthening Judaism in the State of Israel," *Women's League Outlook* 75, no. 3 (2005): 22–26.
2. Lee Israel Levine, "How the 'Tali' Schools Began," *Avar v'Átid* 3, no. 2 (1996): 45–55 (Hebrew).
3. Sharone Maital, in discussion with the author, August 17, 2008.
4. Yosef Regev "Toldot hakehilla" in www.eshelavraham.org/page.php?id=3.
5. *Masorti Foundation for Conservative Judaism* 5, no. 2 (June 2007/5767): 2.
6. Naomi Graetz, *Silence Is Deadly: Judaism Confronts Wifebeating* (Northvale, NJ: Jason Aronson, 1998); *Unlocking the Garden: A Feminist Look at the Bible, Midrash and God* (Piscataway, NJ: Gorgias Pressm, 2005).
7. About Judith Edelman- Green see: http://www.rimonvillage.org/index. php?option=com_content&task=blogcategory&id=28&Itemid=43&lang=en
8. About Gilah Dror, see www.rodefsholomtemple.org/rabbi.htm.
9. For an English synopsis of the responsa see: "vaad hahalakhah-English Summaries The Ordination of Women as Rabbis,"www.responsafortoday.com.
10. For a feminist discussion of *Yalta*, see Rachel Adler, *Engendering Judaism* (Philadelphia: Jewish Publication Society, 1998), 51–59.
11. See Jewish Law Watch, www.schechter.edu/women/aguna.htm.
12. Eliyahu Sapir, "Overview of Guttman Center Data: Religious Observance," Israel Democracy Institute (2007), www.idi.org.il/english/article.asp?id=22112007112505.
13. Aharon David Gordon, *"Leveirur Raayoneinu Miyesodo,"* (Clarifying Our Idea from Its Foundation, 1920), quoted in Einat Ramon, "Equality and Ambivalence: The Political Repercussions of A.D. Gordon's Maternal Ethics," *Nashim: A Journal of Jewish Women's Studies and Gender Issues*, no. 3 (Spring/Summer 5760/2000): 74–103.
14. See Tamar Schechter, "Motherhood: From Personal Experience to Public Expression: The Life and Achievements of Rachel Katzenelson-Shazar," *Massekhet: Say to wisdom, thou art my sister* 7 (Fall 2007/5768): 29–58. I wish to thank Professor Margalit Shilo for the observation on the uniqueness of the Israeli-feminist historical ideals.
15. Ada Maimon, *Chok Batim M'shutafim*, Dealings of the Knesset no. 28, July 1952, page 2730.

The First Decade of the Orthodox Women's Revolution in Israel: The Case of Kolech

MARGALIT SHILO, PhD

1. For previous versions of this chapter, see: "A Religious Orthodox Women's Revolution—The Religious Feminist Revolution: The Case of Kolech (1998–2005)." In *Sev-*

enty Years to "Emuna," edited by Lilach Rosenberg-Friedman, 177–84. Jerusalem: The Religious Women's Movement, 2006 (Hebrew); "The Case of 'Kolech' 1998–2005." *Israel Studies Forum* 21 (July 2006): 81–95; "A Jewish Orthodox Women's Revolution." In *Building Feminist Movements and Organizations: Global Perspectives,* edited by Lydia Alpizer, Anahi Duran, and Anahi Russo Garrido, 25–34. London: Zed Books, 2007.

2. Avraham Grossman, *Pious and Rebellious: Jewish Women in Europe in the Middle Ages* (Jerusalem: Zalman Shazar Center for Jewish History, 2001), 51–62 (Hebrew).

3. Ibid., 266–303.

4. This is the official translation of the name of the organization, as the Hebrew term *dati* is translated: religious, meaning Orthodox.

5. The basic principles of the organization were published in the first leaflet of Kolech, August 23, 1998, 4.

6. I edited the first two volumes of *To Be a Jewish Woman* (Urim Publications, 2001; 2003). The third volume (2005) was edited by Tova Cohen and Aliza Lavie, and the fourth was edited by Cohen. The fifth is being written.

7. Noa Sheshar Atun, "The Impact of Feminism on Religious Zionism," in *Blessed Art Thou Who Made Me a Woman: The Woman in Judaism—From the Bible until Today,* ed. D. Y. Ariel, Maya Leibovitz, and Yoram Mazor (Tel Aviv: Yediot Achronot, 1999), 207–23 (Hebrew).

8. Moshe Meiselman, *Jewish Woman in Jewish Law* (New York: KTAV Publishing House, 1978), 34:42.

9. The first institution for rabbinical advocates was established in 1989 by Nurit Fried. Atun, "The Impact of Feminism on Religious Zionism," 215.

10. On the program, see ibid., 216.

11. H.C. 153/87 *Shakdiel v. Minister of Religions,* P.D. 42(2) 21.

12. Estelle Freedman, "Separatism as a Strategy: Female Institution Building and American Feminism, 1870–1930," in *Feminist Studies,* V (1979), 512–529.

13. "Feminism and Orthodoxy: The Council for the Amelioration of the Legal Position of the Jewess," *Zion* 71, no. 2 (2006): 203–24 (Hebrew).

14. Due to personal reasons, Kehat resigned after six years of intensive work as the head of Kolech. At the fourth international conference, in July 2005, she received the medal of the Founder of Kolech.

15. Kolech's leaflet, no. 90 (2005): 8.

16. Yehuda Gelman, "Religious Feminism and the Theological Challenge," *Shilo* (2001): 39–43 (Hebrew).

17. Rabbi Mordechai Eliahu's ruling was made public in August 2004 in the daily *Hazofe.*

18. Address of the president Carrie Chapman Catt to the Ninth Congress of the International Woman Suffrage Alliance, *The International Woman Suffrage News,* July 1923, 147.

19. This agreement was developed by two rabbis and a rabbinical advocate. Kolech is trying to publicize it. David Ben Zazon, *Agreements for Mutual Respect, Halachic, Moral and Practical Dilemmas, Zohar* 20 (2005): 79–82 (Hebrew).

20. Esther Yeivin, "Twenty-Five Years of the Federation for Equal Rights in Eretz Israel," in *The Federation of Jewish Women for Equal Rights in Eretz Israel: Twenty-Fifth Anniversary Volume,* 8–10.

Gender, Sexuality, and Age
Jewish Feminism, Sexuality, and a Sexual Justice Agenda
MARLA BRETTSCHNEIDER, PhD

1. See, for example, Noel Ignatiev, *How the Irish Became White* (Cambridge, MA: Harvard University Press, 1995).
2. See, for example, Nancy Ordover, *American Eugenics: Race, Queer Anatomy, and the Science of Nationalism* (Minneapolis: University of Minnesota Press, 2003).
3. See, for example, Melanie Kaye/Kantrowitz, *The Issue Is Power: Essays on Women, Jews, Violence and Resistance* (San Francisco: Aunt Lute Books, 1992); Karen Brodkin, *How Jews Became White Folks and What That Says about Race in America* (New Brunswick, NJ: Rutgers University Press, 1998).
4. See, for example, Laura Berlant, *The Queen of America Goes to Washington City: Essays on Sex and Citizenship* (Durham, NC: Duke University Press, 1997).
5. See, for example, Dorothy Roberts, *Shattered Bonds: The Color of Child Welfare* (New York: Basic Books, 2002).
6. See Diane Tobin, Gary Tobin, and Scott Rubin, *In Every Tongue: The Racial and Ethnic Diversity of the Jewish People* (San Francisco: Institute for Jewish and Community Research, 2005).

Koach Banot (Girl Power): Talking Feminism with Jewish Teen Girls
BETH COOPER BENJAMIN, EdD, AND JODIE GORDON

1. Many thanks to Rachel Abeshouse, Tamar Blanchard, and Natasha Bernstein Bunzl for their thoughtful and enthusiastic participation in this project, to their families for their support, and to all our research training interns, whose work has taught us so much about the lives of Jewish teen girls and the future of Jewish feminism.
2. Michelle Fine and Pat Macpherson, "Over Dinner: Feminism and Adolescent Female Bodies," in *Disruptive Voices: The Possibilities of Feminist Research,* ed. Michelle Fine (Ann Arbor: University of Michigan Press, 1992), 175–203.
3. Dan Kindlon, *Alpha Girls: Understanding the New American Girl and How She Is Changing the World* (New York: Rodale, 2006).
4. Fine and Macpherson, "Over Dinner," 175.
5. See Debbie Stoller's introduction to *Stitch and Bitch* for an excellent discussion of feminists reclaiming traditional skills and crafts: Debbie Stoller, "Take Back the Knit: Why Young Women Are Taking Up Knitting Once More," in *Stitch and Bitch: The Knitter's Handbook* (New York: Workman Publishing Company, 2003), 2–13.
6. Girls (particularly privileged white girls) may, in fact, have the admissions deck stacked more steeply against them. Writing in the *New York Times,* Kenyon College dean of admissions Jennifer Delahunty Britz recently explained that despite the fact that they now apply in greater numbers, girls applying to elite U.S. colleges are increasingly being held to a higher standard than their male peers, as the schools strive to maintain an even gender balance in admissions and enrollment. In what is essentially an unintended consequence of women's advancement, admissions

policies are penalizing these girls for surpassing the boys. Jennifer Delahunty Britz, "To All the Girls I've Rejected," *New York Times,* March 23, 2006, A25.
7. Jonathan Sarna, *L'Dor V'Dor (From Generation to Generation): Placing Jewish Youth Philanthropy in an Historical Context.* Lunch and Learn teleconference, Jewish Teen Funders Network, December 13, 2007.
8. Anna Greenberg, *Grande Soy Vanilla Latte with Cinnamon, No Foam: Jewish Identity and Community in a Time of Choice* (New York: Greenberg, Quinlan, and Rosner with Reboot, 2006).

Women and the Denominations

1. Elyse Goldstein, *Revisions: Seeing Torah through a Feminist Lens* (Woodstock, VT: Jewish Lights Publishing, 1998), 14.

Orthodoxy and Feminism

IDANA GOLDBERG, PhD

1. See Michael Silber, "The Emergence of Ultra-Orthodoxy: The Invention of a Tradition," in *The Uses of Tradition,* ed. Jack Wertheimer (New York: Jewish Theological Seminary Press, 1992), 23–84.
2. See, for example, Blu Greenberg, *On Women and Judaism* (Philadelphia: Jewish Publication Society, 1981); Tova Hartman, *Feminism Encounters Traditional Judaism: Resistance and Accommodation* (Waltham, MA: Brandeis University Press, University Press of New England, 2007); Tamar Ross, *Expanding the Palace of Torah: Orthodoxy and Feminism* (Waltham, MA: Brandeis University Press, University Press of New England, 2004).
3. The mission of the Jewish Orthodox Feminist Alliance is "to expand the spiritual, ritual, intellectual and political opportunities for women within the framework of *halakhah.* We advocate meaningful participation and equality for women in family life, synagogues, houses of learning and Jewish communal organizations to the full extent possible within *halakhah.* Our commitment is rooted in the belief that fulfilling this mission will enrich and uplift individual and communal life for all Jews." See www.jofa.org for more on the organization's activities.
4. In the context of this essay, the discussion of halakhically acceptable practices refers to the framework of Modern Orthodox halakhah as it is currently defined.
5. In response, JOFA initiated the Gender and Orthodoxy Curriculum project, which conveys to the students a sense of faithfulness to tradition, but also incorporates ethical messages of gender equality. See www.jofa.org for more about this curriculum and its availability.
6. Two recent examples within the Orthodox community that demonstrate the conservatism of the community include the publication of the Artscroll *Women's Siddur,* which presents a limited view of women's obligations and opportunities in prayer, and the ruling of the National Council of Young Israel prohibiting women from serving as synagogue presidents and prohibiting synagogues from hosting women's prayer services or Megillah (book of Esther) readings.

7. Rabbi J. B. Soloveitchik, *Halakhic Man,* trans. Lawrence Kaplan (Philadelphia: Jewish Publication Society, 1983); see also Abraham R. Besdin, *Man of Faith in the Modern World* (Hoboken, NJ: KTAV Publishing, 1989).
8. Yitz Greenberg, "The Hashkafah of Rav Soloveitchik and Its Potential Application for Feminism" (JOFA 2nd International Conference, New York, February 15–16, 1998). To order an audiotape of these remarks, visit www.jofa.org.

The Changing Status of Women in Liberal Judaism: A Reflective Critique

RABBI RACHEL SABATH BEIT-HALACHMI

1. This article was originally published in *Judaism and the Challenges of Modern Life,* ed. Donniel Hartman and Moshe Halbertal (New York: Continuum Press, 2007). Reprinted in revised form with permission.
2. Resolution passed by the Central Conference of American Rabbis (CCAR) in 1893.
3. Resolution passed by the CCAR in 1922.
4. CCAR platform, 1885.
5. Judith Plaskow, *Standing Again at Sinai: Judaism from a Feminist Perspective* (San Francisco: HarperSanFrancisco, 1990).
6. Ibid., 238.
7. See, for example, Rachel Adler, "Feminist Judaism: Past and Future," *Cross Currents* 51, no. 4 (Winter 2002).
8. Rachel Adler, *Engendering Judaism* (Boston: Beacon Press, 1998).
9. Daniel Boyarin, *Carnal Israel: Reading Sex in Talmudic Culture* (Berkeley: University of California Press, 1993), 227.

Feminism and Halakhah: The Jew Who (Still) Isn't There

RABBI HAVIVA NER-DAVID, PhD

1. Susannah Heschel, ed., *On Being a Jewish Feminist: A Reader* (New York: Schocken Books, 1971).
2. Rachel Adler, "The Jew Who Wasn't There: Halakhah and the Jewish Woman," in *On Being a Jewish Feminist,* ed. Heschel, 13.
3. Chanah Henkin, "Women and the Issuing of Halakhic Rulings," in *Jewish Legal Writings by Women,* ed. Micah Halpern and Chanah Safrai (Jerusalem: Urim Publications, 1998), 285–86.
4. Rachel Adler, *Engendering Judaism: An Inclusive Theology and Ethics* (Philadelphia: Jewish Publication Society, 1998).
5. Judith Plaskow, "The Right Question Is Theological," in *On Being a Jewish Feminist,* ed. Heschel, 224.
6. Adler, *Engendering Judaism,* xiv.
7. Ibid., 28.
8. Ibid., 21.
9. Ibid., xxiv.

10. Ibid., 33.
11. Henkin, "Women and the Issuing of Halakhic Rulings," 287.
12. Tamar Ross, *Expanding the Palace of Torah: Orthodoxy and Feminism* (Hanover, NH: Brandeis University Press, published by University Press of New England, 2004).
13. Ibid., 157–61.
14. Zalman Schachter-Shalomi, *Integral Halakhah: Transcending and Including* (Victoria, Canada: Trafford Publishing, 2007).
15. The phrase "paradigm shift" was coined by scientist Thomas Kuhn in 1962 to describe a change in basic assumptions within the ruling theory of science. It has since been applied to other realms of human experience. Schachter-Shalomi was the first to apply this concept in a Jewish theological context.

Feminism and Jewish Law in Conservative Judaism

RABBI GAIL LABOVITZ, PhD

1. Being called to the Torah, being Torah readers, serving as prayer leaders.
2. Each of the items cited in this paragraph can be found online at the Jewish Women's Archive, www.jwa.org. Dr. Hyman's statement, and links to the original Ezrat Nashim documents, can be accessed at www.jwa.org/feminism/_html/JWA039.htm.
3. *Emet ve-Emunah: Statement of Principles of Conservative Judaism* (New York: The Jewish Theological Seminary of America, the Rabbinical Assembly, and the United Synagogue of America, 1988), 14–15.
4. In the Orthodox world, one could add women's access to the full scope of Jewish learning. The Conservative movement has generally educated its male and female members equally. Indeed, it has been noted that this social fact helped fuel the feminist challenge to the movement; as Ezrat Nashim wrote in 1972, "The Conservative Movement has tacitly acknowledged this fact [women's intellectual and spiritual equality with men] by demanding that their female children be educated alongside the males—up to the level of rabbinical school. To educate women and deny them the opportunity to act from this knowledge is an affront to their intelligence, talents and integrity."
5. There are three exceptions to this rabbinic autonomy, known as "Standards of Rabbinic Practice": a Conservative rabbi may not officiate at or attend a marriage between a Jew and a non-Jew, may only accept as Jewish someone born of a Jewish mother or converted according to halakhic procedure, and may not perform a wedding if one of the parties was previously married Jewishly but did not participate in a Jewish divorce for the prior relationship. A Conservative rabbi who violates one or more of these standards is liable to be stripped of membership in the RA.

    For the RA's description of the current functioning of the CJLS, its decision-making processes, and the relationship between the CJLS and the individual rabbi in his or her community, see "Contemporary Halakhah: The Committee on Jewish Law and Standards," www.rabbinicalassembly.org/law/contemporary_halakhah.html; also David Fine, "The Committee on Jewish Law and Standards and Multiple Opinions," www.rabbinicalassembly.org/docs/CJLS_and_Multiple_Opinions.doc. It should be noted that for a number of years the Israeli branch of the Rabbinical Assembly has had its own Va'ad Ha'Halakhah (Law Committee) that also issued *teshuvot* written and approved by Israeli rabbis affiliated with the Masorti movement (as the Conservative movement is known in Israel and outside of North America); see www.responsafortoday.com/eng_index.html.

6. David J. Fine, "Women and the Minyan," www.rabbinicalassembly.org/ teshuvot/docs/19912000/oh_55_1_2002.pdf. Rabbi Fine's *teshuvah* also provides an extensive history of the development of the movement's views on this question. See also Judith Hauptman, "Women and Prayer: An Attempt to Dispel Some Fallacies," *Judaism* 42, no. 1 (1993): 94–103.

7. Gordon Tucker, "Final Report of the Commission for the Study of the Ordination of Women as Rabbis," in *The Ordination of Women as Rabbis: Studies and Responsa,* ed. Simon Greenberg (New York: The Jewish Theological Seminary of America, 1988), 13.

8. Ibid., 19.

9. Myron S. Geller, "Woman Is Eligible to Testify," www.rabbinicalassembly.org/ teshuvot/docs/19912000/geller_womenedut.pdf (adopted by a vote of 10-5-4), and Susan Grossman, "*Edut Nashim K'Edut Anashim*: The Testimony of Women Is as the Testimony of Men," www.rabbinicalassembly.org/teshuvot/docs/19912000/ grossman_womenedut.pdf (adopted by a vote of 8-7-4).

10. The counterargument, that Conservative divorces are likely to be rejected in Orthodox circles simply by virtue of the fact that they were effected under Conservative auspices has not (yet) brought about a serious reconsideration of this policy, most likely because not all in the Conservative movement itself would accept such divorces.

11. Mayer Rabinowitz and Dvora Weisberg, "Tape Recording and Photography on Shabbat," in *Responsa 1980–1990: The Committee on Jewish Law and Standards of the Conservative Movement,* ed. David J. Fine (New York: Rabbinical Assembly, 2005), 218–21, or available online at www.rabbinicalassembly.org/law/teshuvot_ public.html; adopted in 1984.

12. Because Jewish marriage law originated in a system that allowed for polygamy, the man's relationship with another woman (presuming she is single) is not technically adulterous, and the children do not suffer any legal disabilities as to their status. As noted above, a Conservative rabbi may not officiate at a wedding for either a man or a woman if a previous marriage was not properly dissolved according to Jewish law.

13. Eli Bohnen et al., "T'nai B'kiddushin," *Proceedings of the Rabbinical Assembly of America* 32 (1968): 229–41.

14. Saul Lieberman, "Ketubah," *Proceedings of the Rabbinical Assembly of America* 18 (1954): 66–68.

15. David Aronson, "Kedat Moshe VeYisrael," *Proceedings of the Rabbinical Assembly of America* 15 (1951): 120–40.

16. Elliot N. Dorff, Daniel S. Nevins, and Avram I. Reisner, "Homosexuality, Human Dignity and Halakhah: A Combined Responsum for the Committee on Jewish Law and Standards," www.rabbinicalassembly.org/docs/Dorff_Nevins_Reisner_ Final.pdf (2006): 19.

17. Elliot N. Dorff, Daniel S. Nevins, and Avram I. Reisner, "Summary of Homosexuality, Human Dignity and Halakha, www.rabbinicalassembly.org/docs/Dorff_ paper.pdf (2006).

Women and the Reconstructionist Movement

RABBI BARBARA PENZNER

1. *Exploring Judaism: A Reconstructionist Approach* (Elkins Park, PA: The Reconstructionist Press,2000), 133.
2. Excerpts from "Merger," from *The Dinner Party*, used with permission in *Kol Haneshamah: Shabbat Vehagim* (Elkins Park, PA: The Reconstructionist Press, 1994), 127.

Leadership and Social Justice
Jewish Women's Leadership for the Twenty-first Century

SHIFRA BRONZNICK

1. Shifra Bronznick, Marty Linsky, and Didi Goldenhar, *Leveling the Playing Field: Advancing Women in Jewish Organizational Life* (New York: Advancing Women Professionals and the Jewish Community and Cambridge Leadership Institute, 2008), 17.
2. Catalyst, *The Bottom Line: Connecting Corporate Performance and Gender Diversity* (New York: Catalyst, 2004).
3. Joyce K. Fletcher, *Disappearing Acts: Gender, Power, and Relational Practice at Work* (Cambridge, MA: MIT Press, 1999), 106–129.
4. Joyce K. Fletcher, "The Paradox of Post-Heroic Leadership: An Essay on Gender, Power and Transformational Change," *Leadership Quarterly* 15, no. 5 (2004): 647–61.
5. Didi Goldenhar and Sivanie Shiran, *Cultivating the Talent: Women Professionals in the Federation System: A Research Report* (New York: AWP–UJC, 2007).

Bread, Roses, and Chutzpah:
Jewish Women in American Social Movements

RABBI JILL JACOBS

1. While it is impossible to define precisely who counts as a leader, a number of academic books have noticed the high proportion of Jewish women among the acknowledged leadership of American social movements. See, for example, Joyce Antler, *The Journey Home: How Jewish Women Shaped Modern America* (New York: Schocken, 1997); Debra Schultz, *Going South: Jewish Women in the Civil Rights Movement* (New York: New York University Press, 2002); and Judith Rosenbaum, "Jewish Women as Feminist Pioneers," on www.myjewishlearning.com (available at www.myjewishlearning.com/history_community/Modern/Overview_The_Story_19481980/America/PWPolitics/Feminism.htm).
2. For more on the 1909 strike and on Schneiderman's life, see Annelise Orleck Antler, *Common Sense and a Little Fire: Women and Working-Class Politics in the United States 1900–1965* (Chapel Hill: University of North Carolina Press, 1995), and David von Drehle, *Triangle: The Fire that Changed America* (New York: Grove Press, 2003).

3. Rose Schneiderman with Lucy Goldthwaite, *All for One* (New York: Peter S. Eriksson, 1967), 14.
4. Ibid., 39–40.
5. Ibid., 49–50.
6. Ibid., 35.
7. For background on Jewish women in the civil rights movement, see Schultz, *Going South.*
8. Betty Alschuler, "Notes from the American Revolution—1962," reprinted in *The Jewish 1960s*, ed. Michael Staub (Waltham, MA: Brandeis University, 2004), 12–17.
9. Rosenbaum, "Jewish Women as Feminist Pioneers."
10. "Jewish Roots: An Interview with Betty Friedan," January/Febuary, 1988, 24–26.

Women's Right to a World Free of Violence

RABBI LYNN GOTTLIEB

1. Elisa Klapheck, *Fraulein Rabbiner Jonas,* trans. Toby Axelrod (San Francisco: John Wiley and Sons, 2004), 51.
2. Statistics provided by Just Communities Central Coast, Santa Barbara, California, in Michael Bochenek, *Hatred in the Hallways: Violence and Discrimination against Lesbian, Gay Bisexual and Transgender Youth in U.S. Schools* (New York: Human Rights Watch, 2006), section 6, 11.
3. From a training manual prepared by Transforming Communities: Technical Assistance, Training and Resource Center for the California Department of Health Services, 2007.
4. Judith Herman, *Trauma and Recovery* (New York: Basic Books, 1992), 75–76.
5. Research by advisor to the chief of staff in matters pertaining to female soldiers.
6. Rachel Shabi, in the *Guardian,* April 17, 2006.
7. Idan Halili's story is available online on the American Friends Service Committee website, under the Faces of Hope Campaign www.afsc.org/Palestinian-IsraeliConflict/ht/d/ContentDetails/3552; or through New Profile, at www.NewProfile.org.
8. For more about domestic violence, see: Renita J Weens, *Battered Love: Marriage, Sex and Violence in the Hebrew Scripture* (Minneapolis: Fortress Press, 1995); Marcia Cohn Spiegel, "Bibliography of Sexual and Domestic Violence in the Jewish Community," January 12, 2004, Minnesota Center Against Violence and Abuse's website, www.mincava.umn.edu/documents/bibs/jewish/jewish.html; Jewish Women International, www.jwi.org; the FaithTrust Institute, www.faithtrustinstitute.org, for books, videos, training programs; and Shalom Bayit: Bay Area Jewish Women Working to End Domestic Violence, www.shalom-bayit.org.

Servant before the King: Raising Up the Healer to Leadership

RABBI VALERIE JOSEPH AND RABBI ALANA SUSKIN

1. Rabbi Carla Howard, in personal conversation with *chevruta* Janet Sternfeld Davis and in conversation with Rabbi Valerie Joseph.

2. Rabbi Rachel Cowan, Jewish Women's Archive, November 2007, http://jwa.org/fem.inism/_html/JWA016.htm.

3. Rabbi Lori Klein, in personal conversation with Valerie Joseph.

4. A. I. Slomovitz, *The Fighting Rabbis: Jewish Military Chaplains and American History* (New York: New York University Press, 1999), 124–27.

Post-Triumphalism and the New *Haskalah*

ROSIE ROSENZWEIG

1. Jonathan D. Sarna, *American Judaism: A History* (New Haven: Yale University Press, 2004), 341.

2. See "Our History" at the Third Wave Foundation, www.thirdwavefoundation.org.

3. Pythia Peay, "Feminism's Fourth Wave: A New Activist Movement Is Gathering Women across Faiths," *Utne Reader,* March/April 2005.

4. Frederick M. Schweitzer, *A History of the Jews since the First Century A.D.* (New York: Macmillan, 1971), 161.

5. Ibid., 109.

6. Howard M. Sachar, *A History of Jews in the Modern World* (New York: Alfred A. Knopf, 2005), 31.

7. Mircea Eliade, ed., *The Encyclopedia of Religion* (New York: Macmillan, 1987), 107.

8. Robert C. Lester, *Buddhism* (New York: Harper and Row, 1987), 11. This figure has undoubtedly increased, especially in the United States.

9. During a November 19, 2003, keynote address for the Endowment for Religious Understanding, "Where Is the Love? Can Religions Learn to File Share?" *Milton Magazine,* Spring 2004, 48.

10. Sandra Lubarsky, "Enriching Awareness: A Jewish Encounter with Buddhism," in *Beside Still Waters: Jews, Christians, and the Way of the Buddha,* ed. Harold Kasimow, John and Linda Kennan (Boston: Wisdom Publications, 2003), 64.

11. Peay, "Feminism's Fourth Wave."

Glossary

Aggadah: The homiletic and non-legalistic exegetical texts in classical rabbinic literature, particularly as recorded in the Talmud and Midrash. This compendium of rabbinic homilies incorporates folklore, historical anecdotes, moral exhortations, and practical advice in various spheres, from business to medicine.

agunah, agunot (pl.): Literally "anchored" or "chained"; a halachic term for a Jewish woman who is "chained" to her marriage because her husband's whereabouts are unknown. Used today for a woman whose husband refuses or is unable to grant her an official bill of divorce. See *get.*

aliyah, aliyot (pl.): The honor of being called up to the Torah for the blessings before and after its reading.

Amidah: Literally, "Standing Prayer"; also called the *Shemoneh Esrei* ("The Eighteen Blessings"). This is the central prayer of the Jewish liturgy.

bar mitzvah: A boy child's coming of age at age thirteen, at which time he is permitted to have an aliyah and count in the minyan. *Bar mitzvah* also refers to the ceremony that acknowledges this milestone, as in "I had a bar mitzvah."

bat mitzvah: A girl child's coming of age, traditionally at age twelve, but acknowledged in the liberal communities at thirteen. Bat mitzvah ceremonies began in the 1920s and exist now in almost all denominations in one form or another.

bimah: The platform in the synagogue from which services are led. Usually the rabbi and cantor stand on the bimah, as well as others who have service honors.

brit: Literally "covenant." God makes a *brit* with many biblical characters. Today we usually associate this word with the covenant of circumcision. Pronounced *bris* in Ashkenazi.

brit milah: Literally "the covenant of circumcision." This ceremony is performed at eight days, when the foreskin of the infant boy is removed amid blessings and ritual. Circumcision was commanded to Abraham as a sign of the covenant for all males for all time.

cantor: The person responsible for the musical portions of a prayer service. See *hazzan.*

chavurah, chavurot (pl.): Small groups of people who meet together for prayer and study.

chuppah: Wedding canopy.

cohen, cohanim (pl.): A member of the highest priestly class who served in the desert tabernacle and then in the Temple in Jerusalem. Some people still trace their lineage to the *cohanim* of old, and these modern descendants receive the first aliyah in traditional synagogues, as a sign of honor and respect. Sometimes spelled *kohen*. If there had been female priests the word would have been *cohenet/kohenet*.

daven: To pray or recite Jewish prayers daily.

divrei Torah: Short sermons or explanations of the weekly Torah portions.

Gemara: Part of the Talmud that contains commentary on the Mishnah, part of the Oral Law of the Jewish religion.

get: Official bill of divorce, presented by a husband to his wife on the occasion of their divorce.

haftarah, haftarot (pl.): Portions from the Hebrew Bible, specifically from the books of Nevi'im ("The Prophets"), that are read publicly in the synagogue after the reading of the Torah on Shabbat, as well as on Jewish festivals and fast days. A haftarah usually has a thematic link to the Torah reading that precedes it.

Haggadah: The liturgical book that contains the order of the Passover Seder. Haggadah, meaning "telling," is a fulfillment of the scriptural commandment to each Jew to "tell your child" about the Jewish liberation from slavery in Egypt, as described in the book of Exodus in the Torah.

halakhah: The overall term for Jewish law, codified through the ages, since the Torah. Halakhah is still evolving, in all the denominations.

halakhists: Experts in halakhah.

haredi: Ultra-Orthodox Jews; consider their belief system and religious practices to extend in an unbroken chain back to Moses and the giving of the Torah on Mount Sinai. As a result, they consider non-Orthodox denominations to be unjustifiable deviations from authentic Judaism, both because of other denominations' doubts concerning the divine revelation of the Written and Oral Torah, and because of their rejection of halakhic (or Jewish legal) precedent as binding.

Hasidism: Principles and practices of the Jewish sect founded in eighteenth-century Poland by Baal Shem Tov. Was founded as a movement of the common people to access the joy and spirituality of Judaism as well as its legal aspects; popularized mystical traditions and the ascent of the rabbi to the status of a miracle worker and "rebbe."

Haskalah: The Jewish enlightenment movement in the eighteenth and nineteenth centuries that was influenced by European intellectuals and sought to offer secular education to European Jews.

havdalah: Jewish religious ceremony that officially signifies the end of Shabbat and holidays, and ushers in the beginning of the new week.

hazzan, hazzanim (pl.): A Jewish musician trained in the vocal arts who helps lead the synagogue in songful prayer.

kabbalah: Jewish mysticism, developed throughout the ages but mostly associated with the system popularized in the thirteenth century CE in Safed.

kabbalists: Those who practice kabbalah.

Kaddish: The memorial prayer, said for eleven months after a blood relative passes away. Traditionally, only men are obligated to say this prayer, though for both deceased women and men. In liberal communities it is common for women to say the Kaddish for their loved ones.

kashrut: The body of Jewish dietary law that determines whether something is clean or fit to eat; adherence to Jewish dietary laws.

ketubah, ketubot (pl.): A Jewish wedding certificate, stipulating the promises made by the groom and bride, including material sustenance and sexual satisfaction. The traditional *ketubah* has the groom acquiring the bride for a price. Egalitarian *ketubot* are being written and used today, as well.

kibbutz, kibbutzim (pl.): Cooperative farm settlement in Israel, popular from the 1940s until the 1980s. Many of today's kibbutzim have been privatized to a large extent.

kriyah: The cutting of a garment or black ribbon by mourners.

Levites: Assistants to the priests, they were honored servants of the sacred rites in the desert tabernacle and then in the Temple in Jerusalem. Those people who still trace their lineage to the Levites of old receive the second aliyah in a traditional synagogue.

mechitzah: A wall or screen for separating the genders.

mezuzah: A small box, usually decorated, affixed to the doorpost of a Jewish home. It marks the distinction between the profane outside world and the holy world inside. The box contains a piece of paper with the words of the Shema in Hebrew written on it. Traditional Jews will touch the mezuzah and say a blessing as they go in and out of the house.

Meir, Golda: First female prime minister of Israel, 1969–74.

midrash, midrashim (pl.): A rabbinic story, parable, or interpretation of biblical text, coming from the root *d-r-sh,* which means "to examine." These midrashim help fill in gaps in the text, supply missing details or dialogue, and enliven the text with personal anecdotes. Early midrashim can be found in the Talmud from the second century, but the first actual compendium was edited in the fifth and sixth centuries CE. Modern midrashim are still being written today.

midrashist: A person involved in the writing or creating of midrashim.

mikveh, mikvaot (pl.): A pool of water used for ritual immersions. Comprised of natural rain water plus tap water, built and filled to exact legal specifications, mikvaot are used traditionally to immerse new dishes, brides (and in some cases grooms), converts to Judaism, and women after their monthly menstrual period. Separate mikvaot are used to immerse corpses for final purification before burial.

minyan: A quorum of ten needed for public prayers. In Orthodox services, only men are counted in the ten. In liberal services, either women or men or both together are counted in the ten.

Miriam: The sister of Moses who led the women in song at the Red Sea.

Mishnah: Part of the Talmud consisting of a collection of oral religious laws of Judaism.

mitzvah, mitzvot (pl.): A commandment from the Torah or later enacted by the Rabbis.

niddah: Literally, "separation"; generally considered to refer to separation from ritual impurity.

parshanut: Interpretations of the Torah written by scholars and rabbis.

piyyut, piyyutim (pl.): Liturgical hymns.

rebbetzin: The Yiddish word for the wife of a rabbi.

Rosh Chodesh: The Jewish New Moon, celebrated each month when the moon is darkest, just before the sliver of the new moon is seen. Traditionally understood as a "woman's holiday" because of the confluence of women and the moon. Rosh Chodesh groups began proliferating in the 1960s as women "rediscovered" this woman's holiday.

sabra: Native-born Israeli.

semicha: Ordination of a rabbi.

Shabbat: The Jewish Sabbath, beginning Friday at sundown and lasting until Saturday at sundown.

Shekhinah: The Indwelling Presence of God, a rabbinic notion from the time of the Talmud, later adapted by the kabbalists to evoke a feminine side or feminine presence of God. Sometimes spelled *Shechinah.*

shliach tzibbur: The person who leads the congregation in prayer.

tallit, tallitot (pl.): A prayer shawl worn during daytime services and once a year at night on Yom Kippur. Women have begun making and wearing tallitot in recent times. Pronounced tallis in Ashkenazi.

Talmud: The compilation of Rabbinic law that includes the Mishnah (legal decisions edited in the third century CE) and the Gemara (Rabbinic discussions of those laws, edited in the sixth century CE). In the traditional community, the Talmud is authoritative on matters of daily life.

Tanakh: An acrostic for the whole of the Jewish Bible, which is divided into three sections: Torah (Five Books of Moses), Nevi'im (Prophets), and Ketuvim (Writings.)

t'chinot: Prayers written for or by women.

tefillah: Hebrew for prayer. The Hebrew root means "to think, entreat, judge, intercede," and the reflective means "to judge oneself" and "to pray."

tefillin: Also called phylacteries; a pair of leather boxes containing scrolls of parchment inscribed with biblical verses. Worn traditionally by male Jews and wrapped around the arm, hand and fingers, as well as above the forehead. Today many women are taking on the wearing of tefillin. They serve as a sign and remembrance that God brought the children of Israel out of Egypt. According to halakhah, tefillin should be worn during weekday morning prayer services.

teshuvah: Literally, "to return"; the Jewish concept of repentance. It involves the renunciation of wrongdoing, appeal for forgiveness, and return to God's law. *Teshuvah* serves as the motif of the Ten Days of Penitence. The Yom Kippur prayers focus on this doctrine.

tikkun olam: Literally, "world repair"; has come to connote social action and the pursuit of social justice.

tum tum: The Talmudic term for one whose gender is not clear at birth.

tzedakah: Righteous giving. In the Bible, *tzedakah* means "righteous behavior" and is often paired with "justice." In Jewish thought and tradition, material support for those in need is not a matter of charity but a requirement.

yahrzeit: Anniversary of the death of a relative. It is observed by kindling a light and reciting the Kaddish.

yeshiva, yeshivot (pl.): A school of full-time Jewish learning, for either children or adults.

YHVH: The four-letter Hebrew name of God, commonly pronounced "Adonai."

Suggestions for Further Reading

Torah Commentaries by Women

Cohn Eskenazi, Tamara, and Weiss, Andrea L. eds. *The Torah: A Women's Commentary.* New York: URJ Press, 2008.

Goldstein, Elyse, ed. *The Women's Torah Commentary: New Insights from Women Rabbis on the 54 Weekly Torah Portions.* Woodstock, VT: Jewish Lights Publishing, 2000.

———. *The Women's Haftarah Commentary: New Insights from Women Rabbis on the 54 Weekly Haftarah Portions, the 5 Megillot and Special Shabbatot.* Woodstock, VT: Jewish Lights Publishing, 2004.

Leibowitz, Nehama. *Studies in Bereshit, Shmot, Vayikra, Bamidbar, Devarim.* Jerusalem: World Zionist Organization, 1980.

Zakon, Miriam Stark, trans. *Tzenah U'Renah: The Classic Anthology of Torah Lore and Midrashic Comment.* Jerusalem: Mesorah Publications, 1983.

Zornberg, Avivah. *Genesis: The Beginning of Desire.* Philadelphia: Jewish Publication Society, 1995.

Feminist Biblical Interpretation

Antonelli, Judith S. *In the Image of God: A Feminist Commentary on the Torah.* Northvale, NJ: Jason Aronson, 1997.

Aschkenasy, Nehama. *Woman at the Window: Biblical Tales of Oppression and Escape.* Detroit: Wayne State University Press, 1998.

Bellis, Alice Ogden. *Helpmates, Harlots, and Heroes: Women's Stories in the Hebrew Bible.* Louisville: Westminster John Knox Press, 1994.

Brenner, Athalya, ed. *Feminist Companion to Reading the Bible: Approaches, Methods and Strategies.* Ithaca, NY: Cornell University Press, 1997.

Buchmann, Christina, and Celina Spiegel, eds. *Out of the Garden: Women Writers on the Bible.* New York: Fawcett Columbine, 1994.

Exum, J. Cheryl. *Fragmented Women: Feminist Subversions of Biblical Narratives.* Harrisburg, PA: Trinity Press International, 1993.

Frankel, Ellen. *The Five Books of Miriam.* New York: G. P. Putnam's Sons, 1996.

Frymer-Kensky, Tikva. *Studies in Bible and Feminist Criticism.* Philadelphia: Jewish Publication Society, 2006.

Graetz, Naomi. *Unlocking the Garden: A Feminist Jewish Look at the Bible, Midrash, and God.* Piscataway, NJ: Gorgias Press, 1994.

Handelman, Susan, ed. *Torah of Our Mothers.* Jerusalem: Urim Publications, 2006.

Newsom, Carol A., and Sharon H. Ringe, eds. *The Women's Bible Commentary.* Louisville, KY: Westminster John Knox Press,1992.

Oistriker, Alicia. *The Nakedness of the Fathers: Biblical Visions and Revisions.* New Brunswick, NJ: Rutgers University Press,1994.

Pardes, Ilana. *Countertraditions in the Bible.* Cambridge, MA: Harvard University Press,1992.

Schussler Fiorenza, Elisabeth. *Bread Not Stone: The Challenge of Feminist Biblical Interpretation.* Boston: Beacon Press, 1995.

Trible, Phyllis. *Texts of Terror: Literary-Feminist Readings of Biblical Narratives.* Philadelphia: Fortress Press, 1984.

Female Biblical Characters/Midrash

Adelman, Penina. *Praise Her Works: Conversations with Biblical Women.* Philadelphia: Jewish Publication Society, 2005.

Bach, Alice, ed. *Women in the Hebrew Bible: A Reader.* New York: Routledge Press, 1998.

Bronner, Leila Leah. *From Eve to Esther.* Louisville, KY: Westminster John Knox Press,1994.

Burns, Rita J. *Has the Lord Indeed Spoken Only through Moses.* Dissertation Series. Atlanta: Scholars Press, 1987.

Dame, Enid, Lilly Rivlin, Henny Wenkart, and Naomi Wolf, eds. *Which Lilith? Feminist Writers Re-Create the World's First Woman.* Northvale, NJ: Jason Aronson, 1998.

Diamant, Anita. *The Red Tent.* New York: St. Martins Press, 1997.

Frymer-Kensky, Tikva. *Reading the Women of the Bible.* New York: Schocken Books, 2002.

Hammer, Jill. *Sisters at Sinai: New Tales of Biblical Women.* Philadelphia: Jewish Publication Society, 2001.

Hyman, Naomi Mara. *Biblical Women in the Midrash: A Sourcebook.* Northvale, NJ: Jason Aronson, 1998.

Jeansonne, Sharon Pace. *The Women of Genesis.* Minneapolis: Fortress Press,1990.

Kates, Judith, and Gail Twersky Reimer. *Reading Ruth: Contemporary Women Reclaim a Sacred Story* New York: Ballantine Books, 1996.

Koltuv, Barbara Black. *The Book of Lilith.* York Beach, ME: Nicolas-Hays, 1987.

Labowitz, Shoni. *God, Sex and Women of the Bible: Discovering Our Sensual, Spiritual Selves.* New York: Simon and Schuster, 1998.

Lerner, Anne Lapidus. *Eternally Eve: Images of Eve in the Hebrew Bible, Midrash and Modern Jewish Poetry.* Waltham, MA: Brandeis University Press, 2007.

Meyers, Carol. *Discovering Eve: Ancient Israelite Women in Context.* New York: Oxford University Press, 1991.

Ochs, Vanessa. *Sarah Laughed.* New York: McGraw-Hill, 2004.

Rosen, Norma. *Biblical Women Unbound.* Philadelphia: Jewish Publication Society, 1996.

Sasso, Sandy Eisenberg. *But God Remembered: Stories of Women from Creation to the Promised Land.* Woodstock, VT: Jewish Lights Publishing, 2008.

———. *Noah's Wife: The Story of Naamah.* Woodstock, VT: Jewish Lights Publishing, 2002.

Teubal, Savina. *Sarah the Priestess.* Athens, OH: Swallow Press, 1986.

———. *Ancient Sisterhood: Lost Traditions of Sarah and Hagar.* Athens, OH: Swallow Press, 1997.

———. *Ancient Sisterhood: The Lost Traditions of Hagar and Sarah.* Columbus: Ohio University Press, 1997.

Thaw Ronson, Barbara L. *The Women of the Torah: Commentaries from the Talmud, Midrash, and Kabbalah.* Northvale, NJ: Jason Aronson, 1998.

Feminism and Judaism, Women's Spirituality, Theology

Adler, Rachel. *Engendering Judaism: An Inclusive Theology and Ethics.* Philadelphia: Jewish Publication Society, 1998.

Alpert, Rebecca, and Danya Ruttenberg. "Priority Lists: A Dialogue on Judaism, Feminism, and Activism." In *Righteous Indignation: A Jewish Call for Justice,* edited by Or Rose, Margie Klein, and Jo Ellen Green Kaiser. Woodstock, VT: Jewish Lights Publishing, 2007.

Bernstein, Ellen. *The Splendor of Creation: A Biblical Ecology.* Cleveland: Pilgrim Press, 2005.

———. *Ecology and the Jewish Spirit.* Woodstock, VT: Jewish Lights Publishing, 1999.

Berrin, Susan, ed. *Celebrating the New Moon: A Rosh Chodesh Anthology.* Northvale, NJ: Jason Aronson, 1996.

Cantor, Aviva. *Jewish Women, Jewish Men: The Legacy of Patriarchy in Jewish Life.* San Francisco: Harper and Row, 1995.

Chesler, Phylis, and Rivka Haut, eds. *Women of the Wall: Claiming Sacred Ground at Judaism's Holy Site.* Woodstock, VT: Jewish Lights Publishing, 2003.

Christ, Carol P., and Judith Plaskow, eds. *Womanspirit Rising: A Feminist Reader in Religion.* San Francisco: HarperSanFrancisco, 1979.

Epstein, Julia, and Lori Lefkovitz, eds. *Shaping Losses: Cultural Memory and the Holocaust.* Champagne: University of Illinois Press, 2001.

Firestone, Tirzah. *The Receiving: Reclaiming Jewish Women's Wisdom.* San Francisco: Harper San Franciso, 2004.

Fishman, Sylvia Barack. *A Breath of Life: Feminism in the American Jewish Community.* Waltham, MA: Brandeis University Press, 1995.

Frankiel, Tamar. *The Voice of Sarah: Feminine Spirituality and Traditional Judaism.* San Francisco: Harper and Row, 1990.

Goldman, Karla. *Beyond the Synagogue Gallery: Finding a Place for Women in American Judaism.* Cambridge, MA: Harvard University Press, 2001.

Goldstein, Elyse. *ReVisions: Seeing Torah through a Feminist Lens.* Woodstock, VT: Jewish Lights Publishing, 1998.

Greenberg, Blu. *On Women and Judaism: A View from Tradition.* Philadelphia: Jewish Publication Society,1981.

Grossman, Susan, and Rivka Haut. *Daughters of the King.* Philadelphia: Jewish Publication Society, 1994.

Hartman, Tova. *Feminism Encounters Traditional Judaism: Resistance and Accommodation.* Waltham, MA: Brandeis University Press, 2007.

Heschel, Susannah, ed. *On Being a Jewish Feminist.* New York: Schocken Books, 1995.

Kaye/Kantrowitz, Melanie, and Irena Klepfisz. *The Tribe of Dina.* Boston: Beacon Press, 1989.

Koltun, Elizabeth. *The Jewish Woman: New Perspectives.* New York: Schocken Books, 1976.

Levitt, Laura. *Jews and Feminism: The Ambivalent Search for Home,* New York: Routledge, 1997.

Ochs, Vanessa. *Inventing Judaism.* Philadelphia: Jewish Publication Society, 2007.

———. *Words on Fire: One Woman's Journey into the Sacred.* Jackson, TN: Westview Press,1999.

Orenstein, Debra, and Jane Rachel Litman, eds. *Lifecycles: Jewish Women on Biblical Themes in Contemporary Life.* Vol. 2. Woodstock, VT: Jewish Lights Publishing, 1997.

Plaskow, Judith. *Standing Again at Sinai: Judaism from a Feminist Perspective.* San Francisco: HarperSanFrancisco, 1990.

———. *The Coming of Lilith: Essays on Feminism, Judaism, and Sexual Ethics, 1972–2003.* Boston: Beacon Press, 2005.

———. and Carol Christ. *Weaving the Visions: New Patterns in Feminist Spirituality.* San Francisco: HarperSanFrancisco, 1989.

Peskowitz, Miriam, and Laura Levitt, eds. *Judaism since Gender.* New York: Routledge, 1997.

Prell, Riv-Ellen. *Women Remaking American Judaism.* Detroit: Wayne State University Press, 2007.

Raphael, Melissa. *The Female Face of G-d in Aushwitz: A Jewish Feminist Theology of the Holocaust.* New York: Routledge, 2003.

Reimer, Gail Twersky, and Judith Kates, eds. *Beginning Anew: A Woman's Companion to the High Holy Days.* New York: Touchstone Press, 1997.

Rosenzweig, Rosie. *A Jewish Mother in Shangri-la.* Boston: Shambhala Publications, 1998.

Ross, Tamar. *Expanding the Palace of Torah.* Waltham, MA: Brandeis University Press, 2004.

Ruttenberg, Danya. *Yentl's Revenge: The Next Wave of Jewish Feminism.* Seattle: Seal Press, 2001.

———. "Fringe Me Up, Fringe Me Down: On Getting Dressed in Jerusalem." In *Bitchfest: Ten Years of Cultural Criticism from the Pages of Bitch Magazine,* edited by Lisa Jervis and Andi Zeisler. New York: Farrar, Straus and Giroux, 2006.

Umansky, Ellen, and Diane Ashton, eds. *Four Centuries of Jewish Women's Spirituality: A Sourcebook.* Boston: Beacon Press, 1992.

Weidman Schneider, Susan. *Jewish and Female: Choices and Changes in Our Lives Today.* New York: Simon and Schuster, 1984.

Zolty, Shoshana Pantel. *And All Your Children Shall Be Learned: Women and the Study of Torah in Jewish Law and History.* Northvale, NJ: Jason Aronson, 1997.

On God, God Language, and the Goddess

Campbell, Joseph, and Charles Muses, eds. *In All Her Names.* San Francisco: HarperSanFrancisco, 1991.

Falk, Marcia. *The Book of Blessings.* San Francisco: HarperSanFrancisco, 1996.

Frymer-Kensky, Tikva. *In the Wake of the Goddess.* New York: MacMillan, 1992.

Goldenberg, Naomi R. *Changing of the Gods.* Boston: Beacon Press, 1979.

Gottlieb, Lynn. *She Who Dwells Within.* San Francisco: HarperSanFrancisco, 1995.

Graves, Robert. *The White Goddess.* London: Faber and Faber, 1961.

Hammer, Jill. "An Altar of Earth: Reflections on Jews, Goddesses, and the Zohar." *Zeek,* Fall/Winter 2004, 7–20.

———. "Holle's Cry: Unearthing a Birth Goddess in a German Jewish Naming Ceremony." *Nashim: A Journal of Jewish Women's Studies and Gender Issues* 9 (Spring 5765/2005): 62–87.

———. "Faces of the Shekhinah: Thirteen Archetypes of the Priestess from Jewish Tradition." *Ashe: The Journal of Experimental Spirituality* 5, no. 4 (Winter 2007): 376–90.

Patai, Raphael. *The Hebrew Goddess.* Detroit: Wayne State University Press, 1990.

Stone, Merlin. *When God Was a Woman.* New York: Dial Press, 1976.

Women in Jewish History, Feminism and Jewish History

Baskin, Judith. *Jewish Women in Historical Perspective.* Detroit: Wayne State University Press, 1999.

Bird, Phyllis A. *Missing Persons and Mistaken Identities: Women and Gender in Ancient Israel.* Philadelphia: Fortress Press, 1997.

Brooten, Bernadette. *Women Leaders in the Ancient Synagogue.* Chico, CA: Scholars Press, 1982.

Henry, Sondra, and Emily Taitz. *Written Out of History: Our Jewish Foremothers.* New York: Biblio Press, 1990.

Ilan, Tal. *Jewish Women in Greco-Roman Palestine*. Peabody, MA: Hendrickson Publishers, 1996.

———. *Integrating Women into Second Temple History*. Peabody, MA: Hendrickson Publishers, 2001.

Shepherd, Naomi. *A Price below Rubies: Jewish Women as Rebels and Radicals*. Cambridge, MA: Harvard University Press, 2002.

Women and Ritual

Anisfeld, Sharon Cohen, Tara Mohr, and Catherine Spector, ed. *The Women's Passover Companion: Women's Reflections on the Festival of Freedom*. Woodstock, VT: Jewish Lights Publishing, 2003.

———. *The Women's Seder Sourcebook: Rituals and Readings for Use at the Passover Seder*. Woodstock, VT: Jewish Lights Publishing, 2003.

Berkowitz, Miriam. *Taking the Plunge: A Practical and Spiritual Guide to the Mikveh*. Jerusalem: Schechter Institute of Jewish Studies, 2007.

Berman, Phyllis, and Arthur Waskow. *A Time for Every Purpose Under Heaven: The Jewish Life-Spiral as a Spiritual Journey*. New York: Farrar Straus & Giroux, 2002.

Broner, E. M. *The Telling: Including the Women's Haggadah*. New York: HarperCollins, 1994.

———. *Bringing Home the Light: A Jewish Woman's Handbook of Rituals*. San Francisco: Council Oak, 2005.

Cohen Tamara. *The Journey Continues: The Ma'yan Passover Haggadah*. New York: Ma'yan, 2000.

Hammer, Jill. *The Jewish Book of Days: A Companion for All Seasons*. Philadelphia: Jewish Publication Society, 2006.

Ochs, Vanessa. *Inventing Jewish Ritual*. Philadelphia: Jewish Publication Society, 2007.

Orenstein, Debra. *Lifecycles: Jewish Women on Life Passages and Personal Milestones*. Woodstock, VT: Jewish Lights Publishing, 1994.

Sasso, Sandy Eisenberg. *Unwrapping the Gift in Women and Religious Ritual: An Interdisciplinary Investigation*. Dr. Lesley A. Northrup, ed. Washington, DC: Pastoral Press, 1993.

Women and Jewish Law, Talmud, Rabbinics

Abrams, Judith. *The Women of the Talmud*. Northvale, NJ: Jason Aronson, 1995.

Baskin, Judith R. *Midrashic Women: Formations of the Feminine in Rabbinic Literature*. Waltham, MA: Brandeis University Press, 2002.

Biale, Rachel. *Women and Jewish Law*. New York: Schocken, 1995.

Hauptman, Judith. *Rereading the Rabbis: A Woman's Voice*. Boulder, CO: Westview Press, 2001.

Peskowitz, Miriam B. *Spinning Fantasies: Rabbis, Gender, and History*. Berkeley, CA: University of California Press, 1997.

Suskin, Alana. "A Feminist Theory of Jewish Law." In *The Unfolding Tradition: Jewish Law after Sinai*, edited by Elliot Dorff. New York: Aviv Press, 2005.

Wasserfall, Rahel, ed. *Women and Water: Menstruation in Jewish Life and Law.* Waltham, MA: Brandeis University Press, 1999.

Wegner, Judith Romney.*Chattel or Person? The Status of Women in the Mishnah.* London: Oxford University Press, 1988.

Jewish and Lesbian

Alpert, Rebecca. *Like Bread on the Seder Plate: Jewish Lesbians and the Transformation of Tradition.* New York: Columbia University Press, 1998.

Alpert, Rebecca T., Sue Levi Elwell, and Shirley Idelson. *Lesbian Rabbis: The First Generation.* New Brunswick, NJ: Rutgers University Press, 2001.

Aviv, Caryn, and David Schneer. *Queer Jews.* New York: Routledge, 2002.

Beck, Evelyn Torten, ed. *Nice Jewish Girls: A Lesbian Anthology.* Rev. ed. Boston: Beacon Press, 1989.

Moore, Tracy. *Lesbiot: Israeli Lesbians Talk about Sexuality, Feminism, Judaism, and Their Lives.* New York: Cassell, 1999.

Women as Rabbis

Greenberg, Simon, ed. *The Ordination of Women as Rabbis: Studies and Responsa.* Moreshet Series: Studies in Jewish History, Literature, and Thought 14. New York: Jewish Theological Seminary, 1988.

Klapheck, Elisa. *Fraulein Rabbiner Jones: The First Woman Rabbi.* San Francisco: Jossey Bass, 2004.

Nadell, Pamela Susan. *Women Who Would Be Rabbis: A History of Women's Ordination, 1889–1985.* Boston: Beacon Press, 1998.

———. "Opening the Blue of Heaven to Us: Reading Anew the Pioneers of Women's Ordination." *Nashim: A Journal of Jewish Women's Studies and Gender Issues* 9 (Spring 5765/2005): 88–100.

Ner-David, Haviva. *Life on the Fringes: A Feminist Journey towards Traditional Rabbinic Ordination.* Needham, MA: JFL Books, 2000.

Sheridan, Sybil. *Hear Our Voice: Women in the British Rabbinate.* Columbia, SC: University of South Carolina Press, 1998.

Wisdom You Are My Sister: Twenty-five Years of Women in the Rabbinate. Special issue of CCAR Journal (Summer 1997).

Zola, Gary Phillip, ed. *Women Rabbis: Exploration and Celebration: Papers Delivered at an Academic Conference Honoring Twenty Years of Women in the Rabbinate, 1972–1992.* Cincinnati: Hebrew Union College Press, 1996.

Jewish Women's Music

Ashira (www.cdbaby.com/cd/ashira2).

Cantor Aviva Rosenbloom (www.jewishstore.com/Music/Products.asp?ProdID=SWP-AARM2).

Chana Rothman (www.chanarothman.com)

Charming Hostess (www.charminghostess.us/about.html)

Debbie Friedman (www.debbiefriedman.com)

Geela Rayzel Raphael (www.shekhinah.com)

Hannah Tiferet Siegel (www.hannatiferet.com)

Juliet Spitzer (www.julietspitzer.com)

Linda Hirshorn (www.lindahirschhorn.com)

Margot Stein (www.mirajtrio.com)

Naomi Less (www.myspace.com/naomiless)

Pharaoh's Daughter (www.pharaohsdaughter.com)

Rabbi Shefa Gold (www.rabbishefagold.com)

Rabbi Tirzah Firestone (www.tirzahfirestone.com)

Shabbat Unplugged (www.shechinah.com/unplugged/index.html)

Tziona Achishena (www.koltziona.com)

Yofiyah: (http://www.hebrewkirtan.com)

Printed in the USA
CPSIA information can be obtained
at www.ICGtesting.com
JSHW012018140824
68134JS00033B/2755

9 781683 362203